THE JOURNEY OF LIU XIAOBO

# The Journey of Liu Xiaobo

*From Dark Horse to Nobel Laureate*

EDITED BY JOANNE LEEDOM-ACKERMAN

WITH YU ZHANG, JIE LI, TIENCHI MARTIN-LIAO

TRANSLATED BY STACY MOSHER AND ANDRÉA WORDEN

POTOMAC BOOKS

*An imprint of the University of Nebraska Press*

Library of Congress Cataloging-in-Publication Data
Names: Leedom-Ackerman, Joanne, 1948– editor. | Mosher, Stacy, translator. | Worden, Andréa, translator. | Liu, Xiaobo, 1955–2017. Works. Selections.
Title: The journey of Liu Xiaobo: from dark horse to Nobel Laureate / edited by Joanne Leedom-Ackerman with Yu Zhang, Jie Li, Tienchi Martin-Liao; translated by Stacy Mosher and Andréa Worden.
Other titles: From dark horse to Nobel Laureate
Description: [Lincoln]: Potomac Books, an imprint of the University of Nebraska Press, 2020.
Identifiers: LCCN 2019039069
ISBN 9781640122246 (hardback)
ISBN 9781640122925 (epub)
ISBN 9781640122932 (mobi)
ISBN 9781640122949 (pdf)
Subjects: LCSH: Liu, Xiaobo, 1955–2017. | Political prisoners—China—Biography. | Dissenters—China—Biography. | Nobel Prize winners—Biography.
Classification: LCC CT1828.L595 J68 2020 | DDC 951.05092 [B]—dc23
LC record available at https://lccn.loc.gov/2019039069

Set in Questa by Laura Ebbeka.
Designed by N. Putens.

To PEN members and colleagues worldwide who work on behalf of fellow writers to keep corridors of thought and expression open and who add their voices when others are silenced.

Freedom of expression is the foundation of human rights, the source of humanity, and the mother of truth.

—Liu Xiaobo, "I Have No Enemies: My Final Statement"

# CONTENTS

List of Illustrations . . . . . . . . . . . . . . . . . . . . . . . . . . . . . . . . . . . . . . . . . . . . . xv

Acknowledgments. . . . . . . . . . . . . . . . . . . . . . . . . . . . . . . . . . . . . . . . . . . . . xvii

## Introduction: Unity of Knowledge and Action

Editor's Note. . . . . . . . . . . . . . . . . . . . . . . . . . . . . . . . . . . . . . . . . . . . . . . . . . . 3
*Joanne Leedom-Ackerman*

Foreword. . . . . . . . . . . . . . . . . . . . . . . . . . . . . . . . . . . . . . . . . . . . . . . . . . . . . . 5
*The Dalai Lama*

The Passion of Liu Xiaobo . . . . . . . . . . . . . . . . . . . . . . . . . . . . . . . . . . . . . . . 6
*Perry Link*

Liu Xiaobo's Spiritual Heritage . . . . . . . . . . . . . . . . . . . . . . . . . . . . . . . . . 14
*Zhang Zuhua*

Democracy's Iron Man. . . . . . . . . . . . . . . . . . . . . . . . . . . . . . . . . . . . . . . . . 32
*Cui Weiping*

On the Causes of Controversies about Liu Xiaobo . . . . . . . . . . . . . . . . . . 50
*Yan Jiaqi*

A Brief Biography of Liu Xiaobo. . . . . . . . . . . . . . . . . . . . . . . . . . . . . . . . . 61
*Yu Zhang*

**Why Lui Xiaobo Matters: Black Hand behind a Red Wall**

On the Liu Xiaobo Incident . . . . . . . . . . . . . . . . . . . . . . . . . . . . . . . . . . . . .75
*Yu Ying-Shih*

Liu Xiaobo's Death as an Event of Human Spirit . . . . . . . . . . . . . . . . . . .80
*Teng Biao*

Liu Xiaobo, a Moral Giant of China's Democratic Transition . . . . . . . .88
*Yang Guang*

For Whom the Bell Tolls. . . . . . . . . . . . . . . . . . . . . . . . . . . . . . . . . . . . . . . .97
*Hu Ping*

Liu Xiaobo and His Political Views . . . . . . . . . . . . . . . . . . . . . . . . . . . . . .106
*Bao Tong*

Liu Xiaobo on the Front Line of Ideas. . . . . . . . . . . . . . . . . . . . . . . . . . . .110
*Joanne Leedom-Ackerman*

He Walked the Path of Kang Youwei and Shed the Blood of Tan Sitong. . . 114
*Wang Dan*

Remembering a Hero and a Martyr . . . . . . . . . . . . . . . . . . . . . . . . . . . . .117
*Carl Gershman*

Chinese Culture's Backbone . . . . . . . . . . . . . . . . . . . . . . . . . . . . . . . . . . .125
*Qian Yuejun*

**Youth and University Days: Innocent Hearts to Dark Horse**

Liu Xiaobo's Resistance . . . . . . . . . . . . . . . . . . . . . . . . . . . . . . . . . . . . . . .131
*Shao Jiang*

The Last Idealist . . . . . . . . . . . . . . . . . . . . . . . . . . . . . . . . . . . . . . . . . . . . . .143
*Wang Wei*

I Look Forward to a Magnificent Farewell . . . . . . . . . . . . . . . . . . . . . . . .147
*Ai Xiaoming*

Unfinished Journey............................................160
Mo Zhixu

Liu Xiaobo Turned Radical Suffering into Calm...................170
Su Xiaokang

A Formidable Personality .....................................179
Jean-Philippe Béja


Tiananmen Square and After: No Enemies

In Memory of My "Best Friend," Liu Xiaobo ......................189
Zhou Duo

Liu Xiaobo, Who Has Ascended the Altar........................ 202
Yi Ping

The Values of Peace and Reason Are Eternal......................214
Wu Zuolai

Liu Xiaobo and His View of "No Enemies" ......................219
Jin Zhong

Liu Xiaobo, An Eternal Monument ............................224
Pan Yongzhong

Poems ....................................................231
Shi Tao

Poems ....................................................233
Xu Lin

The Well after Its Name Has Left: In Memory of a Departed Poet ....235
Zi Kang

Message to Liu Xiaobo and Liu Xia ............................236
Tiananmen Mothers

## Politics, People, and PEN: Facing up to and Resisting Reality

Our Last Parting Unexpectedly Became Our Final Farewell . . . . . . . . .239
Wang Debang

Missing My Good Friend Liu Xiaobo. . . . . . . . . . . . . . . . . . . . . . . . . . . . . .250
He Depu

Mourning Little Brother Xiaobo. . . . . . . . . . . . . . . . . . . . . . . . . . . . . . . .254
Cary S. Hung

Some Recollections of Liu Xiaobo . . . . . . . . . . . . . . . . . . . . . . . . . . . . . .256
Zhao Dagong

A Prisoner on His Road . . . . . . . . . . . . . . . . . . . . . . . . . . . . . . . . . . . . . . .261
Ye Du

Liu Xiaobo and I. . . . . . . . . . . . . . . . . . . . . . . . . . . . . . . . . . . . . . . . . . . . .267
Liu Di

The Most Forgiving Opposition . . . . . . . . . . . . . . . . . . . . . . . . . . . . . . .278
Zheng Yi

The Liu Xiaobo I Knew. . . . . . . . . . . . . . . . . . . . . . . . . . . . . . . . . . . . . . 280
Cai Chu

Xiaobo, Tonight I Light a Cigarette for You . . . . . . . . . . . . . . . . . . . . .289
Emily Wu

Liu Xiaobo, Me, and Independent Chinese PEN Center . . . . . . . . . . . .292
Qi Jiazhen

Being-toward-Death: Remembering Xiaobo . . . . . . . . . . . . . . . . . . . . . .301
Xiao Qiao

China's Free Spirit . . . . . . . . . . . . . . . . . . . . . . . . . . . . . . . . . . . . . . . . . .308
Qin Geng

The Final Farewell. . . . . . . . . . . . . . . . . . . . . . . . . . . . . . . . . . . . . . . . . . .312
Yu Jianrong

Profound Memories to Be Cherished Forever...................315
*Yan Jiawei*

Twofold Grievous News, Nothing Can Top It ....................321
*Wang Jinbo*


## Charter 08: No Hatred

Liu Xiaobo's Self-Cultivation in Suffering .......................329
*Xu Youyu*

Deeply Concerned for Liu Xiaobo, on the Verge of Death...........340
*Jiang Qisheng*

On One of Liu Xiaobo's Ideological Legacies .....................344
*Pei Yiran*

Mourning Liu Xiaobo ..........................................349
*Sun Wenguang*

What Liu Xiaobo Means to Hong Kong...........................351
*Albert Ho Chun-yan*

Why I Follow Mr. Liu Xiaobo...................................356
*Lu Yang*

Liu Xiaobo Is a Hero to Hongkongers...........................360
*Tsoi Wing-Mui*

Salute Liu Xiaobo! ...........................................365
*Zhao Changqing*


## Nobel Peace Prize: Empty Chair

The Nobel Peace Prize for 2010 ...............................375
*Norwegian Nobel Committee*

A Good Choice of Nobel Prize for Xiaobo ........................377
*Sha Yexin*

The Spirit of Liu Xiaobo's "No Enemies" Will Exist Forever in Japan... 384
*Makino Seishu and Wang Jinzhong*

China Will Face Dilemma and Inconsistency between the Nobel
Prizes for Literature and Peace: One Thought after the Death of
Liu Xiaobo.................................................................392
*Hori Takeaki*

## Being-toward-Death: Torch in the Darkness

Xiaobo and His Era..........................................................401
*Yu Jie*

A Life like a Symphonic Poem: Farewell to Liu Xiaobo ..............411
*Tienchi Martin-Liao*

Liu Xiaobo Had a Dream ....................................................414
*Kaiser Abdurusul ÖzHun*

Ascending the Altar: Mourning Liu Xiaobo ........................418
*Chen Kuide*

Two or Three Things about Liu Xiaobo ...........................421
*Ai Weiwei*

Liu Xiaobo's Death and Chinese Regime's Fear ................... 426
*Andrew J. Nathan*

Liu Xiaobo's Fight for Freedom ...................................429
*Louisa Greve*

"They Killed Him": Denial of Medical Care in China and the
Literary Conscience .............................................436
*James Tager*

Remembering Liu Xiaobo ......................................439
*Hu Jia*

Elegy for Liu Xiaobo . . . . . . . . . . . . . . . . . . . . . . . . . . . . . . . . . . . . . . . .442
*Liao Yiwu*

Rebirth. . . . . . . . . . . . . . . . . . . . . . . . . . . . . . . . . . . . . . . . . . . . . . . . . . . .444
*Tsering Woeser*

My Brother, Why Have You Gone to Die?. . . . . . . . . . . . . . . . . . . . . . .445
*Du Daobin*

Poems . . . . . . . . . . . . . . . . . . . . . . . . . . . . . . . . . . . . . . . . . . . . . . . . . . . . .447
*Li Yongsheng*

## Conclusion: Heart to Heart

Poems . . . . . . . . . . . . . . . . . . . . . . . . . . . . . . . . . . . . . . . . . . . . . . . . . . . . .453
*Liu Xia*

Preface to Liu Xia's Photo Album. . . . . . . . . . . . . . . . . . . . . . . . . . . . . .456
*Liu Xiaobo*

## Appendix

Xiaobo, a Meteoroid in Darkness. . . . . . . . . . . . . . . . . . . . . . . . . . . . . . .461
*Independent Chinese PEN Center*

Liu Xiaobo—An Exceptional Life, Always Remembered . . . . . . . . . . .463
*PEN International*

Chinese Publisher's Afterword. . . . . . . . . . . . . . . . . . . . . . . . . . . . . . . . .467
*Wang Tiancheng*

To Those Gathered for the Book Launch of Essays
Commemorating Liu Xiaobo and Dialogue on His Legacy. . . . . . . . . .469
*Marco Rubio and Chris Smith*

Letter of Thanks to PEN International Congress . . . . . . . . . . . . . . . . . .471
*Liu Xia*

Additional Statements . . . . . . . . . . . . . . . . . . . . . . . . . . . . . . . . . . . . . . . . 473

Books by Liu Xiaobo . . . . . . . . . . . . . . . . . . . . . . . . . . . . . . . . . . . . . . . . . . 475

Liu Xiaobo's Awards and Honors . . . . . . . . . . . . . . . . . . . . . . . . . . . . . . 477

Chronology . . . . . . . . . . . . . . . . . . . . . . . . . . . . . . . . . . . . . . . . . . . . . . . . . . 479

Charter 08 . . . . . . . . . . . . . . . . . . . . . . . . . . . . . . . . . . . . . . . . . . . . . . . . . . 487

I Have No Enemies: My Final Statement . . . . . . . . . . . . . . . . . . . . . . . 497
*Liu Xiaobo*

List of Contributors . . . . . . . . . . . . . . . . . . . . . . . . . . . . . . . . . . . . . . . . . . 503

# ILLUSTRATIONS

*Following page 236*

1. Liu Xiaobo

2. Liu Xiaobo on Tiananmen Square

3. Independent Chinese PEN Center's second awards ceremony

4. Members of Independent Chinese PEN Center and PEN centers

5. Liu Xia and Liu Xiaobo at Mount Lao in Qingdao

6. Liu Xiaobo and Professor Sun Wenguang

7. Independent Chinese PEN Center's third awards ceremony

8. Professors Ding Ziling and Jiang Peikun

9. Liu Xiaobo at farmyard in Beijing suburbs

10. Liu Xiaobo

11. Liu Xiaobo at Bao Zunxin's funeral

12. Liu Xiaobo speaking

13. Meeting with Japanese congressman to support Liu Xiaobo

14. Nobel Peace Prize Certificate for Liu Xiaobo

15. Empty chair for Liu Xiaobo at Nobel Peace Prize awarding ceremony

16. Independent Chinese PEN Center celebration demonstration in Oslo

17. Demonstration in front of Chinese Embassy in Oslo

18. International Conference of Four-PEN Platform

19. Liu Xiaobo Memorial Award to Dr. Shirin Ebadi

20. Liu Xiaobo's funeral

## ACKNOWLEDGMENTS

Thank you to the Independent Chinese PEN Center, Democratic China, and the Taiwan Foundation for Democracy, which funded part of the translation. A majority of these articles were originally published in Chinese by Democratic China after Liu Xiaobo's death. Gratitude must also go to the Nobel Foundation, Nobel Media, PEN International, and Human Rights in China for their permissions to use their online texts and photos. Profound thanks to fellow editors Yu Zhang, Tienchi Martin-Liao, and Jie Li and to Cai Chu and Yu Zhang, editors of the original Chinese edition, and its publisher, Wang Tiansheng. Much appreciation and recognition are due to translators Stacy Mosher and Andréa Worden and to the many colleagues of Liu Xiaobo who contributed to this book. Gratitude is recurring to agents Peter and Amy Bernstein, who shepherded this manuscript, helped it find a home, and continue to assist as it finds its audience. Finally thank you to the team at Potomac Books and the University of Nebraska Press, including editor Thomas Swanson, editorial assistant Abigail Stryker, publicity manager Rosemary Sekora, manager of editorial design and production Ann Baker, senior project editor Joeth Zucco, and copy editor Sarah C. Smith.

THE JOURNEY OF LIU XIAOBO

# Introduction

*Unity of Knowledge and Action*

## Editor's Note

*Joanne Leedom-Ackerman*

A zoo in China placed a big hairy Tibetan mastiff in a cage and tried to pass if off as an African lion. But a boy and his mother heard the animal bark, not roar. As news spread, the zoo's visitors grew angry. "The zoo is absolutely trying to cheat us. They are trying to disguise dogs as lions!" declared the mother.[1]

In 2009 the Chinese government put Liu Xiaobo, celebrated poet, essayist, critic, activist, and thinker into a cage, labeled him "enemy of the state," charged him with "inciting subversion of state power," and sentenced him to eleven years' imprisonment. Liu Xiaobo was not an enemy, but he was a "lion" the state feared. He challenged orthodoxy and conventional thinking in literature, which he wrote and taught, and authoritarian politics, which he protested and tried to help reshape. His insistence on individual liberty in more than a thousand essays and eighteen books, his relentless pursuit of ideas, including as a drafter and organizer of *Charter 08*, which set out a democratic vision for China through nonviolent change, and finally his last statement, "I have no enemies and no hatred," threatened the Chinese Communist Party and government in a way few other citizens had.

Dr. Liu Xiaobo was the first Chinese citizen to win the Nobel Prize for Peace, in 2010, but he was in prison, was not allowed to attend the ceremony, and died in custody in July 2017.

When news of Liu Xiaobo's death reached the world and in particular the writers and democracy activists who knew him, writers began to write. Tributes and analyses poured in, many sent to the Independent Chinese PEN Center (ICPC), a gathering of writers inside and outside of Mainland China that Liu helped found and served as president. *The Journey of Liu Xiaobo* traces Liu's history and the path of liberalism in China and is perhaps the largest gathering of Chinese democracy activists' writing in one volume. Because of length restrictions, some tributes are listed only by authors' names in the appendix.

A Chinese edition was published in 2017 as *Collected Writings in Commemoration of Liu Xiaobo* by Democratic China and the Institute for China's Democratic Transition. It is hoped that this revised and expanded English edition, organized according to phases of Liu's life and development, will find an even wider audience and offer insight into the person—his ideas, his loves, and his legacy. Some have suggested that because of Liu Xiaobo's death and the economic and political ascendency of the current Chinese regime, Liu's legacy has been reduced to a void. I would recommend that those who claim such consider the longer arc of history. The same was said of visionaries in Eastern Europe when earlier protests were crushed in Poland, East Germany, and elsewhere; the same was said of early martyrs in South Africa, where repression eventually led to widespread civic resistance and in other countries where civilians have challenged repressive systems. Liu Xiaobo was committed to nonviolent engagement and political change. Though he no longer walks the earth, his ideas and writings endure. History will unfold this story. In the meantime the essays in this volume recount one man's journey and commitment to the struggle for the individual's right to freedom.[2]

Societies move forward and are changed by ideas, by leaders, and ultimately by their citizens. None of these essays show Liu Xiaobo aspiring to personal power. But those in power worried about this man of ideas and this activist who set ideas into motion. He didn't need to roar like a lion to garner the world's attention and respect. By his life and his death he holds those in power to account.

NOTES

1. Michael Bristow, "China 'Dog-Lion': Henan Zoo Mastiff Poses as Africa Cat," *BBC News*, August 15, 2013, https://www.bbc.com/news/world-asia-china-23714896.
2. In these collected essays, a number of writers express concern about the fate of Liu Xiaobo's beloved wife, poet and artist Liu Xia, who spent years under house arrest. Since the writing of these articles, Liu Xia has been allowed to go to Germany for medical treatment. As of 2019 she resides in Berlin.

# Foreword

*Shakya Bhikshu Dalai Lama, Tenzin Gyatso*

In contemporary Chinese history, Liu Xiaobo worked greatly for individual freedom and social equality. He was not only someone who struggled for a long time for human rights, democracy, and rule of law in China, but he was also someone who symbolized the Chinese scholar community's recognition of the unequal and unjust situation of present-day Tibet, and he expressed solidarity. Accordingly, I rejoiced when the Nobel Peace Prize was awarded to him. Unfortunately, under restrictions by the Chinese government and in an environment without freedom of expression, he had to be in prison for a long time. It was a matter of regret and sadness that he eventually became ill and passed away in hospital.

I commend the compilation and publication of this book in memory of Mr. Liu Xiaobo by his friends and acquaintances in the Chinese scholar community. The main point of remembering the departed ones is to continue the determination and mission to benefit others that the departed had set for themselves when they were living.

Therefore, I want to make this appeal and prayer: through continued remembrance of Mr. Liu Xiaobo's fearless determination, his reverence for universal values, and his altruistic disposition, it is important to strive at one's ability, like the flow of a river, to fulfill his aspirations.

> *Tibetan Royal Year 2144. November 12, 2017*
> *Translated by Bhuchung Tsering*

# The Passion of Liu Xiaobo

*Perry Link*

From his earliest years, Liu Xiaobo had a characteristic that was so distinctive, and remained so constant, that it almost seems genetic. He was honest. He was blunt. As a preteen, the trait got him into some trouble, both in his family and in his school. In his teens and twenties, his girlfriend Tao Li, whom he married in 1984, seems to have played a role in rounding his rough edges, but later, when he emerged as a brilliant graduate student at Beijing Normal University, the obstreperousness reappeared. Then it subsided again—whether because of his travels abroad, because of his witnessing of the Beijing massacre in June 1989, because of his growing involvement with his second wife, Liu Xia, or because of all these factors, is hard to say. It developed steadily through the 1990s. After 1999, when he emerged from a labor camp (his third incarceration within a decade), he began to write political, social, and cultural criticism that showed his mature thinking. Embracing a pacifist philosophy of "no enemies and no hatred"—but not abandoning his characteristic candor in the slightest—he began to write essays on political, social, and cultural criticism that were remarkable for both their acerbity and their erudition.

By the early 2000s, he had become one of those unusual people who could look at human life from the broadest of perspectives and reason about it from first principles. His keen intellect noticed things that others also looked at but did not see. It seems that hardly any topic evaded his interest, and he could write with analytic calm about upsetting things. One might expect such calm in a recluse—a hermit poet or a cloistered scholar—but in Liu Xiaobo it came in an activist. Repeatedly he went where he thought he should go and did what he thought he should do, as if immune to things like havoc, danger, and the possibility of prison. He seems to have moved through life taking mental notes on what he saw, heard, and read, as well as on the inward responses he felt.

He loved reading. He read quickly, broadly, and with an uncanny ability to remember nearly everything. He stuttered—except when he was lecturing or involved in a passionate argument. In those settings he was quite fluent and resumed stuttering only after reverting to a normal state. He did not care much about dress. His appearance, combined with his no-nonsense temperament, could easily lead a person to underestimate the depth and brilliance of his mind. He wrote about Saint Augustine and Kant, about Zhuangzi, about the rise of great powers, about training for the Olympic Games, about race relations in the mid-nineteenth-century United States, about humor in Czechoslovakia, about the psychology of pornography, about coal miners in Shanxi, about the internet, Jesus Christ, and Tibet.[1] And more. And well.

Luckily for his readers, he always wrote free from fear. Most of his contemporary Chinese writers, including many of the best ones, wrote with political caution in the backs of their minds and with a shadow hovering over their fingers as they passed across a keyboard. How should I couch things? What topics should I not touch? What indirection should I use? Liu Xiaobo did none of that. With him, it was all there. What he thought, you got.

In writing honestly, he did not spare himself. He was constantly self-critical. The only reason we know details of his misbehavior in the early years of the Cultural Revolution, when he was eleven to fourteen years old, is that he later wrote essays about it. He rues the fact that he took up smoking at age eleven, but writes down—and publishes!—how it happened and then goes on to tell us how that misbehavior drew him into two other bad habits. One was stealing, because he had to pilfer money from his father to buy cigarettes; the other was lying, because he had to lie about both the smoking and the pilfering. Perhaps these vices were not too difficult to confess, since they belonged to a child—indeed, a cute child.

More difficult to confess, we must imagine, were details of how he behaved after the June 4 Massacre of 1989. In his retrospective essays on this topic, he blames himself for escaping after the massacre into the quarters of a foreign diplomat, while many others—ordinary citizens—not only remained on the streets of Beijing but risked their lives to rescue the wounded. As he recalls these facts, Liu is mortified. Even more painful was looking back on a confession he wrote under duress during a nineteen-month stay in Beijing's Qincheng Prison, where he was held for having been a "black hand," in the government's lingo, behind the "counterrevolutionary riot" that led to the massacre. We do not have the text of that confession and likely would not even know about it had Liu not written out his repentance.

The first sentence of his final statement at trial in December 2009, when he stood charged with inciting subversion of state power, was "June 1989 has been the major turning point in my life." When his wife, Liu Xia, told him in October 2010 on a visit to him in prison that he had won that year's Nobel Peace Prize, he answered, "This is for those lost souls," meaning the dead at Tiananmen. Each year, on the anniversary of the massacre, he wrote a poem remembering them. We do not know whether, while wasting in prison for the last nine years of his life, he continued to write a poem on each anniversary, but it is hard to imagine that he did not. Below I copy the first of four sections of the poem he wrote in 1999 while imprisoned in a labor camp on the tenth anniversary of the Tiananmen massacre. He called it "Standing in the Execrations of Time":

To me, standing amid the execrations of Time
that day seems so strange

1
Ten years ago this day
dawn, a bloody shirt
sun, a torn calendar
all eyes upon
this . . . single . . . page
the world a single outraged stare
time tolerates no naiveté
the dead rage and howl
till the earth's throat
grows hoarse

Gripping the prison bars
this moment
I must wail in grief
for I fear the next
so much I have no tears for it
remembering them, the innocent dead,
I must thrust a dagger calmly
into my eyes
must purchase with blindness
a clarity of the brain
for that bone-devouring memory
is best expressed
by refusal[2]

Liu's feelings of guilt toward the lost souls seem to have locked him into a sense that the rest of his life must be devoted to them and to what they stood for, regardless of the personal costs to himself. In a letter of January 13, 2000, to his friend Liao Yiwu, he wrote:

Compared to people in other nations that have lived under the dreary pall of communism, we resisters in China have not measured up very well. Even after so many years of tremendous tragedies, we still don't have a leader like Vaclav Havel. It seems ironic that in order to win the right of ordinary people to pursue self-interest, a society needs a moral giant to make a selfless sacrifice. In order to secure "passive" freedom—freedom from state oppression—there needs to be a will to do active resistance. History is not fated. The appearance of a single martyr can fundamentally turn the spirit of a nation and strengthen its moral fiber. Gandhi was such a figure. So was Havel. So, even more, was that humble boy born in a manger two thousand years ago. Human progress is the result of the accident of birth of people such as these. . . . A moral exemplar is needed to articulate principles of conscience that will catalyze the consciences of ordinary people. In China our need for this kind of exemplar is especially strong.[3]

Here Liu seems to be imagining that he or his friend Yiwu might be such an exemplar, ready to pay a fateful price. It would be a serious error to read these words from him as imagining fame for himself. He is wondering whether he has the courage to sacrifice himself for the future of China. Ultimately, that is very close to what happened.

In the spring of 2008, some of his friends conceived the idea of writing a citizens' manifesto calling for free elections and constitutional government in China. They called it Charter 08, in conscious admiration of Vaclav Havel and Czechoslovakia's Charter 77. Liu did not join at first, but in the fall, when the drafting was well underway and momentum was building, he threw his energy into the project. He edited drafts and tried to remove needlessly provocative language that might prevent some people from signing. He then worked hard to solicit signatures—not only from known dissidents but from workers, farmers, state officials, and others willing to gather under the broad tent of asking for a more open and liberal society. The language of the Charter is moderate. Much of it already appears in Chinese and United Nations documents. But a few lines, like "we must abolish the special privilege of one party to monopolize power," went beyond what China's rulers could stomach.

It is clear that Liu's work on Charter 08 led to his eleven-year prison sentence a year later and to his Nobel Peace Prize a year after that. At the Nobel Banquet in December 2010, a member of the selection committee told me that her group had for years been wanting to find a Chinese winner for their prize and that the previous year's events "made this finally seem the right time." Chinese President Hu Jintao and his Politburo were likely annoyed to realize (if ever they did) that their imprisonment of Liu helped pave the way to his award.

It might seem puzzling that an advocate of "no enemies and no hatred" who actually worked to soften the language of the Charter should have been singled out for punishment during the government's crackdown. Several of Liu's colleagues were detained and interrogated and had their computers confiscated, but only Liu was sent to prison. While it is a standard device in Communist Chinese political engineering to "kill a chicken for the monkeys to see," the question remains why a pacifist chicken would be their choice. One reason, almost certainly, was that Liu had been to prison before. The party normally comes down harder on recidivists than others. If they have shown they cannot be intimidated, they are more dangerous.

Another reason, almost certainly, was that the charter movement was viewed as an unauthorized "organization" of which Liu was the leader. The men who rule China had been showing that they could tolerate tongue-lashings from the populace so long as they came from isolated individuals. But an unauthorized organization, even if moderate, had to be crushed. In 2005 Hu Jintao issued a classified report called "Fight a Smokeless Battle: Keep 'Color Revolutions' Out of China." It said people like Nelson Mandela, Lech Wałęsa, and Aung San Suu Kyi are dangerous. If similar movements appeared in China, Hu instructed, "the big ones" should be arrested and "the little ones" left alone. In November 2008, when Chinese police learned that people were signing Charter 08, the Charter was officially labeled an attempt to start a "color revolution." That made Liu Xiaobo a "big one" who needed to be brought down. There are signs that Liu himself understood this mechanism. When he joined the Charter effort, he told his friends that, in addition to editing and gathering signatures, he would "take responsibility" for the Charter—in effect, he would risk being a "big one."

Why Hu Jintao and his people decided on a sentence of eleven years—not ten, twelve, or some other number—was a mystery at the time and remains so now. Of the many guesses that have been offered, one was that eleven years is 4,018 days and there are 4,024 Chinese characters in Charter 08. Thus: one day for every character you wrote, Mr. Liu, and we'll waive the final six. (This was a guess, but not a joke. That sort of petty-minded and highly personal kind of thinking is common in elite Chinese politics.)

The combination of Charter 08 and a consequent Nobel Prize seemed, for a time, to open a new alternative for China. Chinese citizens had long been accustomed to the periodic alternations between "more liberal" and "more conservative" tendencies in Communist rule and had often pinned hopes on one or another high official, but Charter 08 seemed to say that there could be another way to be modern Chinese.

It was hard to find people who disagreed with the Charter once they read it, and it was precisely this potential for contagion that most worried regime leaders. That was their reason (not their stated reason but their real one) for suppressing the Charter, for imprisoning Liu, and for denouncing his Nobel Peace Prize. Their efforts were effective: most young Chinese a decade later did not know who Liu Xiaobo was, and older ones who did were well aware of the cost of saying anything about him in public.

Controls on Chinese society tightened during the last few years of Liu Xiaobo's life, which were also the first few years of Xi Jinping's rule. Society moved in the opposite direction from what Charter 08 had called for. This raises the questions, "Was the Charter movement killed? Was the whole effort in vain?" These are difficult questions, but my answer would be no. The organization had been crushed, but its ideas were not. The government's continuing efforts—assiduous, inveterate, nationwide, and very costly—to repress anything that resembled the ideas in Charter 08 is evidence enough that the men who ruled were quite aware of the ideas' continuing appeal. It would have been wonderful to hear Liu Xiaobo's own answer to the question of whether the Charter movement died, but China's prison system silenced him in his final years. What did he think during those last eight years? What did he foresee for a world in which China's Communist dictatorship continues to grow?

Liu Xiaobo has been compared by some (implicitly, by the Chinese regime itself) to Nelson Mandela, Vaclav Havel, and Aung San Suu Kyi, each of whom accepted prison as the price for pursuing more humane governance in their homelands. But Mandela, Havel, and Suu Kyi all lived to see release from the beastly regimes that repressed them, and Liu Xiaobo did not. Does this mean his place in history will fall short of theirs? Is success of a movement necessary in order for its leader to be viewed as heroic?

Perhaps. It may be useful, though, to compare Liu Xiaobo and Xi Jinping. The two were separated in age by only two years. During Mao's Cultural Revolution both missed school and were banished to remote places. Xi used the time to begin building a résumé that would allow him, riding the coattails of his elite Communist father, to one day vie for supreme power; Liu used the time to read on his own and learn to think for himself. One mastered the skullduggery and sycophancy that a person needs to rise within a closed bureaucracy; the other learned to challenge received wisdom of every kind, keeping for himself only the ideas that could pass the test of rigorous independent examination. For one of them, value was measured by power and position; for the other, by moral worth. In their final standoff, one "won"; the other "lost." But two hundred years from now, who will recall the names of the tyrants who sent Mandela, Havel, and Suu Kyi to jail? Will the incisive glint of Liu Xiaobo's intellect be remembered, or the cardboard mediocrity of Xi's?

## NOTES

1. Zhuang Zhou (Chuang Tzu, c. 369 BC—c. 286 BC), often known as Zhuangzi (literally Master Zhuang), was one of most influential Chinese philosophers and litterateurs. His classic work *Zhuangzi*, a philosophical, literary, and religious collection of his writings, is regarded as one of the foundational texts of Taoism.—Ed.
2. Liu Xiaobo, "Standing in the Execrations of Time," trans. Isaac P. Hsich, in *Liu Xiaobo: No Enemies, No Hatred*, ed. Perry Link, Tienchi Martin-Liao, and Liu Xia (Cambridge MA: The Belknap Press of Harvard University Press, 2012), 16.—Ed.
3. Liu Xiaobo, "A Letter to Liao Yiwu," trans. Perry Link, in Link et al., *Liu Xiaobo*, 287.—Ed.

# Liu Xiaobo's Spiritual Heritage
*Zhang Zuhua*

On July 13, 2017, Dr. Liu Xiaobo, a Nobel Peace Prize laureate, passed away after suffering long-term political persecution, literary inquisition, and imprisonment. Widely knowledgeable, exceptionally brilliant, highly enthusiastic, and extraordinarily energetic, Liu Xiaobo had dedicated the sixty-one years of his precious life to the great cause of struggling for freedom, defending human rights and dignity and achieving constitutional democracy. He was not only a standard-bearer of contemporary liberalism in China and a key campaigner in democracy movements but also an outstanding spiritual leader in upholding universal values and a moral conscience against totalitarianism and autocracy in today's world.

The untimely passing of Liu Xiaobo filled people of conscience all over the world with deep grief and indignation, and they have used various ways to commemorate, mourn, acknowledge and enshrine him, praying sincerely for him and his family. As his colleagues and comrades-in-arms, we are obliged to carefully parse his spiritual, intellectual, and political legacy to pass on the torch of his ideals and morality. What follows are my views for the reference of others.

## The Spirit of Inheriting and Upholding Liberal Ideas

Throughout his life, what Liu Xiaobo valued most was liberty, and what he hated most was the dictatorial system restraining liberty. Having accepted and embraced liberalism in his youth, he never wavered in holding high the banner of liberalism, upholding and passing along liberal ideas, bravely defending liberal doctrine, and persistently speaking about and practicing liberalism.

What is liberalism? Liberalism is a mainstream value and a fundamental principle of today's civilized world, as well as a powerful weapon against all forms of absolutism, totalitarianism, and authoritarianism. In more than three hundred years of development, through the efforts of John Locke, Montesquieu, David Hume, Adam Smith, George Byron, Percy Shelley, Edmund Burke, Wilhelm von Humboldt, Benjamin Constant, Alexis de Tocqueville, Immanuel Kant, John Stuart Mill, John Dalberg-Acton, Thomas Paine, Thomas Jefferson, Friedrich Hayek, and Karl Popper, liberalism has gradually acquired four aspects. The first is political liberalism, with the basic notions of establishing constitutional politics, implementing representative democracy and rule of law, and protecting human rights. The second is economic liberalism, with the core connotations of protecting private property, implementing market economy, and minimizing the state's interference in and control of economic activities. The third is social liberalism, which is concerned with social justice and protecting the basic living conditions and rights of the disadvantaged. The fourth is individual liberalism, with an emphasis on individual values and rights and on the individual receiving the highest respect and enjoying basic human rights and dignity. The fundamental tenets of liberalism, including individual freedom and dignity, freedom of speech, religious tolerance, popular sovereignty, universal human rights, rule of law, transparent and open government, restrictions on governmental power, protection of private property, basic equality, free market economy, and free trade, have rooted themselves in the minds of people in most countries and have made liberalism a universally acknowledged mainstream civilization.

As Li Shenzhi pointed out, liberalism is not a tradition in the thousands of years of Chinese civilization but an outcome of Western learning that spread to the East. It was introduced to China a little more than a hundred years ago. The first person who introduced the concept of liberty to China was Yan Fu. He translated John Stuart Mill's *On Liberty* and brought the classic definition of liberty to China: "A person should be free to do as he likes in his own concerns; (but he ought not to be free to do as he likes in acting for another under the pretext that the affairs of another are his own affairs)." Furthermore, "he must not make himself a nuisance to other people." In 1895, facing the critical condition of China after its defeat in the First Sino-Japanese War and summarizing historical experience since the Opium Wars, Yan Fu published *On the Speed of World Change*, which explicitly stated that the crux of the difference between the prosperous and powerful West and the weak and impoverished China was "whether or not there is freedom."

Following Yan Fu, Liang Qichao published his essay *On Liberty* in May 1902, pointing out that Patrick Henry's statement "Give me liberty or give me death" was what nations in Europe and America were founded on during the eighteenth and nineteenth centuries. Further, in *On the New People*, Liang stated, "Is the sense of liberty applicable to today's China? Liberty, as a common notion in the world and essential element of human life, is applicable everywhere."

Cai Yuanpei, who became the president of Peking University in 1917, used a policy of "including great classics, collecting various schools, freedom of thought, and inclusiveness" to transform Peking University into a truly modern university and a base for introducing and promoting liberalism in China.

As a result, Yan Fu, Liang Qichao, and Cai Yuanpei are considered the founders of Chinese liberalism, as well as representatives of China's first generation of liberalism. Following Yan, Liang, and Cai, the next person taking up the banner of liberalism was Hu Shih, who throughout his life championed freedom of thought, speech, religion, and politics. Hu Shih is therefore widely regarded as the main representative of the second generation in the historic development of liberalism in modern China.

The year 1949 was a historical turning point. As the Chinese Communist Party (CCP) took power through unlawful and violent revolution, a large number of liberal intellectuals such as Hu Shih moved to Taiwan. "The father of the Republic of China's Constitution," Zhang Junmai (Carsun Chang), and other renowned scholars went into exile overseas. From then on, the flowers and fruits of liberalism in China were scattered and faded into a backdrop of devastation. Under the continuous political suppression of CCP totalitarianism, the liberal intellectuals who remained in Mainland China were without exception brutally suppressed through "class struggle" and "proletariat dictatorship," jailed on trumped-up charges or labeled and forced to undergo thought reform. After the Anti-Rightist Campaign in 1957, liberal intellectuals were reduced to silence and isolation. It was not until the early 1970s that the sprouts of liberalism began reappearing, making a subtle debut during the April 5 Movement in 1976 and gradually becoming a formidable ideological weapon against autocracy and totalitarian rule.[1]

From the April 5 Movement to the Democracy Wall Movement in the late 1970s, then on to the ideological enlightenment and ideological liberation movements of the 1980s and the 1989 Democracy Movement, a new group of liberal intellectuals emerged in Mainland China, forming the third generation of Chinese liberalism and causing a revival of liberalism that had a significant and far-reaching ideological impact on social transformation and political reform in China. I consider the representative figures of Chinese liberalism during this period to be Hu Ping, Chen Ziming, and Liu Xiaobo.

Hu Ping (born on August 18, 1947, now living in New York) completed his long essay "On Freedom of Speech" in July 1975. The fourth edition of his article was published as a special issue of a privately published magazine *Fertile Soil* during the Democracy Wall Movement in Beijing in February 1979. Its fifth edition was completed in early 1980, and when in November he sought election as deputy of the People's Congress of Haidian District, where he was a student at Peking University, the article was copied onto big-character posters and distributed around the campus as campaign material. Afterwards, a mimeographed version was disseminated overseas and published in installments in several issues of *The Seventies* monthly magazine (later renamed *The Nineties*) in 1981. In 1986 the article was printed in letterpress for the first time in Mainland China in the July and September issues of *Youth Forum* magazine in Wuhan. Copied and distributed on campuses throughout the country, Hu Ping's essay contributed significantly to the revival of liberalism in China. Since then, Hu Ping has become a prolific writer, but his departure from China many years ago and authorities' censorship of his articles have limited his influence in China.

Chen Ziming (January 8, 1952–October 21, 2014) was a veteran of the April Fifth Movement, the Democracy Wall Movement, the ideological liberation movement, and the 1989 Democracy Movement. Although repeatedly imprisoned, he was a prolific author who wrote and compiled a large number of well-received works on political liberalism, the theory of constitutional democracy, and the history of democracy movements in China. His works were eventually compiled into a twelve-volume collection as well as in other publications. Regrettably, due to censorship by the authorities, Chen Ziming could only publish in Mainland China under a pen name. It was the advent of the internet age that enabled the circulation of Chen Ziming's articles and thinking.

Liu Xiaobo was youngest of the three. He was part of the first group of students admitted to college under the National Higher Education Entrance Examination, which resumed in 1977 after the Cultural Revolution. He received his master's and doctoral degrees in literature in 1984 and 1988, respectively. During the 1980s, he published *The Critique of Choice: Dialogues with Li Zehou* (1988), his doctoral thesis *Aesthetic and Human Freedom* (1988), *The Fog of Metaphysics* (1989) and *Going Naked toward God* (1989). Chinese authorities designated *The Critique of Choice* "for internal circulation," while the other three were banned soon after their release. *Going Naked toward God* was recalled and destroyed even before it reached the market. The publication of these books marked Liu's transformation from a leftist youth deeply influenced by Marxism to a liberal intellectual.

If regarded as an academic liberal before 1989, his experience of the 1989 Democracy Movement quickly made Liu Xiaobo a political liberal advocating human rights, democracy, rule of law, and constitutionalism. After the 1989 Democracy Movement, Liu Xiaobo penned more than a thousand articles on current affairs. In particular his masterpiece *Civil Awakening: The Dawn of a Free China* and Charter 08, which he took part in drafting and initiating, profoundly expound on the universal values and basic principles of political liberalism and have had a great far-reaching influence on the constitutional democracy movement in Mainland China, making him worthy to be a standard-bearer of contemporary liberalism in China.

In his book *Civil Awakening*, Liu Xiaobo wrote that "private property is the foundation of liberal constitutionalism." He also put forward nine political demands central to the fight for civil rights: 1) economic reform, 2) legal reform, 3) administrative reform, 4) media reform, 5) reform of the people's congresses, 6) electoral reform, 7) finance and tax reform, 8) military reform, and 9) education reform. He defended the legal right of members of the public to participate in public affairs and strongly criticized the "theory of gradual development of democracy."

Charter 08 points out: "Freedom is at the core of universal human values. Freedom of speech, freedom of the press, freedom of assembly, freedom of association, freedom in where to live, and the freedoms to strike, to demonstrate, and to protest, among others, are the forms that freedom takes. Without freedom, China will always remain far from civilized ideals."[2] In particular, Charter 08 presents several political recommendations (Recommendations 7–14) to implement the principle of freedom.

Liu Xiaobo was arrested and tried for his involvement in drafting and initiating Charter 08. In court, he read out his stirring "I Have No Enemies: My Final Statement":

> Free expression is the base of human rights, the root of human nature, and the mother of truth. To kill free speech is to insult human rights, to stifle human nature, and to suppress truth.
>
> I feel it is my duty as a Chinese citizen to try to realize in practice the right of free expression that is written in our country's constitution. There has been nothing remotely criminal in anything that I have done, yet I will not complain, even in the face of the charges against me.[3]

Facing trumped-up charges and imprisonment, Liu Xiaobo didn't think of his own safety but of ending the literary inquisition in China and of bringing about freedom of speech and the free expression of alternative values, ideas, beliefs, and political views. This fully demonstrates his awe-inspiring upholding of justice, sacrifice for righteousness, and soaring morality of friendship.

Contemporary China has a large number of intellectuals who have contributed to the revival of liberalism.[4] In terms of social influence in combining knowledge with action, however, no one has surpassed Liu Xiaobo. That is why Liu Xiaobo is an outstanding representative of the third generation of liberal intellectuals in Mainland China and deserves to be called the standard-bearer of contemporary Chinese liberalism.

### Dauntless Spirit of Unifying Knowledge with Action and Daring to take Responsibility

It should be particularly pointed out that the liberalism Liu Xiaobo espoused consistently rejected cynicism. Under the coercive rule of totalitarianism and autocracy, non-involvement in current affairs and a play-it-safe cynicism have prevailed in Chinese society, but Liu Xiaobo was overflowing with a dauntless spirit of unifying knowledge with action; fearing no risk, he "took up morality and justice on iron shoulders, and wrote with a ruthless pen."[5]

In his 2002 essay "The Poverty of China's Popular Opposition: On the 13th Anniversary of June 4th," Liu Xiaobo wrote:

> The philosopher Wang Yangming, celebrated for his "School of Mind" and "the unity of knowledge and action," said, "Knowledge without action is mere ignorance." Unfortunately, most Chinese intellectuals exist in this "ignorant" state of "knowledge without action." In today's world, where division of labor is becoming increasingly exhaustive, intellectuals' unity of knowledge and action means not being controlled by any external authority and truthfully expressing your knowledge. In the context of contemporary China, however, where intellectuals are intimidated and obstructed with systemic terror and lies, intellectuals' unity of knowledge and action means truthfully expressing your knowledge with conscience and courage in the face of terror. This is the sacred mission of intellectuals.

Liu Xiaobo both spoke and acted this way. In April 1989, when the Tiananmen Democracy Movement broke out, Liu Xiaobo was a visiting scholar at Columbia University, but he flew from New York to Beijing and involved himself in this earthshaking democracy movement, holding fast to the frontline from beginning to end and becoming one of the key intellectual representatives in the movement. After the June Fourth Massacre, when others chose to leave the country to seek asylum or even abandoned the democracy movement, he chose to shoulder the dual responsibilities of justice and politics in spite of the attendant humiliations and insisted on remaining in China to continue the struggle. He spent the next twenty-eight years in and out of prison and most of the time in custody. He spent his time outside of prison dashing off emphatic appeals for freedom, democracy, and human rights while defying danger and hardship on the frontline of the social movement for freedom and democracy, taking part in nearly every battle.

Not long after being released from prison in 1991, Liu Xiaobo went to the home of Professor Ding Zilin, whose son had been killed in the June Fourth Massacre.[6] In her memoir, Ding writes:

That day, Jiang [Peikun] briefly told him about Lian'er joining the student movement and the situation before and after his death. [Liu] turned and excused himself, and half an hour later came with a bouquet of fresh flowers and suddenly fell to the floor weeping before Lian'er's tablet. . . . We were all plunged in unrestrained grief. The next day, he came again to our home, and before Lian'er's tablet he read out the poem he had written the night before, "To the Seventeen-Year-Old." His voice was choked with sobs; it was unbearable.[7]

After that, Liu Xiaobo continued to take enormous risk in his unsparing efforts to help the families of victims and the Tiananmen Mothers in their rights defense struggle. He wrote many articles to gain support for the families and the Tiananmen Mothers in the international community, and he took the lead in nominating the Tiananmen Mothers for the Nobel Peace Prize. After Liu Xiaobo died, the ailing Ding Zilin represented the Tiananmen Mothers in expressing condolences: "Although you lost your freedom and lost your life, you still possess the great love of the world, which no one on Earth can match. In our hearts, you live eternally."[8]

On February 20, 1995, Liu Xiaobo joined with Bao Zunxin, Wang Ruoshui, Chen Ziming, Xu Wenli, and others in drafting and signing the "Anticorruption Proposal to the Third Plenary Session of the Eighth National People's Congress," which proposed seven items for short-term reform and five for long-term reform. Liu Xiaobo also joined Bao Zunxin in issuing an open letter demanding that Chen Ziming be released on medical parole and collected signatures from prominent intellectuals. In May 1995 Liu Xiaobo joined Chen Xiaoping in drafting "Drawing from a Lesson Paid for in Blood and the Process of Promoting Democracy and Rule of Law: An Appeal on the Sixth Anniversary of June 4th" and gathered signatures.[9] Before the statement was formally issued, Liu Xiaobo was held in solitary confinement under "residential surveillance" in the Beijing suburbs by the Beijing Municipal Public Security Bureau and wasn't released until February 1996.

In August 1996 Liu Xiaobo met with the famous dissident Wang Xizhe in Guangzhou, and after discussing some issues of common interest, they decided to submit "Views on Certain Major Affairs of Our Country" to the Kuomintang (Nationalist Party of China) and the Chinese Communist Party. Issued on the fifty-first anniversary of the Double Tenth Agreement the two parties had signed on October 10, 1945, it was called the Double Ten Declaration and touched on a political foundation for cross-strait reunification, the issue of Tibet, strengthening the system of the National People's Congress, and the issue of the Diaoyu Islands.[10] Two days before this declaration was formally issued, the Beijing Municipal Public Security Bureau once again detained Liu Xiaobo, and he was eventually sentenced to three years of reeducation through labor (RTL) on the charge of "causing a social disturbance." He was held in the Dalian RTL Center until he completed his sentence in October 1999.

In his article "The Internet and I," Liu Xiaobo wrote, "When I finished my three years in prison on October 7, 1999, I returned home to find a computer that a friend had given to my wife. Soon after my return, the computer became my writing tool." From then on, he used the computer and the internet to churn out and post more than a thousand current affairs commentaries promoting universal values, freedom, democracy, human rights, rule of law, and constitutionalism, which had an enormous influence on society.

With the beginning of the new century, Liu Xiaobo constantly stood at the forefront of the democracy and rights defense movements. From supporting the Four Gentlemen of the New Youth Study Group to rescuing the Stainless Steel Rat (Liu Di), Du Daobin, and other victims of literary inquisition, from supporting persecuted Falun Gong practitioners to protesting the death of Sun Zhigang, from protesting the government's blocking of the internet to calling for the abolition of the crime of "inciting subversion of state power," from protesting the Shanwei shootings and the closure of the *Century China* website to protesting the government's persecution of the blind rights defender Chen Guangcheng and human rights lawyers Gao Zhisheng and Teng Biao, and finally taking part in the Same World, Same Dream, Same Human Rights signature campaign, Liu Xiaobo was constantly dashing off articles and taking part in open letters and appeals that had considerable social influence.[11] Adhering to the notion of liberty and human rights above all, Liu Xiaobo wrote more than a hundred commentaries targeting the CCP authorities on issues such as pressuring Taiwan on its democracy, stripping Hong Kong of its freedoms, and violating the human rights of people in Tibet and Xinjiang. After the crackdown in Tibet in March 2008, Liu Xiaobo joined with Wang Lixiong and others in issuing a twenty-one-point opinion paper on how to handle the situation in Tibet, the first time Mainland Chinese citizens had issued a joint statement on the Tibet issue. Commenting on Liu Xiaobo's death on July 14, 2017, His Holiness the Dalai Lama issued a statement:

> I am deeply saddened to learn that fellow Nobel Laureate Liu Xiaobo has passed away while undergoing a lengthy prison sentence. I offer my prayers and condolences to his wife, Liu Xia and to other members of his family.
>
> Although he is no longer living, the rest of us can best pay honor to Liu Xiaobo by carrying forward the principles he has long embodied, which would lead to a more harmonious, stable and prosperous China.
>
> It is my belief that Nobel Laureate Liu Xiaobo's unceasing efforts in the cause of freedom will bear fruit before long.[12]

In an article commemorating Liu Xiaobo, the Xinjiang Uyghur leader Mehmet Emin Hazret wrote, "Liu Xiaobo was the intimate friend of the Uyghur people. The article 'The Right to Autonomy,' which he published in November 2000, demanded that the Chinese Constitution and Law on Regional National Autonomy protect the right to genuine autonomy of the Uyghur and Tibetan people."[13]

In July 2001 Liu Xiaobo took part in establishing what is now known as the Independent Chinese PEN Center. He was elected the second president of ICPC in November 2003 and reelected on November 2, 2005. When he finished his second term in October 2007, Liu Xiaobo continued to serve on the ICPC board until he was arrested again in December 2008. In the four years Liu Xiaobo served as president, the ICPC experienced rapid growth. Members living in Mainland China began to outnumber those living overseas, and ICPC's growing reputation and influence within China led to an unprecedented number of appeals for freedom of expression and freedom to write. This is one reason why CCP authorities began to fear Liu Xiaobo and became determined to eliminate him.

While Liu Xiaobo continued to invest himself wholeheartedly in the cause of China's freedom and democracy, he also had the humanist sentiments of a world citizen. The day after the September 11, 2001, terrorist attacks on the United States, Liu Xiaobo and his friends jointly issued an open letter to President George W. Bush and the citizens of the United States expressing sympathy and support for the American people and vehement condemnation of international terrorism's violence against humanity. The open letter was posted on the internet and collected 673 signatures.

For this reason, Liu Xiaobo's death drew not only heartfelt condolences and reminiscences from China's democracy activists, rights defenders, and liberal intellectuals but also high appraisals of him from international human rights organizations and champions of justice.

### An Indefatigable Spirit for Exploring the Road to Constitutional Politics

After experiencing the 1989 Democracy Movement and June Fourth Massacre, Liu Xiaobo pondered how to confront the CCP's totalitarian rule and violent culture. He chose feasible means to mobilize popular forces to join in promoting the progress of China's democratization and explored the path for maximizing nonviolent and peaceful means to achieve democratic transformation and establish a constitutional state. To this end, he spent his last twenty years writing articles expounding on the ideology of constitutional democracy and the road to China's democratic transformation, which were collected and published in 2005 as *Civil Awakening*. In this book, he comprehensively explored the optimal conditions for China to carry out political reform: the rise of civil rights and corresponding decline in bureaucratic powers, reform of property rights, awakening consciousness of human rights, the rise of worker movements, practicing grassroots democracy and autonomy, the popular movement to protect freedom of expression on the internet, a popular impetus toward journalistic reform and the rise of dissenting views within the system. He systematically expounded on the development of various facets of Chinese society and the way these related to China's political democratization. He believed that China had experienced complications and learned lessons in its hundred-year effort to modernize from 1848 to 1949 but had ultimately taken the worst possible path by choosing the Soviet model of Communist totalitarianism. Mao's death by natural cause was followed by a new modernization effort as the CCP of the post-Mao era pursued the lame reforms launched by Deng Xiaoping. At the outset of the twenty-first century, although China's modernization was still not on the right track, its internal and external environments presented a golden opportunity as favorable international trends and an awakening domestic popular society joined to push China back in the right direction.

To harness the collective wisdom of the general public for in-depth exploration of the path toward China's democratic transformation and to facilitate the establishment of a constitutional and democratic political system, Liu Xiaobo, Cai Chu and I established the *Democratic China* electronic journal overseas in October 2006. Liu Xiaobo served as chief editor and set the goal of *Democratic China* as "liberty, democracy, human rights, rule of law and constitutionalism." He personally took charge of the e-journal's work plan and external liaison work, organized a crack editorial team and high-quality advisory board, and contacted and invited a large number of scholars, political commentators, and democracy activists to write articles for the journal. Since then, *Democratic China* has published more than six thousand articles commemorating the anniversary of June 4, describing the current situation and prospects of China's democratic transformation, and exploring possible paths toward this transformation. The journal commemorated the hundredth anniversary of the Xinhai Revolution, commenting on the international fourth wave of democratization and China's democratic transformation. It analyzed the relationship between democratic transformation and systemic reform, civil society, social movements, the internet age, and the magazine's editorial motto. All-inclusive, multi-faceted study and discussion of the various problems and difficulties of China's democratic transformation have raised many valuable ideological viewpoints. About 90 percent of the writers for *Democratic China* are in Mainland China, with the remaining 10 percent residing all over the world. All of this effort is aimed at pushing forward China's democratization, ending the single-party autocracy, and contributing valuable theoretical guidance and rich accumulated experience for establishing constitutional politics.

Around 2005 Liu Xiaobo and I and a few other like-minded friends began mulling over crafting a political program to maximize consensus among the popular democratic forces to draw together China's scattered popular democratic forces, rights defenders, and liberals to jointly push forward the process of China's constitutional democracy. This programmatic document was Charter 08, which was issued on December 9, 2008.

Liu Xiaobo participated throughout the process of creating Charter 08, from considering, planning, drafting, discussing, revising, and soliciting views on the content to finalizing and collecting signatures. Because Liu Xiaobo was president of the ICPC and chief editor of *Democratic China* at that time, he had many tasks to deal with, so our friends chose me to produce the initial draft (temporarily entitled "Political Document") with the help of He Yongqin (who wrote under the pen name Wen Kejian) and Wang Zhijing (who used the pen name Wang Debang). Bao Zunxin did the overall planning and direction, while Xiaobo was responsible for contacting people from all fields and collecting their views for incorporation into revision of the text. The initial draft was divided into a general program for politics, economics, society, and culture. Because I lacked expertise on economic issues, I asked He Yongqin, who had studied economics, to draft that part. Most of the content was on politics, and when I had difficulty dealing with a particular issue, I consulted Liu Junning, who was very helpful. Wang Zhiqing helped me convene many online discussions of the text and collected feedback suggesting a number of revisions. Jiang Qisheng was also one of the earliest participants and provided pertinent views that were incorporated into the text. At the last stage, Zhao Changqing filled in gaps in the conclusion of the text. Election expert Yao Lifa played a key role in contacting people throughout the country and collecting signatures.

From the outset, the participants unanimously agreed to draft a strategic programmatic document with clearly demarcated clauses, like the American Declaration of Independence (1776) and the French Declaration of the Rights of Man and of the Citizen (1789), and the 1948 Universal Declaration of Human Rights. We wanted a document that could provide principled guidance for China's current democracy movement, as well as fundamental points for establishing constitutional politics under a democratic China of the future.

The drafting process referenced a large number of key documents relating to democratic transformation and human rights safeguards in countries all over the world. The first draft was written at the end of 2005 with a total of sixty articles and more than ten thousand characters. During discussion, Bao Zunxin, Liu Xiaobo, and other friends suggested that the document was too long and its clauses too numerous, that it should be more succinct, and that some of its formulations required further deliberation. Incorporating the suggestions of Liu Xiaobo, Bao, and other participants, I carried out seven or eight revisions in 2006, reducing the text to a little more than four thousand words and thirty-five articles. At that time, we estimated that we could collect one hundred signatures but decided not to publish it in late 2006 because some participants felt it wasn't an optimal time. We held several discussion meetings in 2007 to further revise the text. One meeting, in June of that year, was held at the country home of Ding Zilin at Yanqing County's Xiaying village in Beijing. The participants included Liu Xiaobo, Bao Zunxin, Ding Zilin, Jiang Peikun, Jiang Qisheng, Mo Shaoping, Yang Jianli, me, the father of June 4 victim Zhao, and others.

The participants reached a high degree of consensus on endorsing universal values and establishing a constitutional democratic system, and there were only some differing views on issues such as a federal system, totalitarianism, the land system, Falun Gong, and popular religious beliefs. People also had their own views and suggestions on some specific articles and phraseology. After each meeting, everyone's opinions and suggestions were incorporated into another revision of the text. In this way, the text underwent numerous revisions in 2007, and the total number of articles was reduced to about twenty. We once again considered publishing the document at the end of 2007, but some participants felt the time was still not ripe and proposed expanding the range of participants to include some influential proponents of democracy, business figures, and public intellectuals within the public system. That brought us into 2008.

Liu Xiaobo put an enormous effort into collecting signatures. He and I went together to visit Mao Yushi, Bao Tong, Jiang Ping, and other prominent people of integrity and prestige within the public system. Furthermore, Xiaobo personally took printed copies of the text and privately met with more than seventy people, patiently explaining the articles to them one by one and collecting views for revision as well as signatures. He also entrusted friends in other cities to visit prominent people in their places of residence and collect signatures. Coupled with the effort of other participants in recommending the text, we collected the first round of 303 signatures from all over the country, more than triple our initial projection of 100 signatures.

The year 2008 was the 100th anniversary of China establishing a constitution, the 60th anniversary of the Universal Declaration of Human Rights, the 30th anniversary of the birth of Democracy Wall, and the 10th anniversary of the Chinese government's signing of the International Covenant on Civil and Political Rights. We unanimously decided to issue the document on December 10, the 60th anniversary of the Universal Declaration of Human Rights, and to call it Charter 08. It was Liu Xiaobo who finalized the text, painstakingly fine-tuning of the draft based on everyone's suggestions in an effort to make it fitting, succinct, and refined. That's how it became Charter 08, with nineteen articles (recommendations) totaling 4,024 characters.

Many people from all walks of life took part in the process of drafting, discussing, revising, and shaping Charter 08 and provided valuable views and suggestions. In this sense, Charter 08 was the crystallization of group knowledge and the result of long-term pondering and deliberation. As Xu Youyu said, "It could be considered the group product of Chinese intellectuals pursuing freedom and democracy, and the history exam paper they turned in following the June Fourth Massacre. It also reflected Xiaobo's personal effort, change in direction and improvement."[14]

As of July 16, 2017, Charter 08's signature collection team had published thirty-six batches of signatures, bringing the total number of people signing Charter 08 to 13,520, and signatures continue to be added. The signature campaign will continue until China implements constitutional politics and joins the ranks of democratic countries.

It is under such extraordinarily arduous conditions that China's liberal intellectuals such as Liu Xiaobo have spent and sometimes sacrificed their lives in search of how to achieve freedom and liberation, how to effectively safeguard human rights and human dignity, how to establish a constitutional democratic political system, and how to lead China onto the path of modern civilization. Bao Tong points out, "Liu Xiaobo found the path of least resistance and the path with the most grounds. His ultimate goal was one that no one dared to publicly oppose. If China really embarks on the road to democracy, then it will not only be for the well-being of the Chinese people, but the whole world will also benefit from a responsible, big country. This can play a major positive role in the common development of human civilization."[15]

Liu Xiaobo's spirit of persistently continuing his struggle in pursuit of liberty in spite of all setbacks, of unifying knowledge with action, turning words into deeds, fighting for democracy, and defending human rights and human dignity, and of tenaciously exploring China's path to constitutionalism are the precious spiritual legacy he has left for us. Liu Xiaobo offered up his life in struggling for the great cause of freedom and democracy. United with the sea, he will enrich the great land of China and extend the benefit to world civilization. Freedom's fire burns eternal; "the torch is passed on, and we don't know where it ends."[16]

*Translated by Stacy Mosher and Yu Zhang*

## NOTES

1. See Bao Zunxin, "The Spectrum of the Development of Liberalism in China" (in Chinese), Independent Chinese PEN Center, July 24, 2019, http://www.chinesepen .org/blog/archives/79853.
2. "China's Charter 08," trans. Perry Link, *New York Review of Books*, January 15, 2009, http://www.nybooks.com/articles/2009/01/15/chinas-charter-08/.—Trans.
3. Liu Xiaobo, "I Have No Enemies: My Final Statement," trans. Perry Link) in *Liu Xiaobo: No Enemies, No Hatred*, ed. Perry Link, Tienchi Martin-Liao, and Liu Xia (Cambridge MA: The Belknap Press of Harvard University Press, 2012), 326.—Trans.
4. Rong Jian, "The 'Third Wave' of Liberalism in China" (in Chinese), *Boxun*, November 2013, https://blog.boxun.com/hero/201311/rongjian/29_1.shtml.
5. This expression originates with Ming dynasty statesman Yang Jisheng (1516–55) in his book *Yang Zhongmin gong ji*. It refers to taking on the task of saving the nation and the people.—Trans.
6. Ding Zilin (b. 1936) and her husband, Jiang Peikun (1934–2015), were among the founders of the Tiananmen Mothers, a group of family members of June 4 victims seeking justice for the victims and a reassessment of the democracy movement and the government's violent crackdown.—Trans.

7.  Ding Zilin and Jiang Peikun, "Our Acquaintance and Friendship with Liu Xiaobo" (in Chinese), *Democratic China*, January 14, 2010, http://minzhuzhongguo.org/MainArtShow.aspx?AID=13095.

8.  As translated by Human Rights in China elsewhere in this volume.—Trans.

9.  "Drawing from a Lesson Paid for in Blood and the Process of Promoting Democracy and the Rule of Law: An Appeal on the Sixth Anniversary of June 4th," at "Appeals for Justice," Human Rights in China, May 29, 2008, https://www.hrichina.org/en/content/3725.

10. China and Japan have been engaged in a dispute over the Diaoyu Islands, also known as the Senkaku Islands, since the 1970s. Japan claimed sovereignty over the uninhabited archipelago in the East China Sea in 1895.—Trans.

11. The New Youth Study Group was established in 1999 by Yang Zili (b. 1971), Xu Wei (b. 1974), Jin Haike (b. 1976), and Zhang Honghai (b. 1973) to discuss political issues. All four were arrested in March 2001 for "subversion of state power." Liu Di (b. 1981) became a symbol of free speech after being detained in 2002 for writings she posted on the internet under the pen name Stainless Steel Rat (after a character in a Harry Harrison science fiction story). Du Daobin (b. 1964) was arrested in October 2003 for posting articles on the internet advocating democracy and human rights.

    Sun Zhigang (1976–2003), a university graduate and migrant worker, was beaten to death in a custody and repatriation center in March 2003 after being detained in Guangzhou for lacking the appropriate residential permit. A public uproar about the case led to abolition of the custody and repatriation system.

    In December 2005 the People's Armed Police opened fire on residents of Shanwei Village, Guangdong Province, who were protesting the construction of a wind-power generator on agricultural land without proper compensation being paid to displaced farmers. The authorities acknowledged three people killed and eight injured as a result of the shooting.

    The *Century China* website, which focused on China's social development and culture, was forced to close down in July 2006.

    Chen Guangcheng (b. 1971) is a blind self-taught lawyer who was subjected to repeated detention and house arrest because of his rights defense work; he obtained political asylum in the United States in 2012. Gao Zhisheng (b. 1964) is likewise a rights defense lawyer who has been repeatedly imprisoned and placed under house arrest. Teng Biao (b. 1973) is a U.S.-based Chinese scholar and human rights lawyer.—Trans.

12. "His Holiness the Dalai Lama Deeply Saddened by Liu Xiaobo's Passing Away," His Holiness the 14th Dalai Lama of Tibet, July 14, 2017, https://www.dalailama.com/news/2017/message-from-his-holiness-the-dalai-lama.

13. Mehmet Emin Hazret, "With Liu Xiaobo's Death, the Conscience of 1.3 Billion Chinese Has Died" (in Chinese), *Boxun*, July 23, 2017.

14. Xu Youyu, "Liu Xiaobo and Charter 08," *China in Perspective (Zonglan Zhongguo)*, July 16, 2017 (also collected in this book).

15. Bao Tong, "Liu Xiaobo and His Political Stands," *Radio Free Asia*, July 13, 2017 (also collected in this book).

16. Adapted from Zhuangzi (Chang Tzu), *Nourishing the Lord of Life*, translated by James Legge (1815–97), https://www.taoistic.com/chuangtzu/chuangtzu-03.htm. The entire sentence goes, "What we can point to are the faggots that have been consumed; but the fire is transmitted (elsewhere), and we know not that it is over and ended."—Trans.

# Democracy's Iron Man

*Cui Weiping*

> As when the frailest person falls asleep,
> Torrential rain poured on our country that night;
> It was his tears at parting with humanity.
> "I'm not the person you imagined."

The final statement Liu Xiaobo was unable to read out in court at the end of 2009 included his formulation "I have no enemies," which had first appeared in" The June 2nd Hunger Strike Declaration" of the Four Gentlemen of Tiananmen Square in 1989. Many people have forgotten that historical declaration from so long ago, but Liu Xiaobo remembered it clearly. Among the "basic watchwords" that declaration announced, the first was "We have no enemies. We must not let hatred or violence poison our thinking or the progress of democratization in China."[1] Facing the same impasse and the same moment of truth twenty years later, Liu Xiaobo once again grasped the opportunity to proclaim, "I have no enemies and no hatred. . . . Hatred only eats away at a person's intelligence and conscience, and an enemy mentality can poison the spirit of an entire people."[2]

Today some sneer at this statement of Liu Xiaobo, which shows that they have never faced the kind of hopeless situation he faced on June 4—an army's suppression, being surrounded by strange faces so close that they could see each other's eyes and noses and hear each other breathing, and at such an obvious disadvantage in terms of strength as to be no match for the army. Should he surrender his life or hold it fast? It would be decided in a twinkling. In a situation where lives were hanging by a thread, he needed to find a solid ground—he needed to say, "The earth beneath your feet is also for me to stand on; the sky above your heads is also for me to enjoy."

Wielding his last and only opportunity, Xiaobo said, "Merely for express-ing different political views and for joining a peaceful democracy movement, a teacher lost his right to teach, a writer lost his right to publish, and a public intellectual could no longer speak openly. Whether we view this as my own fate or as the fate of a China after thirty years of 'reform and opening,' it truly is a sad fate."[3] Perhaps Xiaobo also wanted to loudly proclaim, "I am not the enemy you imagine me to be." He had reason to say so. No crimes could be found in his history, and he wasn't acting in his personal interest. Please allow him to counterattack in the way that was possible for him at the time. Compared with the self-defense of "I am not the enemy," isn't "I have no enemies" even more powerful? Or was he supposed to say, "Yes, I am that enemy you speak of," and to accept that groundless charge?

He viewed the world through boundaries of his own making. Whatever he wouldn't allow into his life, he was also unwilling to allow into the world. For instance, if he didn't have violent tendencies in his own life, he would not let the behavior of others impose violence on him. If he valued freedom and autonomy, he would not become mired in hatred because of the crimes of others, since hateful people were dominated by values opposed to freedom and autonomy. If he experienced the good things and positive feelings of human life, he knew all the more that he must allow what was good and open to take root in himself, not what was biased and narrow minded. His life was oriented toward love and light, not toward hatred and darkness. This was his own decision and what he was willing to take upon himself; every person writes his own history. Other people could choose to go along with Xiaobo or advance alongside him, but there was no need to feel that this was an error or flaw that he must correct or surmount. Twenty years passed like a day, and he was a trailblazer for people who insisted on their own ideas. China lacks trailblazers like Xiaobo, and that is what allowed him to become a standard-bearer for the Chinese democracy movement and gain the widespread endorsement of the international community.

I became acquainted with Xiaobo at a late stage, after he was released from reeducation through labor in 1999. I don't even remember some of our get-togethers apart from photos sent by friends. I have a deeper impression of several walks in the suburbs. One time we somehow ended up near Qincheng Prison in the northern suburbs, and he and young Liu Di pointed out the positions of their former cells and took photos as a souvenir.[4] The last time I met him was to sign Charter 08 in early November 2008. It was at a restaurant near the Xizhimen subway station, and Xu Youyu, Leung Man-tao, and others were also there.[5] He suddenly asked me, "Why is it that the government absolutely must 'protect the eight'?" I didn't respond at first. What he referred to was the government's insistence on maintaining GDP growth of 8 percent.[6] The perplexed and insistent expression on his face at that time is the last I recall of Xiaobo.

On two occasions he said seriously to me, "Weiping, you and I are all that's left from the literary circles of the 1980s." What he meant was that the literary people of the 1980s had moved on, and many familiar faces had departed. That was also why I had to make telephone calls on his behalf to locate those old friends after he was sentenced to eleven years in prison. In 2010 a policeman asked me, "How did you become acquainted with Liu Xiaobo?" I answered, "We studied the same major." Both of us graduated with degrees in Chinese literature in 1982, he at Jilin University and I at Nanjing University, and we had studied in a dense atmosphere of historical introspection. The social consensus of that period was to abandon the previous doctrine of fight-to-the-death class struggle and return to human feeling and tolerance, as Xiaobo made a point of mentioning in both "The June 2nd Hunger Strike Declaration" and his "My Final Statement." We continued our graduate studies in the same specialized area—the trend toward Western literary theory in literature and art. Professor Jiang Peikun, who supervised Xiaobo in defending his dissertation in 1988, had taken the same boat as me from Chongqing to Nanjing in 1982 after a conference on literary theory.

Xiaobo was half a year older than me, and like me he had been in elementary school during the Cultural Revolution; our parents were away from home, classes were suspended, and for a time we lived a free and carefree existence, the historical burden before us relatively light. When we were in our teens, he accompanied his parents when they were sent to the countryside. There were some other comical similarities because we were both the youngest in our families. Finally, we both suffered from cancer, a disease that tests people in ways that are worse than death. Of course his situation was much more serious.

## From Sensate Individual to Iron Man of Democracy

Xiaobo's essay that created such an uproar in the 1980s had a title that seems obscure nowadays: "A Dialogue with Li Zehou: The Sensate, the Individual, My Choice." What is meant by "the sensate," or "the individual"? This was his starting point, and it is also the starting point for understanding him. Liu Xiaobo was first and foremost this kind of sensate individual, although that might not be common knowledge to his scholar friends.

Recently a mutual friend, the poet Jian Ning, wrote a short essay about the first time he met Xiaobo in October 1986, at a small conference during which Xiaobo tearfully read an excerpt from *Radish.*[7] Xiaobo was a savage critic of everyone notable in literary theory or creation at that time, but the one writer he liked was Mo Yan, whose early novels displayed an unusually dazzling sensuality. Jian Ning recalls Xiaobo taking off as a "dark horse" at that conference, and he continued in the same vein afterwards. At dinner, the host seated people by seniority and status according to usual practice, but Xiaobo threw a fit and walked out in tears, saying, "Even at this kind of conference, dinner has to follow rank!" The young people present were mesmerized by his actions, and some got up in front of everyone and followed him out. They then went to another friend's home to eat dumplings. At dinner he bragged to the young poets about smoking marijuana. At that time I was in the vanguard poetic circles and had seen a lot of that kind of thing, so I understood those things but didn't like them.

Xiaobo's personal temperament was still dominated by the intellectual. Intellectually stimulating activities made him genuinely happy, and ideas were always behind his actions meant to shock and astound. It was this energy that set him apart from other intellectuals. Do you want freedom? Then act with freedom. Do you want dignity? Then abandon some things and act like a dignified person. A lot of people have mentioned that there were two Liu Xiaobos, before and after, but I believe that without the sensate individual Liu Xiaobo who came before, the active Liu Xiaobo would not have emerged later. His starting point as an activist had been set back in the 1980s; his character and his fate ran through him from beginning to end.

During the hunger strike at Tiananmen Square, Liu Xiaobo and others came up with the slogan "We announce a hunger strike. We protest, we implore, and we repent!"[8] These four phrases targeted the long-term spineless inactivity of intellectuals. Xiaobo's 2001 essay "The Power of Freedom Is in Practice" ended with a loud appeal: "If freedom is only words that don't need to be put into practice, then freedom is not moral, let alone powerful!"

Perhaps in the eyes of the average Chinese, what Xiaobo experienced seemed more like an "accident," a chain of mishaps, setbacks, or red lights. Totalitarianism's perfectly linked chain repeatedly dropped off of him. Among our friends, it was his unique life more than anyone else's that revealed the essence of totalitarianism and our personal situations—conflict was unavoidable. In this sense, one of the struggles against totalitarianism was to turn one's single life into a series of deeds that could be narrated.

It should be said that as a scholar or thinker, Xiaobo didn't demonstrate a very strong ability to set the topic of conversation, but he always embodied the truth he embraced and put his ideas into practice in perceptible action. This led him to constantly lash against the bottom line of this regime, using his own behavior to expand the boundaries of social space and civil action. The 1989 hunger strike was aimed at "publicizing our political stands on the Square to impress them on the hearts of the people and give them greater influence." He was labeled a "black hand" and sent to Qincheng Prison, and in January 1991 he was tried for "counterrevolutionary propaganda and incitement," but because he had led the students to peacefully with-draw from the square, he was not subjected to criminal penalty. In 1995 he drafted and issued two important statements: "Anti-corruption Proposal to the Third Plenary Session of the Eighth National People's Congress" and "Drawing from a Lesson Paid for in Blood and the Process of Promoting Democracy and Rule of Law: An Appeal on the Sixth Anniversary of June 4th." As a result, the Beijing Municipal Public Security Bureau held him in solitary confinement in the form of residential surveillance in the Beijing suburbs for several months. Because he and another issued the Double Ten Declaration on the issues of Taiwan and Tibet in 1996, he was sent to three years of RTL on the charge of "disturbing public order." He was detained in 2008 because of Charter 08 and eventually sentenced to eleven years in prison for "inciting subversion of state power," and he died in custody.

It's hard enough for a person to be imprisoned even once under China's brutal prison conditions, but he was in and out repeatedly over the years, as well as suffering countless instances of harassment, constant surveillance, and strict limitations on his everyday activities, but he never gave up. He should be given the title of Iron Man of Democracy.

In terms of putting ideals into action, Liu Xiaobo's name ranks with those of Vaclav Havel, Nelson Mandela, Mahatma Gandhi, and Aung San Suu Kyi.

## Tamed by Love

People always talk about how Xiaobo's character was displayed in his actions. Was he a very "genuine" person? If so, it should be said that there were two genuine people: One was sincere, guileless, and effortlessly authentic, without even knowing how to care about what others thought of him. The other pursued truth in a process of cutting and polishing. A person can approach the authentic self through conscious improvement, or by seeking out and making manifest the most authentic of various distracting thoughts that appear at the same time. Xiaobo belonged to the latter category. He constantly pursued truth, but the process of seeking may also have been a process of distortion: When an individual wants to demonstrate that he is authentic, he loses authenticity. When he carries out exaggerated actions and becomes immersed in a dramatic performance, he should know that he has become distorted, yet he works hard to make this distortion look real. This creates a void, requiring him to take further steps to seek the authenticity he has lost.

In this way, wanting to indicate an intense spirit of introspection, Xiaobo would look at himself in the mirror and constantly warn and correct himself to restore what had become distorted. As Hu Ping has said, "Xiaobo was not without flaws, but I know he had a fine quality: Xiaobo had a strict spirit of introspection. He placed very high demands on himself and was willing to devote constant effort toward that." This gave him a quality of growth and openness, as well as a special personal charm. The way I see it, there was an external and an internal Liu Xiaobo. The Liu Xiaobo on stage in the spotlight couldn't avoid dabbing on a little greasepaint, and his actions might look a little funny; while at the same time the Liu Xiaobo backstage intently watched the one on stage, examining him, ridiculing him, booing at him, and putting pressure on him.

In his 1993 confession regarding June 4, *The Monologues of a Doomsday's*

*Survivor*, Xiaobo created considerable controversy by describing some negative behavior at Tiananmen Square in a harsh and nitpicking way while even more brutally analyzing himself. I read it only recently. There is room for discussion on certain details, including a possibly biased understanding of the movement itself. In fact, after he was released from prison in 1999, he made a major adjustment and treated the victims' sacrifice with humility and respect. Regardless, this book has the kind of psychological authenticity that is quite shocking and rare in the Chinese literary world. It may be the calmest, most restrained, most profound, and most compact text of Xiaobo's tumultuous life and should not be written off because of its superficial flaws.

This short book is permeated with self-reproach because he was still alive while others had died. As a "June 4 celebrity," he had lived while ordinary people had died. He wrote in *The Monologues*, "What had happened to the young man who stood with his arms spread wide in front of the tanks? Had all of your blood been shed in vain? Had your courage, conscience and spirit of self-sacrifice been turned into a joke? Some people manage to turn suffering into fame, and sacrifice becomes fodder for attaining status and wealth; the sorrow of our entire race may have merely enriched a handful of cowards and swindlers, myself among them." Before the lives of ordinary people, he bowed his unruly head. The guns of June 4 in fact caused people like us to realize a simple truth: the bullets that pierced the bodies of others could similarly pierce our own brains.

It is hard to avoid writing a statement of repentance while behind prison walls. Things said under pressure don't count, and anyone could excuse himself for it, but Xiaobo took it to heart. Imagining all kinds of possibilities and impossibilities, he went back and forth examining himself. What if he hadn't written the statement? But if he had refused to repent, it would not have been "respecting truth for the sake of conscience, protecting my conscience and insisting on justice, but rather for the sake of my public image, social fame and long-term interests." Yet this "public image" didn't belong to himself alone; it was something the government helped to create and was related to officially created delusions and lies. When they searched for enemies that didn't exist, they at the same time created "heroes," which meant that this hero was tainted. He wrote in *The Monologues*, "If the Communist Party had been just a little smarter, today's China would not have dissident heroes. The Communist Party's stupidity, intolerance and fabrications created many heroes, and these bogus heroes are an integral part of the Communist Party's culture of lies. While deceiving itself, the Communist Party also deceives the public. Ironically, the positive self-perceptions of those heroes are also the result of being misled by the Communist Party's lies." I've always been interested in how Soviet or Eastern European dissidents understand themselves, but I've never seen such a profound viewpoint. While exposing the government's lies, he also exposed the hollowness of heroes and of himself and pulled himself down from the position of hero on a dramatic stage.

What caused him to undergo a fundamental change was his wife, Liu Xia. Liu Xia is an unusual woman who writes poetry, makes films, draws, and is addicted to books. She eats little and is so thin that she looks like the wind could carry her away, but she has an enormous spiritual energy. The two of them married in spring 1996 and visited both sets of parents, but at that time Xiaobo lacked a residency permit and was unable to obtain a marriage certificate. In the last half of 1996, Xiaobo was sent to RTL, so to qualify for legal visiting privileges, they obtained a marriage certificate with the help of a lawyer and shared a meal at the RTL center in a sort of second marriage ceremony. Liu Xia went to see Xiaobo every month with a backpack full of books. During those three years, Xiaobo once again immersed himself in reading—Hayek, Habermas, Heidegger, Dostoyevsky, Dworkin, Bonhoeffer, Saint Augustine, and others—and in the elegant wielding of language. The dozens of poems he wrote to Liu Xia in prison are the height of his linguistic abilities and further tempered his emotions and character. He had earlier lived the life of an unruly poet, but it was behind bars that he truly wielded language to become a poet better than many other poets. Years from now, when his rapid-fire news commentaries have been forgotten, people will remember his poems.

Liu Xia is a very serious creator of art who makes every word and brush stroke count. She once told me that she spent an entire year "writing four poems," which shows her perseverance. She seldom went out and seldom attended Xiaobo's outside get-togethers; she had her own rich world. If it is said that there are two types of contemporary artist, one indulgent and the other ascetic, Liu Xia belongs to the latter category. Her temperament is Kafkaesque right down to her marrow; she devotes her full effort to defending herself and preserving her authenticity. As Xiaobo was buoyed up on the tidal wave of his era and then sank into the deep in the blink of an eye, Liu Xia kept to herself, instinctually resisting the fuss and commotion. This is one of Liu Xia's earliest poems to Xiaobo, dated June 2, 1989, the day the Four Gentlemen went on hunger strike:

> Before I had time to talk to you,
> you became a man in the news . . .
> The best I could do was escape from the crowd
> smoke a cigarette
> and look at the sky.

In a poem entitled "Dislocation," she writes,

> At the moment of unguarded frailty
> an unrehearsed drama was performed . . .
> No costume or greasepaint
> could disguise you
> As the audience disperses
> we stand shoulder-to-shoulder on stage
> one with a tear-soaked face
> the other laughing loudly.

In August 1989 she even wrote a poem called "Empty Chair," which makes her look like a prophet:

> Empty chair empty chair
> so many empty chairs
> all over the world
> the empty chair painted by van Gogh is especially alluring.

She didn't need to seek validation from the outside world and kept aloof from uproar and disturbance. In terms of character, she was probably more genuine and down-to-earth than Xiaobo. She was like Xiaobo's other self, his innermost self, and because of that he gave her his greatest tribute:

You always appear at
the ultimate moment
making me look up and swoon
legs too weak to climb
a gaze filled with dread.

This poem is dated December 28, 1996, the first birthday Xiaobo spent in the RTL center. In his poems he repeatedly expressed that he only wanted to be with her, even if this world was closed to him for the time being:

Casting off hypothetical martyrdom
I long to lie at your feet
apart from tangling with death, this is
the only duty
and when the heart is like a mirror
an enduring happiness.

("Longing to Escape—To My Wife," December 8, 1999)


The outside world is bright and splendid
so bright that it scares me
so splendid that it exhausts me
my gaze only desires your darkness—
pure and inseparable.

("I Am Your Lifelong Captive," January 1, 1997)

Liu Xia was his "magic needle that stills the oceans."[9]

The relationship between the two of them made me think of the word "tame" in *The Little Prince*—tamed by love. The fox told the Little Prince he was not tame. The Little Prince asked, "What does that mean—tame?" The fox replied, "It means to establish ties."[10] A person becomes unique not only through his upbringing but also through the taming influence of love. Being tamed is a kind of openness to life. Through this openness and dialogue, two people bind their lives together at the roots. As Xiaobo wrote in February 1997,

> Who is willing to take on my crimes
> isn't it the woman moved by me?
> It is you! I can tell by the clay that it is you . . .
> You are the woman molded by me
> and who molded me.

There's an old Chinese saying: "Everyone has their match." Some friends say that they were astonished and mystified that Xiaobo was "vanquished" by Liu Xia. It was Xiaobo's good fortune. This man who wanted to tame rulers and power was first tamed by a woman and subdued the unruly and strident parts of himself. When someone cannot escape being the target of hatred and enmity, love eliminates them.

> Dear one, you should get up
> The bridge to the abyss is about to collapse
> With your explosion grip my will
> Doubt begins with Sisyphus's stone
> Faith begins with you throwing away the key to home
> All of my terror and hatred
> I hand to you and you alone
> Let my head once more
> Be lifted nobly, up until
> The darkest moment descends.
> *("With Your Explosion—To Xia," January and February 1997)*

### Democratic Politics Changes Enemies into Friends

"I Have No Enemies" issued an intense appeal, provided a new political culture, and created a new political space.

It is said that after 1989, Xiaobo's thinking evolved from radical to moderate, and that's how it looks on the surface. But I want to point out a misunderstanding. The Xiaobo before 1989 was mainly engaged in cultural criticism and the pursuit of esthetic emancipation. That made for a heedless style, coming and going as he pleased and taking personal responsibility for whatever he said. Once politics became involved, the circumstances were very different. It could be said that once Xiaobo became involved in politics, that is, in 1989, he was moderate. By "moderate" I don't mean endorsing the official standpoint and taking the government's side but rather adopting a channel that was moderate and pragmatic. At a certain time in 1989, a temporary and moderate political space existed, and once Xiaobo stepped into it, that space became the starting point for his subsequent political activity.

Zhou Duo, who joined Xiaobo on the hunger strike at Tiananmen Square, recalls that he invited Liu Xiaobo to take part in a United Front Work Department meeting on May 13, 1989. In fact, the United Front Work Department had two meetings on that day. The first was held at noon by the department's deputy director, Tao Siliang, and the department's director, Yan Mingfu, soon came over from another meeting. The meeting was held in hopes that Zhou Duo, Zheng Yafu, Zhang Lifan and others in attendance would be able to convince the students to leave the square before Soviet leader Mikhail Gorbachev arrived for his state visit to China. This would avoid the party's reformist faction being put at a disadvantage and purged. In the afternoon, Zhou Duo and the others went out to find people, and Zhou Duo found Xiaobo to see if he could bring student leader Wu'erkaixi to the United Front Department for an informal discussion. Xiaobo himself also accepted the invitation. The United Front Department held its second meeting at 7:30 that night, and all of the student representatives came, even representatives of the official Communist Youth League. Yan Mingfu himself presided over the meeting. This was a meeting of a political nature, a temporary political space that was very rare at that time.

On the one side were open-minded officials such as Yan Mingfu, and on the other side were hunger-striking students, while Xiaobo, Deng Zhenglai, and other young university instructors, in Zhou Duo's words, played the role of "mediators" in an attempt to make both sides engage in dialogue, communicate, and understand each other. Compared with the erstwhile cynical and antisocial poet Xiaobo was known as, Xiaobo's identity underwent an obvious change and incorporated new content.

Xiaobo's memoirs state that Zhou Duo asked him to come to the meeting and speak. Xiaobo started out by criticizing the government's April 26 editorial as wrong and said that the government needed to acknowledge the legitimacy of the Students' Autonomous Federation.[11] He then called on the students to learn "compromise, yielding ground and tolerance." He wrote in *The Monologues of a Doomsday's Survivor* that there was an "enemy mentality" among the students: "Enemy mentality and preserving face at all costs will destroy the existing atmosphere of mutual understanding. If the students won't compromise or yield ground, they will gradually lose the support and sympathy of the open-minded faction within the Party and government. The student movement shouldn't become embroiled in the Party's internal factional struggle, but must fight for the broad support of all sectors of society, especially support from within the Party."

After he finished speaking, Yan Mingfu smiled and said, "Don't speak too transparently; hints are enough." A little after 2:00 a.m. on May 14, Xiaobo jumped onto a flatbed tricycle and gave a speech calling the students to be reasonable when Gorbachev arrived, and he criticized some students for interrupting the remarks by government representatives: "This is not democracy, but enmity." People in the crowd yelled, "Coward, fuck off!" and "What turned the dark horse into a sheep?" Xiaobo faced these same criticisms when he organized the peaceful withdrawal from the square, and people derided him as a "coward," "chicken," and "traitor." Those who now deride Xiaobo because of his stance of "I have no enemies" belong to the same "holy family" as these people back then.

Xiaobo felt aggrieved. Had he come all the way from the United States just to listen to students' catcalls and boos? Yet, even while being castigated, he didn't feel a need to backpedal. He knew clearly what he was and what he wanted. After that, on May 15, he refused a request to revise a petition drafted by some famous writers and scholars because he felt it was utilizing the party's ideological language ("since Liberation," "the laboring people," "Long Live the People"), indicating that these people had many conscious and unconscious ties with the old order, while Xiaobo had completed his baptism of independence and was a free agent. This freedom manifested itself in that although he was in the system, his thinking and position went beyond the system, and since he was free, he was beyond taking sides. In fact, it was quite possible for someone to be outside of the system but to share the thinking of the system. Xiaobo said that "the basic content [of 'The June 2nd Hunger Strike Declaration'] was arrived at by discussion between Zhou Duo and me" and that Hou Derchien had also added some points. He said that he penned the declaration himself, but he didn't distinguish among the viewpoints. Zhou Duo's memoirs state that Xiaobo suggested the hunger strike and that his acceptance of Xiaobo's invitation to take part in the hunger strike was conditional: "We have to issue a declaration stating that our objective is not incitement but reconciliation, and we need to use it to publicize a new political culture of no enemies; I also suggested two slogans: 'We have no enemies,' and 'China's progress is everyone's responsibility.'" Zhou Duo also said, "I drafted an outline, and Xiaobo wrote it out." Zhou Duo thought that if he took part in the hunger strike, he could keep Xiaobo from doing anything crazy. When Xiaobo's wife at the time heard that Zhou Duo was also taking part in the hunger strike, she breathed a sigh of relief, feeling that if anything happened, only Zhou Duo could influence Xiaobo. It could be said that upon entering the political space, a mutual taming occurs in the relationship between individuals—that is, establishing profound ties for taking both personal and mutual responsibility. That was the case with Xiaobo and Zhou Duo back then.

There is a matter to be clarified. Some Western media and authors have described Xiaobo as the last person on the square to negotiate with the martial law troops, but in fact that's not true—the people who stepped forward to negotiate were Hou Derchien and Zhou Duo, and all three of them (Xiaobo, Zhou Duo and Hou Derchien) have written that in their memoirs. Zhou Duo said it was he who suggested evacuating the square and going to negotiate with the martial law troops, and finally the three of them with Gao Xin unanimously made the decision, including whom to send to talk. Xiaobo later vividly described his feelings as he witnessed the two negotiators going forward: "Watching them climb down from the Monument step by step, my heart tugged painfully; I didn't know if the two of them would come back alive or in one piece." Staying behind, Xiaobo continued anxiously dealing with any weapons that might be left on the square and smashed a semiautomatic rifle on the railing of the monument, the reverberations causing the crotch of his thumb and his arms to tingle. Before then, he, Zhou Duo, and Hou Derchien had successfully convinced several Beijing residents to discard a heavy machine gun that they'd grabbed after obstructing a tank. It is hard to imagine the heavy backlash if that gun had been fired, and how many students and ordinary citizens might have died. In fact, it's a mystery how that gun fell into the hands of civilians; perhaps a historian will be able to explain it someday. When Xiaobo was interviewed by Hao Jian in December 2008, two days before he was arrested, he said on camera that smashing the gun had symbolic meaning—"non-violence."[12]

Raising these details is not to undermine Xiaobo's significance at Tiananmen Square but rather to highlight his valuable political character. It's possible for one person to go to prison or to sacrifice himself or herself, but politics isn't created by an individual; politics is a relationship between people, a shared fate, breathing together. It requires constructing a platform and enlarging it as much as possible to accommodate even more people's views and conform to even more people's interests. At that moment, Zhou Duo, Liu Xiaobo, Hou Derchien, and Gao Xin were able to join four pairs of hands and create a human bridge that allowed safe passage to even more lives. As soon as they reached a mutual decision and acted together, each of them individually contributed the same force, without any one being more important than the others. Xiaobo's self-restraint was especially valuable. In fact, he initially opposed withdrawing and negotiating, but as he wrote in his memoirs, he finally agreed out of respect for the democratic principle of "the minority submitting to the majority." In a political movement, the ability to listen to the views of others is more important than exercising one's own unrestrained will.

Politics isn't an individual composition, and the original copyright isn't important. Whoever agrees with certain reasoning takes ownership of that reasoning and then proceeds to put it into practice. Whoever has practice has politics. From this perspective, signing a petition or declaration is undeniably a political act. It's inviting more people to speak out on the same platform, and expanding the discourse platform expands the political platform. Xiaobo was detained again in 1995 and 1996 because of writing texts and gathering signatures. Some have attacked him for doing nothing but "petitioning" and continuing to harbor illusions toward the system, but this idea isn't even worth refuting; the government knows this better than they do. The fact that Xiaobo went to prison three times shows the significance of his efforts. Under a system of control aimed at dividing and conquering, bringing together people of different identities and status is the greatest politics.

Charter 08 can be understood as a discourse platform as well as a political platform. Although the text of the Charter itself isn't perfect—in the past I've even said that it doesn't have any new ideas but just repeats boilerplate expressed by various other people over the years—it was the first time that all of this boilerplate had been assembled and placed on the same platform. I agree with the view of Perry Link, the English translator of Charter 08, who says, "Chinese citizens had long been accustomed to the periodic alternations between 'more liberal' and 'more conservative' tendencies in Communist rule, and had often pinned hopes on one or another high official, but Charter 08 seemed to say that there can be another way to be modern Chinese."[13]

In fact, the text of Charter 08 wasn't even drafted by Xiaobo but by someone else; he joined in the effort later on. But as soon as he became involved, he brought enormous enthusiasm to his work. He went all around Beijing personally asking others to sign it, patiently explaining its importance, and successfully convincing many people and winning their support. He also wrote many emails and repeatedly explained it, including to young people. He was always very humble toward everyone when approaching them. It's hard to imagine who but Liu Xiaobo could have collected the first 303 signatures. To be able to unite oppositionists inside and outside of the system, in different fields and from different eras, on the same platform and preserve their differences while issuing a joint statement—I can't see anyone else being able to do what he did in the subsequent ten or even fifteen years. This was the political capital that Xiaobo had accumulated over all those years. Through his sacrifice, his learning, and his inclusiveness he had acquired an extensive relationship network. He had dropped out of the system, but he created new strong and durable ties for himself and brought different people together on another platform. Starting out with an independent esthetic liberation, he moved toward earnest and down-to-earth political liberation.

The most distinctive aspect of Xiaobo's spiritual legacy is this political legacy—political language and political action. Charter 08 is first of all a political text, not a moral text. Of course, under totalitarianism, moral courage is always important and precious, and a capacity for dauntless action is most important of all. Xiaobo embodied the spirit to fight on in spite of all setbacks, yet he also had a valuable political consciousness. He devoted himself to building a new political platform and forging a new political space, expanding civil society and carrying out dialogue and establishing ties within the opposition faction, especially with various forces in society. Does Charter 08 still have meaning? This is a question that should be asked of each of us who signed it; it depends on the effort of each of us signatories in the future and in the present. If we can carry on its spirit and act according to its spirit, then it has meaning. Only through our continued and constant effort can it become a legacy.

Regarding the expression "I have no enemies," the international community has accepted its message, while some who profess to be Xiaobo's comrades-in-arms have resisted and even ridiculed him on this point. They are willing to contest his banner and castrate his thinking and are anxious to surpass him. Even after his death, Xiaobo cannot avoid being attacked from both the front and the rear. He lost his freedom at the time of his greatest honor and left behind an immense responsibility for us to take on. We are obliged to advocate politics in an environment with no politics, to push forward the birth of democracy where there are no conditions for democracy, and to struggle to promote rule of law where no rule of law exists. Apart from this, what else can we do?

Democracy doesn't mean having no enemies but rather turning enemies into friends, just as Xiaobo always did.

In his memoir of June 4, Xiaobo ridiculed the day's personalities, including himself, as "heroes descending the cross." This time he didn't descend the cross but died nailed to it. His departure brings us once again to the ultimate questions: What is the purpose of life? How can we live a meaningful life? How can we bring our scattered lives together and do something meaningful?

Rest in peace, Xiaobo!

*Translated by Stacy Mosher*

Originally published by Initium Media (Hong Kong).

1. "The June 2nd Hunger Strike Declaration," trans. Perry Link, in *Liu Xiaobo: No Enemies, No Hatred*, ed. Perry Link, Tienchi Martin-Liao, and Liu Xia (Cambridge MA: The Belknap Press of Harvard University Press, 2012), 282.—Trans.

2. "I Have No Enemies: My Final Statement," trans. Perry Link, in Link et al., *Liu Xiaobo*, 322.—Trans.

3. "I Have No Enemies," 322.—Trans.

4. See essay by Liu Di (b. 1981) in this volume. She became a symbol of free speech after being detained in 2002 for writings she posted on the internet under the pen name Stainless Steel Rat (after a character in a Harry Harrison science fiction story).—Trans.

5. See essay by Xu Youyu in this book—Trans.

6. This policy, lasting from 2005 to 2012, was seen as a means of maintaining social stability. See Eve Cary, "Goodbye Bao Ba," *The Diplomat*, April 3, 2012, https://thediplomat.com/2012/04/goodbye-bao-ba/.—Trans.

7. *Radish* is a 1985 novel by Mo Yan, who won the Nobel Prize for Literature in 2012.—Trans.

8. "June 2nd Hunger Strike Declaration," 277.—Trans.

9. In the classic novel *Journey to the West*, this "magic needle that stills the oceans" was a magical iron rod the Monkey King "borrowed" from the Dragon King of the Eastern Sea.—Trans.

10. Antoine de Saint-Exupéry, *The Little Prince*, ch. 21.—Trans.

11. The editorial published on the front-page article of *People's Daily* on April 26, 1989, defined the student movement as a destabilizing anti-party revolt that should be resolutely opposed at all levels of society.

12. Hao Jian (b. 1954) is a Beijing-based film studies professor and human rights defender.—Trans.

13. Perry Link, "The Passion of Liu Xiaobo," *New York Review of Books*, July 13, 2017, http://www.nybooks.com/daily/2017/07/13/the-passion-of-liu-xiaobo/.—Trans.

# On the Causes of Controversies about Liu Xiaobo
*Yan Jiaqi*

Liu Xiaobo is not a saint but an ordinary person. I'm one of the many participants in the 1989 Tiananmen Incident who fled China, while Liu Xiaobo stayed behind and was imprisoned and lost his life for the cause of reversing the verdict on June 4 and for Charter 08. From 1993 onward, it was the Tiananmen Mother Ding Zilin and Liu Xia who gave Liu Xiaobo a new life, and Liu Xiaobo fully deserved the Nobel Peace Prize.

Liu Xiaobo was sentenced to eleven years in prison for "inciting subversion of state power." Now, as Liu Xiaobo died after long-term persecution, countless people in China and worldwide mourn and commemorate him, but many controversies around him have occurred overseas. Some people call him a saint, and others regard him as an opportunist. The process of how Liu Xiaobo became a Nobel Peace Prize laureate and the matter of how to fully evaluate him are significant for understanding Chinese politics today.

Four major events cast Liu Xiaobo into the public spotlight. The first was during his youth, when he challenged a leading authority on aesthetics, Li Zehou. The second was on the eve of the June Fourth Massacre, when he stood out from the crowd by declaring a hunger strike. The third was when he established the Independent Chinese PEN Center and the online magazine *Democratic China*, and the fourth was when he was persecuted to death after winning the Nobel Prize for Charter 08.

### Challenging Li Zehou
Li Zehou, twenty-five years older than Liu Xiaobo, is a famous philosopher and authority on aesthetics in China. In the 1980s Li Zehou published highly influential books such as *A Critique of Criticizing Philosophy*, *The History*

of *Beauty*, and *An Intellectual History of Ancient, Recent, and Contemporary China*. Li Zehou had accumulated many academic accomplishments over the course of decades, and none of his colleagues in the field would have thought of challenging him. Liu Binyan, who shortly after the Cultural Revolution was transferred to the Institute of Philosophy and did translation work in the Foreign Philosophy Research Division, felt nothing but respect for Li Zehou. In the tenth issue of *China* magazine in 1986, Liu Xiaobo published an article entitled "Dialogue with Li Zehou: The Sensate, the Individual, My Choice," in which he issued a challenge to Li Zehou.

Li Zehou critically interpreted Kant and Hegel and established an aesthetic theory of cultural "sedimentation," but Liu Xiaobo, citing Freud and Sartre, established an aesthetic theory that could be referred to as "individual breakthrough." Without going into the specific content of these two theories, I will just point out that Li Zehou had long lived in philosophical circles that appealed to rationality, and suddenly there arrived Liu Xiaobo, a passionate and poetic research fellow in aesthetics. How could the rationalist Li Zehou come to grips with someone who desired breakthrough as intensely as Liu Xiaobo? In his article, Liu Xiaobo wrote, "In philosophy and aesthetics, Li Zehou has a standard in terms of society, rationality and essence, but I do in terms of the individual, sensibility and phenomenon; he emphasizes and projects integral subjectivity [*zhutixing*], but I emphasize and project individual subjectivity, and his vision shifts to the past through 'sedimentation,' but my vision points to the future through 'breakthrough.'"

### Creating the "Greatest Dance of Life"

The 1989 Tiananmen Incident was a turning point in contemporary Chinese history, the point at which the twentieth-century International Communist Movement began heading toward extinction.

The key to Liu Xiaobo's approach to participating in the Tiananmen Incident can be found in his article "Dialogue with Li Zehou." Liu Xiaobo regarded "rational sedimentation" as "fetters." He wrote, "As soon as the fetters of rationality fall apart, one faces a brand new cosmos full of vitality. The inebriated Bacchus created the greatest dance of life." Scanning Liu Xiaobo's life, we can see that he was first and foremost a poet and writer, and the life goal deepest inside of him was to smash the "fetters of rational sedimentation" and create the "greatest dance of life."

How could he create the "greatest dance of life" for himself in the millions-strong mass movement at Tiananmen Square? Liu Xiaobo spoke of the conflict between his "two selves": "One self is rational and sober, wanting to just watch from the sidelines and not get involved, because I respect the free and intelligent individual and despise large-scale mass movements, feeling that carrying out large-scale mass movements in China cannot have positive significance. The other self is emotional and heedless, eagerly getting involved in every stage of the movement and wanting to occupy a prominent position in the movement, greedily watching over the fanatical crowd, and thinking how Liu Xiaobo could not leave his mark on such an unprecedented movement."

The 1989 Tiananmen Democracy Movement was a movement of students as its main party. Wang Dan, Wu'erkaixi, Chai Ling, Feng Congde, Zhang Boli, Xiongyan, and Xiang Xiaoji, among others, became widely known for their participation in the dialogue. The hunger strike of thousands of students at Tiananmen Square attracted the attention of all China and the whole world, but no one would pay attention to a student who didn't take part in the dialogue. Liu Xiaobo had an extraordinary sense for major historical incidents and involved himself in the mass movement he disdained in such a way as "to leave a mark for Liu Xiaobo." Just as Liu Xiaobo had attracted the attention of the aesthetic circle by challenging Li Zehou, he used the Four Gentlemen of Tiananmen on hunger strike to attract the attention of the world and in his own special way wrote the formulation "I have no enemies" into "The June 2nd Hunger Strike Declaration." By these actions, Liu Xiaobo smashed the "fetters of rational sedimentation" and created his "greatest dance of life."

Zhang Boli asked me to take part in the opening ceremony for the Tiananmen University of Democracy at 10:00 at night on June 3, 1989. After I gave a speech, two students from the Beijing Institute of Physical Education (now Beijing Sport University) helped me leave the square, which by then was packed with humans, and I returned to my home at Jianguomen a little after 11:00. By then, the slaughter had already begun far away, outside Fuxingmen. The June Fourth Massacre killed or wounded thousands of innocent civilians and resulted in the imprisonment of tens of thousands of peaceful protesters. Liu Xiaobo courageously faced the red terror and was arrested while I ran away from Beijing on the morning of June 4.

### Forging a New Path by Imitating Rousseau's *Confessions*

Two days after the June Fourth Massacre, Liu Xiaobo was arrested. The official media publicly accused him of being a "black hand" manipulating the student movement. On June 24 *Beijing Daily* published an article entitled "Seizing Liu Xiaobo's Black Hand." Under pressure, Liu Xiaobo appeared on China's official China Central Television (CCTV), testifying that he hadn't seen People's Liberation Army soldiers killing anyone at Tiananmen Square. In September 1990 Liu Xiaobo was dismissed from his civil service position, and in January 1991 the Beijing Municipal Intermediate People's Court found him guilty of "counterrevolutionary propaganda and incitement." Because he had "rendered major meritorious service" by convincing the students to leave the square, he was released without further criminal penalty. After leaving prison, he became a freelance writer in Beijing and took part in the human rights movement. In 1993 Liu Xiaobo's version of Rousseau's *Confessions*, *The Monologues of a Doomsday's Survivor*, was published in Taiwan. In it he confessed to protecting himself by testifying that he hadn't seen killings by the People's Liberation Army at Tiananmen Square while defending himself. This book is key to understanding Liu Xiaobo's inner world. I believe that when Liu Xiaobo wrote this book, he had lost faith in his political future and intended to blaze a new path for himself outside of politics by using the French philosopher's approach and returning to the life of a poet, writer, and commentator.

*The Monologues of a Doomsday's Survivor* contains many of Liu Xiaobo's self-focused dictums. For example,

> At every major historical juncture, participants embrace their personal objectives in using historical opportunities. Opportunistic winners will gain various honors and benefits, while opportunistic losers will be criticized, and those who missed the opportunity will regret it. . . .
>
> Regardless of what others may argue, I firmly believe that it was very much worth grasping the opportunity of the 1989 protest movement,

and that God blessed me with this opportunity, and even if criticized as a political opportunist, I'm at peace with it and have no regrets. . . .

In the depths of my heart, I believed that I would become an overnight sensation, that this was my instinct, talent and destiny. . . .

I despise the crowd and regard society as a rabble, and I respect the creative ability of the talented individual. The objective of my entire life is to find out which is greater: a creative solitary talent or the mass of living things.

Liu Xiaobo never glossed over his own motivations, and he analyzed his inner world as Rousseau did. He exposed and criticized the darkness of China's traditional politics while at the same time declaring, "I have no enemies," with the same sense of agape he embraced when writing love poems to Liu Xia. This was the monologue of a romantic writer pursuing inner freedom. When Liu Xiaobo won the Nobel Peace Prize, many long-suffering Chinese democracy activists harshly criticized him, mistakenly regarding his monologue of a romantic writer as the guiding principle of the Chinese democracy movement. This is now the main source of the endless controversy surrounding "I have no enemies."

## Liu Xiaobo's Rebound and Transformation

Liu Xiaobo's actions during the 1989 Tiananmen Democracy Movement and afterward are well known. After leaving prison, he saw how the Tiananmen Mothers had suffered for many years, and he began contacting other June 4 victims in Beijing. Under the influence of Ding Zilin and Jiang Peikun, he became reactivated, making appeals for a reappraisal of the June Fourth Incident and writing about China's future. Wang Juntao says that the Tiananmen Mothers changed Liu Xiaobo from a "madman" into a courageous warrior fighting for China's democratic future.

Liu Xia's love was also a factor in Liu Xiaobo's transformation. Liu Xia entered Liu Xiaobo's life after June 4, 1989, after he was dismissed from his position at Beijing Normal University and his marriage broke up. In May 1995 Liu Xiaobo was placed under house arrest for writing an appeal for the sixth anniversary of June 4 along with Wang Dan, Chen Xiaoping, Zhou Duo, and others. Eventually, in 1996 he was sent to Dalian for three years of reeducation through labor, and Liu Xia took a train from Beijing to Dalian once a month to visit him. Liu Xia is an outstanding contemporary Chinese poet who disdains and transcends politics. She is someone who believes in love above all. Liu Xiaobo and Liu Xia's poems show the purity of their love and a noble realm that transcends political advantage and disadvantage.

In her poem "Wind: To Xiaobo," Liu Xia writes:

You are fated to be like the wind,
blown all about,
playing among the clouds.
I once imagined being with you
but what kind of home
could accommodate you?
Walls suffocate you.
you are the wind, and the wind
has never told me
when it comes or goes.
When the wind comes, I cannot open my eyes,
and when the wind goes, dust covers the ground.

In 1996 Liu Xiaobo and Liu Xia obtained a marriage certificate at the Dalian RTL Center and were formally married, allowing Liu Xia to visit Liu Xiaobo as his wife. After Liu Xiaobo finished his sentence, they settled down in Beijing, and Liu Xiaobo established himself as a freelance writer. From then until 2008, under the constant surveillance of the police and state security apparatus, Liu Xiaobo devoted his efforts to the Independent Chinese PEN Center and the online magazine *Democratic China* and to demanding a reassessment of the Tiananmen Incident while joining Liu Xia to pursue a life detached from everyday hardship.

## The Only Person Giving His Life for Charter 08

Charter 08, the Magna Carta of contemporary China's progress toward democracy, is a document of immense historical significance. The drafter of Charter 08 was Zhang Zuhua, who once served as secretary of the Central State Organs' Committee of the Communist Youth League of China.

Zhang Zuhua had left his position after coming under attack after June 4. He engaged in advanced studies in jurisprudence and constitutional theory at the graduate school of the China University of Political Science and Law. By 2005 he had written the tens of thousands of words that came to be known as Charter 08. In a video interview with Ai Xiaoming on April 2, 2010, Liu Xia said, "Xiaobo didn't draft Charter 08."

Charter 08 was to be issued at a press conference scheduled to be held in Beijing on December 10, 2008, the sixtieth anniversary of the Universal Declaration of Human Rights, but Zhang Zuhua and Liu Xiaobo were simultaneously detained on December 8. China's then-leader, Hu Jintao, was well acquainted with Zhang Zuhua from working at the Youth League's central committee, so Zhang was released, but Liu Xiaobo was sentenced to eleven years in prison. Liu Xiaobo won the Nobel Peace Prize because of his imprisonment and his collection of signatures for Charter 08. The judgment of the Beijing First Intermediate People's Court states, "The testimony of witness Zhang Zuhua shows: At the end of 2008 he and Liu Xiaobo together finished drafting Charter 08. He also collected signatures, after which Liu Xiaobo published Charter 08 on foreign websites."[1] Zhang Zuhua issued a public statement saying that this was fundamentally untrue and that when subpoenaed by the police on December 8, 2008, and asked whether others, including Liu Xiaobo, had taken part in drafting Charter 08, he had answered, "I don't know." He only answered questions about what he himself had done, and he refused to answer questions about what others had done. Zhang Zuhua said, "When the police detained Xiaobo and me at the same time on December 8, Charter 08 had not yet been made public so how could I state that 'Liu Xiaobo published Charter 08 on foreign websites?'"

Although Zhang Zuhua drafted Charter 08, its enormous influence on China and the world today is closely related to Liu Xiaobo and Ding Zilin. It was Ding Zilin who urged Liu Xiaobo to get more people to sign the Charter. In his recollections of Liu Xiaobo, Jiang Qisheng said, "When Charter 08 was finalized, I added one sentence, which was 'abolish single-party monopolistic ruling privilege.' After I added this sentence, Xiaobo was very happy, and it was also endorsed by the people who subsequently signed it."

Some people say that Charter 08 was "petitioning the emperor," but

Jiang Qisheng said, "Charter 08 wasn't petitioning or admonishing the emperor. Charter 08 aims at all of society as a revolutionary text, one that will contribute to the transformation from a single-party autocracy to a democratic constitutional government." Liu Xiaobo was not only a victim of June 4 but also the only person to give his life for Charter 08.

Not all leading figures in human history have aimed to change the world. Hu Jintao was a leading figure with no great ideals and therefore shortsighted, weak, and incompetent, bullying the weak and fearing the strong. Hu Jintao's field of vision went no further than *The Story of Zoya and Shura*, so he imprisoned a writer and poet who wanted nothing but freedom of expression, as a result of which Liu Xiaobo won the Nobel Peace Prize.[2]

In December 2012, 134 Nobel laureates called on the Chinese government to "immediately free Liu Xiaobo and his wife Liu Xia." Three days later, I wrote an article entitled "Four Major Steps for the Revival of the Chinese People," which expressed the hope that the newly elected general secretary of the Chinese Communist Party, Xi Jinping, would listen to this appeal and release Liu Xiaobo. These laureates, who had made enormous contributions to humanity in the fields of physics, chemistry, economics, medicine, and literature and promoting world peace, were issuing the appeal on the basis of human conscience. The whole world knew that the Chinese government had convicted Liu Xiaobo of the "crime" of expressing words prohibited by the Hu Jintao–Wen Jiabao regime. Convicting Liu Xiaobo on this basis was like the cruel torture inflicted on Galileo in the seventeenth century for promoting Copernicus's theory, forbidden by the Roman Catholic Church that the sun was at the center of the universe. To this day, under CCP rule, China has had no Nobel laureates in economics or the natural sciences, and one of the main reasons for this is that China's lack of freedom of thought also constrains people in the scientific realm.[3] Likewise, the main reason China has not been able to step out of its "cycle of order and disorder" even a century after the Qing dynasty died out is that its governments have never allowed the Chinese people to use their brains to explore the maladies of the Chinese political system. Any criticism of China's political system has been categorized as "subverting the regime."

Liu Xiaobo spent his life fighting for democratic politics, prosperity, and strength for China, and he gave his life for a reappraisal of June 4 and for Charter 08.

## Liu Xiaobo's Guilt and the Tragedy of the Chinese People

Success in any undertaking cannot compensate for failure in family life. This is an adage throughout the world. Lacking this awareness, China's Communist leaders have often destroyed their families in their pursuit of supreme power. Mao's pursuit of dictatorial power resulted in a sentence of life in prison for his wife, Jiang Qing; she ultimately killed herself, effectively making the Great Leader a "family member of a counterrevolutionary." Lin Biao was next in line for succession after Mao but ended up dead with his family and with no final resting place. How could Liu Xiaobo not know that when he created his "greatest dance of life," he would inflict untold misery on his wife and son and the rest of his family?

Of course it's the Chinese autocratic system that created unhappiness for Liu Xiaobo and his family, but Liu Xiaobo didn't avoid it. Only at the end of his life did Liu Xiaobo acknowledge that he had wronged his former wife, Tao Li, and admit that he was "filled with remorse" toward Liu Xia: "A person like me, so dissolute and hungry for social fame, isn't equipped to have a family, is unworthy to be a responsible husband and father, and didn't deserve Tao Li's love. . . . I gained fame for engaging in the civil rights movement. What about Tao Li? She gained nothing but suffering, fear and anxiety, and she was not only reduced to skin and bones, but had to devote all her strength to raising our child. She was fully justified in divorcing me."

Liu Xiaobo once said, "I have an intense desire to explore the different kinds of beauty in thousands of women." It wasn't until he fell in love with Liu Xia that Liu Xiaobo changed. He said, "I've finally found all the beauty I want in one woman." Liu Xiaobo transformed from a vagrant and prodigal in the 1980s into a devoted husband. Liu Xiaobo's essay "I Have No Enemies," published before he entered Jinzhou Prison in 2010, stated that his greatest happiness over the previous twenty years was the selfless love he received from his wife Liu Xia.

Liu Xiaobo wrote:

I have been held in tangible prisons, while you have waited for me within the intangible prison of the heart. Your love has been like sunlight that peeps over high walls and shines through iron windows, that caresses every inch of my skin and warms every cell of my body. It has bolstered my inner equanimity while I try to stay clearheaded and high-minded; it has infused with meaning every minute of my stays in prisons. My love for you, on the other hand, is burdened by my feelings of guilt and apology. These are so heavy that they sometimes seem to make me stagger.[4]

Liu Xia's love for Liu Xiaobo shook heaven and earth, transcending prisons and shackles to reach the heart of the one she loved.

After Liu Xiaobo died, a democracy activist who had suffered a long stretch in prison wrote in an essay posted online, "Seven years ago, Liu Xiaobo used fraudulent means to swindle his way to the Nobel Peace Prize." The fact is that Liu Xiaobo never aspired to the Nobel Peace Prize. After Liu Xiaobo was arrested because of Charter 08, Yang Jianli, Li Xiaorong, and others joined with Vaclav Havel, the Dalai Lama, and other Nobel laureates to nominate Liu Xiaobo for the Nobel Peace Prize. Liu Xiaobo's essay "I Have No Enemies," like the love poems he wrote for Liu Xia, was not written as the "guiding principle" for China's democratic revolution but to create his "greatest dance of life." When 134 Nobel laureates called on the Chinese government to "immediately release Liu Xiaobo and his wife Liu Xia" in December 2012 and when 154 laureates from around the world issued an open letter to Chinese leader Xi Jinping in June 2017 demanding that Liu Xiaobo and his ailing wife Liu Xia be allowed to seek medical treatment in the United States on humanitarian grounds, Xi Jinping ignored them. It is none other than the CCP, in its deviation from the high road of human civilization, that magnified the greatness of Liu Xiaobo, full of human weakness as he was, in his pursuit of love and agape.

Feng Youlan said that human life has four realms: the natural, the utilitarian, the moral, and the universal.[5] The "sage" is the standard of the moral realm; a sage is "morally perfect." People living in the universal realm pursue sainthood. "What a saint does is the same as what ordinary people do, but a saint has a high degree of understanding whatever is done." Liu Xiaobo is not comparable to India's Mother Teresa in that he hasn't achieved sainthood. Liu Xiaobo was an ordinary person pursuing love and agape, a "man writ large" who gave his life for Charter 08. That the CCP would imprison a poet who proclaimed, "I have no enemies," and who venerated love, and abuse him until he died only adds a new layer of grief to the Chinese nation, which has already had their fill of grief. As Liu Xiaobo's friend Chen Jun once said, "It is because of Liu Xiaobo that our era has not collapsed in its defense of conscience. Liu Xiaobo's witness to hardship, his steadfastness in the darkness, and his martyrdom have raised the sufferings of the Chinese nation to the level of collective memory of humanity and at the same time infused the common pursuits and ideals of our several generations with an even nobler spiritual quality and beauty."

*Translated by Stacy Mosher*

## NOTES

Written on July 27, 2017, in Washington DC. Published in the September 2017 issue of Hong Kong's *Qian shao (Frontline Magazine)*, published here with a few additions and edits.

1. "The Criminal Verdict," trans. Perry Link, in *Liu Xiaobo: No Enemies, No Hatred*, ed. Perry Link, Tienchi Martin-Liao, and Liu Xia (Cambridge MA: The Belknap Press of Harvard University Press, 2012), 331.—Trans.

2. Zoya Kosmodemyanskaya was an eighteen-year-old Russian woman who was executed by the Germans as a Soviet partisan in 1941. She was lauded as a national hero, and her mother, Lyubov Kosmodemyanskaya, contributed to her fame with the book *The Story of Zoya and Shura*, about Zoya and her brother Alexksandr (Shura), who died on the Eastern Front in World War II at the age of nineteen. They were held up as models for youthful emulation in China.—Trans.

3. Two Chinese citizens, Yang Chen-ning (b. 1922) and Lee Tsung-dao (1926), won the Nobel Prize in Physics, while two others of Chinese birth, Daniel Tsui (b. 1939) and Charles Kao (b. 1933), were foreign citizens when they received the prize. One Chinese citizen, Tu Youyou (b. 1930), won the Nobel Prize in Physiology or Medicine in 2015. Chinese citizen Mo Yan (b. 1955) won the Nobel Prize for Literature in 2012, and the China-born Gao Xingjian (b. 1940) received his prize in 2000, though he was a French citizen at the time.—Trans.

4. Liu Xiaobo, "I Have No Enemies," trans. Perry Link, in Link et al., *Liu Xiaobo*, 325.—Trans.

5. Feng Youlan (1895–1990) was a scholar who was instrumental in reintroducing the study of Chinese philosophy in the modern era.—Trans.

# A Brief Biography of Liu Xiaobo

*Yu Zhang*

## A Member of the "Innocent Hearts" Poetry Group

Liu Xiaobo was born on December 28, 1955, in Changchun, in China's northeastern Jilin Province, the third of five brothers. His father, Liu Ling, was a teacher at Northeast Normal University and then a guest lecturer at Choibalsan University in Ulan Bator, the capital of the Mongolian People's Republic. The family lived in Mongolia for three years before returning to China in 1959.

In 1969, while Liu was still in middle school, China's universities closed down for the Cultural Revolution, and Liu's family moved to the Dashizhai People's Commune in the Horqin Right Front Banner of the Inner Mongolia Autonomous Region. Four years later, in 1973, Liu's family returned to Changchun as some universities resumed classes, and Liu continued his studies at the Attached Middle School of Northeast Normal University. After graduating in July 1974, he went to the countryside as an "educated youth" to be reeducated at Shan'gang People's Commune in Nong'an County, Jilin Province. In November 1976, two months after Mao's death and one month after the arrest of Jiang Qing and her Gang of Four brought an end to the Cultural Revolution, Liu was assigned to do plastering for the Changchun City Construction Company.

Liu Xiaobo was admitted as a student of Chinese literature at Jilin University in 1978, and two years later joined the Innocent Hearts (Chi Zi Xin), a poetry group created by six schoolmates. After graduating with a BA in literature in 1982, he began graduate studies at the Chinese Literature Department of Beijing Normal University. He married his university classmate, Tao Li, who was teaching at the Beijing Language Institute, and their son Liu Tao was born the following year.

## A Literary Dark Horse

In April 1984 Liu published his debut article, "On Artistic Intuition," in the *Journal of the University of International Relations*, followed by an essay on the ancient philosopher Zhuang Zhou in the bimonthly *Social Science Front*. That same year, he received his MA in literature and became a teacher of Chinese literature at Beijing Normal University. He continued publishing articles and reviews in various academic journals, expressing the rebellious spirit of "New Literature" against the mainstream and its tolerance of humiliation. This "Liu Xiaobo Phenomenon" sent shockwaves through Mainland China's literary circles.

In September 1986 the Institute of Literature at the Chinese Academy of Social Sciences held a symposium in which Liu Xiaobo gave an impromptu speech entitled "The New Period Literature Is Facing a Crisis." Liu referred to China's mainstream May 4 literature and Western modernist literature in terms considered shocking at the time, which he applied to Chinese cultural and intellectual circles generally:

> The national inertia of Chinese intellectuals is even more deeply entrenched than that of the general public! . . . Chinese writers still lack a sense of individuality. At a deeper level, this lack of individuality is a withering of vitality, or a rationalization and dogmatism of vitality. The development of Chinese culture has always restricted sensibility with rationality, and has framed the free development of individual consciousness within moral standards. . . . Until we break through tradition, thoroughly negate traditional, classical culture as during the May Fourth era, and cast off the fetters of rationality and dogmatism, we will not be able to shake off this crisis.

Liu's speech was published by *Shenzhen Youth Daily* in early October and soon reprinted by many domestic and overseas presses, earning him the title of "literary dark horse." That same month, he published another article, "Dialogue with Li Zehou: The Sensate, the Individual, My Choice," showing his development from literary reviews to ideological and cultural criticism. Liu continued research for his PhD in literary theory while publishing literary, aesthetic, and ideological critiques in various publications.

Liu's first book, *The Critique of Choice: Dialogue with Li Zehou*, was published in January 1988 and soon became a bestseller for Liu's comprehensive criticism of Chinese tradition and his blunt challenge to Li Zehou, a rising star exerting major ideological influence on China's young intellectuals. In 1988 *The Hundred* (*Bai Jia*), a new literary bimonthly, launched a special column, "One Hundred and One," which published Liu's article "On Loneliness" and essays by other young scholars discussing the Liu Xiaobo Phenomenon. In June Liu published his doctoral thesis as his second book, *Aesthetics and Human Freedom*, defending it before a spontaneous audience of hundreds of college students and obtaining the unanimous approval of a panel of nine prominent literary critics and aestheticians to receive his PhD in literature. He then became a lecturer in the same department.

In August 1988 Liu was invited to serve as a visiting scholar at the University of Oslo, the University of Hawaii, and Columbia University in New York City. At the same time, he began publishing groundbreaking political essays with titles such as "The Demon King of Chaos: Mao Zedong" in Hong Kong publications, in particular *Emancipation Monthly* (later renamed *Open Magazine*). In an interview entitled "Literary 'Dark Horse' Liu Xiaobo," he was quoted as saying:

> Marxism-Leninism in China is not so much a faith as a component of autocracy. Marxism-Leninism is not a faith but rather a tool for rulers to carry out ideological dictatorship.
>
> China's cultural legacy has been to oppose only foolish monarchs and corrupt officials rather than the autocratic and imperial powers. . . .
>
> It took a century of colonialism to make Hong Kong what it is today. Given China's size, it would need three centuries of colonialism to become what Hong Kong is today. I even wonder if three centuries would be enough.

In the interview, Liu Xiaobo also sharply criticized several prominent "thought leaders" and "youth mentors," namely Liu Binyan, Li Zehou, Jin Guantao, and Liu Zaifu, who were well respected among Chinese dissidents, especially young people. His comments attracted considerable concern and countercriticism. In particular, Liu Binyan had won great respect and sympathy both at home and abroad, and Liu Xiaobo's ridicule, coming two years after Liu Binyan had been expelled from the CCP for his courageous public comments, was considered lacking in compassion and a ploy to gain fame by disparaging prominent individuals.

## The Four Gentlemen of Tiananmen Square

When public morning for the death of ousted CCP general secretary Hu Yaobang developed into the 1989 Democracy Movement, Liu Xiaobo, then a visiting scholar at Columbia University, took part in solidarity activities by overseas Chinese students and scholars.

On April 20 Hong Kong's *Ming Pao* reported, "Hu Ping, Liu Xiaobo, Chen Jun and seven others have jointly published 'Reform Suggestions' urging the CCP to reflect on and correct its errors . . . expressing concern about the current student movement in mainland China," demanding that the Chinese authorities "reexamine . . . the 1983 Anti-Spiritual Pollution Campaign and the 1987 Anti-Bourgeois Liberalization Campaign and related issues" and also amend the constitution by abolishing the "Four Cardinal Principles" and inserting language to safeguard human rights, allow private publications, end the conviction of people based on their words, and implement genuine freedom of speech and of the press.

On April 22 Liu suggested in an article entitled "Reflections on the Phenomenon of Hu Yaobang's Death" and published in the U.S.-based *World Journal (Shijie Ribao)*, "Abandon the reform model of seeking an enlightened monarch, and try the path of transforming China institutionally. . . . If college students and intellectuals pursuing democracy in mainland China can openly support the liberal faction within the CPC while also openly helping Wei Jingsheng, Beijing Spring and others overseas, this will certainly speed up the democratization process." On the same day, Liu drafted "An Open Letter to College Students in China" with seven suggestions on how to carry out the student movement, which he distributed in China with the help of other overseas Chinese students and scholars, including Hu Ping, chairman of the overseas Chinese Alliance for Democracy.

Liu then changed his original plan to return home in 1990 and instead left the United States on April 26, arriving in Beijing the following day. He immediately joined the student movement, passing along thousands of dollars donated by overseas students and scholars to the Student Union of Beijing Normal University.

On May 13 hundreds of Beijing college students began a sit-in and hunger strike at Tiananmen Square, and Liu began helping them with publicity, writing, lectures, and fundraising. On June 2 Liu Xiaobo, Zhou Duo, Gao Xin, and Taiwanese singer Hou Derchien declared a hunger strike, through which they earned the trust of the protesting students and came to be known as the Four Gentlemen of Tiananmen Square. Liu called on both the government and the students to abandon the ideology of class struggle and to adopt a new political culture of dialogue and compromise. Although unable to prevent the massacre that began outside the square on the night of June 3, Liu and his colleagues successfully negotiated with the commanders of the martial law troops to allow thousands of students to peacefully withdraw.

On the same day, Liu Xiaobo heard that martial law troops had begun arresting people, and he went with Hou Derchien to the Diplomatic Residence Compound, where they hid in the apartment of sinologist Zhou Si (Nicholas Jose), the cultural counselor of the Australian Embassy in China.

Zhou Si was about to return to Australia, and he proposed that Liu take refuge in the Australian Embassy and seek political asylum abroad. Liu considered Zhou's offer, but mindful that few of the other Four Gentlemen would be able to escape, he declined Zhou's proposal on June 6. He was arrested just outside the embassy gate and detained in Beijing's infamous Qincheng Prison.

Afterwards, Liu was accused in official media of being a "black hand" manipulating the student movement to overthrow the government and socialist system. In late June the government published a critical anthology, *Liu Xiaobo: The Man and His Deeds*, and Liu was expelled from his university in September. His third book, *The Fog of Metaphysics*, a comprehensive review on Western philosophy, came out that year but was immediately banned with his other published works and a fourth book in press, *Going Naked toward God*. Still, many of his works were republished in Taiwan.

## A Doomsday's Survivor

In September 1989 China Central Television in Beijing broadcasted an interview during which Liu Xiaobo described what he had witnessed while the martial law forces cleared Tiananmen Square and testified that "no one was killed in Tiananmen Square."

Under pressure from prison administrators and family members, Liu Xiaobo wrote his "statement of repentance" in November that year. The authorities printed off his statement as propaganda material for the political and ideological education of students in China's universities.

Liu Xiaobo and Tao Li divorced in August 1990, and Tao eventually immigrated with their son to the United States. In January 1991 the Beijing Intermediate People's Court found Liu guilty of "counter-revolutionary propaganda and incitement," but he was exempted from further punishment due to his "major meritorious act" of persuading the students to leave Tiananmen Square. After his release, he resumed writing as a freelancer in Beijing and continued his involvement in human rights activities. However, his actions while in prison drew disappointment and criticism from many people both at home and abroad.

In January 1993 Liu Xiaobo was invited to Australia and the United States for showings of a documentary film, *The Gate of Heavenly Peace*. Although many friends advised him to seek political asylum abroad, he returned to China in May. On June 5 he published an essay entitled "We Were Knocked Out by Our 'Justice'" in Taiwan's *United Daily News*, and soon afterward published a confessional and critical memoir, *The Monologues of a Doomsday's Survivor*, which caused considerable controversy among dissidents at home and abroad with its negative comments on the 1989 Democracy Movement.

### Learning the Lessons of Blood

On February 20, 1995, Liu Xiaobo joined eleven other intellectuals in issuing an "Anti-corruption Proposal to the Third Plenary Session of the Eighth National People's Congress," suggesting five short-term and seven long-term goals for reform. Another joint statement followed in May, "Drawing from a Lesson Paid for in Blood and the Process of Promoting Democracy and Rule of Law: An Appeal on the Sixth Anniversary of June 4th," but Liu was detained before its formal publication and held under residential surveillance for nine months.

In August 1996 Liu Xiaobo and the well-known dissident Wang Xizhe made plans for a joint statement to the CCP and Taiwan's KMT on cross-strait relations and other cross-border issues as well as political reform.

Two days before the declaration's planned release on October 10, Liu was detained and sentenced to three years of RTL for "disturbing social order." While at the Dalian RTL Center, Liu wrote hundreds of thousands of words.

Following his release on October 7, 1999, Liu resumed his freelance writing, quickly publishing three volumes of political and cultural criticism and poetry in Mainland China, Hong Kong, and Taiwan, respectively: *A Belle Gave Me a Knockout Drug* (under penname Lao Xia and coauthored with Wang Shuo), *Selected Poems of Liu Xiaobo and Liu Xia*, and *A Nation That Lies to Conscience*.

During this period, Liu Xiaobo's image was restored. In 1999 Liu Bin-yan, serving as a visiting scholar at the Asia-Pacific Center of Stockholm University in Sweden, commended Chinese intellectuals' constant issuing of joint letters. Discussions of influential figures particularly cited Liu Xiaobo's development after 1995, and he was expected to make even greater progress after standing up to RTL.

### Golden Years of the Independent Chinese PEN Center

In July 2001 Liu Xiaobo helped found the Independent Chinese PEN Center, known in Chinese as China Independent Writers PEN (Zhongguo Duli Zuojia Bihui). PEN International's archives shows that on July 23, its headquarter received a list of thirty-one founding members of ICPC. Among them, Liu Xiaobo and his wife, Liu Xia, a poet, were the only two independent writers residing in Mainland China, thus distinguishing ICPC from the other Chinese PEN centers existing at the time. Among them, the long-standing Taipei Chinese PEN Center was composed of writers living in Taiwan; the Hong Kong Chinese-speaking PEN Center was established in the 1950s as a group of writers in Hong Kong; the China PEN Center, Shanghai Chinese PEN Center, and Guangzhou Chinese PEN Center were all founded in the 1980s as subordinate groups to the official China Writers Association; and Chinese Writers Abroad PEN Center (formerly known as Chinese Exiled Writers PEN Center) consisted of overseas and exiled Chinese writers. Without the participation of Liu Xiaobo and Liu Xia at its founding, ICPC would have had difficulty justifying its existence, as the others members could have joined an existing PEN center rather than establishing a new one.

Due to its membership distribution, ICPC's earliest efforts were limited to the United States. In December 2002 two prominent U.S.-based exiles, Liu Binyan and Zheng Yi, were elected chairman and vice chairman, respectively. The executive director, Huang Beiling, and other staff members all resided in the United States. By the time ICPC held its first membership assembly online in November 2003, its membership had grown to sixty-seven, with about one-third residing in Mainland China, nearly half of them recommended by Liu Xiaobo, including the well-known dissident writers Liao Yiwu and Yu Jie. The membership assembly adopted the ICPC Charter and change ICPC's Chinese name to Independent Chinese Writers PEN (Duli Zhongwen Zuojia Bihui) in acknowledgment that most of the members were not in China and some weren't even Chinese citizens. At the same time, the membership assembly elected a president and board of directors. Supported by Liu Binyan, Zheng Yi, and most of the founding members, Liu Xiaobo was elected president with forty-four out of forty-seven votes. Of the seven board members, Liu Xiaobo and two others were in China, while the other four, including vice president Cai Chu and Chen Maiping, were overseas.

After taking up the presidency, Liu Xiaobo recommended a large number of Mainland-based writers to join ICPC and actively supported the establishment in December of its Writers in Prison Committee (WiPC), of which I was appointed coordinator in January 2004. ICPC's Writers in Prison Committee was a subordinate branch of PEN International's most influential committee. Its focus on long-neglected writers in prison and the relevant issues of freedom of expression and literary inquisition quickly made the WiPC a vital institution. As ICPC entered the rapidly developing internet era and the international community of PEN International, it grew from a small circle of underground and exiled writers mainly focusing on their past accomplishments into the most influential member-based NGO supporting independent writers and prisoners of writing in China.

On October 30, 2004, Liu Xiaobo chaired ICPC's ceremony of the second Freedom to Write Award, held at a restaurant in suburban Beijing. The sixty-two attendees included the awardee, Zhang Yihe, and other prominent figures. It was the first time Liu Xiaobo had made a speech at a gathering of more than thirty people since his arrest in

1989 and also the largest number of participants at an ICPC gathering in Mainland China.

In May 2005 I joined Kjell Holm, the international secretary of Swedish PEN, Zhou Si, the former president of Sydney PEN, and Chip Rolley, the chairman of the WiPC of Sydney PEN in Beijing for a dinner party on May 13 with Liu Xiaobo and Liu Xia, ICPC Director Yu Jie and his wife Liu Min, deputy secretary-general Wang Yi, chief editor Yu Shicun, and former prisoner Li Baiguang, who was out on bail. I had another opportunity the next day to have dinner with Liu Xiaobo, as well as Holm and a writer from the China Writers' Association, never imagining that I would never meet Liu Xiaobo again.

When Liu Xiaobo presided over the second ICPC membership assembly over the internet in October, membership had grown to 140, with more than half of the members residing in Mainland China, including many influential internet writers, reflecting the shift of ICPC's main focus to China. In accordance with the PEN International's recent reforms and the development of ICPC, the membership assembly amended its charter and changed its Chinese name to enlarge the scope of its membership to those who write, edit, translate, research, and publish literary works in Chinese. The shift in focus toward Mainland China was further reflected in the election of five Mainland residents to the nine-member board of directors, including reelected President Liu Xiaobo and Vice President Yu Jie. Then Liu Xiaobo appointed me as the secretary-general with the board's approval.

On January 2, 2006, Liu Xiaobo held ICPC's third Freedom to Write Award and its first Lin Zhao Memorial Award in Beijing, with all five Mainland board members attending the event. Despite intensified efforts by the authorities to suppress such activities, Liu managed to get permission to organize a private dinner party for the New Year, with slightly fewer participants than the year before. From then on, as the authorities began cracking down in preparation for the 2008 Beijing Olympics, the domestic situation became increasingly tense, and pressure on Liu also grew to the point that even private gatherings of this type became impossible. ICPC's next award ceremony had to be delayed and held in Hong Kong in February 2007. In October 2006, Liu Xiaobo was invited to become chief editor of the U.S.-based website Democratic China.

When Liu Xiaobo presided over the third ICPC membership assembly on the internet in October 2007, the number of members had grown to 220, nearly quadruple the number four years before. Although the proportion of mainland members was still a little over half, the proportion of well-known writers, academics, journalists, and dissidents among the new members had greatly increased, mostly on Liu's recommendation. Liu did not run for president again but continued to serve as a board member for the next two years. In particular, he devoted much more time to supporting and participating in the WiPC's rescue missions, including contacting the families of imprisoned ICPC members.

## Harsh Sentence for Initiating Charter 08

In 2008 Liu Xiaobo took part in drafting and launching Charter 08, a manifesto calling for political reform, human rights protection, and gradual implementation of a constitutional democracy in China, in the style of Czechoslovakia's Charter 77. Charter 08 was to be released on the sixtieth anniversary of the adoption of the Universal Declaration of Human Rights on December 10.

On December 8, two days before the scheduled publication of Charter 08, Liu Xiaobo was summoned for questioning by the Beijing Municipal Public Security Bureau, and his home was searched. The next day, Charter 08, initially signed by 303 Chinese citizens, was issued one day early. Up to now, in 2017, it has gained more than thirteen thousand signatures.

Liu Xiaobo was held in an undisclosed location until formally arrested on suspicion of inciting subversion of state power on June 23, 2009. Liu was put on trial at the Beijing Municipal First Intermediate People's Court on December 23, 2009, represented by lawyers Ding Xikui and Shang Baojun. About twenty people were allowed to attend the hearing, including Liu Xiaobo's younger brother and brother-in-law, while his wife Liu Xia was forcibly taken as a prosecution witness and was not allowed to enter the courtroom. Many individuals barred from attending the hearing waited outside the court, including media reporters and a dozen foreign diplomats from the embassies of the United States, Germany, and Australia, among others. Liu pleaded not guilty but was allowed to speak for only fifteen minutes during the two-hour trial, and the judge interrupted him before he could finish reading out his two prepared statements, "My Self-Defense" and "I Have No Enemies: My Final Statement." On December 25 the court held its final hearing to deliver its verdict, based on a total of 224 words extracted from six of the thousands of articles Liu had published over the years, along with Charter 08, produced as evidence of "rumors, defamation," and "seditious remarks." In its verdict, the court ruled, "The defendant Liu Xiaobo is guilty of the crime of inciting subversion of state power and sentenced to eleven years' imprisonment and two years' additional deprivation of political rights." Liu's appeal was dismissed by the Beijing Municipal High People's Court in February 2010, and in May 2010 Liu was transferred to Jinzhou Prison in Liaoning Province to serve his sentence.

### Nobel Peace Prize Laureate: "I Have No Enemies"

Ever since 1989, human rights organizations worldwide had expressed concern and solidarity with Liu Xiaobo, and he had won many international awards. Starting in 2009 a number of groups and individuals, including Nobel laureates and national parliaments, joined in nominating Liu for the Nobel Peace Prize. On October 8, 2010, the chairman of the Norwegian Nobel Committee, Thorbjørn Jagland, announced that the Nobel Peace Prize was awarded to Liu Xiaobo "for his long and nonviolent struggle for fundamental human rights in China."

Liu Xiaobo was unable to attend the Nobel Peace Prize Ceremony in Oslo on December 10, and the Chinese government also prevented his wife, Liu Xia, and others from leaving China to attend. On that day, Liu Xiaobo was represented by an empty chair on the podium while the Norwegian actress Liv Ullmann read out an English translation of his essay "I Have No Enemies: My Final Statement." In addition, a commemoration exhibition of the 2010 Nobel Peace Prize laureate was also opened to the public, a concert celebrating Liu Xiaobo was held the following night, and a Nobel Foundation documentary of Liu Xiaobo was issued, all based on the theme "I have no enemies!"

In early June 2017, Liu Xiaobo was granted medical parole after being diagnosed with terminal liver cancer in prison. He was transferred to the First Affiliated Hospital of China Medical University in Shenyang for medical treatment under isolation from the outside world. At 5:35 p.m. on July

13, the hospital announced that Liu Xiaobo's condition had deteriorated and that he had died of multiple organ failure at the age of sixty-one. On the morning of July 15, 2017, Liu's remains were cremated, and his ashes were buried at sea at noon on the same day.

In addition to publication in Hong Kong and Taiwan, Liu Xiaobo's works have been translated into English and other foreign languages for publication abroad.

*Translated by Stacy Mosher*

## NOTE

Revised and updated from the author's book, *From Wang Shiwei to Liu Xiaobo: Prisoners of literary Inquisition under Communist Rule in China*, Volume 1 (1947–2010).

## BIBLIOGRAPHY

Bao Zunxin. "Anti-corruption Proposal." *Beijing Spring*, April 1995.
Beijing Municipal First Intermediate People's Court. "Verdict against Liu Xiaobo." 2009.
Fan Xing. "Cultural Whirlpool at the End of the Century." *Literature and Art Criticism* (Wenyi Pinglun) 5 (1996).
Hu Ping. "My Association with Liu Xiaobo (Part 1)." *Beijing Spring*, November 2010.
Jin Zhong. "Literary 'Dark Horse' Liu Xiaobo." *Emancipation Monthly* (Hong Kong), December 1988.
Liu Xiaobo. *The Collected Works of Liu Xiaobo*. Hong Kong: New Century Press, 2010.
——— . "Crisis! The Crisis Facing New Literature." *Shenzhen Youth Daily*, October 3, 1986.
——— . "Dialogue with Li Zehou: The Sensate, the Individual, My Choice." *China* 10 (1986).
——— . "The File of Liu Xiaobo." *Democracy Forum*, November 28, 2000.
Qian Wei. "Human Rights Organizations Put Liu Xiaobo Forward for the Nobel Peace Prize." *Voice of America*, July 19, 2009.
State Education Commission Ideological and Political Work Office. *Fifty-Six Hair-Raising Days: A Daily Record of the Events from April 15 to June 9, 1989*. 1989.
Wen Ping. "From Nationalistic Nihilism to Treason: A Critique of Liu Xiaobo's Bourgeois Liberalist Fallacies." *People's Daily*, November 7, 1989.
Wu Renhua. *Chronicle of the 1989 Tiananmen Incident*. Edoors.com, 2011.
Yu Jie. *I'm Innocence: The Story of Liu Xiaobo*. Taipei: China Times Publishing House, 2012.
Zheng Wang and Ji Kuai. *Liu Xiaobo: The Man and His Deeds*. Beijing: China Youth Press, 1989.

# Why Liu Xiaobo Matters

*Black Hand behind a Red Wall*

# On the Liu Xiaobo Incident
*Yu Ying-Shih*

When Liu Xiaobo was diagnosed with liver cancer, it was already at the terminal stage, so the Communist Party transferred him from prison to a hospital but maintained close watch on him. We overseas were able to observe only one instance of Liu Xia going to visit him, but we could see that Liu Xiaobo was already emaciated, and I surmised that his condition was serious. The fact that Liu Xiaobo contracted liver cancer after so many years in prison makes me think it was related to the pressure and harsh treatment the Communist Party imposed on him. His spirits must have been very low since cancer is often affected by mood. Although Liu Xiaobo was sentenced only to eleven years in prison, it was tantamount to a death sentence. The Communist Party wasn't about to let him enjoy easy days in prison. Over time, if he wasn't struck by heart disease it would be by some other illness, and in this case it was cancer. Once cancer reaches the terminal stage, it is extremely hard to treat. The Communist Party didn't grant him early release but kept him under a multitude of restrictions, simply exchanging an actual prison for a hospital. This shows how cruel and merciless the Communist Party is.

The most important point in the Liu Xiaobo incident was the worldwide reaction. I took note of the reaction in Europe and Japan and among various people in the United States. People were virtually unanimous in calling for Liu Xiaobo to be released and allowed to receive treatment in the United States. The U.S. State Department also directly or indirectly expressed to the Chinese government the wish that Liu Xiaobo be brought over for treatment. The Communist Party was uncompromising on this point and absolutely refused to relax Liu Xiaobo's punishment on the grounds of his illness. Leaving China was therefore impossible.

Of course there was considerable pressure from the international community, but a show of benevolence could not be expected, given that ruthlessness has been the Communist Party's basic principle all along. Liu Xiaobo's fate was therefore effectively decided. Even so, the pressure may have prompted a softer tone. Eventually the Chinese government said that foreign specialists would be allowed to treat Liu Xiaobo if they were willing to go to China. This was the least that could be hoped for—if foreign specialists weren't allowed to go China to treat him, that would mean the government wanted him dead. In order to avoid this even more serious accusation, the government offered a buffer.[1] Even so, everything remained under the Communist Party's control. The Liu Xiaobo incident therefore leads us to understand the Communist Party even better.

Many people continued to hope that Xi Jinping would cushion the blow. By then he had achieved the status of supreme leader, with close to the level of power Mao Zedong once enjoyed, and he should have been able to show some leniency. The reality was completely different, however, mainly because Xi Jinping still didn't have great confidence in his grasp on power. This became clear in the series of broadcasts by Guo Wengui in the United States, saying that the upcoming Nineteenth Party Congress posed an enormous threat to Xi.[2] Although Guo was basically targeting Wang Qishan and Fu Zhenghua, it gradually also involved the position of president and who could take over.[3] If Wang Qishan was unable to accept a position on the Central Politburo Standing Committee after the Nineteenth Party Congress, who would replace him? That was a very important question.

For this reason, the Liu Xiaobo incident was not a simple matter. Many friends in Mainland China telephoned me and said that even though the government had never issued any kind of report, and newspapers weren't allowed to report on Liu's health, word got around through private channels and couldn't be effectively blocked. Many people sympathized with Liu. So while it has been said that the Communist Party's long-term suppression has kept most people from knowing who Liu Xiaobo was, information couldn't be suppressed to the point of persecuting him to death. The name of Liu Xiaobo and his actions and his behavior related not only to the constitution but also to human rights, a basic liberal democratic system and rule of law, which everyone wants. This earned Liu Xiaobo an exalted status among the intellectuals I know. Furthermore, he had reached the age of sixty-one and might have lived only one or two years more. If he died, everyone would deeply mourn him, but his name would remain immortal throughout history.

In truth, the historical status of today's party leader, compared with that of Liu Xiaobo, will present a stark contrast, one positive and one much more negative. I therefore feel that the Liu Xiaobo incident should not be viewed only from the present or as a matter of life and death. Life or death no longer mattered to Liu Xiaobo, whose challenge to this totalitarianism achieved an immortal historical status. Whoever writes the history of the Chinese Communist Party's decades of rule will have to mention Liu Xiaobo and do so in an increasingly positive light, as was the case for Lin Zhao during the Anti-Rightist Campaign. Lin Zhao was a Peking University student who was eventually executed for opposing the totalitarian regime. Now people are starting to take notice of her. People are constantly going to her grave in Suzhou to pay their respects, and we're hearing more reports about her. Liu Xiaobo's influence far outweighs Lin Zhao's, besides which he is the only Chinese to have been awarded the Nobel Peace Prize. Even while dying after nine years in prison, Liu Xiaobo highlighted the essence of CCP rule in a way that could not be clearer.

I feel that the sheer idiocy of the Communist Party reached its apogee at this point; it would have been impossible to more completely bungle this matter. Releasing Liu Xiaobo or relaxing the conditions for his medical treatment would have ensured a much more positive reputation for the CCP in the international community. People would have felt that there was some humanity in the CCP, but the way they actually treated Liu Xiaobo made them look utterly inhumane. Liu Xiaobo had nothing to lose by that point; he had already reached the pinnacle of his achievement. For such a person to emerge in China showed that China's intellectuals had not completely capitulated to the Communist Party. Even though Chinese intellectuals remain under tremendous pressure and people don't dare express their views publicly in Mainland China, there is still resistance in private. Under these conditions, the CCP's insistence on thoroughly suppressing Liu Xiaobo and blocking all information about him only shows lack of confidence in the stability of its own regime.

I believe that the Communist Party's biggest problem is that it knows it holds all the power and that it can suppress the entire country with its millions of troops and millions of police officers, but it cannot achieve true legitimacy in the hearts of its people. Many people go along with the CCP for the sake of their own survival but do not embrace this regime in their hearts. Of course, there are many people who do support the regime, but we can see that these people tend to be those in the Fifty Cent Party and the wealthy because the CCP regime has become a big bourgeois dictatorship.[4]

It's the same in every large city or region, including Hong Kong. Xi Jinping's incident in Hong Kong also reflects his fear for his own political power.[5] He was unwilling to meet with Hong Kong's pan-democrats or enter into dialogue with them. He spoke instead of using the People's Liberation Army as a backup force to deal with protests in Hong Kong. The people were not subdued by him. Friends I telephoned in Hong Kong felt that Xi Jinping's visit did not increase positive feelings toward the Beijing regime among ordinary Hong Kong residents but rather made them fear it all the more. Under these circumstances, I feel it was notable that while Hongkongers were protesting against Xi Jinping, the first banner I saw them carrying on television said "Free Liu Xiaobo." This shows that Liu Xiaobo was embraced by the people to the extent that even though he had nothing to do with Hong Kong, one of the first things Hongkongers thought of as a condition for accepting the CCP regime was the need to free Liu Xiaobo. This shows the importance of the name Liu Xiaobo.

If the CCP insists on continuing along the same lines, it will isolate itself from the people, and they will refuse to submit. Ostensibly people accept the CCP's violent rule, but how long that rule can continue is something only heaven knows. That's why I feel that we cannot regard the Liu Xiaobo matter as one of an individual's life and death. Even if Liu Xiaobo could have been cured, the Communist Party wouldn't have granted him freedom. Liu Xiaobo cannot play a role in future political movements. His Charter 08 caused a stir for a time, but that moment has passed, and his work in China's political and social movements has ended. His personal morality and his greatest political accomplishments have also reached their pinnacle, and there's nothing to regret in that. What is regrettable is that he lived under a regime more ruthless than any that has ever ruled China. This should distress all of China's people.

*Translated by Stacy Mosher*

NOTES

Adapted from an essay posted on the Radio Free Asia website.

1. Steven Jiang, "Foreign Doctors Say Liu Xiaobo Can Travel Abroad for Cancer Treatment," CNN, July 10, 2017, https://www.cnn.com/2017/07/09/china/liu-xiaobo-doctors-travel/index.html. In spite of the statement by the German and American specialists who examined Liu Xiaobo, the Chinese government did not allow him to travel abroad for treatment.—Trans.

2. Guo Wengui (b. 1967), also known as Miles Kwok, is a former state security operative turned billionaire who took refuge in the United States and in 2017 began offering sensational revelations about the Chinese government.—Trans.

3. Wang Qishan (b. 1948), former secretary of the Central Commission for Discipline Inspection, has been the vice president of the PRC since 2018. Fu Zhenghua (b. 1955), a deputy minister of public security at the time that Liu Xiaobo died, is the minister of justice.—Trans.

4. "Fifty Cent Party" (*wumao dang*) is a Chinese expression for people paid by the Chinese authorities to post comments on the internet with the aim of manipulating public opinion, reputedly for fifty cents per posting.—Trans.

5. Xi Jinping met with protests during a three-day visit to Hong Kong to mark the twentieth anniversary of China's resumption of sovereignty over the former British colony on July 1, 2017. In his speech, Xi said that "any attempt to . . . challenge the power of the central government . . . is an act that crosses the red line and is absolutely impermissible." See Austin Ramzy, "Xi Delivers Tough Speech on Hong Kong, as Protests Mark Handover Anniversary," *New York Times*, July 1, 2017, https://www.nytimes.com/2017/07/01/world/asia/hong-kong-china-xi-jinping.html.—Trans.

On the Liu Xiaobo Incident   79

# Liu Xiaobo's Death as an Event of Human Spirit
*Teng Biao*

When I came to know Liu Xiaobo's name, the CCP had already labeled him as a behind-the-scenes "black hand" of the 1989 "counter-revolutionary riot." Initially, my understanding of his views and ideas unexpectedly came from just a few words of official propaganda I read. That "counter-revolutionary riot" was later called the "turmoil," then the "political disturbance," and then, in the end, it became a sensitive word. "Liu Xiaobo" became a restricted area. His body disappeared again and again inside iron walls. His writing was heavily blocked by the Red Wall. It was difficult for his ideas and spirit of resistance to break through the cage, but he nevertheless inspired a handful of "unwise" rebels.

Having grown up in a remote mountainous area of China in the 1970s, I didn't have an opportunity to get a taste of this universally shocking "dark horse of the literary scene" of the 1980s. It was in 1996, in the documentary *Tiananmen*, which was then quietly circulating among people in Mainland China, that I first saw the stuttering Liu Xiaobo. In the beginning of that year, he had just emerged from more than six months' jail time, but before the year's end, he was given a three-year term of reeducation through labor.

By the time his RTL term was completed in 1999, China already had the internet as well as a firewall. Liu Xiaobo was, of course, one of the names that the authorities were most keen on people not being able to retrieve. There were not that many people who were willing to have contact with him. Those who knew him affectionately called him Stammer Liu. This is probably the inevitable lonely fate of a rebel under a dictatorship: his body is imprisoned and ruined, his speech is prohibited from circulating. He's harassed in his daily life, and cynical people avoid him like the plague.

The first time I met Liu Xiaobo in person was in 2004, at a dinner party.

At that time, the rights defense movement was just emerging. He was very concerned about the movement and wrote many articles, one after the next, with commentary on rights defense events and figures. The New Youth Study Group case, Taishi Village case, Chen Guangcheng incidents, the Black Brick Kilns Scandal, the Yang Jia case—for almost every important, hot case, one can see his incisive commentary.[1] From the time of our first meeting until just before he went to jail at the end of 2008, we were often together, drinking, chatting, and participating in prodemocracy activities. I also introduced rights lawyers such as Gao Zhisheng and Li Heping to Liu Xiaobo, Zhang Zuhua, and others in their circle. The dividing line between "human rights defenders" and "pro-democracy activists" at that time had already started to slowly fade. In March 2008, the first time I was abducted and detained, Liu Xiaobo wrote an article titled "The Insanity of the Dark Forces: Reflections on Teng Biao's Abduction" and denounced the authorities' wanton trampling of human rights.

Liu Xiaobo showed me a draft of Charter 08, and I made my suggestions to him in person. At that time, in the version that I read, there were twenty "Fundamental Recommendations." I said that was too many—the main points weren't prominent and that ten were enough. Later, the formally released version had nineteen provisions. Charter 08, with freedom and human rights as its core and the establishment of a democratic constitutional government as its goal, reflects the basic consensus of Chinese civil movements on the direction of China's political future and is a historic political text issued by some Chinese people who were not in favor of the government. The Charter 08 movement was a concentrated display of people power accumulated since the 1970s through the prodemocracy movements and rights defense movement and brought the post-1989 civil liberalization movement to a new level.

My name was mentioned in Beijing No. 1 Intermediate People's Court's criminal verdict of Liu Xiaobo. I also published an essay "Testimony on My Testimony," in which I wrote:

> I suggested some revisions, such as removing the content about environmental protection and social security, etc., and reducing the number of clauses in order to focus on the human rights, rule of law and political

framework. My point is that it's unreasonable for you to take Xiaobo into custody and not me. Xiaobo was not the only person to participate in the drafting of *Charter 08*; I am also willing to assume legal responsibility relating to *Charter 08*. . . . If Liu Xiaobo committed a crime, then I am an "accomplice." As one of the first group of signatories of *Charter 08*, if you count the promotion of *Charter 08* as a crime, I demand to bear the same responsibility. If signing and disseminating *Charter 08* constitutes inciting subversion of state power, I also signed it, disseminated it, and will continue to disseminate it. I demand to share Mr. Liu Xiaobo's suffering because that is tantamount to sharing his honor. To stand on your defendant's dock and live in your jail is not my disgrace.

Because I signed Charter 08, I was suspended by the China University of Political Science and Law. But Liu Xiaobo was sentenced to eleven years' imprisonment; he paid an enormous price. However, before July 2017, no one knew—including Liu Xiaobo himself—that the price he would pay was his life.

Why is Liu Xiaobo important? Among China's freedom and democracy fighters, Liu Xiaobo is irreplaceable:

1. Mature and profound thought. He was a dark horse in literary circles with a PhD in literature. As a scholar, writer, poet, and teacher, it was easy for him to undertake criticism in the fields of literature, art, aesthetics, and culture. His essence was that of a free and unconstrained, willful poet and an unconventional and pioneering writer, but the political reality caused him to become a dissident, prodemocracy activist, political commentator, human rights activist, and prisoner of conscience. Both in and out of prison, he was diligent in his reading and writing, enriching his own knowledge reserves and theoretical weapons and gradually sharpening himself into a mature thinker. One can see from his essays that he was not limited to preaching morality, making ethical judgments, and analyzing aesthetics, but he also absorbed and applied knowledge from political science, philosophy, law, history, economics, sociology, psychology, and other disciplines. Moreover, this was reflected through infectious text, rich in his distinct

personal characteristics. His articles were sharp, rational, and firm, and they were permeated with a deep concern for humanity. They became his most important weapon of resistance. He had a profound understanding of democracy, nationalism, liberalism, human nature, and human rights and was filled with a spirit of self-criticism and self-examination. All of these are rare, important qualities.

2. Complete opposition to autocracy. Unlike many liberal intellectuals, his criticism of autocracy and totalitarianism was thorough. Not only on a theoretical level, but also from the aspects of politics, human nature, aesthetics, and practice, he comprehensively subverted absolutism. He did not hold illusions nor fall short on his commitment; he was not afraid of losing his platform to speak nor of being unemployed or jailed. However, some people, because of their level of understanding, are unable to completely break with the CCP's autocratic regime. There are also some people, because of their interests, or fear, who need to conduct self-censorship to some extent.

3. Enormous courage and long-term persistence. He had experienced weakness and made concessions, but after reflecting, he didn't flinch. After drawing lessons from painful experiences, his spirit was raised to a higher level. On two occasions, he gave up the opportunities to obtain asylum abroad and without hesitation returned to China. Again and again, he was subjected to house arrest, disappearance, searches, reeducation through labor, prison sentences, long-term harassment, isolation, and misunderstanding, but none of these challenges made him give up the struggle. The longer he fought, the more courageous he became. There weren't any sensitive meetings that he didn't dare organize and participate in, nor were there any topics or figures that he was afraid to comment on. The general secretary, the one-party system, corruption, Tiananmen massacre, prisoners of conscience, Falun Gong, Tibet, Xinjiang, nationalism—he recorded all of them faithfully. With respect to the dark forces, he mercilessly exposed and criticized them, and he paid ardent attention to the weak and the sufferers and appealed for them. There are some fighters who, for various reasons, have retreated or gone into exile, and there are some people who have given up because of fear and despair, even a few who

have been lured by gain and surrendered to the dictatorship, but Liu Xiaobo persisted.

4. Extensive contacts. At a young age, Liu Xiaobo became famous throughout the country. He took part in the 1989 Democracy Movement and organized the Independent Chinese PEN Center. Time and time again, while engaged in resistance activities, Liu Xiaobo accumulated extensive contacts both inside and outside the system. He became an important bridge and hub, linking reformers within the party, liberal intellectuals, independent writers, political prisoners, families of the Tiananmen massacre victims, democracy activists, human rights lawyers, petitioners, grassroots NGOs, entrepreneurs, university professors, young students, and more. Although Liu Xiaobo was not the main drafter of Charter 08, nevertheless, it was because of Charter 08 that he was sentenced to eleven years' imprisonment. The most important reason was that without the authorities knowing, he had launched this Charter that sought the establishment of the Federal Republic of China and moreover collected signatures nationwide from 303 intellectuals, democracy activists, and human rights defenders as initial sponsors of the Charter. This could not but cause great panic among the CCP authorities.

5. Widespread international recognition. After 1990 Liu Xiaobo won numerous international human rights awards and received the attention of the media, human rights organizations, and some Western governments. After winning the Nobel Peace Prize in 2010, he received even more reports, attention, and respect from around the world. His biography and collections of his works have been translated into many languages, and he has become the most famous of China's democracy fighters.

6. Rich experience and outstanding ability to act and lead. Since the 1980s, Liu Xiaobo transformed from an unruly, arrogant, and obstinate dark horse in intellectual circles to a mature, self-disciplined freedom warrior who was prepared for loneliness and constantly sacrificed himself. His long-term resistance career, suffering in prison, and brutal reality gave Liu Xiaobo a wealth of political wisdom and fighting experience and made him a democracy movement leader with extraordinary ability in action.

Some Chinese democrats and political opponents may meet two to three or even four to five of the six characteristics mentioned above, but it is hard to think of anyone other than Liu Xiaobo who could conform to all of these aspects. In this sense, Liu Xiaobo is almost irreplaceable. The fact that he was persecuted to death is a tremendous loss to China's cause of freedom and democracy. Kindhearted people once expected Liu Xiaobo to play an important role in China's political transition once he walked out of the dark prison after eleven years. However, Liu Xiaobo could not wait for that day. More accurately, the CCP, out of fear, deliberately did not let Liu Xiaobo wait until that day.

Like the events such as the collapse of the Berlin Wall, the 9/11 terrorist attacks on the United States, Tibetans' self-immolations, and the plight of the Syrian refugees, in my opinion, Liu Xiaobo's death was one of the most important events of the human spirit in world history after 1989.

After the Tiananmen massacre in 1989, when the bloodstains of the CCP's victims were not yet dry, all the democracies in the West, one after the next, tossed the CCP an olive branch. They couldn't wait to welcome the dictators and executioners with flowers and a red carpet. Trade and human rights were severed. The CCP was allowed to enter the World Trade Organization, allowed to host the Olympic Games and the World Expo, and was elected again and again to the UN Human Rights Council. As the second-largest economy in the world, China plays an increasingly unreasonable and provocative role internationally; it even wants to replace the United States and the West as the global leader on some important issues.

The West is meek with respect to the CCP and doesn't dare to promote the democratization of China. It is not even willing to sternly criticize the Chinese government on human rights issues. Scholars, research institutes, the media, publishing companies, and commercial organizations have all adopted self-censorship to maintain their relations with China or to enter the Chinese market. Some companies have even cooperated with the CCP to do evil: helping the CCP to develop censorship software or giving customer information to the CCP's national security apparatus. The West's long-term appeasement policy toward the CCP's autocratic regime has already resulted in evil consequences and threatens the value of Western liberal democracy. There are many examples at hand: cross-border kidnapping of activists, Confucius Institutes that threaten academic freedom, cyber-attacks, infiltration of free media, international bribery, attempting to control democratic elections, helping pro-CCP politicians enter Western politics, purchasing movie theater chains, promoting the concept of "human rights with Chinese characteristics," preventing overseas Tibetans' freedom of speech and right from demonstrating, monitoring the speech of Chinese students studying abroad by the Chinese students and scholars associations, and so on. However, few observers and politicians in the West have given sufficient attention to the seriousness of this issue.

China is the largest autocracy in the world, and Liu Xiaobo was the first Chinese citizen to win the Nobel Peace Prize. It's clear that he has become an important symbol. For such a saint-like victim, a hero who promoted the cause of human freedom and democracy—although the international community gave him substantial attention and support—it was far from enough. The CCP turned a deaf ear to the calls of support and concern; it even scoffed at them and intensified the long-term strict house arrest of Liu Xiaobo's wife, Liu Xia. The international community looked on helplessly as Liu Xiaobo received a heavy sentence, was imprisoned and subjected to liver cancer, and was unable to obtain freedom until the moment of his death. People usually compare Liu Xiaobo to Carl von Ossietzky, a German journalist and writer who won the Nobel Peace Prize while he was in a Nazi concentration camp. However, Ossietzky died in a hospital a year and a half after being formally released. Liu Xiaobo remained in strict police custody until his death. To date, he is the only Nobel laureate to have died in custody. Even after Liu Xiaobo died, his ashes were forcibly cast into the sea. He died without a burial place. Even after he died, CCP authorities continue to subject his widow Liu Xia to house arrest and disappearance.[2]

Liu Xiaobo's death was a global live stream of a murder foretold. Western democracies did not have a strong desire to help Liu Xiaobo obtain freedom. Even as Liu Xiaobo passed away, Western leaders were drinking with CCP leaders and signing one deal after another, and even though they orally expressed some demands, they lacked practical ways to pressure the CCP. Amid the arrogance and dominance of the CCP, people around the world had no choice but to watch Liu Xiaobo be sadistically killed, watch Liu Xia be disappeared, and watch even more prisoners of conscience arrested, imprisoned, and tortured.

The death of Liu Xiaobo is also a huge symbol of suffering, symbolizing the rising CCP's autocratic regime's enormous ridicule of humanity's justice and conscience, and the evil consequences of the West's appeasement policy toward China and the even greater threat to the future. In this sense, people will gradually realize that Liu Xiaobo's death is a shocking event in the history of the human spirit since the end of the Cold War.

*Translated by Andréa Worden*

NOTES

1. Four members of the New Youth Study Group, which focused on political reform, were arrested in 2004. Taishi Village in Guangdong Province became a flashpoint for political reform when villagers tried to recall a corrupt village head. Chen Guangcheng, a blind self-taught lawyer in Shandong Province, was subjected to house arrest and imprisonment before escaping and seeking refuge in the U.S. Embassy in Beijing in April 2012. The Black Brick Kilns Scandal refers to the discovery of forced labor in Shanxi in 2007. Yang Jia was executed in 2008 for killing six Shanghai police officers in revenge for his treatment in detention.—Trans.

2. In August 2018 Liu Xiaobo's wife, Liu Xia, was allowed out of China and flew to Finland and then to Germany.

# Liu Xiaobo, a Moral Giant of China's Democratic Transition
*Yang Guang*

## A Disheartened Advocate of Wholesale Westernization

Before 1989 Liu Xiaobo had become known to the world as a "literary dark horse" due to his unconventional thinking, radical remarks, and inappropriate language. He took a ruthless and thoroughly negative attitude toward the Chinese literary tradition represented by Qu Yuan and Du Fu, the Chinese philosophical tradition represented by Confucianism, the Chinese political tradition represented by absolute imperialism, and the contemporary political tradition represented by Mao Zedong and the Chinese Communist Party.[1] Liu Xiaobo also directed freezing irony and burning satire at (or simply refused to consider) the so-called Four Great Youth Mentors of the New Enlightenment period of that time.[2]

Liu Xiaobo closely examined the multilayered reasons for China's backwardness, which he did not believe was a matter of modern history; rather, he believed that throughout history, China had never been "advanced," from its system and culture to the "character" and "race" of the Chinese people. He said, "This may have something to do with race," therefore leading to the "300 years of colonialism" quote—colonialism rooted in the white race's theory of superiority and the rationalization of an advanced race's discrimination against and enslavement of backward peoples. This idea was clearly at odds with his subsequent insistent belief that "all people are created equal" per Thomas Jefferson's U.S. Declaration of Independence and the universal values of freedom, human rights, constitutional government, and democracy.

The Liu Xiaobo of that earlier time was not a genuine proponent of freedom and democracy but only a radical anti-traditionalist and proponent of wholesale westernization. His remarks were similar to those of the Japanese enlightenment thinkers at the outset of Japan's Meiji Restoration period, who advocated "breaking away from Asia and joining Europe."[3] He even made "treasonous and heretical" remarks such as "If I could manage [foreign] languages well enough, I would have nothing to do with China," and "If you say I'm a traitor, then I am," which were simply the indignant outpouring of frenzied hatred due to the depths of his love for the nation. In fact, when China was in crisis in 1989, Liu Xiaobo, for all his appearance of thoroughly detesting everything Chinese, didn't take the opportunity to break off relations with China but rather put his life at risk for the cause of China's human rights and democracy. Liu Xiaobo can be considered our generation's most steadfast and determined and greatest patriot.

Some say that before the 1989 Democracy Movement, Liu Xiaobo was like the haughty, narcissistic, virulently outspoken Li Ao of Taiwan's Martial Law period. There are in fact similarities in rhetorical style, but Liu Xiaobo himself said he was more like the nineteenth-century German philosopher Friedrich Nietzsche, who expressed his extreme disappointment with history and current reality by declaring "God is dead" and calling for "revaluation of all values."

### A Proponent of Freedom and Democracy Forged in Blood and Fire

The 1989 Democracy Movement was a watershed in China's era of reform and opening and also a turning point in Liu Xiaobo's ideological ideas. Mao Zedong said, "The salvoes of the October Revolution brought us Marxism-Leninism." Borrowing from Mao we could say, "The shouts of the 1989 Democracy Movement brought us freedom and democracy." For the generations of Chinese who in the post–Cultural Revolution era searched for the path to China's modernization, the 1989 Democracy Movement was our self-study course in democracy and tutorial in human rights, the seeder of freedom and catalyst for constitutional government.

When Hu Yaobang's death triggered the student movement, Liu Xiaobo was still in the United States as a visiting scholar. He was immediately drawn to this enormous and impressive mass movement. Resolutely abandoning his overseas academic career, he took the risk of returning to China and throwing himself into the flood of democratic protest at Tiananmen Square. In fact, this peaceful protest movement that sprang up on university campuses and erupted into the streets almost instantaneously overturned

Liu Xiaobo's extremely pessimistic prejudices toward the Chinese people, Chinese culture, and the road to China's modernization. He had never stubbornly stuck to his own opinions, although unlike Mahatma Gandhi, he didn't take delight in publicly exposing his own errors and "scandals." He discovered that China was not beyond salvation, that Chinese people were not hopelessly apathetic, that freedom, human rights, constitutional government, and rule of law were not unsuited to China, that China did not lack a path to modern civilization and that "300 years of colonialism" was not the only way to get there. The 1989 Democracy Movement was ironclad proof that China could be saved and that there was hope for democracy and freedom.

That massive peaceful protest movement ultimately failed under the Chinese government's armed suppression, and China's political and social situation experienced a huge regression. Most of those who came to prominence in the 1989 movement scattered with the four winds and disappeared from the stage of China's reforms. Imprisoned, Liu Xiaobo also fell into a dejected silence for a while, but he soon extricated himself from his frustration and fear. He became reactivated after coming to the profound realization that someone had to bear the intellectual elite's responsibility toward the ordinary participants in the 1989 movement and the responsibility of the survivors toward the victims of June 4. If everyone chose to go into exile or fell silent or withdrew, the torch of the 1989 Democracy Movement would be extinguished, and the sacrifice of the victims of June 4 would come to naught. Liu Xiaobo therefore chose to hold fast, struggle, sacrifice himself, and take on the burden.

When the government's tyranny, the soldiers' cruelty and the ruthlessness of the tanks and grenades drove others to despair, Liu Xiaobo was one of the few who observed how panic-stricken and intrinsically debilitated the single-party autocracy was in the face of nonviolent resistance. He saw the latent courage and enormous power in civil society. More crucially Liu Xiaobo saw in the mass emotion of the street movement and its stirring defeat under blood and fire, the distant hope of a free China and a future of democratic transformation. He clearly distinguished the future direction of China's social transformation: "A future free for China is among the people."

## Living for the Dead of June 4th, Dying for Charter 08

June 4 changed Liu Xiaobo's personal fate. As China's most famous prisoner of conscience, he spent almost the last half of his life in prison or on
his way there. Of course, he could have chosen to leave China and go into
exile—the life chosen by the vast majority of the heroes on the square and
the "black hands" who supported them behind the scenes. A few promises
to the authorities would have been enough to allow him to immediately
take up a new life, or he could have chosen to "see which way the wind
blows," bowed his head to the authorities, and chosen to forget June 4 and
abandon his struggle. But that was not Liu Xiaobo.

After June 4 China entered a long and depressing period of political
decay and a low tide in the democracy movement. Reform never stopped,
but it was limited to economic reform. Political reform died as "stability
overrode everything else"—the "China model" that Liu Xiaobo evocatively
referred to as "lame reform." After Deng Xiaoping's 1992 Southern Tour
and China's accession to the World Trade Organization, China's increasing
market orientation and openness to the outside world gave the nation the
second-highest GDP in the world, while its freedom of expression, rights
of religious belief and association, progress of grassroots elections, access
to public positions, separation of the party from the government, and
public policy-making all regressed from the situation before June 4. The
line from Deng Xiaoping to Jiang Zemin to Hu Jintao and Xi Jinping was
largely one of monotonous systemic decline. "Lame reform" was accompanied by worsening omens in the political ecology and social structure
from top to bottom: ideological emptying, profitization of the ruling clique,
corruption in the bureaucratic ranks, increasingly sinister enforcement
organs, growing cynicism among the intellectual elite, a growing vassal
mentality among the capitalistic elites, polarization in the social structure,
and a younger generation increasingly focused on entertainment. Under
these conditions, members of the public who had taken part in the 1989
Democracy Movement began to distance themselves from the cause of
freedom and democracy, and even student leaders and intellectual elites
who had shouted and waved banners back then became disheartened,
abandoned their ideals, and retreated to the fringes.

"When the seas are in turmoil, heroes are on their mettle."[4] Confucius speaks of one "who keeps working towards a goal the realization of which he knows to be hopeless."[5] Mencius said, "I will go forward against thousands and tens of thousands."[6] Kṣitigarbha Bodhisattva (Dizang Pusa) said, ""If I don't go to hell, who will?"[7] Liu Xiaobo chose to live for those who died on June 4, devoting all his effort to completing his last watch for the 1989 Democracy Movement. Like Nelson Mandela, Aung San Suu Kyi, Vaclav Havel, and Lech Wałęsa, who refused to go into exile or to accept awards overseas for fear of not being allowed to return to their countries and who preferred to go to prison, Liu Xiaobo made prison his chief battleground in his fight against tyranny. In fact, ever since Mahatma Gandhi created the modern nonviolent civil disobedience movement, leaders of resistance movements and their followers have willingly gone to prison for peaceful noncompliance, the main content of this resistance method. In South Africa, Gandhi boycotted the poll tax on Asians and the discriminatory Identity Card Law, and in India he resisted the Salt Law and launched the independent liberation movement, all of which involved resisting evil laws, self-sacrifice, and mass jailings. Mandela and Suu Kyi gained the world's sympathy and respect as moral heroes mainly because they spent such long periods of time in prison or under house arrest.

Once imprisoned the fourth time, because of Charter 08, Liu Xiaobo never came out again, ultimately dying in cold and lonely confinement as the last martyr of the 1989 Democracy Movement and the first martyr of Charter 08.

Liu once said that the optimal hypothetical after June 4th would have been "if Fang Lizhi had left the U.S. Embassy and faced trial under the CCP, and if everyone had stayed behind and filled the CCP's prisons, and if Zhao Ziyang had openly broken with the ruling party as Yeltsin had," then the 1989 Democracy Movement would certainly not have been so easily extinguished by the CCP's primitive blockading and "stability maintenance." He observed that Poland had a Wałęsa, Czechoslovakia had a Havel, South Korea had a Kim Dae-jung, South Africa had a Mandela, the Philippines had Corazón Aquino, and Myanmar had an Aung San Suu Kyi, but that no such individual had emerged in China after so many political disasters, and that "one Aung San Suu Kyi was worth more than a dozen of China's dissident. . . . History is not fated. The appearance of a single martyr can fundamentally turn the spirit of a nation and strengthen its moral fiber," he wrote in a letter to Liao Yiwu.[8]

In fact, Liu Xiaobo was wrong. China's cause of democracy and human rights has not lacked moral giants, and Liu Xiaobo was one of them. Liu Xiaobo was not in any way inferior to Mandela or Aung San Suu Kyi. The CCP government he faced was far more evil than the white Afrikaner government or Myanmar's military junta, and Mandela and Aung San Suu Kyi were backed by the highly organized African Congress and Burmese National League for Democracy, while Liu Xiaobo was backed by only a small group of widely dispersed people with shared goals. Comparatively speaking, the value of Liu Xiaobo's steadfastness and sacrifice and his spirit of justice were even greater than that of Mandela and Suu Kyi.

### "I Have No Enemies" and Nonviolence

Liu Xiaobo's most famous and also his most controversial saying was "I have no enemies." This sentence first came out in "The June 2nd Hunger Strike Declaration" in 1989 and became widely known through the statement he delivered at his trial, "I Have No Enemies: My Final Statement." Clearly, unlike "300 years of colonialism," "I have no enemies" was not a slip of the pen, a blurted comment, or words spoken in the heat of the moment but rather his carefully considered and long-maintained political and moral principle. But while these words helped Liu Xiaobo win the 2010 Nobel Peace Prize, they also drew countless opposing voices from within his camp.

In "The June 2nd Hunger Strike Declaration," Liu Xiaobo wrote,

Thousands of years of Chinese history are filled with instances of hatred between adversaries and the use of violence to battle violence. By the dawn of the modern era an "enemy mentality" had taken root in Chinese political thinking, and after the Communist victory in 1949 slogans like "Take class struggle as fundamental" pushed the traditional hate psychology, enemy mentality, and battling of violence with violence to new extremes. The current martial law is a manifestation of "class struggle" thinking. By our hunger strike we appeal to our fellow Chinese to begin immediately to move away from, and eventually to completely abandon, the enemy mentality, hate psychology, and "class struggle" political culture. Hatred leads only to violence and dictatorship. We must begin to build democracy in China in a spirit of tolerance and with conscious cooperation.[9]

Liu Xiaobo said, "We advocate the spread of democracy in China through peaceful means and we oppose violence in any form" because "a democratic society is not built on hatred and enmity; it is built on consultation, debate, and voting that are carried out on a basis of mutual respect, tolerance, and willingness to compromise."[10] This clearly eliminates all ambiguity in the statement "I have no enemies." It doesn't mean ending struggle, nor is it appeasement, and even less is it "capitulation" or "currying favor with the CCP"; rather, it refuses to divide political society and civil society into the enemy and us and refuses to apply the "philosophy of struggle" and enemy mentality to any Chinese citizen, whether an ordinary person or one with special status such as the Chinese citizen Li Peng.

Unlike Gandhi or Martin Luther King Jr., Liu Xiaobo did not expound on his ideology of nonviolence or its strategy of struggle, but with "I have no enemies" as its principle of political ethics, nonviolent resistance was the sole struggle approach he could accept. In his essay "Revenge in the Style of Yang Jia is Primitive Justice," Liu Xiaobo stated that he opposed the government's violent "stability maintenance" but also opposed private citizens using violence to defend their rights and extract revenge. He said, "Yang Jia is not a hero or a knight-errant because he ended six lives. . . . When justice cannot be achieved through legal means, how can it be considered justice to destroy the lives of others (even the lives of instruments of dictatorship) in order to achieve justice?" Apart from publishing commentaries on the Yang Jia case, Liu Xiaobo carried out even more in-depth discussion of "fundamental choices on the route to China's transformation." He held that China's democratic transformation could only be achieved through peaceful and nonviolent means because "replacing violence with violence has already become an extremely outdated approach of regime change, while nonviolent transformation conforms to the moral standards of human civilization as well as to the beneficial principles of social development, and that is why it has increasingly become the world trend." He believed that the "accumulated pressure of persistent nonviolent resistance" would result in a more positive, lasting, and desirable transformation than a tumultuous and violent revolution.

For Nelson Mandela, nonviolence was a means and not an end. In fact, Mandela early on organized and led an underground militant group called Spear of the Nation, which planned to bomb military and transportation installations and other such violent activities, and one explosion accidentally resulted in the deaths of two innocent white people. It was not until he went to prison that Mandela established his strategy of nonviolence. The reason that Mandela and F. W. de Klerk were jointly awarded the Nobel Peace Prize in 1993 wasn't because of Mandela's early years resisting apartheid but because after leaving prison he led reconciliation among the South African people without regard to race. For Gandhi and Martin Luther King Jr., nonviolence was both a means and an end. Gandhi believed that nonviolence was God's decree, that it was "truth" and an inviolable belief, that it was "the weapon of the strong" as those imposing violence were the ones who were selfish, cowardly, and weak. Gandhi would rather end a resistance movement to prevent mass violence and would cooperate with the rulers than see the spread of a violent movement. In his later years, Gandhi repeatedly went on hunger strike to dissuade people from violent uprisings, achieving an almost unbelievable moral feat. In his steadfast adherence to a peaceful road to China's democratic transformation, Liu Xiaobo can in a sense be considered modern China's Gandhi and Martin Luther King Jr.

*Translated by Stacy Mosher*

NOTES

1. Qu Yuan (340–278 BC) was a poet and minister of the Warring States period who killed himself after being slandered and sent into exile. Du Fu (712–70) was a famous Tang dynasty poet who also failed in his desire for public service.—Trans.
2. The Four Great Youth Mentors were Li Zehou (b. 1930), Jin Guantao (b. 1947), Liu Binyan (1925–2005), and Liu Zaifu (b. 1941). No matter how insufficient and deficient in their words and deeds, there is no doubt that they played in enormous role in leading the young post–Cultural Revolution generation to cast off the ideological shackles of Maoism and in creating space for lively discussion and collective activities

on university campuses in the 1980s. The emergence of the 1986 and 1989 student movements was very closely related to the ideological enlightenment represented by them and a large number of other open-minded scholars.

3. This idea originated with the Japanese author, journalist, entrepreneur, and liberal ideologist and activist Fukuzawa Yukichi (1835–1901), who is considered one of the founders of modern Japan.—Trans.

4. A quote from a poem by Guo Moruo (1892–1978), which is translated in Mao Tse-tung, *Ten More Poems of Mao Tse-tung* (Hong Kong: Eastern Horizon Press, 1967), 31.—Trans.

5. Confucius, *Analects*, trans. D. C. Lau (London: Penguin Classics, 1979), book 14, ch. 38.—Trans.

6. *The Work of Mencius*, trans. James Legge (Scotts Valley CA: Createspace Independent Publishing Platform, 2010), book 2, part 1, Kung-sun Ch'au, chapter 2.—Trans.

7. Han Xin, Well-Known Temples of China (Shanghai: The Eastern Publishing Company, 2006). See "Hall of Kshitigarbha," Wikipedia, https://en.wikipedia.org/wiki/Hall_of_Kshitigarbha.—Trans.

8. Translated by Perry Link, "A Letter to Liao Yiwu" (January 13, 2000), in *Liu Xiaobo: No Enemies, No Hatred*, ed. Perry Link, Tienchi Martin-Liao, and Liu Xia (Cambridge MA: The Belknap Press of Harvard University Press, 2012), 288.—Trans.

9. Link et al., *Liu Xiaobo*, 278.—Trans.

10. Link et al., *Liu Xiaobo*.—Trans.

# For Whom the Bell Tolls

*Hu Ping*

This is a sorrowful time: at 5:35 p.m. on July 13, 2017, Liu Xiaobo died of belatedly treated liver cancer in Shenyang, China. The whole world watched helplessly as a Nobel Peace Prize laureate died at the hands of Chinese tyranny. It was only after Liu Xiaobo died that Western leaders publicly spoke his name and paid tribute to him—but without harshly criticizing the Chinese government for keeping this Nobel laureate in prison until he died. Due to years of suppression by the authorities, only a small number of people in China mourned Liu Xiaobo; the majority were apathetic or silent. Consequently, quite a few people regard the undertaking to which Liu Xiaobo devoted himself as a small bubble outside of China's mainstream.

But that's not true at all. We must not forget the peaceful democracy movement of unprecedented scale that broke out in China twenty-eight years earlier. On April 27, 1989, the day that Liu Xiaobo flew back to China from New York, a massive demonstration flooded Chang'an Avenue with people and banners as far as the eye could see. The 1989 Democracy Movement was powerful evidence that freedom and democracy were not the pursuit of just a handful of dissidents but the common aspiration of hundreds of millions of people, first and foremost the younger generation. The unimaginably brutal methods that China's hardliners, led by Deng Xiaoping, used to crush the democracy movement resulted in an unprecedented split in the CCP's ruling clique and unanimous condemnation from the international community. That same year brought tremendous change to the Soviet Union and Eastern Europe. The international Communist camp disintegrated, and the United States became the world's sole superpower. As the forces of freedom and democracy scored a historic and glorious victory, it was commonly believed that the days were numbered for China's autocratic Communist regime.

Yet twenty-eight years have passed, and the Chinese Communist autocratic regime is still standing and is stronger than ever before. In particular, its sustained economic development has exceeded most people's expectations. Likewise unanticipated is the CCP regime's refusal to launch political reform along with its deepening economic reforms. Rather than growing milder and more tolerant with its enormous economic success, it has become even more overbearing and high-handed and has abandoned the policy of "maintaining a low profile" in international affairs in favor of a more aggressive approach.[1] At the same time, democratic countries, including the United States, have encountered all kinds of difficulties. In a short period of fewer than thirty years, we have witnessed repeated astonishing reversals of the kind that used to be rare in human history, and the rise of autocratic China has become today's most serious challenge to universal values.

Liu Xiaobo wrote ten years ago, "What concerns me is that in facing today's most powerful dictatorship, China, Westerners may once again commit a great error." He warned the international community:

> The truth that international mainstream society must take very seriously is that today's chess game between the Chinese dictatorship and the free world is completely different from that with the traditional totalitarian Soviet communists. The Chinese Communist Party is no longer firmly entrenched in ideology and military competition, but rather is devoting its effort to developing its economy and forsaking ideological friendships; in the economy it is carrying out reforms toward marketization and striving to merge into the global community, while on the political front it is tenaciously defending its dictatorial system and forcefully countering any West-driven peaceful evolution. It's clear that the CCP regime, with its bulging wallet, is engaging in dollar diplomacy with the world, becoming a blood-transfusion machine for other dictatorships while using economic and trade interests to break up Western alliances and using its huge market to lure and coerce big capital in the West. In the face of the rapidly increasing economic power of this dictatorship,

failure to impose forceful external restraints while continuing to adopt policies of appeasement will result in a historic reversion that will bring disaster not only on the Chinese people, but also on the globalization of liberal democracy. Given the need to contain the adverse effects that a rising dictatorship can have on world civilization, the free world must help the world's largest dictatorship transform into a free and democratic country as soon as possible.[2]

From his stirring performance at Tiananmen Square to his solitary death at the First Affiliated Hospital of Shenyang's China Medical University, Liu Xiaobo was fated not only to reflect the plight of China's democracy but also to sound a warning to the world. Twenty-eight years ago, who would have imagined what the world has become today. If the trend continues, the world twenty-eight years from now will be too dreadful to contemplate. For whom does the bell toll? We can only hope that Liu Xiaobo's death marks the beginning of a reversal.

## Liu Xiaobo's Political Last Words

Liu Xiaobo died under the CCP's tight control. He was not even allowed to leave last words for the public. Fortunately we still have Liu Xiaobo's final statement from when he was on trial. In it, Liu Xiaobo uses the language of a prose poem to express his dreams and hopes.

Liu Xiaobo said:

I look forward to the day when our country will be a land of free expression: a country where the words of each citizen will get equal respect; a country where different values, ideas, beliefs, and political views can compete with one another even as they peacefully coexist; a country where expression of both majority and minority views will be secure, and, in particular, where political views that differ from those of the people in power will be fully respected and protected; a country where all political views will be spread out beneath the sun for citizens to choose among, and every citizen will be able to express views without the slightest of fears; a country where it will be impossible to suffer persecution for expressing a political view. I hope that I will be the last victim in China's long record of treating words as crimes.[3]

When reading this statement by Liu Xiaobo, one can't help but think of Martin Luther King Jr.'s famous "I Have a Dream" speech. In it, King says,

> I have a dream that one day this nation will rise up and live out the true meaning of its creed: "We hold these truths to be self-evident: that all men are created equal." I have a dream that one day on the red hills of Georgia the sons of former slaves and the sons of former slave owners will be able to sit down together at the table of brotherhood. I have a dream that one day even the state of Mississippi, a state sweltering with the heat of injustice, sweltering with the heat of oppression, will be transformed into an oasis of freedom and justice. I have a dream that my four little children will one day live in a nation where they will not be judged by the color of their skin but by the content of their character.

Liu Xiaobo's final statement is as good as Martin Luther King's speech in its connotations and its expression and may be even richer. Someday it will be printed in high school textbooks along with King's speech and be passed down through the generations.

In "I Have No Enemies: My Final Statement," Liu Xiaobo writes, "Free expression is the base of human rights, the root of human nature, and the mother of truth. To kill free speech is to insult human rights, to stifle human nature, and to suppress truth. I feel it is my duty as a Chinese citizen to try to realize in practice the right of free expression that is written in our country's constitution. There has been nothing remotely criminal in anything that I have done, yet I will not complain, even in the face of the charges against me."[4]

Back when he was in college, Liu Xiaobo conceived of the ideal of fighting for freedom of expression in China and resolved to put his beliefs into practice in public words and actions. At first glance, freedom of expression seems very mild, but it has lethal power against Communist autocracy. Liu Xiaobo wrote, "For both officials and ordinary citizens, promoting an open press and freedom of expression on the mainland is in fact the chief goal for promoting the stable transformation of Chinese society. The ban on opposition parties can be ignored for now, but we cannot wait another moment to remove the ban on speech." Freedom of speech is enough to cause the collapse of autocratic rule "Once the ban on speech is lifted, a free China will surely arrive." Accordingly, Liu Xiaobo proposed that civil rights defense efforts should make the fight for free expression its breakthrough point.

What must be made clear is that fighting for freedom of expression doesn't require everyone to fearlessly express all of their viewpoints. It only requires boldly stepping forward whenever freedom of expression is violated.

When Liu Xiaobo was handed his heavy prison sentence at the end of 2009, Cui Weiping of the Beijing Film Academy asked her colleagues in intellectual and cultural circles to discuss their views of the Liu Xiaobo case. Some didn't respond at all, but almost all of those who did respond expressed opposition to the sentence imposed on Liu Xiaobo. Some respondents stated that they disapproved of Liu Xiaobo's views and even strongly opposed them, but they could not accept his being convicted on the basis of his speech. Some of them quoted Voltaire: "I disapprove of what you say, but I will defend to the death your right to say it."[5] I don't know if those people really opposed Liu Xiaobo's views. It could be that some agreed with them but didn't dare say so or even falsely claimed not to agree with them to avoid trouble for themselves. That's beside the point. What matters is their defense of Liu Xiaobo's rights and his freedom of expression.

This is the secret of fighting for free expression—minimizing risk. When you don't express agreement with a dangerous "reactionary viewpoint" and even "draw a clear distinction" from reactionary expression, what can the authorities do to you? This is a risk most people can take, and it's very easy to do this much. If more people take this stand, true freedom of expression will come closer to reality.

Make fighting for freedom of expression the first step in vanquishing totalitarian rule and continue take a stand for freedom of expression. These are the political last words that Liu Xiaobo left for us.

### Some Minor Details That Reveal Liu Xiaobo's Character

I've read many essays commemorating Liu Xiaobo, and some of them talk about certain incidents in Liu Xiaobo's life that are deeply moving.

The veteran Beijing democracy activist He Depu was sentenced to eight years in prison on November 6, 2003. He wrote in social media that as his wife, Jia Jianying, was on her way home after the sentencing, she received a phone call from Liu Xiaobo, who invited her to his home for dinner. Liu Xia cooked dinner while Liu Xiaobo talked with Jia Jianying. After Liu Xiaobo was arrested, Jia Jianying sewed him a thick quilt according to the measurements that He Depu provided her from prison. Liu Xiaobo supported the families of many political prisoners who were handed heavy sentences in the early 2000s.

After He Depu posted this account, the Sichuan-based dissident Ouyang Yi and several others also posted messages about the great support they'd received from Liu Xiaobo and expressed regret that there was nothing they could do to support him now.

Yu Zhijian was one of three men who splashed paint on Mao's portrait at Tiananmen Square during the 1989 Democracy Movement. Yu died in 2017, and when his widow, Xian Gui'e, learned of Liu Xiaobo's death, she was extremely sad and wrote an article in his memory. Xian Gui'e noted, "When we got married in 2006, he telephoned us. Zhijian conversed with Mr. Xiaobo in a respectful and excited tone of voice, and I was dancing with happiness."

Liu Xiaobo held fast in China and maintained contact with dissidents inside the country. Many persecuted dissidents had never had anything to do with Liu Xiaobo or even met him in person, but Liu Xiaobo treated them like brothers, and apart from using ICPC resources to serve writers in prison, he also spent his own earnings to help them. Many families of people convicted of speech crimes, including the wives of Yang Zili and Du Daobin and Liu Di's grandmother, received phone calls and emails from Liu Xiaobo inquiring after their welfare. The writer Shi Tao, handed a ten-year prison sentence for articles he'd posted on overseas websites, had never been in direct contact with Liu Xiaobo, but when his mother went to visit him in prison, he told her quietly that if there was a problem she should go to see "Bo." This shows how much Shi Tao trusted Liu Xiaobo.

It must be emphasized that this trust wasn't based on Liu Xiaobo's parading around and making a big show; rather it resulted from many small things done outside of public view that had spread by word of mouth over the years. It's a powerful testament to Liu Xiaobo's character.

These episodes would never have been made public if Liu Xiaobo hadn't died, and outsiders would never have been aware of them. For a long time, a small number of people have spread inaccurate and intentionally fabricated stories attacking and disparaging Liu Xiaobo's character, but none of the accusations hold water, as is obvious from the widespread and enormous trust Liu Xiaobo enjoyed. One example is the number of people who signed Charter 08. We know that Liu Xiaobo personally recruited more than 70 of the 303 initial signatories, more than anyone else. Some people signed it as soon as Liu Xiaobo contacted them, without even reading it in detail, because they completely trusted Liu Xiaobo.

## Liu Xiaobo as Saint

After Liu Xiaobo died, many people wrote articles lauding and praising him, and some suggested erecting a monument to him or naming a street or square after him. Then someone warned, "Don't turn him into a saint." Having experienced the personality cult of the Mao era, people were especially sensitive to deifying anyone. But the activities we're carrying out in praise of Liu Xiaobo are fundamentally different from the deification campaigns of the Mao era.

I remember that at the outset of the Cultural Revolution, in response to Western criticism of the CCP's personality cult, Mao told the American journalist Edgar Snow, "I'm said to have a personality cult, but you Americans have more personality cults! Your national capital is called Washington. The place where Washington is located is called the District of Columbia." Mao said, "Are you, Snow, happy if no one worships you? If every governor or president or department head in America doesn't have people who worship them, how can they carry on?"[6]

Mao seemed to have a point, but his argument doesn't hold water. The crux is that allowing people to worship you is one thing, but disallowing people from not worshiping you is another. The problem with the Communist Party was not its excessive praise of its leader but its use of power to punish those who refused to praise or worship Mao for speech crimes. Deng Xiaoping was a CCP leader who reportedly never imposed a personality cult and even opposed it, but all it took was for Wei Jingsheng to write a single big-character poster criticizing Deng Xiaoping and Deng ordered him arrested and imprisoned. The crux of the matter is therefore not whether a person is deified but whether freedom of expression is safeguarded and whether people are punished for speech crimes.

Now some people are giving Liu Xiaobo an extremely high appraisal and are preparing to establish some form of memorial for him. There is nothing in this that forces people to regard Liu Xiaobo as a great man or a saint; everyone is free to maintain their own views. There is nothing in this that negates freedom of expression or persecutes or convicts people who hold alternative views. It is completely different from what the CCP has been imposing.

In fact, giving some individuals an extremely high appraisal as saints has been a long tradition both in the East and West. For example, the Roman Catholic Church has a tradition of canonizing saints. Famous examples include Saint Francis, Saint Anthony, and Saint Augustine. Saints are not necessarily people who have never done anything wrong in all their lives. For example, Saint Augustine was wild in his youth and only became a faithful Christian in middle age, when he went to live in a monastery and devoted the remainder of his days to good works. In ancient China Mencius said, "All men may be Yaos and Shuns."[7]

Wang Yangming has a famous quote: "The streets are full of saints."[8] That is to say, people have the potential for goodness, and if they persist in their efforts, they can transcend the ordinary and reach the realm of saints and sages.

In the film *The Lady*, Aung San Suu Kyi says, "Saints are sinners who go on trying." I feel this is an excellent saying. Among the dissidents I have known, quite a few are people of moral rectitude and steadfast will. Among them, Liu Xiaobo was not necessarily the most outstanding. But all of these people have gone into exile, one after another, and they can't make the most of their abilities in a free society. Furthermore, while Liu Xiaobo was not without flaws, he had a rigorous spirit of introspection, and his expression did not stay on paper but was carried out in practice. The majority of the various schools of spiritual self-cultivation in the past and present, in China and overseas, emphasize putting beliefs into practice—living according to your principles and turning your principles into a way of life. As long as you honor the demands of your principles in leading a different life, then even if you lose your way to some extent at first, with persistence, all those things will naturally fade away over time, and your soul will become pure. For more than twenty years, Xiaobo devoted himself to China, and his steadfast resistance and calm in the face of suffering gradually raised his spiritual realm to a higher level.

Saints are sinners who go on trying. Liu Xiaobo persisted to the very end. If he wasn't a saint, then who could ever be? Saints are tempered in this way. No one is born perfect; perfection is embodied in the constant pursuit of perfection. Those who spend their lives pursuing perfection are perfect.

*Translated by Stacy Mosher*

## NOTES

1. In the early 1990s, Deng Xiaoping advocated the policy of *taoguang yanghui, yousuo zuowei*—keeping China's capabilities under wraps in international affairs while trying to accomplish something on the economic front.—Trans.
2. Liu Xiaobo, "The Western Left, Lost in the Embrace of Tyrants" (in Chinese), posted on *Boxun* and available on the website of the Independent Chinese PEN Center, https://blog.boxun.com/hero/liuxb/377_1.shtml.
3. Liu Xiaobo, "I Have No Enemies: My Final Statement," trans. Perry Link, in *Liu Xiaobo: No Enemies, No Hatred*, ed. Perry Link, Tienchi Martin-Liao, and Liu Xia (Cambridge MA: The Belknap Press of Harvard University Press, 2012), 325–26.—Trans.
4. Link et al., *Liu Xiaobo*, 326.
5. This quote, attributed here to Voltaire, is believed to have actually originated with his biographer, British historian Evelyn Beatrice Hall (1868–1956).—Trans.
6. For the full record of Mao's interview with Edgar Snow on December 18, 1970, see "Abstract of Mao Zedong's Conversation in a Meeting with Snow—Regarding the Cultural Revolution, Personality Cult and Plans" (in Chinese), *Baidu*, December 31, 2010, https://wenku.baidu.com/view/6fff31d436ocba1aa811da95?fr=prin.—Trans.
7. Mencius (372–289 BC) was a Chinese philosopher regarded as the most famous Confucian after Confucius; Yao and Shun were legendary monarchs ranked by Confucius as the highest saints.—Trans.
8. Wang Yangming (1422–1529) was a philosopher who stressed intuition in contrast with the philosopher Zhu Xi's "investigation of things."—Trans.

# Liu Xiaobo and His Political Views
*Bao Tong*

At the end of 1986, during the student movements that took place in Anhui, Nanjing, Shanghai, and Beijing, I learned about Liu Xiaobo, but we had never met. Before 2007 Liu Xiaobo came to see me twice; both times he was blocked by the police, so he had no choice but to leave. I got acquainted with Liu Xiaobo in 2007 and 2008, and we soon became good friends.

Liu Xiaobo's expertise was literary theory. In college, he studied the theoretical school of Nicolai Dobrolyubov, Vissarion Belinsky, and Nicolai Chernyshevsky, but he was not satisfied.[1]

He liked to lead a carefree and unrestrained life and liked to make friends and chat. In terms of his temperament, he was not a man of politics. We discussed everyday matters of ordinary people, and talked about everything under the sun, from ancient times to the present, but rarely touched politics. Incidentally, when we drank tea and talked, there was always someone close by listening to us.

After we'd become acquainted, like clockwork, we would get together to drink tea once a month. But for various reasons, it was not always possible to meet up. He knew that I practiced tai chi every day in Yuyuantan Park, and sometimes he stopped by the park to see me. Once in 2008, he came to the park and said that several friends were drafting Charter 08, and he wished to discuss it with me. After that, we met more often than once a month.

Charter 08 was not drafted by Liu Xiaobo alone; he managed the effort, but everyone consulted with each other. He listened attentively to various opinions, and he listened particularly carefully to differing opinions. He also debated but was not stubborn; he chose the right course and followed it. Whatever it took to get more people to agree on the text, he agreed that was how it should be written.

Liu Xiaobo's personality is moderate, not going to extremes, neither subjective nor radical. His subsequent article "I Have No Enemies" truly reflects his character and position.

When drafting Charter 08, he also sought my opinion, but my opinion was very simple. It was only one sentence: the simpler, clearer, and more moderate, the better. Besides that I had no other opinion. A few friends consulted about it together; they were busy as bees, but he was the busiest.

Liu Xiaobo was smart and knew that things must be done according to the law. In this way, more people would participate and there would be less resistance. The contents of Charter 08 were almost all already addressed in China's Constitution. We were only demanding that they be implemented and enforced in earnest; there was otherwise nothing new. Under normal circumstances, it goes without saying, all of it would have been acceptable to the authorities, and there would have been no reason for them to reject it.

For example, all power in the People's Republic of China belongs to the people, who enjoy the freedoms of speech, the press, assembly, association, procession, and demonstration. All of these things are expressly included in the constitution and should be guaranteed by the government; there's nothing subversive about them.

At that time, it was reckoned that there were two issues that might be more difficult to accept. One was that "the military should be made answerable to the national government," and the other was the demand for "a federated republic." At first, it had been considered whether or not to include these two issues, but the common conclusion was that for the love of the country, they must be addressed. It was our responsibility as patriots not to be perfunctory.

If the military is not made answerable to the national government, might it be privatized or subject to a political party or warlord control? This should not be. The national defense forces must naturally be made answerable to the national government, which was a consistent proposition of Mao Zedong and Zhou Enlai from 1937 to 1946, and from which there should be no wavering.

Federalism is the foundation of a democratic system. If China, as big as it is, does not implement a federated system, then it is governed by a centralized authority. Beginning with Emperor Qin Shihuang, all absolutism has been linked with the centralization of authority; therefore, a federation is actually an effective prescription for governing a big country. The successful experience of the United States proves that if there is no federation, and if there is no local autonomy, then "of the people, by the people, and for the people," will certainly fail.

Historically, the CCP had advocated for the autonomy of united provinces. But that was something programmatic, a position advanced by the ancestor of the CCP. When Mao Zedong was in Hunan, he even mentioned that Hunan should be independent, an idea that was radical and outside the norm. A federation is absolutely not the same thing as a nation split. The United States is a federation. Who can split her?

The road taken by Liu Xiaobo was well thought out: everything was based on legality, peace, and nonviolence. It was moderate and not radical, and there was a good foundation, based on the current laws and in accordance with historical records.

At that time, everyone was relatively optimistic because it was said that China was going to become a "harmonious society." There was already a constitution. Although it was not perfect, there were some good things in it. There should have been relatively light resistance to implementation of the good things, and there would be more people in favor of it. There should have been no reason to oppose it. So everyone was pretty optimistic, as was I.

Liu Xiaobo's wife, Liu Xia, always listened quietly. She loves to laugh and smiles brilliantly. But she is a melancholic person. She is a poet, an artist, and enjoys photography. The tone of her work is melancholic and sad—it laments the state of the world. After Charter 08 was published, the authorities unexpectedly detained Liu Xiaobo and sentenced him. I don't know if Liu Xia had a premonition. I was really not mentally prepared for it.

Why was Liu Xiaobo convicted of a crime and given a heavy sentence? He was guilty of patriotism and upholding the constitution. I still find this incomprehensible. At that time, there was a professor at Tsinghua University, Hu Angang, who said that the Politboro Standing Committee system of the Chinese Communist Party is a collective presidential system. After those words were published in the *Global Times*, no one in China criticized the idea. Obviously, it was serious and had a consensus. At the time of the CCP's Sixteenth and Seventeenth National Congresses, each standing committee member likely controlled his own fief. When Liu Xiaobo was arrested, Zhou Yongkang was the secretary of the Central Political and Legal Affairs Commission. Therefore, I can only understand it this way: the arrest and punishment of Liu Xiaobo was due to outrages committed by the corrupt element, Zhou Yongkang.[2] The real truth of the matter, I believe, will be made clear in the future.

Later, Liu Xiaobo won the Nobel Peace Prize, an honor deserved for his true achievement. Liu Xiaobo found the path of least resistance and the path with the best foundation. His ultimate goal was one that no one dared to publicly oppose. If China really embarks on the road to democracy, then not only will it be for the well-being of the Chinese people, but the whole world will also benefit from a large, responsible country. This can play a major positive role in the common development of human civilization.

With this essay, I wish to commemorate the great patriot—Liu Xiaobo.

*Translated by Andréa Worden*

NOTES

1. The aesthetic school of Nicolai Chernyshevsky of the 1850s (anticipated by Vissarion Belinsky in the 1840s and later elaborated and radicalized by Nicolai Dobrolyubov and Dmitry Pisarev) held that human beings have objective needs that must be satisfied, and the existence of these requirements provide an infallible test of the value of every cultural practice and social institution.—Trans.
2. Zhou Yongkang was placed under investigation for abuse of power and corruption in late 2013 and on June 11, 2015, was sentenced to life in prison after being convicted of bribery, abuse of power, and the intentional disclosure of state secrets.—Trans.

# Liu Xiaobo on the Front Line of Ideas

*Joanne Leedom-Ackerman*

I never met Liu Xiaobo, but his words and life touch and inspire me. His ideas live beyond his physical body. I am among the many who wish he survived to help develop and lead democratic reform in China, a nation and people he was devoted to.

Liu's "I Have No Enemies: My Final Statement," delivered December 23, 2009, to the judge sentencing him, stands beside important texts that inspire and help frame society, as Martin Luther King Jr.'s "Letter from a Birmingham Jail" did in the United States. King addressed fellow clergymen and also his prosecutors, judges, and the citizens of the United States in its struggle to realize a more perfect democracy.

I hesitate to project too much onto Liu Xiaobo, but I can offer my own context and measurement as a writer and as an activist through PEN, an organization that works on behalf of writers whose words set the powers of state against them.

Liu Xiaobo said June 1989 was a turning point in his life, when he returned to China to join the protests of the democracy movement. In June 1989 I was president of PEN Center USA West. It was a tumultuous year: the fatwa against Salman Rushdie was issued in February, and PEN, including our center, mobilized worldwide protest.

In May 1989 I was a delegate to the PEN Congress in Maastricht, Netherlands, where PEN Center USA West presented to the Assembly of Delegates a resolution on behalf of imprisoned writers in China, including Wei Jingsheng.[1] We called on the Chinese government to release these writers and lobbied our own governments to take action in support of them. The Chinese delegation, which represented the government's perspective more than PEN's, argued against the resolution. Poet Bei Dao, who was a guest of the congress, defended our resolution, with Taipei PEN translating.[2]

When the events of Tiananmen Square erupted a few weeks later, my first concern was whether Bei Dao was safe. It turned out he had not yet returned to China. PEN Center USA West, along with PEN centers around the world, began going through the names of Chinese writers taken into custody so that we might protest and speak out on their behalf. I remember reading through these names written in Chinese, sent from PEN's London headquarters, and trying to sort them and get them translated. Liu Xiaobo, I am certain, must have been among them, though I didn't know him at the time.

In his "My Final Statement" to the court twenty years later, Liu told the consequence for him of being found guilty of "the crime of spreading and inciting counterrevolution" at the Tiananmen protest: "I found myself separate from my beloved lectern and no longer able to publish my writing or give public talks inside China. Merely for expressing different political views and for joining a peaceful democracy movement, a teacher lost his right to teach, a writer lost his right to publish, and a public intellectual could no longer speak openly. Whether we view this as my own fate or as the fate of a China after thirty years of 'reform and opening,' it is truly a sad fate."[3]

During the years I chaired PEN International's Writers in Prison Committee (1993–97), Liu served time in prison, and PEN worked on his behalf. During the years I served as international secretary of PEN International (2004–2007), Liu Xiaobo served as president of the newly formed Independent Chinese PEN Center. Though I met and worked with many of his colleagues and attended conferences in Hong Kong, he and I never met in person because he was not allowed to leave the mainland, and I did not visit the mainland during that period.

I finally did meet Wei Jingsheng after years of working on his case. He was released and came to the United States, where we shared a meal together at the Old Ebbitt Grill in Washington DC. I was hopeful I might someday also get to meet Liu Xiaobo, or if not meet him in person, at least continue hearing more from him through his poetry and prose.

His words are now our only meeting place. His writing is robust and full of truth about the human spirit, individually and collectively, as citizens form the body politic. I expect that both his poetry and the famed Charter 08, of which he was one of the drafters and which more than fourteen thousand Chinese citizens have now endorsed, will resonate and grow in consequence.

Charter 08 set out a path to a more democratic China that I hope will one day be realized:

> The political reality, which is plain for anyone to see, is that China has many laws but no rule of law; it has a constitution but no constitutional government," noted Charter 08.

> The ruling elite continues to cling to its authoritarian power and fights off any move toward political change. . . .

> Accordingly, and in a spirit of this duty as responsible and constructive citizens, we offer the following recommendations on national governance, citizens' rights, and social development: a New Constitution . . . Separation of Powers . . . Legislative Democracy . . . an Independent Judiciary . . . Public Control of Public Servants . . . Guarantee of Human Rights . . . Election of Public Officials . . . Rural-Urban Equality . . . Freedom to Form Groups . . . Freedom to Assemble . . . Freedom of Expression . . . Freedom of Religion . . . Civic Education . . . Protection of Private Property . . . Financial and Tax Reform . . . Social Security . . . Protection of the Environment . . . a Federated Republic . . . Truth in Reconciliation."[4]

Charter 08 addresses the body politic. Liu Xiaobo's "I Have No Enemies: My Final Statement" addresses the individual and for me resonates most profoundly. Its call doesn't allow readers to depend on others but on themselves for execution. Liu warned against hatred:

> Hatred only eats away at a person's intelligence and conscience, and an enemy mentality can poison the spirit of an entire people (as the experience of our country during the Mao era clearly shows). It can lead to cruel and lethal internecine combat, can destroy tolerance and human feeling within a society, and can block the progress of a nation toward freedom and democracy. For these reasons I hope that I can rise above my personal fate and contribute to the progress of our country and to

changes in our society. I hope that I can answer the regime's enmity with utmost benevolence, and can use love to dissipate hate.[5]

At a conference two months after Liu Xiaobo died in 2017, a participant asked if Liu might have changed this statement if he understood how his life would end. A friend who knew him assured that he would not for he was committed to the idea. Liu Xiaobo's commitment to "no enemies and no hatred" does not accede to the authoritarianism he opposed but instead resists the negative. He aligns with benevolence and love as the powers that nourish the human spirit and ultimately allow it to flourish. Liu's words and the ideals he lived offer us all a beacon and a guide.

## NOTES

1. Wei Jingsheng (b. 1950) is a Chinese human rights activist and was a political prisoner in 1979–93 and 1994–97, spending a total of eighteen years in prisons. He was deported on medical parole to the United States on November 16, 1997.—Ed.
2. Bei Dao (b. 1949), born Zhao Zhenkai, is a Chinese poet, professor at Hong Kong University, and the most notable representative of the Misty Poets, a group who reacted against the restrictions on art and literature during the Cultural Revolution.—Ed.
3. Translated by Perry Link, in *Liu Xiaobo: No Enemies, No Hatred*, ed. Perry Link, Tienchi Martin-Liao, and Liu Xia (Cambridge MA: The Belknap Press of Harvard University Press, 2012), 322.—Ed.
4. Link et al., *Liu Xiaobo*, 303–9.—Trans.
5. Link et al., *Liu Xiaobo*, 322.—Trans.

# He Walked the Path of Kang Youwei and Shed the Blood of Tan Sitong

*Wang Dan*

As soon as I heard the news of Liu Xiaobo's death, I immediately reported it on my Facebook. Many netizens left comments expressing their grief over his passing. I want to share with everyone one netizen's comments, that Liu Xiaobo "walked the path of Kang Youwei and shed the blood of Tan Sitong."[1]

The reason I decided to share these words is because I think they are very insightful and deserve our consideration. In saying Liu Xiaobo "walked the path of Kang Youwei," obviously this writer didn't mean that Liu Xiaobo had been a royalist or advocated for constitutional monarchy but rather that Liu Xiaobo's political propositions and his basic position were actually very moderate, just like those of Kang Youwei in the late nineteenth century. Liu Xiaobo never advocated for revolution; indeed, he even advocated that "I have no enemies." As a result, however, his ending was just as tragic as that of Tan Sitong, whom the authorities persecuted to death in 1898 because he had sought reform and progress. Sometimes history really does repeat itself.

However, the death of Liu Xiaobo also tells us a fact that is actually very clear but that everyone is unwilling to acknowledge: for the Chinese Communist Party, even the most moderate proposition—as long as it is based on constitutional democracy—is unacceptable. No matter how mild these propositions are or how those who put them forward express their good intentions, the CCP regards all these proponents as "enemies of the state" and will not be satisfied until all of them are dead. From former general secretary Zhao Ziyang within the system to dissident Liu Xiaobo outside the system, it's always been like this, without exception.

What does this indicate? This indicates that all of those who place hope on the CCP proactively leading political reform, all those beliefs in the assessment that as long as economic development reaches a certain stage, the CCP will move toward democracy, and all those expectations that Xi Jinping will perhaps lead China to a rule of enlightened despotism are all completely wrong, extremely naïve, and, it can even be said, ignorant. The death of Liu Xiaobo has once again proven it.

This is very important for the following reason: since China is a big country, its future process of transition—whether or not it's smooth—will have major implications for neighboring countries and the whole world. As the ruling party, if the CCP is willing to accept the views of a moderate opposition, the future transition may possibly be a smooth and peaceful one. But if the CCP cannot even tolerate mild opposition like Liu Xiaobo and persecutes such figures to death, the only possibility left is to cut off any road of the moderates and accumulate hatred in society. Cutting off the road of reform, China will have a confrontation between the state and society and a bloody revolution. Such a prospect is, of course, not one that we wish to see, but as soon as it happens, China's interior will inevitably sink into turmoil, and this internal chaos will invariably trigger external effects that will directly affect neighboring countries and even the whole world. This is what the death of Liu Xiaobo has given us—an even deeper level of thinking and concern.

Liu Xiaobo's tragic end was without a doubt the result of the CCP's ruthless and inhumane persecution, but as Professor Jerome Cohen of New York University Law School pointed out, Western countries have become increasingly indifferent to China's human rights' issues, almost to the point of giving up. This kind of indulgence and policy of appeasement also has to bear some of the blame. The death of Liu Xiaobo will inevitably set off great waves in the international community, and the voices calling for a review of human rights policy toward China will also gain a greater say.

In the face of the tragic death of a Nobel Peace Prize laureate, pro-China political parties and politicians are probably only stupefied and rethinking their position. In other words, the death of Liu Xiaobo is likely to become a turning point in the rise of China. The CCP, which has always used the image of its rapidly developing economy to buy popularity throughout the world, will bear the burden of Liu Xiaobo's death for a long time to come;

its image will be greatly damaged and its arrogance will also plummet. This is, of course, something that we'll be glad to see, but the price we've paid for it is Liu Xiaobo's life, which is, indeed, an unbearable weight and a tragedy of the times.

That Liu Xiaobo used his life and his last breath to tell us the fact that the CCP had already become a neo-Nazi gang—this is hopefully something that will make the whole world ponder.

*Translated by Andréa Worden*

## NOTES

Originally printed in *Apple Daily*, July 15, 2017.

1. Kang Youwei (1858–1927) was a scholar and political reformer of the late Qing dynasty. Tang Sitong (1865–98) was also a Qing reformist but was executed for his part in a failed reform movement.—Trans.

# Remembering a Hero and a Martyr

*Carl Gershman*

In the debate over the compatibility of democracy and Asian values that Kim Dae-jung had with Lee Kuan Yew two decades ago, Kim said that his fundamental reason for optimism about the prospect for democracy in Asia was "this increasing awareness of the importance of democracy and human rights among Asians themselves."[1] Nothing demonstrates more powerfully the depth of this commitment to democratic values than the life and courageous struggle of Liu Xiaobo, who in the years following the Tiananmen massacre in 1989 became the world's most eloquent and impassioned voice for democracy and human freedom.

Liu understood the enormity of the challenge he faced as a dissident democrat defying the power of the authoritarian Chinese state. He mourned the victims of the Tiananmen crackdown, which he said was "the major turning point" in his life, and he realized that rising Chinese power could blot out their legacy. But he remained hopeful about the prospect for democracy in China because he saw the economic, ideological, and political pillars of Chinese totalitarianism eroding under the impact of the forces of modernization and technological change. He believed that such forces were changing not just the institutions of China but also the consciousness of the people.

In his famous essay "To Change a Regime by Changing a Society," published in 2006, Liu wrote that dissidents could no longer be cowed into submission by the repressive regime. "Political persecution can still bring economic loss and the loss of personal freedom, but it can no longer destroy a person's reputation or turn a person into a political leper. Indeed, today it can have the opposite effect—not merely failing to destroy one's dignity or spirit but actually helping a person to achieve spiritual wholeness, and even, in the view of others, to rise to the status of 'conscience of the people' or 'hero of truth.'"[2]

This essay, with its reference in the title to changing the regime, was used by the Chinese authorities at Liu's trial as evidence of his guilt of "the crime of inciting subversion of state power." The regime also charged that he was the lead author and organizer of Charter 08, a manifesto for democracy and constitutional government that was signed at great personal risk by more than ten thousand Chinese citizens. But far from destroying him, his imprisonment only increased his stature and made him into the "conscience of the people," as he had said it would. As a result, he also became renowned internationally and was awarded the Nobel Peace Prize in 2010.

At the Nobel ceremony, which neither Liu nor his wife, Liu Xia, was permitted to attend, Norwegian actress Liv Ullmann read Liu's final trial statement, in which he said, "China will in the end become a nation ruled by law, where human rights reign supreme."[3] He also called for an end to "the enemy mentality of the regime" that "poisons" the spirit of the nation, "incite[s] cruel mortal struggles," destroys the society's tolerance and humanity, and hinders the country's progress toward freedom and democracy.

This statement was not the first time Liu had pointed to the danger of regime-fomented enmity. He had continuously called for an end to hatred and "class-struggle thinking," most notably in "The June 2nd Hunger Strike Declaration" that he authored in Tiananmen Square less than two days before the regime crushed the nonviolent uprising with massive force. The poisonous culture created by the regime's stoking of such enmity, he believed, prevented his fellow countrymen from becoming engaged and responsible citizens.

Liu responded by trying to "dispel hatred with love." But he was far from a naïve or quixotic idealist. He saw a terrible danger coming for both China and the world if China failed to democratize and continued to rise economically and militarily as a dictatorship. He worried that "the great powers in human history that rose as dictatorships— . . . Hitler's Germany, the Meiji Emperor's Japan, and Stalin's Soviet Union—all eventually collapsed, and in doing so brought disaster to human civilization."[4] And he warned that "if the Communists succeed in . . . leading China down a disastrously mistaken historical road, the results will not only be another catastrophe for the Chinese people but likely also a disaster for the spread of liberal democracy in the world."[5] He believed, therefore, that it was in the vital interest of all democratic countries and freedom-loving people "to rescue the world's largest hostage population from enslavement."[6]

It's been more than a decade since Liu issued this warning about the danger that China's rising as a dictatorship posed to liberal democracy and global security. Virtually no one in the West heeded Liu's warning because the overwhelmingly dominant view at the time was that China's rise was something to be welcomed and not feared. U.S. Deputy Secretary of State Robert Zoellick voiced the conventional wisdom when he said that bringing China into the rules-based liberal international order would make it a "responsible stakeholder" in the international system and that economic growth would inexorably liberalize China by producing a middle class that would demand political participation and reform.

But instead of promoting liberalization, China's dramatic economic growth has had the opposite effect of reinforcing the regime's belief in the legitimacy and superiority of its state-driven economic model. In addition, the wealth China has amassed as a result of its economic growth has enabled it to play a much more assertive role internationally, totally upending the delusion that China's growth would be good for democracy and the rules-based global order. Reflecting the disillusionment of the U.S. foreign-policy establishment, former State Department Asia hand Kurt Campbell recently observed that "the liberal international order has failed to lure or bind China as powerfully as expected. China has instead pursued its own course, belying a range of American expectations in the process." Following Xi Jinping's announcement in February 2018 that the Chinese constitution would be changed to allow him to remain as president indefinitely, *The Economist* magazine bluntly stated, "The West's 25-year bet on China has failed."

Liu Xiaobo was in prison until his death in 2017, so his voice was silenced during his final years when China's power grew and the scales fell from the eyes of Western leaders and policy makers. Though he could not comment on the consequences of China's rise during these years, they were anticipated in his earlier writings:

The restoration under Xi Jinping of Mao-like personalistic rule, which enables Xi to control all the levers of power in the state and the Communist Party, including the military and the police.

The establishment of a repressive surveillance state that uses digital imaging, facial recognition technology, and unprecedented amounts of data about people's financial and social interactions to monitor the behavior of all individuals and to regulate their access to economic and social benefits according to their loyalty to the state.

China's $1 trillion Belt and Road Initiative, seven times larger than the Marshall Plan in postwar Europe, which uses massive infrastructure development in sixty-four countries to advance Chinese military and geopolitical goals, including securing access to strategic resources, gaining control by Chinese state-owned enterprises of strategic ports and terminals, using partnerships with governments and national media to export Chinese techniques of state surveillance and to disseminate Chinese media content, and establishing a system of dispute resolution for initiative projects that promotes Chinese rules as an alternative to Western legal norms.

China's continued fortification of reefs in the disputed Spratly Islands, in defiance of a ruling by an international tribunal, leading Admiral Philip Davidson of the U.S. Pacific Command to say, "China is now capable of controlling the South China Sea in all scenarios short of war with the United States."

Its comprehensive economic and military buildup, which a Pentagon study (mentioned in an article by David Ignatius entitled "China's Plan to Rule the World") described as "perhaps the most ambitious grand strategy undertaken by a single nation-state in modern times."

In sum, China's emergence as a political and ideological rival of the West, using economic leverage, military power, and sharp-power information tools to promote its model of authoritarian development as an alternative to democracy—"a new option for other countries," as Xi Jinping declared at the Nineteenth Party Congress.

China's continued rise, along with Xi's radical centralization of power, are not inexorable developments. They could encounter setbacks and complications in the period ahead. As Susan Shirk noted in her recent article in the *Journal of Democracy*, "The Return to Personalistic Rule," under Xi Jinping "the more autocratically a leader behaves, the more likely other politicians are to try to bring him down." A power play of this magnitude, therefore, may spark elite conflict and resistance from rival leaders, which could lead to a return to collective leadership and even to an unanticipated political opening for reform.

In addition, China's push for global leadership has already produced a backlash that *The Economist* has called "the starkest reversal in modern geopolitics." This has led to a proliferation of proposals and initiatives in the United States and other countries to counter and contain China's expansionism. These range from supporting the efforts of Asian countries and Australia to balance China militarily in the South China Sea and other potential conflict zones to calls for a policy of "reciprocity" that would apply a single standard to dealings with China—from screening its investments in the United States to block access to Chinese companies that is denied to U.S. companies in China, to monitoring cultural programs like Confucius Institutes to ensure that they are not used as sharp-power tools of political influence and insisting that U.S. cultural centers have equal access to Chinese universities.

So far the response to China as a rising authoritarian power has been reactive and defensive. The focus, not surprisingly, has been on the security threat posed by assertive Chinese actions in a growing number of potential conflicts zones, as well as on the political challenge that China presents, which includes its use of economic leverage and sharp power to demand compliance with its position on issues like Tibet and Taiwan. What is not being addressed, though, is the issue that Liu Xiaobo considered to be the central and decisive question—whether China could take a different and more democratic path than its current obsession with concentrating dictatorial control at home and pursuing geopolitical hegemony abroad.

Right now, it appears extremely unlikely that China will reverse its current path. Under Xi Jinping, Beijing has stepped up repression dramatically, cracking down on civil society activists and online bloggers and journalists, arresting hundreds of human rights lawyers, passing new laws that suppress online freedom of expression and subject international

NGOs to unprecedented control by the Chinese security services, severely increasing repression over the Uyghur and Tibetan minorities, and tightening control over basic freedoms in Hong Kong, including the forcible disappearance of five employees of an independent bookstore.

But such repression, while intended to strengthen the hand of the central government, actually demonstrates its deep insecurity, its classification of any independent voice as a dangerous threat to its power and to the social order itself. Were the regime really confident about its power and legitimacy, it wouldn't need to silence a dissident writer like Liu Xiaobo (and even his widow, Liu Xia), or to eliminate a human rights lawyer like Li Baiguang, or to expunge any memory of the Tiananmen uprising in 1989.[7]

Nothing more clearly exposes the regime's deep insecurity than a new law it passed in 2018 criminalizing criticism of the "heroes and martyrs" of China's Communist past. In effect, the law is an attempt to whitewash such Maoist disasters as the Great Leap Forward, which led to massive famine and tens of millions of deaths, as well as the Cultural Revolution, a "spiritual holocaust" during which China descended into chaos, mass violence (more than one million people were killed and tens of millions were tortured and humiliated), and ideological madness.

Perry Link has noted that the Heroes and Martyrs Protection Act has nothing to do with protecting history "and everything to do with maintaining the party's power and control today." He said that Liu Xiaobo drew inspiration from historical figures such as Lin Zhao, Yu Luoke, and Zhang Zhixin, all of whom were executed during the Cultural Revolution "for expressing truths the party did not want to hear. The fact that the present law will have nothing to do with protecting the reputations of those [true] martyrs says all one needs to know about the purpose of the law."[8] Xi has campaigned against any honest accounting of these horrors, calling them an indulgence in "historical nihilism" that would damage the legitimacy of the Communist Party. The party, in other words, requires the denial of truth and the rewriting of history in order to survive.

This is not a strategy that can work in the long run because it depends upon the Chinese regime's ability to impose its version of the truth on everyone it deals with, from its subjects at home to foreign business leaders, government officials, and academics. Legitimacy cannot be achieved through coercion. It requires the capacity to project ideas and values that are persuasive and attract genuine loyalty. The disclosure of the famous Document No. 9 revealed that the regime has declared war on so-called Western ideas such as universal values, civil society, and free media, which it sees as a threat to the Communist Party's social foundation. But if it wants to suppress such ideas, it will need alternative ideas with which to replace them. The problem is that it has no ideas, which is why it has stoked nationalism to fill the void left by the death of Communist ideology.

Political scientist David Shambaugh has written, "Until China develops values that appeal universally, it will lack one of the core features of global leadership." Until then, it will continue to be a global bully, trying to impose its will on a cowed but disbelieving international community. And it will try to maintain absolute control internally, fearful that the whole system will unravel the moment the government loosens its iron grip.

Liu Xiaobo saw the vulnerabilities of such a system, which is why he wrote that "even the most vicious tyranny will be short-lived" the moment that people decide to oppose it "to the bitter end." There are people in China who have such determination, and their numbers could grow if the alarm over China's belligerence persuades the world's democracies that defending democrats in China is consistent not just with our values but with our interests as well. This was Liu's central message—that our freedom is linked to his and, by extension, to freedom in China. In remembering Liu Xiaobo, we are affirming and defending our common future.

NOTES

1. Kim Dae-jung, "A Response to Lee Kuan Yew," *Foreign Affairs*, November/December 1994. Kim Dae-jung (1924–2009) was president of South Korea from 1998 to 2003 and the 2000 Nobel Peace Prize laureate; Lee Kuan Yew (1923–2015) was the first prime minister of Singapore, from 1959 to 1990, senior minister from 1990 to 2004, and the minister mentor from 2004 to 2011.—Ed.

2. Liu Xiaobo, "To Change a Regime by Changing a Society," trans. Perry Link, in *Liu Xiaobo: No Enemies, No Hatred*, ed. Perry Link, Tienchi Martin-Liao, and Liu Xia (Cambridge MA: The Belknap Press of Harvard University Press, 2012), 24.—Ed.

3. Liu Xiaobo, "I Have No Enemies: My Final Statement," in Link et al., *Liu Xiaobo*, 232.—Ed.

4. Liu Xiaobo, "Behind the Rise of the Great Powers," trans. Josephine Chiu-Duke, in Link et al., *Liu Xiaobo*, 237.—Ed.

5. Xiaobo, "Behind the Rise," 239.—Ed.

6. Liu Xiaobo, "The Negative Effects of the Rise of Dictatorship on World Democratization," trans. Human Rights in China, based on a translation by Paul Frank, Human Rights in China, April 9, 2010, https://www.hrichina.org/en/content/3202.—Ed.

7. Li Baiguang (1968–2018) was a Chinese legal scholar, human rights activist, and member of the Independent Chinese PEN Center. On February 26, 2018, he reportedly died of liver disease, his death widely considered to be suspicious.—Ed.

8. Lin Zhao (born Peng Lingzhao, 1932–68) was a female student from Beijing University who was labeled as a rightest in 1957, imprisoned in 1960, and executed in 1968. Yu Luoke (1942–70) was a worker, writer, and popular thinker known for his treatise "On Family Background" at the outset of the Cultural Revolution; he was arrested in 1968 and executed in 1970. Zhang Zhixin (1930–75) was a female cadre of CCP, imprisoned in 1969 for criticizing the idolization of Mao Zedong and the ultra-left and executed in 1975.—Ed.

# Chinese Culture's Backbone

*Qian Yuejun*

It was shocking to learn that Dr. Liu Xiaobo had been diagnosed with terminal liver cancer, and I could hardly believe it. With only three years left of his prison term, how could it suddenly be announced that he would die there?

People scurried about and issued appeals for Liu Xiaobo to be released from prison and sent to Germany for treatment, and Germany and the United States prepared medical teams as well as chartered flights to bring the Nobel Peace Prize laureate to them. Even if there was no miraculous cure that could save him, at least he could breathe his last in freedom.

It can be imagined that if he had gone to Germany, the world's media would have gathered at the airport, and he would have been headline news in Europe and the United States, at least. If he had died in Germany, many overseas comrades would have attended his memorial service to see him on his last journey, and many writers and Nobel laureates would have sent floral wreaths. Perhaps even the German prime minister or foreign minister would have attended, and he would have been given a dignified grave in a Berlin cemetery. As poet Bei Dao wrote, "Debasement is the password of the base, Nobility the epitaph of the noble."[1]

Yet all was for naught. Although medical specialists from Germany and the United States went to China to diagnose Liu Xiaobo and confirmed that his health would tolerate his removal from China, all wishes were mercilessly denied by the Chinese government: Liu Xiaobo must die in China!

I was even more shocked to read on Facebook that he was to be buried at sea. I immediately posted, "Even if he's not buried, he should not be given a sea burial! His martyr's remains must be left behind." During the Nazi era, the German authorities persecuted Nobel Peace Prize laureate Carl von Ossietzky to death. He died in a civilian hospital but under surveillance. Liu Xiaobo was the first Nobel Peace Prize laureate to die in custody. The Nazis allowed Ossietzky a proper burial, although without his name carved on his gravestone, and his wife was forced to change her name in hope that "the world would forget him forever." Although not necessarily trying to be more shameless than the Nazis, the CCP was just as shameless by imposing a "sea burial" on Liu Xiaobo's remains. They wanted there to be no trace of Liu Xiaobo left in this world and to eliminate all evidence of his existence. That in the 9.6 million square kilometers of Chinese territory not even an urn of ashes could be permitted is more outrageous and tragic than words can express.

Liu Xiaobo was thrown into prison for organizing the signature campaign for Charter 08. He never aspired to the Nobel Peace Prize. When it was awarded to him, he wept and said that the prize had not been conferred on him but rather on the dead of Tiananmen. I think so too. The June Fourth Massacre not only washed China in blood but was a tragedy that shocked the world, and the most notable of all awards, the Nobel Peace Prize, had never reflected this tragedy. Finally twenty years later they chose Liu Xiaobo: Liu Xiaobo was not only a key participant in the 1989 student movement but also remained active in China's current rights defense movement. Liu Xiaobo seemed to be the only choice who served both purposes.

Of course, no one would have imagined that winning the prize would change his life trajectory and doom him to never leaving the prison gates alive. Such a person could not remain in China, nor could he be allowed to go overseas. After Liu Xiaobo's death, Guo Wengui revealed that when he talked about Liu Xiaobo with the State Security Ministry head several years ago, the minister made a hand motion meaning "death." Guo asked with surprise, "How will he die? From execution?" The minister just laughed. This shows that back then the black hands of villainy had already decided that Liu would die before completing his sentence; it was just a matter of working out the method and timing.

Liu Xiaobo's tombstone cannot be erected on his grave but is etched in the hearts of all those who share his belief in freedom, as grand and stirring as Yan Zhenqing's "Draft of a Requiem to My Nephew" and more brilliant than the scarlet sunset on the ocean's horizon.

*Translated by Stacy Mosher*

NOTE

1. These are the first two lines from Bei Dao's poem "The Answer," trans. Bonnie S. McDougall, in *The August Sleepwalker* (New York: New Directions, 1990).—Trans.

# Youth and University Days

*Innocent Hearts to Dark Horse*

# Liu Xiaobo's Resistance

*Shao Jiang*

Liu Xiaobo's childhood and youth spanned the rise and fall of the Mao era's centralized system. His independent thinking began with the Democracy Wall period, which challenged Deng Xiaoping's remolding of the centralized system. From 1978 onward Liu Xiaobo used self-enlightenment through literature and aesthetics to practice and maintain the freedom to criticize. In 1989 Liu Xiaobo abandoned the secure development of his academic career overseas to throw himself into China's democracy movement, putting civil resistance into practice. After the June Fourth Massacre, Liu Xiaobo turned his introspection during each spell of imprisonment into the starting point for the next round of continued resistance. He revealed how the dictatorship's omnipresence molded and alienated people. He explored how to jump out of the autocratic loop and cast off the condition of enslavement. Liu Xiaobo's resistance was closely related to dissemination through nongovernment-printed publications and the internet. The rights to association and to peaceful assembly that he put into practice were aimed at establishing an autonomous and independent civil community.

Liu Xiaobo's resistance began in the latter part of the Mao era, after the massive manmade calamities ended. When the emergence of Democracy Wall dragged the CCP into a crisis of legitimacy, Deng Xiaoping reshaped a neototalitarian political system under continued party rule. In economic terms, China was merged into the global capitalist system, while in terms of social control it employed high-pressure preventative measures. As the Chinese economy grew rapidly and China greatly increased its share of the global economy and invested in developed and developing countries, the elites in those countries wined and dined the elites in China's official, production, academic and media sectors and engaged in exchanges of interest, enjoying global supremacy and privilege together.

In the latter part of the Jiang Zemin era and in the Hu Jintao–Wen Jiabao era, Liu Xiaobo, once again released from prison, used the internet to exercise the rights of expression, association, and assembly. As a result, he was sentenced to eleven years in prison, and his wife, poet Liu Xia, was placed under house arrest. Liu Xiaobo was the first Nobel Prize laureate to be killed by the CCP, who had his corpse obliterated and evidences destroyed. The CCP have deprived his wife of her freedom and subjected her to physical and mental devastation, all as the world media watched. The direction the world takes will be symbolized by the handling of Liu Xiaobo's legacy and Liu Xia's fate.

Liu Xiaobo's lifelong practice was what Hannah Arendt called "attentive facing up to, and resisting of, reality—whatever it may be."[1] The resistance Arendt referred to targeted empire, including the Nazi empire and Soviet-style totalitarianism. The Mao-Deng centralization that the CCP has thoroughly combined is a blend of the Nazi and Soviet models, the larger background of which is the comprehensive aggregation of power and globalization of capital led by today's empires. Liu Xiaobo has left us the most important legacy of resistance for this turbulent world.

## Practicing the Freedom of the Press and of Speech

From the late 1970s to the early 1980s, Liu Xiaobo was a writer and editor for the literary journal *Innocent Hearts* (*Chi Zi Xin*), accumulating experience in creating public space through magazine production. He and his fellow writers used literature as the starting point and fulcrum for understanding the self, exposing current conditions of human survival, and exploring the relationship between literature, politics, and society. In the mid- and late 1980s, Liu Xiaobo enhanced the meaningfulness of his life through aesthetic exploration and imagination, revealed the relationship between the intellectual and the official system, practiced the freedom to criticize, and fought for space for freedom of speech.

In the late 1970s, *Innocent Hearts*, like other student literary journals, was allowed to use Jilin University's mimeograph equipment to print copies. The magazine's regular publication and related activities shaped into a gathering space for the university's poets, writers, and literary youth. Some magazines regularly published drawings and related writings that departed from the official style. Such magazines were mailed back and forth between different universities and exchanged among readers, forming an alternative literary discourse outside of the CCP's censorship system and generating a public forum.

In 1979 student literary journals at thirteen universities, including *Innocent Hearts*, jointly published a new magazine, *This Generation*. *This Generation* took the April 5 Movement as the hallmark of a generation and constructed this generation's subjective mentality through resisting autocracy.[2] *This Generation* put transregional association into practice, violating the greatest taboo in the CCP's control of society. The suppression that followed led this journal to nearly die in the womb, but through the persistence of students at Wuhan University, the first issue was finally published and disseminated in fragmented form. This was an important attempt at transregional association during the Democracy Wall period and supplied an important lesson and experience for the subsequent All-China National Association of Independent Magazines and other transregional civil society organizations or networks.

The self-published magazines of university students worked in concert with the off-campus Democracy Wall Movement of that time to form moveable letterpress publications. The democracy walls in various places were like an enormous magazine bringing together the journals produced by university students, urban workers, and intellectuals as well as the big-character posters put up by other social strata. The walls provided a public platform for exchange and resonant interaction between the various social strata, directly challenged and bypassed the censorship system, and became venues for unofficially initiated assemblies. The various democracy walls served as links for forming transregional association and assembly spaces.

At the end of 1979, the CCP carried out a thorough crackdown on the democracy walls in all localities. Universities also began shifting toward campaigns for local people's congresses, turning the moveable unofficial publications of the democracy walls into independent election publications. Participants in off-campus democracy walls continued to publish underground. Semi-underground private magazines, combined with Hong Kong magazines and overseas publications such as *China Spring*, circulated on the mainland. These, along with moveable unofficial publications that disseminated through multiple channels, became the main public sphere for popular exchange.

In 1980 the CCP began a purge of the literary and arts circles. Many literary magazines dealt with this metaphorical winter by seeking free expression within their tighter confines, forming a linguistic resonance between purged works such as "General, You Cannot Do This" and *The Sun and Man*.[3] The expressive forms of *Innocent Hearts* tended to be more diverse. Among them, Liu Xiaobo's works focused more on exploring the independent character and self-accountability.

The continuous disasters created under thirty years of CCP rule had made a wreck of official ideology. The pendulum of centralized propaganda swung between monopolistic interpretation of communism and socialism on one side and patriotism and nationalism on the other. In an attempt to adapt to the bankruptcy of its ideology, the CCP turned some popular "scar literature" into propaganda specimens and sought out the cooperation of the intellectual community. Through its narrative of sufferings, this kind of propaganda model evaded the relationship between calamities and the CCP system. It transferred an individual's affection and ethics toward family to autocracy, thus indulging in an elusive passion for suffering. Centralized power was abstracted as contention toward the mother and the motherland became the source of seeking the roots of excessive emotion. Nostalgia and contention became a hotbed for romantic accommodation of tyranny, thereby creating a mirage in which ardent love for the motherland was inseparable from loyalty to the dictatorship.

This kind of propaganda was coordinated with the "elimination of spiritual pollution." Following the CCP's suppression of the Democracy Wall Movement, this combination of incantations to shackle intellectuals and implementation of an even more systematic censorship system became the main method for the CCP to control society through a combination of modernized propaganda, cooperation, censorship, and suppression. During that same period, broad-minded people in the fields of aesthetics, literature, philosophy, physics, journalism, and publishing counterattacked and deconstructed the retrenchment and encirclement during the modernization of autocracy.

Compared with the discussion of aesthetics in early 1957, the discussion of aesthetics in the mid-1980s was a direct breakout from the encirclement of the CCP's "elimination of spiritual pollution" campaign. The intellectuals of this period took greater initiative in rejecting the CCP's 1950s model of ideological remolding, enlarged the scope for challenging official limits, and created multiple loopholes in the official censorship system. Discussion of aesthetics could also be expanded through official or semi-official dissemination channels to universities in various places and to factories in metropolitan areas. Disseminated through paper media and symposiums, aesthetics and literature were transformed into discussion forums related to politics. These discussions gained an even more extensive social reading and response.

Liu Xiaobo's speech "The New Period Literature Is Facing a Crisis," delivered at a symposium on New Period Literature hosted by the Institute of Literature at the Chinese Academy of Social Sciences, went from academic discussion straight to publication in *Shenzhen Youth Daily*. This kind of non-mainstream discourse was reproduced and disseminated using official and non-official channels. It shaped into a gray area for extensive and diverse discussion of literature, aesthetics, and politics. The relationship between traditional culture and modernization and the role of intellectuals and the freedom to criticize had a major influence on the disenchantment and disambiguation of generations of people under centralized power.

In 1986 Liu Xiaobo most frequently gave public lectures on literature and aesthetics. At the end of that year, he accepted an invitation to deliver a talk on aesthetics and literature at Peking University. During the question-and-answer period, students who disagreed with Liu Xiaobo shouted at him, "Liu Xiaobo, I want to beat you up!" Liu Xiaobo shouted back, "Come on up. . . . Let's have a debate. I disagree with what you say, but I defend your right to say it." What had started out as intermittent catcalls and booing turned into cheering and applause.

In the 1980s there formed a space for commentaries, multiple channels for replication and dissemination, resistance against those who controlled discourse, and the freedom to exercise criticism, which also resembled the New Culture Movement of the May Fourth Era. Liu Xiaobo's PhD dissertation went deeper into what he had expressed in his previous publishing, writing, and public speaking and carved out the meaning of life through the pursuit of freedom, imagination of space, and resistance on his path in literature and aesthetics.[4] His dissertation defense turned a narrow academic topic into a public issue, and the discussion during his defense extended into that of the current state of humanity.

While a visiting scholar overseas from 1988 to April 1989, Liu Xiaobo published articles in *Emancipation Monthly* and other overseas publications that even more directly and explicitly spoke of China's current system and how to resist it, a system that included "congenital racial flaws such as 'blind devotion,' 'the group above all,' 'egalitarianism,' 'nationalism,' etc. But in terms of China's present reality, all of these can be traced back to one point: the force to negate autocracy cannot been found within the autocracy."[5]

## Creating Space for Association and Assembly

Liu Xiaobo went back to China to take part in the 1989 Democracy Movement and gave speeches at Beijing Normal University, at Tiananmen Square, and on the broadcast vehicles. After martial law was imposed, he organized and took part in the hunger strike by the Four Gentlemen. After martial law troops killed peaceful protesters on Beijing's streets, the Four Gentlemen and many participants at Tiananmen Square insisted on nonviolent resistance. After martial law troops surrounded the square and were prepared to use any means and pay any price to clear the square, the Four Gentlemen negotiated with the army and convinced the thousands of protesters to withdraw from the square.

After the June Fourth Massacre, Liu Xiaobo was detained for twenty months. Following his release in 1991, he was dismissed from his university; his writings were banned from publication, and his space for existence and resistance was greatly reduced. Over the next twenty-odd years, Liu Xiaobo wrote articles for a dozen or so overseas publications and published books. He helped establish internet forums within China and online publications overseas that connected the internal and external resistance spaces.

Following release from his first imprisonment, he took a brief trip overseas. It was the only time after June 4 that he traveled overseas. From then on he was banned from leaving the country. From early 1990 onward, under the stability maintenance system that Deng Xiaoping established to nip unrest in the bud, the greatest challenge for a warrior who practiced freedom of expression and freedom to criticize and who insisted on continuing the struggle under totalitarian rule was how to continue creating various kinds of space under this centralized regime. The creation and expansion of space relied on exercising the rights to assembly, association, and speech.

Jiang Peikun, a professor on Liu Xiaobo's doctoral dissertation committee, was also one of the founders of the Tiananmen Mothers. After Liu Xiaobo left prison for the first time, his starting point for repentance, introspection, and seeking a new path for resistance was the investigation of June 4 victims Ding Zilin and other Tiananmen Mothers carried out. At this stage, Liu Xiaobo's participation in statements by dissident groups looked like petitions to the government, but in fact the statements were directed at society as a means of expanding the network.

After 1989 the space for popular gatherings was largely restricted, and the venues were often changed to hotels, restaurants, parks, or the homes of friends. I went to several of the same gatherings as Liu Xiaobo. The longest was in 1993, when Liu Xiaobo and Zhou Duo restlessly returned to Beijing after their last overseas travel. They talked all night long about what they had seen and heard overseas, and they commented on books that couldn't be published in Mainland China. The last such meeting was at a restaurant in Shenzhen at the end of August 1996. Liu Xiaobo suggested that each person tell a joke. One joke was about Deng Xiaoping, Jiang Zemin, and Li Peng traveling in the same car and encountering a fork in the road, and Deng Xiaoping saying to put on the left turn signal and then turn right. Liu Xiaobo commented that the CCP could take all benefit from going either left or right. Another joke was about Reagan, Gorbachev, and Deng Xiaoping telephoning God and asking when each of their countries would implement democracy.[6] Liu Xiaobo didn't comment on that joke at the time. After the gathering, Liu Xiaobo asked me if there were any people locally who could both speak and act. As a result, he met with Wang Xizhe in Guangzhou's Orchid Garden, and they jointly issued the Double Ten Declaration. Soon after the declaration was issued, Liu Xiaobo was detained and sentenced to three years of reeducation through labor, and Wang Xizhe was forced into exile. This was the longest time that Liu Xiaobo was imprisoned after June 4 and before Charter 08, when Liu Xia repeatedly took the "train to the concentration camp."

After Liu Xiaobo was again released back to the big prison in 1999, even more social problems were evident. Social stratification was more obvious, and the intellectual community was more divided than ever. Liu Xiaobo's anonymous dialogue with Wang Shuo, a book entitled *A Belle Gave Me a Knockout Drug*, was published through gray channels in an even more indifferent consumer environment. Discourse in this space had become much more insubstantial than in the 1980s, and it was very hard to form sustained discussion on public topics. Liu Xiaobo, who had never avoided being present at certain events because he feared to hear about the literary inquisition, used his political commentaries to open up new space. He wrote current affairs commentaries about interest groups of the centralization system, illusory prosperity, and popular resistance, and he made them topics of public discussion on the internet.

Unlike in the 1980s, when scholars with opposing viewpoints could meet face-to-face for exchanges and debates, Liu Xiaobo could only publish his comments on the internet. At a time of transition from print media to the internet, the government usually suppressed or abolished opposition parties and underground magazines, scholarly journals with a critical mentality, media breaking out of official strictures, newly generated gray spaces, independent communities, and independent media before they could develop an extensive discussion. The growth of an independent society relies on linking different resistances and using different forms to break through the siege. Liu Xiaobo criticized autocracy and supported the fight for their rights by other people whose views differed from his.[7] This was his way of linking the trajectories of fragmented social strata and groups.

Liu Xiaobo's apparently earthshaking discourse was in fact a continuation of the propositions some scholars took during the May Fourth New Culture Movement, such as his view that China would need three hundred years of colonialism like Hong Kong. This proposal provided another model to cast off China's long-term autocracy and the fascistization of the Chinese empire. The wholesale westernization in the New Culture Movement and Liu Xiaobo's statements of this kind could be intertextually interpreted as a proposal to change the loop of autocracy and reform society. Lu Xun made a pertinent appraisal of such discourse: "By temperament the Chinese love compromise and a happy mean. For instance, if you say this room is too dark and a window should be made, everyone is sure to disagree. But if you propose taking off the roof, they will compromise and be glad to make a window. In the absence of more drastic proposals, they will never agree to the most inoffensive reforms."[8] If Liu Xiaobo's viewpoints are analyzed from the perspective of autonomous resistance, autonomous resistance should be practiced based on the understanding of how the oppressed have been oppressed, how the oppressive system has been caused and operated, and how the oppressed can practice their autonomous resistance through self-education.

Liu Xiaobo's three hundred years of colonialism was meant to borrow external forces to resist China's autocratic nationalism that had enslaved people for a thousand years. But the problem at present is the hegemonic control of global capital and collusion in the division of spoils by China's centralized empire and other powerful empires. If the model of capital and power politics dominating globalization does not change, democratic countries will be unable to eliminate systemic privilege, and the people will be unable to effectively and directly participate in public affairs. As the ruling interest groups of powerful centralized nations cooperate further with the privileged and elite strata in the existing democratic systems, the centralized systems will cause the gradual evolution of the present democratic systems and take them ever further from democratization.

Autonomous resistance isn't using powerful rival tigers against each other but rather putting all of the tigers of the world into cages. Otherwise, humanity can only continue trudging among various forms of barbarism and the law of the jungle. Putting their faith in various kinds of power-holders, the oppressed cannot fundamentally change their fate of enslavement. Walter Benjamin revealed the relationship between willing slaves and rulers: "All rulers are the heirs of prior conquerors. Hence, empathizing with the victor invariably benefits the current rulers."[9] For this reason, the resistance aiming at mastering one's fate and shaking off enslavement means both resisting centralized power and opposing empire.

Most worth emphasizing is that the last chapter of Liu Xiaobo's PhD dissertation called for casting off hopelessness regarding enslavement: "Even if it's a futile effort, we must struggle against it." From the year 2000 onward, looking back on Lin Zhao's resistance became an important resource for popular autonomous resistance. Liu Xiaobo drew a lesson from Lin Zhao's resistance in his ongoing practice of resistance: establishing a subjective popular resistance and relying on the autonomous and conscious effort of citizens to change the regime and politics.[10] As with Lin Zhao's resistance, Liu Xiaobo constantly faced up to power, tested himself in resistance, and engaged in introspection during struggle. This is the enlightenment that Liu Xiaobo and all people who have resisted with their lives have brought to this age.

Liu Xiaobo participated in establishing the Independent Chinese PEN Center, not only practicing freedom of association, but also expanding the public space for freedom of expression in Mainland China. By exercising the rights of association, assembly, and speech, the establishment of the ICPC has been a transregional resistance on an even greater scale. Liu Xiaobo put freedom of speech and humanitarianism into practice by helping to rescue imprisoned writers, by opposing literary inquisition and supporting independent writers in China. He established a model for transnational and intergenerational joint resistance.

Charter 08, in which Liu Xiaobo played a part, started out as an open platform to a certain degree with different layers of political propositions linking fragmented social groups and different ethnicities. Discussion and criticism of Charter 08 have reflected civil society's vitality and diversity. The dissemination of Charter 08 has also reflected the diversity and mobility of popular publications. These qualities are the most important sustaining energy for joint resistance against centralized power and for preserving the autonomy of civil society. The CCP was terrified of Liu Xiaobo collecting signatures for Charter 08 and even more afraid of the snowball effect of Chinese civil society exercising the right to assembly and association and of China's popular resistance joining in the global struggle to bury centralized power and empire.

## Spiritual Home

Liu Xiaobo and Liu Xia's poetry and letters to friends explored and constructed their spiritual home. Liu Xiaobo's reading, reflecting, writing and speaking in custody are the most important legacy of resistance that he left behind for this era. Liu Xiaobo and Liu Xia's correspondence was their resistance of alienation and their struggle to survive and practiced an aesthetic life of spiritual transcendence in confinement amid autocracy's modernization.

Those resisting totalitarianism are not only political dissidents; they are lifestyle dissidents who create a dignified way of life with the capacity for independent thought and action that transcends the confinement or subtle influence of a centralized system.

During his last eight years in prison, Liu Xiaobo constantly examined himself and resisted. The spiritual home that Liu Xiaobo and Liu Xia established, their poems, photographs, and letters, were their way of facing up to power and resisting brutality while practicing freedom and aesthetics. Liu Xia, the poet and photographer under house arrest, joined Liu Xiaobo in creating a spiritual home that was vast and boundless. In his steadfast resistance, Liu Xiaobo made himself a torch in the darkness, being-toward-death.[11]

*Translated by Stacy Mosher*

## NOTES

1. Hannah Arendt, *The Origins of Totalitarianism* (New York: Shocken, 2004), preface, 7.—Trans.
2. *Inaugural* introduction: "Truly, it's hard to imagine, if not for April 5th, our descendants would say of this generation, 'They handed in a blank examination paper!' A blank test paper representing shame, covered up this generation's inflexible face" (*This Generation* 1 [November 1979]).
3. "General, You Cannot Do This" was the most influential work by the poet Ye Wenfu (b. 1944). *The Sun and Man* is a film by Bai Hua (b. 1930) and Peng Ning (1942–2004) based on Bai Hua's novel *Unrequited Love* (Kulian).—Trans.
4. Liu Xiaobo, *Aesthetics and Human Freedom* (Beijing: Beijing Normal University Press, 1988).
5. Liu Xiaobo, "The Devil Incarnate, Mao Zedong." *Emancipation Monthly* (later renamed *Open Magazine*), November 1988.—Trans.

6. The jokes go as follows: 1) Deng Xiaoping, Jiang Zemin, and Li Peng were taking the same car when they encountered a fork in the road. Li Peng said to turn left, Jiang Zemin said to turn right, and when neither would give ground they requested instructions from Deng Xiaoping. Deng said to turn on the left blinker and then turn right. 2) Reagan, Gorbachev and Deng Xiaoping agreed to telephone God together and ask when each of their countries would have democracy. God said the United States needed fifty years, and Reagan said, "I hope I can see that day." When it was Gorbachev's turn, God said the Soviet Union would need one hundred years, and Gorbachev wept, saying, "There's no hope that I'll live to see it." When Deng Xiaoping asked the question, God wept.

7. Liu Xiaobo, "The Paradox of China's Maoists Challenging the Current Regime," *BBC Chinese*, August 13, 2007, http://news.bbc.co.uk/chinese/simp/hi/newsid_6940000 /newsid_6944300/6944348.stm.

8. Lu Xun, *Silent China*, trans. Gladys Yang (New York: Oxford University Press, 1973).—Trans.

9. Walter Benjamin (1892–1940) was a Marxist German Jewish philosopher and theorist who killed himself in September 1940, when his attempt to flee Nazi Germany was thwarted. Walter Benjamin, "On the Concept of History," in *Selected Writings*, Vol. 4, *1938–1940*, trans. Edmund Jephcott, Howard Eiland, and Michael W Jennings (Cambridge MA: Harvard University Press, 2003), 391.—Trans.

10. Liu Xiaobo, "To Change a Regime by Changing a Society," *China Observer*, February 26, 2006.—Trans.

11. A concept of German philosopher Martin Heidegger (1889–1976).—Trans.

# The Last Idealist

*Wang Wei*

In 1983 I was a graduate student in Chinese literature at Beijing Normal University. Liu Xiaobo was a year ahead of me, and we both lived in Building 2 of the student dorms. Liu Xiaobo was a big wit, with the unconventional elegance of a celebrity, willful and natural, informal and unshaven every day. He wore slippers and big pants when going to the cafeteria to get food or to the boiler room to get boiled water. In the summer he was shirtless, cooling himself off in the washroom. He spoke with a stutter, but his voice was very loud. Various stories about him circulated on campus. One of them said that once on his way to take a bus, he saw a girl, caught up to her, and earnestly said, "I'm sorry to bother you. You're so beautiful." He was a maverick and straightforward in this sort of way.

One day in 1985, he told me that Li Zehou would come to campus the next day, and he invited me to attend a debate between him and Li.[1] At that time, Li Zehou was very influential, an idol worshiped by the students. I was excited and called my friend Dahe from across the city of Beijing to come listen to the debate with me. It was only after our arrival that I learned that Li Zehou had not come but had only sent one of his students. The debate took place in Xiaobo's dormitory, and seven or eight people were present. Liu Xiaobo talked nonstop, criticizing Li Zehou, saying that Li's book was not only full of loopholes but also conceptually out of date and that his way of thinking about unearthing the essence of Chinese tradition had substantial negative ramifications for the development of Chinese society. I was dumbfounded; I thought how fortunate that Li Zehou had not come, or else, I don't know how he would have been able to get out of the situation gracefully. That was the first time I regarded this stuttering and eloquent senior schoolmate of mine with a newfound respect.

In 1986 Xiaobo graduated and stayed on at the university, and I went to work at a magazine at the Chinese Academy of Social Sciences (CASS). During those few years, the social trend of thought surged like a gathering storm, and the intellectual world was both exciting and dynamic but also superficially followed whatever was in fashion at the time. In September the Institute of Literature at CASS convened a large-scale conference on the ten years of New Period Literature and invited experts from all over to gather in western Beijing. I bumped into Xiaobo in the hotel corridor. We were happy to see each other because it had been a long time since we last saw each other. As we were talking, the director of the Institute of Literature, Liu Zaifu, walked by and said "You must be Liu Xiaobo, your articles are very well written."

That evening Liu Zaifu hosted an informal discussion. Everyone spoke freely, eager to praise the achievements of the New Period Literature. At this point, Liu Xiaobo stood up, and with a northeastern accent and his stutter, said, "You all talked about how good Chinese literature is during the past decade, but I think it's just dog shit." The whole place was silent and everyone looked at each other. For the next fifteen minutes, Liu Xiaobo enumerated the shortcomings of contemporary literature and demonstrated why those of the "roots-searching school" and the modernists were full of dog shit. It was as if there was no one else present; his words electrified the listeners. The next day, *Shenzhen Youth Daily* published a full-page interview with Liu Xiaobo on the front page. The topic was "Crisis! The New Period Literature Is Facing a Crisis." This was the first time Liu Xiaobo entered the national media and attracted widespread attention. He was called a "dark horse," an emerging talent.

Two months later, his famous article "Dialogue with Li Zehou" was published, causing a sensation. The article comprehensively criticized Li Zehou's theoretical system, which was built on Confucian rationality and essentialism. Liu Xiaobo instead advocated sensibility and individuality to return to life, resistance to tradition, and total westernization. Li Zehou's dominance in Chinese academic circles was thus challenged. Liu Xiaobo's criticism of the entire intellectual community was extremely sharp and attracted official attention. In 1987 the then–minister of culture, Wang Meng, criticized Liu Xiaobo by name, saying that socialist universities cannot cultivate their own gravediggers, and threatened to expel Xiaobo as a student. (At the time he was working on his PhD.)[2]

In the subsequent anti-bourgeois liberalization movement, Liu Xiaobo became a model for criticism, and all of his articles and books were banned. However, he was widely known among young students. In 1988, when Liu Xiaobo defended his dissertation, it became major news on campus. I was not in Beijing at the time and thus unable to be present for the big occasion. It was said that because too many people showed up to participate, at the last minute the defense committee changed the location for the defense to an amphitheater that held four hundred people. The room was packed. The minister of education specifically sent people to monitor, and the size of the audience created a record for Beijing Normal University (or perhaps for any university in China). His doctoral dissertation, "Aesthetics and Human Freedom," was highly praised by the committee and passed unanimously.

In 1989, with the Four Gentlemen's hunger strike and other actions on Tiananmen Square, Xiaobo became the leader of the movement. I was also continually on the square as Xiaobo's foot soldier. On the night of June 1, several colleagues from CASS and I repeatedly discussed and agreed that the military had already entered Beijing and that the situation was on the brink of crisis. We needed to think about the long term and believed it was necessary to withdraw and return to campus. In the middle of that night, we decided to look for the leaders on the square and try to persuade them. The headquarters tent of the Beijing University Students' Autonomous Federation (gaozilian) was at the base of the monument, and there was layer upon layer of identification checks at the checkpoints. I said that we were from CASS and that we were looking for Liu Xiaobo. The students were all respectful and led us into the tent. At the last sentry post, they said they were in a meeting, and we couldn't see him. Through the tent, I could hear Liu Xiaobo's loud voice talking. Waiting and waiting with no end, there was nothing we could do; we had to give up. It was the last time I heard Xiaobo's voice.

Several of us from CASS insisted on staying on the square until the last moment and then withdrew. I only learned later that it was Liu Xiaobo who had negotiated and reached an agreement with the military to let the people on the square withdraw peacefully. Xiaobo saved my life and the lives of thousands of students and avoided bloodshed on Tiananmen Square. Thinking back today, was this final compromise on the square a blessing or a curse for China, for history?

Liu Xiaobo was a nonconformist among Chinese intellectuals. In his early years, he was unconventional and unrestrained and made a rallying cry like a bolt of thunder and lightning in an iron room. After participating in politics, his thinking was, as always, profound and forward-looking, but his feelings became deeper and more profound, and his mind became broader, his character more sophisticated, and his theory more mature. He was a rare charismatic leader who combined in the same person both a thinker and an activist. His sincerity and courage, his down-to-earth attitude, his spirit of sacrifice—"If I don't go to hell, who will?"—his indomitable character of daring to be first in China, and his selfless and fearless personality and charm, made him second to none among contemporary Chinese figures. He was fully deserving of the Nobel Peace Prize. And in time, he will become China's Gandhi, Mandela, and Aung San Suu Kyi. Disaster is striking China; it is an unlucky year when a great man of our time died at an early age. China is sinking and the night is endless. There is no sign of democracy, just an abyss of suffering. What sorrow, what pain!

The departed are merciless, and the living are guilty. Xiaobo, go well.

*Translated by Andréa Worden*

NOTES

1. Li Zehou is a prominent scholar of philosophy and intellectual history.—Trans.
2. For more on Wang Meng's criticism of Liu Xiaobo, see Zha Jianying, "Servant of the State," *New Yorker*, November 8, 2010.—Trans.

# I Look Forward to a Magnificent Farewell

*Ai Xiaoming*

1

This article is so hard to write; I've already postponed it for quite a while. But the delay wasn't relaxing. Every day I was thinking, if I couldn't write something, then I would just let go of this burden. But without writing a little text, I'd feel I would be letting Xiaobo down, and there would be a lot of guilt.

The days are ordinary, as the anxious, scorching awaiting recedes together with the hot summer. Your ashes sank into the sea and then flowed into an ocean of ice. Where should one go to look for the sunken jar, which will reveal tracks of when you began to be forced to suffer liver cancer? The Chilean film director Patricio Guzman made a documentary about a pearl button that was salvaged from a beach in Chile in 2004, which led to the discovery of the secret history behind a disappeared victim of political persecution whose corpse had been dumped into the sea from the dictator's plane.[1] But the final journey to your death, on the face of it, was not secret. For more than ten days, the hospital issued a daily report about a prisoner's critical condition. This unprecedented solicitude as you approached the end of your life was both sincere and bizarre. As you struggled between life and death, our memories, responsibilities and sadness were manipulated, and in the end, suffocated again behind the closed iron curtain.

We have been forced to become accustomed to living an ignoble existence, living in shame, living amid ridicule; living in the process of being raped, adulterated, or being compelled to comply because the rapist is too powerful.

When dissidents are isolated, it's only the stability maintenance personnel assigned to them, or plainclothes police officers performing "customer service," who'll often laugh and talk with them at ease––that's of course the moment when the Stockholm syndrome has taken effect. Rape turned into adultery, and then into an act of two accomplices, so that the victimizer and victim coexist in a courtesy of forgiveness without any principle of right and wrong. This kind of shame is deeply engraved into our lives. I said "our" and perhaps that's not precise, but, at the very least, this is not an experience unique to me.

How can I write your name with a clear conscience or even call out your name? I am unworthy. As a friend of mine who lives overseas reprimanded me several months ago: when he was imprisoned, he had already been locked up for nearly nine years. Where were these so-called friends of yours? Good question. Where were we, the first batch of more than three hundred people who were the first to sign Charter 08? Did we scatter in all directions?

## 2

You are my fellow alum, but we are also almost familiar strangers.

In the spring of 1985, I went to the Chinese Literature Department of Beijing Normal University to pursue a doctorate. My major was modern Chinese literature. I came to Beijing from another province. At that time, I was conventional and well behaved and was considered a good student. Another fellow alum, who was senior to me, Professor Wang Furen, was already a member of the academic advisory committee, and we studied together under Li Helin. It was an era when people used ultra-leftism and liberalism to judge right and wrong. On our campus, where the tide of freedom of thought was surging, various famous faculty members often gave lectures. The classroom was packed with students; some students stood on the steps between seats and some surrounded the windows outside, listening to Furen's passionate lecture about his study of Lu Xun.

At that time, upon your graduation, you had already become a faculty member in the Chinese Literature Department. For your doctorate, you specialized in the study of literature and art. We rarely intersected, but your reputation was soaring. At the time, I didn't understand at all why you would have challenged the academic authorities of the time, Li Zehou or Liu Zaifu. I thought that since my major was modern history, I neither desired nor had the ability to get involved in the fierce disputes of the contemporary literary circles.

We only had one conversation, and that was during the conference of comparative literature held in Shenzhen in 1985. The young people who participated in the conference danced in the café at night and exchanged information about going to Shatoujiao (Sha Tau Kok) to buy stockings. I happened to be dining with you at the same table. You said you'd gone on a very exciting roller coaster ride.

This little discussion is really about some trivial details in an insignificant part of your life but sufficient to show how rare our contacts were. You had your own home on campus. We graduate students from the provinces lived in Building 12. We strived to breathe in the open air of the capital, riding our bikes to rush around to the libraries on and off campus, and we went to the Film Archives at Xinjiekou to watch foreign movies. Listening to the renowned scholars, we felt the superiority of being located in the academic center, enjoying the privilege of freedom. Beijing really was a city that people didn't want to leave once they got there.

We graduated one after another, and I also stayed in Beijing to teach. Soon it was that seething summer. One afternoon, I went to look for Furen, and learned that he had taken a Sha blanket to the square. He might have gone to advise students to return to school or to resist the army's attempt to enter the city. My memory is a bit hazy about this. Martial law had already been declared, and thousands upon thousands of people had been protesting the martial law order on the streets for several days. I took part in the demonstrations, and the lenses of video cameras flashed incessantly in front of our team. The next day, I biked to the square because I wanted to find my "big brother," Wang Furen. It was so crowded that there was no way I could get close to the monument. At that time, I didn't know that you were just then moving toward your own destiny. You were in the center of the square.

Afterward there was a massacre, mass arrests, and a big purge. You became a wicked black hand. Those days are long past; we have survived in the gap between defense and compromise. I never watched your testimony on television. In those days, our inner anger and sorrow were repeatedly suppressed. We waited, we sneered and felt that all of these setbacks were so untrue: how could this be? The reality was so irrational and untrustworthy. But those who did not flee or go abroad tried hard to survive amid the political cleansing. They did not want to lose what they had: teaching, work, and all the conditions for survival.

Later, on an afternoon in the 1990s, we passed each other in a corridor of the campus dormitory. You had been released from your first imprisonment and were going to have a meal at the home of another teacher at our university who similarly was a veteran of the square. I suddenly recognized you and said "Ah, Xiaobo, hello." Nothing more than that, I turned to go back home, without even a ripple in my life.

Just like this, millions of people took to the streets in Beijing. Countless intellectuals, innumerable famous scholars, professors, and artists, and every major central-level agency . . . became silent after the storm, and let life continue.

## 3

At that time, I never thought that we could be friends like this. At the last moment of your life, only four alumni came forward and called out: Free Liu Xiaobo!

We share a common learning bond with you, and we used this bond to show the interdependency of our friendships, unending in life and death. In our hundred-year-old school, fellow alumni can amount to tens of thousands, but when you were on your deathbed, there were just four of us who called out to all the alumni on your behalf. Among us, Guo Yuhua and I are both university professors, and Wen Tao is a journalist. We all graduated from the Chinese Literature Department of Beijing Normal University (in order not to bring trouble to another currently employed professor, the fourth alum's name is, for the time being, omitted here).

In my memory, we began to get closer years after I had left the university and Beijing. Perhaps it was in 2008 when we were all using Skype. We exchanged greetings when we saw each other online. I sent you my documentaries, *Taishi Village, The Epic of the Central Plains*, and so on. We once had a voice call on Skype. I remember you asked me a question, "How can you bear so much suffering?"

This question was what I really wanted to ask you. After you died, I read some of your commentaries and poems you wrote in prison. I think you've performed the ethical responsibility of thinkers with such humility, perseverance, and earnestness: to take on the hardships and pain of a nation and of social change. You are not at all like the young man who was brash and unruly in the 1980s.

As a filmmaker, it's not that I really took on that much suffering. We are only bystanders or gleaners of suffering, and it's the power of the media to arouse a sympathetic response. This kind of media conveys the breadth of human emotions––happiness, anger, sorrow, and joy––of those interviewed. We've arrogated to ourselves the credit that belongs to them.

It was not only the internet that brought us closer, but more important, the rise of social movements and the transformation of ideas. I never used to feel that politics was part of my life. Just as Wang Xiaobo said in his recollection, the instruction from our parents was not to study liberal arts.[2]

Not to study liberal arts meant to stay out of politics. Our parents were repeatedly attacked in political movements since the 1950s. The lesson they hoped to pass on to us was just avoidance. Parental instruction from when we were children erased our political rights. I remember that during my childhood primary schools also had to develop militias to liberate Taiwan. At the dining table, the teachers talked loudly about participating in the militia and practicing shooting. I said to my father, who was the vice principal of the elementary school, "I also want to shoot a gun." My father thundered loudly, "It's none of your damn business!"

My father wanted his children to accept class discrimination and stay away from political dissent. The way to steer clear of politics was to follow the party, but this would inevitably become a paradox because the party was inextricably linked with mobilizing political struggles. Having experienced the Cultural Revolution and then the rehabilitation and redress of individual injustices, we grew up and learned to be suspicious of and distance ourselves from politics. It was very difficult to return to my individual standpoint. I never realized that also concealed under the cloak of independent academics was the automatic abandonment of political responsibility. It took many years until I was able to reflect on this political apathy syndrome, which was at the same time a rights consciousness disability and was contrary to the moral conscience of intellectuals. The lesson of our fathers—keeping a distance from politics—perhaps survives in difficulty, but ceding civil and political rights will not allow us to free ourselves from the fate of political refugees.

I saw in your relevant recollections and poems the shared background of our parents. Maybe your family was more fortunate (or more unfortunate)? The way you unhesitatingly threw yourself into political movements, you must have had an innocent heart. Well, this can be blackened as "wild ambition," and you strongly criticized this yourself. However, is it worse to have a such a heart than to remain silent and passive during a big tragedy? To get involved in social movements in this politically high-risk reality, how much trust must you have in justice and the public? Isn't this just idealism?

At that time, I still remembered the collective fanaticism during the Cultural Revolution and was to some degree against political and social actions due to my sense of individualism. This may also have been because of the influence of a Milan Kundera novel I was fervently reading at that time. I didn't make any effort to enter into the politics of the square. However, if it had happened by chance, who could guarantee that I would not have been swept along and drawn into it? Now that I think about it, the more effective obstacle came from fear. Many adults around me, after they expressed their sense of righteousness, retreated, and didn't take a more radical step. In a deep place in our hearts, there was a strong knot. We did not believe that the army would kill people, or we believed that the army would definitely kill people. Not believing was a formulation that accorded with our ideological education; believing, on the other hand, was an echo from experience. We could not rely on reason, nor could we avoid experience. Between the two, I went to the square and wanted to find our students. I wanted to discourage them, hurry back to school, and stop your persistence.

And what if this happened today? What would I do? Would I be like you, standing among the students on the square, negotiating with the army, and leading thousands of students off the square? Or like the righteous Beijing citizens who later were detained and beaten, blocking military vehicles, rescuing the injured? Or like the righteous person from far away below Jinshui River, at a cost of twenty years in jail for banners proclaiming, "Five thousand years of dictatorship comes to an end at this point," and "Personality cults may cease from now on"?[3] Or, would I be like the relatives in the Tiananmen Mothers' movement, weeping through their long lives, then dying in sorrow?

We should return to the source so that all of this would have been avoided, no autocracy or personality cults; we should turn toward democracy and an open society so that parents will never again have to teach the family not to study liberal arts and be apolitical, instead enabling children to cast off political apathy and naturally enjoy their civil and political rights.

## 4

I left Beijing in 1994. Before that, we had passed each other in the corridor. In the autumn of 2008, maybe in September, we finally met and talked. It was a run-of-the-mill restaurant in Beijing's Haidian district; you also invited Zhang Zuhua and Yu Jie. I have an impression that the lawyer Mo Shaoping was also there. This was the only time in our lives that we had what could be called an in-person conversation. Who would have thought it would also be the last time!

At that time Charter 08 had already been circulated on Skype. I saw the draft of the Charter, and I remember that I made some suggestions for changes in the wording. In the few years preceding this, there had already been many signature appeals relating to political rights. Our earlier political participation began with the 2003 appeal regarding the murder of Sun Zhigang.[4] The government's decision to abolish the custody and repatriation system inspired us to imagine an optimistic future for civic movements.

In those years, I taught and filmed in the south; you wrote and explored social transformation in the north. You used your sharp style of writing to enter discussions about the path for China's political reform, human rights, and constitutional democracy. You held great hope for those dissident intellectuals within the government system. You never complained in the least that fate was unfair. You had been imprisoned for many years and lost all guarantees while your classmates and fellow alumni stepped up into the elite strata within the system and were crowned as top academic leaders and PhD advisors and given other dazzling laurels. Of course, the darkness and hostility you encountered will eventually descend upon these people, but in those few years, our common ideals allowed us to share the same path.

In December 2008, on International Human Rights Day, Charter 08 was made public. I signed this document along with more than three hundred others, but it became the reason you were sentenced to eleven years of imprisonment, something I never expected. You lost your freedom. This matter became an important political case. Many of those who signed were investigated and interrogated, but no one lost more than you. In a public statement, 165 Charter signatories jointly stated that we were willing to share the responsibility together with you. I also signed this statement. A year later, you were sentenced to eleven years' imprisonment. The following year, you won the Nobel Peace Prize. You were serving your sentence in Jinzhou, Liaoning Province, and then there was no more news.

On April 1 or 2, 2009, Cui Weiping, some other friends, and I met with Liu Xia. This was the first time I saw your wife, Liu Xia. Also present were Mo Shaoping, Liu Di, and others (as well as the plainclothes police officers who were nearby monitoring us). Weiping and lawyer Mo Shaoping brought Liu Xia information about the People in Need's Homo Homini Award Ceremony, held in the Czech Republic. In March of the same year, at the international Film Festival One World, held in Prague, former Czech president Vaclav Havel personally presented the Homo Homini Award to Liu Xiaobo and to the group of the initial signatories of Charter 08. That day there was something wrong with Liu Xia's leg. She said that she had been drinking with Liao Yiwu the day before; he had picked her up in a bear hug and whirled her around, and she accidently suffered a sprain. During the return trip, plainclothes police followed Weiping, Liu Di, and me the entire way until we transferred subway lines.

I once asked Liu Xia if during Xiaobo's imprisonment, I could come and interview her once a year. Liu Xia smiled and said, "Okay." Her voice was gentle and the expression in her eyes resolute and straightforward. However, after 2010 I wasn't able to see her until a winter day in2012, when I saw the video of Xu Youyu and Hu Jia breaking through the tight encirclement to visit Liu Xia. Liu Xia looked alarmed and frightened, like a totally different person.

This is the sacrifice you and your wife have made for all of us. Some friends had promised each other that we would accompany Liu Xia to Dalian every year. We had said with certainty that we would share this responsibility together. And the result? I won't speak for all of us, just myself. It was like seeing a distressed child overwhelmed beneath a huge building in an earthquake. In futile sorrow, she can't lift the heavy burden, and we can't share the burden of your long sentence, which you took on for us.

## 5

What's more, you were not a distressed child who had stopped breathing. You had such a rich inner world and sensibility. You were imprisoned until the ninth year. In your last few dying days, your writing was still free to unfold. Seeing the draft of the preface you wrote for Liu Xia's book was like seeing an ice sculpture, sparkling, translucent, and pristine. Even under the tight scrutiny of the monitoring probe, at the place where you start to write about your love, its force penetrates the back of the paper––as a song, as a cry. Imprisoning such a soul, how cruel a crime this is. This is not the Middle Ages!

In the video that was deliberately released of your life in prison, I saw you wearing a prison uniform. You were jogging, and your movements were mechanical; you were sweeping snow, and you received a medical examination. But I didn't see any frames of you receiving books, reading, or writing. If we could have sent books to you, the time in prison would have been so much better. Now none of us knows how you survived the long night of the past nine years, and whether you left any records. And if you did, whether you gave your notes to Liu Xia.

From the day you lost your freedom for the last time until the day you died, there were more than three thousand days and nights. Compared to you, how could we not count every day that we spend in freedom as happiness? This is not to say that there weren't suppression and setbacks or that no one continued to lose his or her freedom or that no one was imprisoned or silenced. But rather, comparing life outside to an invisible prison is somewhat exaggerated. During more than three thousand days and nights, we had WeChat, WhatsApp, and everyone's dramas. . . . How much could we read, create, and share with our circles of friends? We could visit relatives and travel, exercise, and shop on

Taobao--beautiful clothing and food. . . . Most of the time, how could we share the pains and difficulties of those who were imprisoned? We chose to ignore them in our helplessness, one fewer was just less. The cheering on the night the Nobel Peace Prize was announced was really a short-lived moment, here.

My fellow alum, I'm unable to call out your name due to my own inaction and powerlessness to do anything for you in your difficult situation. And being inside, how did you imagine the outside world? You must have known you had enormous moral support, but that brilliant award did not even shorten your sentence by one day. And we as signatories can still enjoy freedom at all because you took the responsibility upon yourself. When I think of you, I think of what Lu Xun said in his essay, "How Do We Behave like a Father Today?" Carrying the heavy burden of old patterns and models and shouldering the floodgate of darkness to let them (i.e., children) go to a broad and bright place; afterward, they will spend their days in happiness, and behave rationally.

Once you wrote in a letter to your friend Liao Yiwu: "Even after so many years of tremendous tragedies, we still don't have a moral leader like Vaclav Havel. It seems ironic that in order to win the right of ordinary people to pursue self-interest, a society needs a moral giant to make a selfless sacrifice. In order to secure 'passive freedom'--freedom from state oppression--there needs to be a will to do *active* resistance. History is not fated. The appearance of a single martyr can fundamentally turn the spirit of a nation and strengthen its moral fiber."[5]

In my mind, you have achieved the image of a moral giant that this nation lacks. Before you, there were Lin Zhao, Huang Lizhong, Yu Luoke, and so on. And with you at the same time are Tang Jingling, Chen Yunfei, Liu Xianbin, and others. But did our souls change because of them? This is the hard question we must ask ourselves now.

6

We--your friends and I--will remember this deeply anxious July of 2017. I didn't understand until later that the bullet was already aimed at your heart; it was just that its speed was being precisely controlled. The bullet slowly traced its arc in its orbit, and from the news of June

26 to the end of your life on July 13, the warhead flew in the air for eighteen days.

In these eighteen days and nights, it was like we were crazy, returning to that schism of reason and emotion twenty-nine years ago: the tiger must eat people, the tiger does not eat people. I wrote that open letter, stood up and shouted, "Free Liu Xiaobo!" Our fantastical myth appears. I want to become a witch with the most magical flying broom to cross over. You and your wife and relatives flew to the other shore of freedom. At the grand welcoming ceremony, you saw your glory and were relieved you could leave it as your final wish to the world.

For this reason, I painted again and again the appearance of birds of paradise; the flower leaves of saffron and bluish-white stripes belong together with the colors in your hospital ward. Birds of paradise spread their wings to fly; they brook no delay. Now these paintings could only be given to the participants of the Guangdong sea ceremony to commemorate the moment of their expression with the price of imprisonment.

In those days you were besieged on your sickbed, and indeed, your friends came from long distances to fulfill the promises they once made. From the time they heard the news to when your ashes left Shenyang and sped toward Dalian, every day there were people looking for you. In the off-limits areas of the ward and at the entrance to the hospital, there were bouquets offered for you. . . . After your ashes were thrown into the sea, some of your friends swam along the coast for more than an hour in the direction of the burial boat, to pay homage at the place where the jar of your ashes sank into the sea.

I remember when I learned the news that you had been released for medical treatment but we wouldn't be able to visit you. The former lawyer Pu Zhiqiang, whose freedom was restricted, sent a message that he wanted to say this to you: "Friends are all here." The various efforts mentioned above are proof, Xiaobo, that it cannot be said that your friends fled in all directions. They were in the closest place to your hospital ward and the closest place to your ashes and are your kindred spirits. Even if separated by thousands of miles, during those days, you were more important than all of our closest family members.

What's more, there are more young people who never saw and will never again have an opportunity to see your glowing high spirits but are using coded language to circulate your news and poetry and to light candles for you in their circles of friends.

In the blink of an eye, it's your hundredth day of death. In these one hundred days, your image is more prominent than ever before. Although your name and Liu Xia's have no sound, as if buried with the dead, we know that your spirit is still here with us, as is hers. Those of us who've benefited because of you will continue to discuss your choice and your ideal. We are thinking about how to bear our own moral responsibility.

I look forward to a grand farewell, one that is worthy of your sacrifice and the glory you brought to this nation. I look forward to being able to embrace Liu Xia in the sunshine and personally pay my respects and express my gratitude to her. I look forward to this farewell not only for you, but at the same time for the countless souls behind you, and for the tens of millions of compatriots who were deprived of their lives by the totalitarian Communists, and for all of those who died without a place of burial and to whom the living were too late or unable to bid farewell. I look forward to the white roses like mountains and seas covering the grief and memories they are due.

Xiaobo, may your soul come back!

*Translated by Andréa Worden*

NOTES

Written October 2017, on Xiaobo's 100th day of death.

1. Patricio Guzman, *The Pearl Button*, 2015. One of the main topics of the documentary is the forced disappearances and political killings that occurred in Chile under General Augusto Pinochet's regime, particularly during the 1970s.

2. Wang Xiaobo, "Why Do I Write—Preface," *The Ages Trilogy* (Guangzhou: Flower City Publishing House, 1997).—Trans.

3. In May 1989 three men in their twenties from Hunan Province, Yu Dongyue (b. 1964), Yu Zhijian (1963–2017), and Lu Decheng (b. 1963), came to Beijing to voice support for the democracy movement at Tiananmen Square and hung two banners on each side of Tiananmen Gate. After that they threw eggs filled with red paint at Mao's portrait hanging above Tiananmen Gate. They were subsequently arrested and imprisoned, Yu Zhijian for life, Yu Dongyue for twenty years, and Lu Decheng for sixteen years.—Trans.

4  Sun Zhigang (1976–2003), a university graduate and migrant worker, was beaten to death in a custody and repatriation center in March 2003 after being detained in Guangzhou for lacking the appropriate residential permit. A public uproar about the case led to abolition of the custody and repatriation system.—Trans.

5  Liu Xiaobo: "A Letter to Liao Yiwu," January 13, 2000, originally published on *Boxun*, translated by Perry Link, in *Liu Xiaobo: No Enemies, No Hatred*, ed. Perry Link, Tienchi Martin-Liao, and Liu Xia (Cambridge MA: The Belknap Press of Harvard University Press, 2012), 287–88.—Trans.

# Unfinished Journey
*Mo Zhixu*

It has already been a month since Xiaobo left us. Grief and anger have gradually subsided, but my yearning is the same as before. At this time, writing down some words may perhaps make the memories of him last forever and my mind feel calmer.

## The Legend of Liu Xiaobo

Before I met Xiaobo, I had known his name for fourteen years.

In September 1986 I had just begun studying at Xiamen University. Soon our dormitory building had the first female dorm rooms. Compared with the unsophisticated boys in our computer science department, most of the female students majoring in international finance came from Beijing, Shanghai, or other similar big cities. Their perspective and contacts were broader than ours. Once at a gathering, a female student took out a stack of copied pages and explained to us that it was a speech given in Beijing by the most popular "dark horse" at the time. Today, looking back, this should be a quick discourse of Xiaobo's rebuke of contemporary Chinese literature. However, at the time, I didn't exactly understand "culture fever" (*wenhua re*), and I couldn't understand where his speech was good, where it was delightful, and how it was pioneering. Instead, what I remember is the name Liu Xiaobo and the nickname "dark horse."

In the blink of an eye it was June 2, 1989. I once again heard on the radio the name Liu Xiaobo as well as the names of the others who constituted the Four Gentlemen. Dozens of hours later, it was indescribable shock, grief, anger, and powerlessness. Liu Xiaobo, together with the others' names, was deeply imprinted in my memory. Later, on the radio or in the press, I also heard or read articles that criticized the "black hands" and the news that he was released because of "meritorious acts." However, during those tumultuous years of being investigated after 1989, then graduating and seeking to survive after my life was abruptly changed due to participation in the student movement, these things flashed by without leaving much of a trace. The youthful era was stifling and depressive. I was not aware that Xiaobo was at that time continuing to devote his efforts to promoting the human rights cause and to pursuing historical justice. He was consequently in and out of jail.

It is worth mentioning that as spring turned into summer in 1990, I discovered by chance the book, *The Fog of Metaphysics*, in my good friend Haizi's dorm room. As an engineering student who had no foundation in the humanities, I persisted in finishing this thick book, which was hundreds of pages long. I did so because of two words: Liu Xiaobo. As for the content of the book, I could barely understand it; I was only faintly aware that it was a theoretical criticism of the ideology of the party-state.

Six months later, because I became acquainted with Mao Yuyuan and Wang Kang, I began the long journey of reading, observing, and thinking about contemporary Chinese issues. Having had the experience of reading *The Fog of Metaphysics*, I admired Xiaobo's ability to use a theoretical weapon to criticize the ideology of the party-state, but I felt even more intellectually frustrated because of my shallow understanding. However, this gap also kindled my thirst for knowledge and stimulated me to follow my colleagues' example. (The other work that stimulated me at that time was *Sacrifice to Utopia* by Su Xiaokang, who is in exile overseas.)

The enlightenment liberalization in the 1980s was the direct impetus for the 1989 student movement. Students in my age, despite their lack of consciousness, eventually were affected by Xiaobo's generation. This point became crystal clear after we experienced the suppression on June 4. I remember in the spring of 1990, I woke up one morning with a hangover, and I didn't know what was wrong. I grabbed a copy of a book my lower bunk classmate had on hand, *Selected Poems by Five Poets*, and casually flipped through the pages. It began with a few poems by Bei Dao, which I had actually read long before, but at that earlier time not only was I unclear about the meaning of the poems, but they also didn't leave much of an impression. However, on that morning in 1990, as a young student who had experienced the impact of the suppression of June 4, I felt suddenly as if I had received an electric shock and understood every single word of Bei Dao's poetry:

Let me tell you, world,
I—do—not—believe!
If a thousand challengers lie beneath your feet,
Count me as number thousand and one.[1]

Isn't this the heartfelt voice of a youth who had begun to thoroughly break away from the system and come out from his previous blind faith?

The results from the reflections made by the generation of Xiaobo, Su Xiaokang, and Bei Dao on the totalitarian system were the starting point of my generation's awareness and thinking. And yet the common position on the totalitarian system, especially the resolute condemnation of the system's brutality, which was exposed during the June 4 crackdown, is also a common understanding between Xiaobo's generation and me. In this sense, I've long had an inextricable spiritual connection with the legendary dark horse Liu Xiaobo and the black hand Liu Xiaobo.

## My Friend Liu Xiaobo

In early 1998 I came to Beijing again. This time, I was an editor of *Strategy and Management*, and I started to have many contacts with the remnants of the post-1989 liberal intellectual groups and opposition circles. I had quite a bit of interaction with He Jiadong and Chen Ziming because of their manuscripts. Xiaobo at that time was still in the Dalian Center of RTL.

In or around the year 2000, enthusiasm for the internet continued to rise, and freedom of speech enclaves on online Bulletin Board Systems (BBS) suddenly popped up, as if out of nowhere, and attracted more and more people. Some liberal intellectuals crowded together on the "Century Salon" BBS. After a period of anonymous exchanges and confrontation, they gradually revealed their true identities and began to meet offline and dine together. One day that winter, after I was invited to the home of my online friend "snoopy" (Cui Weiping), I discovered, with a shock, that one of the guests was none other than the dark horse and black hand I had known about for many years—Liu Xiaobo.

Cui Weiping was our mutual friend. In her home, the atmosphere was casual from the beginning. Although Xiaobo and I were very far apart in terms of age and experience, we had both a common inscription in our memories—June 4, 1989, and the same fundamental stance toward the totalitarian system. During nearly ten years of reading and reflecting, I had ingested nourishment mainly from the achievements of the enlightenment liberalization since the 1980s. I had read almost all of that generation's books and articles. Therefore, Xiaobo and I had not only similar values but also an overlapping genealogy of knowledge. There wasn't a need for too much "code." The atmosphere at the dinner table was harmonious. During our verbal exchanges, a tacit understanding had already been established; it was then very easy to regard each other as a kindred spirit.

Although in my heart, I think of Xiaobo as an older mentor, I have never called him Teacher Xiaobo. Rather we have always called each other Xiaobo and Old Mo. The onetime dark horse and black hand of legend, Liu Xiaobo, became "my friend Liu Xiaobo."

## Fellow Colleague Liu Xiaobo

China around the year 2000 had a dual orientation: the authorities still maintained the post-1989 policy of suppression and showed absolutely no mercy with respect to various social changes. For example, the suppression of Falun Gong, heavy sentences for the members of the China Democracy Party and the New Youth Study Group case, and so on, one after another. On the other hand, because of the deepening of marketization and the successes of becoming a member of the WTO and winning the bid to host the 2008 Olympics, profound economic and social transformation was underway. People generally had more optimistic expectations about the progress of the times.

At this time, Liu Xiaobo, or rather all the opposition and pan-dissident groups, were actually pulled in both directions. In the face of the party-state that still insisted on dictatorial rule, it was necessary to stick to the tradition of dissent and opposition, to persist in civil subjectivity, and to emphasize that "the future of free China exists in civil society." At the same time, the tragic memory of the June 4 suppression was still an aching, dull pain. Xiaobo needed to work together with the Tiananmen Mothers group to pursue the realization of historical justice. All of this prompted Xiaobo and his fellow colleagues who persisted in their dissent to stick to moral values and the pursuit of historical justice.

But with respect to the other direction, Xiaobo was also fully aware that the realization of historical justice and moral values was inseparable from fundamental institutional transformation. This required more extensive social momentum. In Xiaobo's view, if we were going to keep pace with the profound economic and social transformations, we had to make great efforts to form links with a wider range of social groups. We had to combine the positions and morals held by dissenting groups with the rising social forces that were just then emerging and ultimately help bring about the transition to a liberal democracy, including with the authorities themselves.

Xiaobo's own dissenting political commentary, his co-founding of the Independent Chinese PEN Center as a freelance writers' organization, and his participation in and taking the helm of the Democratic China website as a platform for dissenting views and expression demonstrated the hard work of Xiaobo and the group of pan-dissidents and opposition in the first direction. Moreover, his continuous online signature appeals, his support for, and participation in, the rights defense movement, and finally, the drafting of Charter 08 and organizing the collection of signatures for it, demonstrated the intention of Xiaobo and the pan-dissident group who were trying to grasp the progress of the times. He and they reached out to a wider range of social groups and then through the "interaction between government and people" sought to promote the transformation.

During this period, I was energetically slinging bricks (i.e., posting comments) on the internet and was also involved in editing *Strategy and Management*. I also served as the head of the commentary department of a newspaper. My social identity could be classified as a rising media and internet commentator. Because of the experience of 1989, in a certain corner of my heart, the flame of seeking historical justice had never been extinguished. I inherently held a position of dissent and opposition. Therefore, I inadvertently spanned the two directions that Xiaobo and the pan-dissident group had worked hard to achieve. I had a wide overlap of interests and topics to discuss with Xiaobo. We had quite a few circles in common, and our interactions gradually became closer.

In the spring of 2005, I moved to Chegongzhuang in Xicheng District in Beijing. Xiaobo and his wife lived near the Garden Bridge. Since we lived close to each other, our contacts became even closer. At the same time, under the relatively relaxed atmosphere before the Olympics, Xiaobo also had more freedom in his activities which enabled him to communicate with a wider range of groups and have more frequent social activities. In my network and media gatherings, I would try to invite Xiaobo to participate. As an '89 student, I was often invited by Xiaobo to attend parties that tended to have a dissident quality about them.

Of course, we also had some relaxing times. Hao Jian and Cui Weiping would take us on excursions to the mountains, and Bei Zhicheng, Wang Xiaoshan, and I often accompanied Xiaobo and his wife for wine tasting— Red Fort (a kind of sparkling wine) at Zhongzhong's shop, who was often waiting for us to stop by.

"No wine untasted," in the generally still oppressive atmosphere of the era, we had our own little world where we could temporarily escape and listen to Xiaobo talking about his favorite poems, novels, and movies and proudly looking back on his golden age of the 1980s.

### I, Subtly Influenced

Maybe it was because he understood the hardships on the road of dissent and, accordingly, its unsustainability that Xiaobo did not want us '89 students to embark on this road. Rather, he suggested that we first have suitable work and corresponding social roles, especially independent financial ability, that we "buy a house when one should, buy a car when it's needed." I heard him say words like this to people many times. To me, he also half-jokingly said: "Old Mo, properly make books and just like today, it's okay to have money to invite me for a meal."

In the many years we had contact before he went to prison, Xiaobo's influence on me was more of an imperceptible, subtle nature. It was so subtle that for quite a long time, I didn't realize as I changed how much influence Xiaobo had had on me. I, who am a bit arrogant at heart, am always more inclined to see these changes as a result of my own proactive choices. But now, in retrospect, I understand this was not the case.

First of all, I joined the Independent Chinese PEN Center completely because of Xiaobo. Now that I've mentioned it, there is another story here. On October 30, 2004, ICPC held the second Freedom to Write Award ceremony in the outskirts of Beijing. Since many people were invited in advance, it was expected to be a grand gathering. The day before the meeting, Xiaobo sent me a text message inviting me to participate. However, the next day I didn't attend because I was going to participate in the Beijing Paowang team's soccer match. On the surface, I regarded my playing a soccer match as a justifiable reason, but I also knew more or less that not to participate in the ceremony was to avoid it and that I didn't want to get involved in the dissident circle.

Perhaps out of guilt after the soccer game, I called Xiaobo to invite him to participate in a dinner party that some *Guantian* netizens and I were holding.[2] I knew this was an activity he enjoyed attending. Because the location of the Bamboo House Restaurant, in Sweet Nectar Park, was very far away from the place where the award ceremony was held, Xiaobo was quite late when he arrived. I still remember the first words he said when he got out of the car: "Old Mo, I came from so far away, and you only invited me here for a 36-yuan roast duck dinner?"

During subsequent dinner parties, Xiaobo often brought up this story poking fun at me, along with my evasion of the award ceremony, to "enliven the atmosphere," which made me feel embarrassed. So when Xiaobo once again teased me with this story during a dinner party, I decided that in order to preempt Xiaobo, I might as well join the Independent Chinese PEN Center!

Second, my writings of dissent actually started because of a push from Xiaobo. Although I had joined ICPC, I was only a bystander compared to Old Liao Yiwu, Zhang Zuhua, Jiang Qisheng, Yu Jie, Wang Yi, Yu Shicun, Ye Du, and others in the group. These were friends who worked with Xiaobo at the time. At the same time, as a writer, I basically didn't write any so-called sensitive articles. Besides writing commentary for news media such as *Southern Metropolitan Daily*, I was even more content to say whatever I wanted on the internet and be a "famous online brick" (i.e., comment poster). I was immensely pleased with myself at being described "the only figure using comment posts to become famous on the Chinese Internet."

Until July 2006, due to my involvement with Chen Guangcheng's trial, I went to Linyi, in Shandong Province, with Gao Zhisheng and several other friends.[3] After I returned, I talked with Xiaobo on MSN about the trip. During our discussion, Xiaobo encouraged me to write about it. In the end, Xiaobo personally edited my article, titled "Recalling a Joyful Trip," and published it on the Democratic China website. The concluding paragraph, which was also the most outstanding, was, in fact, written by Xiaobo:

> From repression for speaking out with the force of justice to the intimidation and threats that were both comical and ridiculous; these probably indicate both the helplessness of the doomsday dictatorship as well as the helplessness of the civil resistance. There is no doubt how this farce will eventually end, but the way it ends will still be a comedy, using the famous poet T. S. Eliot's well-known phrase—the doomsday dictatorship collapses, "not with a bang but a whimper."

This was my first article formally published on a dissident platform. Coincidentally, the editor who published this article was Su Xiaokang, who was in exile overseas. It can be said that from that time on, from becoming a member of ICPC to writing essays of dissent, I began an unconscious transformation into a dissident.

In the end, my "being made sensitive" (*bei mingan*) was also because of Xiaobo. At a party held before June 4, 2007, Xiaobo asked me to write a June 4 elegy. In the middle of the night on June 2, because I launched an online piece of performance art titled "Crossing the Metropolis: From Beijing University to Tiananmen Square," I was taken into custody by the Beijing Municipal Public Security Bureau's domestic security unit (*guobao*) and was then sent back to my hometown. Due to my inexperience, when I was seized, I did not act quickly enough to shut down my mobile phone, and the police grabbed it. Just at this time, Xiaobo, who was a night owl, sent a text asking me if "the elegy was finished or not." Since then, as a member of ICPC and Xiaobo's friend, I became a monitoring target of the *guobao*, and judging from various signs, it was because I was seen as someone close to Xiaobo that I became a priority monitoring target. Since those monitoring me were the *guobao* officers focusing on the June 4 and ICPC groups, in my long-term dealings with them, what we talked about the most were Xiaobo, June 4, and ICPC.

## Continuing the Unfinished Journey

Next came Xiaobo's detention and sentencing. Consequently, I got more involved in appeals and calls for support and took the initiative to participate in ICPC's elections so that I was, to an even greater extent, irreversibly drifting further away.

Back then, if there had been no Xiaobo, would I have joined ICPC? If there had been no Xiaobo, when would I have written my first article expressing dissent? If there had been no Xiaobo, would I, because of my writing, have become a target of monitoring by the *guobao*, and thus more irreversibly shift toward dissent? And if the follow-up brought by Xiaobo's detention and sentencing hadn't occurred, what kind of situation would I be in today?

Looking back on that first meeting in the winter of 2000, I can't remember what we talked about, but now that I'm reminded of the meeting, it may be the most important day of my life. Although Xiaobo never actively pushed me to do anything, without my interactions with Xiaobo, everything that happened later would not have happened. In fact, Xiaobo's influence on me was not through any direct impetus but rather through his very existence. Xiaobo's existence was to me both an example and a benchmark. Similarly, from that day we first met until now, I wonder, if someone like Liu Xiaobo can do 100 percent, why can't I just do 1 percent?

From the time I learned of the name "dark horse" until today, thirty-one years have passed, spanning my youth, adulthood, and prime of life until today's "being-toward-death," until Xiaobo's final farewell. It wasn't until now that I finally realized that Xiaobo's influence in my life was so huge, so irreplaceable, and so completely cherished.

Today, Xiaobo has left us forever, but the moral values that Xiaobo and I and many more colleagues have insisted on, the historical justice we have pursued, and the liberal democratic transition we have strived to promote, all still seem exceedingly remote. However, just in the way Xiaobo's resolve manifested as a willingness "to die a thousand times without regret," the journey of seeking justice will often transcend an individual's life. The important thing is not necessarily the result. As Xiaobo wrote, "People are destined to die, certainly it is so. But even if one is to perish, one should perish while resisting death."[4] Perhaps, in the journey of pursuing justice, we should, like Xiaobo, resemble the legendary Sisyphus, work hard, and make sacrifices, regardless of results, until the last moment of life.

*Translated by Andréa Worden*

NOTES

1. Excerpt from Bei Dao, "The Answer," trans. Bonnie S. McDougall, Poetry Foundation, https://www.poetryfoundation.org/poems/50088/the-answer -56d22cd8d69d0.—Trans.
2. *Guantian* was a current affairs e-magazine on the Tianya BBS.—Trans.
3. Chen Guangcheng (b. 1971) is a blind self-taught lawyer who was subjected to repeated detention and house arrest because of his rights defense work. Chen obtained political asylum in the United States in 2012. Gao Zhisheng is likewise a rights defense lawyer who has been repeatedly imprisoned and placed under house arrest.—Trans.
4. This was the penultimate sentence of Liu Xiaobo's PhD dissertation.—Trans.

# Liu Xiaobo Turned Radical Suffering into Calm

*Su Xiaokang*

How can we measure the distance from Liu Xiaobo's "China Needs 300 Years of Colonialism" to "I Have No Enemies"? It's the distance between culture and politics, between Nietzsche and Gandhi, and between a rebelliousness and arrogance against everything, and self-examination, humility, and a willingness to descend into hell.

Liu Xiaobo was criticized for being "culturally radical" but also for being "politically moderate." Who else in China has been attacked for both?

The Liu Xiaobo who led students out of Tiananmen Square in the early hours of June 4 as soldiers fired on protesters was different from the Liu Xiaobo who won the Nobel Peace Prize while in prison twenty years later. Although as untamed as ever, he had developed an inner calmness.

## The Dark Horse at the End of the Cultural Fever

Sometime in late summer 1988, Liu Dong and I teamed up to draft a synopsis for a television documentary on the May Fourth Movement. Liu Dong was a PhD student under Li Zehou, and out of respect for his teacher, he delivered a written challenge to Liu Xiaobo for a debate at the Chinese Academy of Social Sciences.[1] I didn't attend the debate, but people told me it ended in a draw and that both of them stammered a bit, which made the debate more interesting. This was during the final flowering of China's "cultural fever," and Liu Xiaobo, known as a "dark horse," was one of the earliest examples of what later became known as China's "angry youth."

After decades of exhausting reversals, brutality, and famine, culture suddenly became fashionable in the 1980s, and everyone seemed compelled to an ideal of "If my lines don't startle others, in death I'll find no rest." *River Elegy* was considered the epitome of this movement and raised eyebrows inside and outside of China by flogging tradition and lauding westernization. But Liu Xiaobo just snorted contemptuously:

> Behind its oral commentary and visuals, *River Elegy* encapsulates millennia of Chinese vanity rather than thoroughly acknowledging China's backwardness. For example, the dragon dance at the beginning is filmed in a rousing and exciting way, very powerful. If I had filmed it, I would have shown how shriveled, weak and fucked up Chinese are without a single word of commentary. But *River Elegy*'s hidden meaning is that China is a great nation. The disparity between the listlessness of 99 percent of the Chinese and the mental state depicted in that footage is just too great. In my essay "The Crisis of New Period Literature," I point out that Chinese have all become impotent, both physically and spiritually!

Chinese scholars in Hong Kong, Taiwan, Europe, and North America were unanimous in pointing out *River Elegy*'s radical cultural bent, but Liu Xiaobo was even more radical:

> I admit that my study of Chinese culture ultimately reached a dead end. If you attribute the problem to political corruption coupled with cultural corruption, you'll ask, why has Confucian thinking been able to dominate China for so many years, with its evil influence remaining even now? I can't answer. I've said that it may be possibly related to race. I absolutely do not believe that China's backwardness was created by a bunch of fatuous and self-indulgent rulers; everyone had a part in it, because a system is created by people. All of China's tragedies have been crafted, directed, acted and enjoyed by the Chinese themselves. There's no use complaining about others.

These quotes come from the November 1988 issue of *Hong Kong's Emancipation Monthly* (the precursor to *Open Magazine*), in an interview with Liu Xiaobo by chief editor Jin Zhong. Liu's arrogance in this extraordinarily shocking conversation makes the laments in *River Elegy* pale in comparison. The most famous quote from the interview is of course Liu's assertion that "China needs 300 years of colonialism." If only a few of Chinese classic quotations from the 1980s are to be selected, this will absolutely have to be one of them.

Liu Xiaobo's dark horse image carried the rebellious undertones of a Nietzsche, a Foucault, or a Sartre, even though he did not read Nietzsche until he went to prison. He wrote, "The first time I read Foucault was in 1994. His *Madness and Civilization* and *Discipline and Punish* are deeply stirring. Even my wife, who seldom reads theory, was thoroughly engrossed when I read them out loud to her." His reading was more a way of sorting out his own extremes. In terms of the radicalization that Yu Ying-shih traces in his history of modern Chinese thought, the most extreme figure is Tan Sitong, who kept one foot on the collapsing ruins of tradition. The anti-traditionalists of subsequent generations would not even brush the edge of tradition, maintaining that everything had to come from the West; Liu Xiaobo's infatuation with Foucault's "critique of power" is one example.

By the end of 1988, the cultural fever was waning. It might be said that the fever produced political ague; otherwise Liu Xiaobo might have taken even more daring cultural leaps. But the withdrawal of culture coincidentally led the feverishly restless literary scholar Liu Xiaobo onto another battlefield, where things got out of hand and brought him to the brink between life and death several times. . . .

## A Moth to the Flame

François Mignet's *History of the French Revolution* holds that revolution broke out against autocracy just as it became willing to carry out reform. This applies to China in 1989. But China had another special characteristic at that time: just when the public became most fearless, intellectuals were the most cautious, possibly out of a combination of weariness with revolution, dread of politics, and hope for peaceful evolution. The storm blew up on the capital's largest political space, where all kinds of revolutionary demons had performed their mad dance and where the lost souls of the inebriated fluttered. The angry students were ready to stake their lives against the Communist Party, while the "long beard" intellectuals were generally in a state of "political stupidity syndrome," cheering and advising from the sidelines but unwilling to join the kids in the trenches. It was at this moment that Liu Xiaobo rushed to Beijing from New York like a moth to the flame, and without a word threw himself in with the students, although berated for "kicking up a fuss" and booed for "putting on a show." The fact that the entire elite stratum at that time was unable to perform such a simple action shows that the literati, scared straight by Mao's campaigning masses, were incapable of creating democracy.

Liu Xiaobo's lack of an elite bearing was secondary; he knew to seek equal standing from the student movement. Around two weeks later this standing enabled him, as the field army's tanks and machine guns surrounded Tiananmen Square from Chang'an Avenue West, to convince thousands of students to accept his negotiation with the apparatus of slaughter and follow him in withdrawing from the square on that somber dawn.

It was the only successful negotiation out of many that occurred during the 1989 student movement. Liu Xiaobo not only rescued the crazed students from certain death but also saved Deng Xiaoping and Yang Shangkun from carrying out a mass slaughter beneath the Memorial to the People's Heroes. Carried out without fanfare, this act of virtue was worth half a Nobel Peace Prize in itself.

But no one credited Liu Xiaobo with this meritorious act at the time. Instead, the Chinese authorities arrested him. This man had managed against all odds to prevent a slaughter at the square, and they had to make use of him to tell the world that no one had been killed in Beijing. I don't know if Liu Xiaobo would rather die than obey, but the truth was that he didn't see anyone killed on the square. The bloodbath had occurred on Chang'an Avenue West, so what was he supposed to say? He let the killers use him, for which the victims could never forgive him and which he deeply regretted. But this knotty problem, on which history has yet to reach a verdict, completely changed Liu Xiaobo. From then on his wild arrogance began to wind down, leaving room for modesty.

He was used to firing off at both left and right, and in his *The Monologues of a Doomsday's Survivor*, published in 1993 after he left prison in January 1991, he castigated the students he'd rescued:

> After 1976 the complete ethical collapse wrought by the disintegration of moral order that Communist beliefs had imposed on the Chinese people was also demonstrated at the roiling Tiananmen Square during the 1989 protest movement; the unbearable filth of the place was the best demonstration of this. They could engage in revolution, rebellion

and hunger strikes while ignoring the most basic moral standards . . .
There was rubbish on every square meter of the square . . . Another major
characteristic on the square was the shocking waste . . . Some students
actually believed that the whole world owed them something for taking
part in the hunger strike . . . I hated those students and myself . . . It
was well deserved! Who made me strive for fame and compliments?
Writing this much, I feel the pen trembling in my hand.

## Standing with the Victims

Liu Xiaobo's moral indignation brought him under even greater moral
accusation by others. He was always instinctively berating people, and his
actions always went too far. Even now, it is by a moral standard that the
Chinese judge him, which means that not only are China's intellectuals
"politically immature," but the general public is also "morally infantile."

Liu Xiaobo had only one form of humility: facing a lost soul. That lost
soul was only seventeen years old. Seventeen years was a symbol. It symbolized the innocence of the dead, the cowardice of the living, and the
tyranny of the powerful:

> I haven't the right or the courage
> to proffer flowers and a poem
> to the seventeen-year-old's smile
> even though I know
> the seventeen-year-old bears no grudge
> . . . . . . . . . . . . . . . . . . . . . . . . . . . . . . . .
> Transcending age
> transcending death
> seventeen years old
> has become eternal.2

"To the Seventeen-Year-Old" shows us a humble Liu Xiaobo for the
first time. After leaving prison in 1991, Liu went to visit Ding Zilin and
Jiang Peikun, "as a student, and as a culpable member of the younger
generation."[3] As soon as he saw their son Jiang Jielian's urn, "he turned
and excused himself, and half an hour later came with a bouquet of fresh

flowers and suddenly fell to the floor weeping before Lian'er's tablet." When he left prison for the second time, on Lunar New Year's Eve in 1999, he once again visited Ding Zilin and Jiang Peikun and obtained a record of Inquiry listing 155 victims:

> As soon as I came in the door, without even taking time to drink some water, I hurriedly began reading "Witnessing the Massacre and Seeking Justice," and with the first page my eyes were wet. In tears I read it out loud to Liu Xia. After almost every paragraph I had to stop because I was choking with sobs. I don't know how often I stopped, and each time I did, the silence was like death. I could hear the souls of the dead crying out for justice in the underworld, so weak, so helpless, so heartbreaking.4

In China speech is tightly controlled, and information is blocked. Even in the case of a home-grown Nobel Peace Prize laureate, there is little material on his achievements or upbringing. Among the very few texts that describe Liu Xiaobo, "Our Acquaintance and Friendship with Liu Xiaobo," by Ding Zilin and Jiang Peikun, is extremely valuable in depicting a flesh-and-blood Liu Xiaobo.

I've discovered that the dark horse of incomparably intense anti-traditionalism revealed in his writings was in fact very traditional. He always addressed Ding and Jiang as his parents, and it mattered a great deal to him that most of the dead were children. He expressed regret: "For ten years I've been constantly wracked with guilt. In Qincheng Prison I sold out the blood of the dead and wrote a statement of repentance." In China, this humanitarian spirit is expressed as treating people appropriately, as when they are elderly or very young, but placing human life above all else is very Western.

Although repeatedly imprisoned, he refused to go into exile until on the verge of death. Rather than say that he chose to accompany the mothers of the victims, it is more that he accompanied the dead, and no one knew the price he paid for it. Before Charter 08 was published, Liu Xiaobo regularly Skyped with me, and he once spoke of something that had just happened: The police at the neighborhood police station constantly harassed him, searching his home and detaining him, but he always tried his hardest to befriend the police chief, although the man was an utter scoundrel. The police chief had recently brought several thugs along to provoke Liu Xiaobo by punching him in the face, then took him back to the police station and held him for more than ten hours. Liu Xiaobo returned home infuriated and was determined to submit an official complaint, but the police chief came running to his home and knelt down and begged his forgiveness. This was an episode of torment (physical and mental), and I could hear in it a hellish humiliation. For Liu Xiaobo, there was no torment in prison, where he could commune with Foucault and Sartre. But being released from prison was torture because he faced the dead. No wonder that when he heard he'd won the Nobel Prize, he blurted out, "This prize belongs to the dead of June 4."

### Crown or Crucifix?

The Nobel Peace Prize is said to be "emperor level." When China's younger generation learned of it, they were very excited, but they didn't know who Liu Xiaobo was. "He must be one of our great party members, a great official . . . and a great leader who does great deeds for his people."[5] There were quite a few opposing voices in China and abroad. Given how enormously controversial Liu Xiaobo was, it would have been strange if no one expressed doubts.

I don't dare predict how much Liu Xiaobo's Nobel Prize will affect China's actual politics. The pleasant surprise of the Chinese was accompanied by a significant degree of admiration and even "national pride," but very few people really understood Oslo's meaning. This situation makes the recipient bear a heavy debt of honor.

While Liu Xiaobo was in prison, the international community and the Chinese civil movement placed great hopes in him, but what could he do? The international level was too complex for deep discussions, and in any case, the West still wanted to do business with China, with no better place for investment at that time. Within China itself the difficulties were great, its politics reprehensible and popular sentiment in disarray, so where was an active and organized force to come from?

Purely from the perspective of the Nobel Peace Prize, China's twenty years of rapid economic growth, massive corruption, and suppression had beyond all hopes produced a peace prize laureate engaged in "long and nonviolent struggle."[6] At the same time, the civil anti-tyranny movement was accompanied by an intense rebellious mentality that was sparking prairie fires. The nonviolent concept of gradual progress, moderation, and dialogue was rapidly being cast aside as worthless. According to statistics from the Ministry of Public Security, there were more than 8,700 instances of protest in China in 1993, while by 2008 this number had grown to more than 120,000. This exponential increase resulted in the CCP spending roughly as much on "stability maintenance" as on national defense, while the civil movement shifted from waiting for an "Uprising of Chen Sheng and Wu Guang" to directly calling for another 1911 Xinhai Revolution.[7] Those advocating "peaceful transformation" were disparaged by some radicals as the "nonviolence collaborationist faction" or "pro-CCP reformist faction." Charter 08, emerging in this political climate, also came under attack and was labeled as part of a "capitulationist ideological line." At the time that Liu Xiaobo achieved his greatest honor, he also faced an even tougher mission.

Ding Zilin once advised Liu Xiaobo to write scholarly works and spend less time writing news commentaries that "just annoyed people." Liu Xiaobo replied, "I can't turn back," and joked that he wanted to earn some royalties for Liu Xia in case he went to prison again. In fact, he wanted to post news commentaries on the internet to plant seeds of rationality, moderation, and nonviolence in China. Having experienced the desolate days of the Tiananmen massacre and witnessed the heartbreak of mothers mourning their children, Liu Xiaobo tempered his arrogance and radicalism and also used philosophical principles to rationalize how gradual and peaceful transformation would benefit Chinese society as a whole. His PhD studies weren't wasted; a foundation in philosophy helped him explain his thinking clearly and colloquially, even if no one appreciated it at the time.

In a certain sense, the 2010 Nobel Peace Prize had been won on the seething square and bloodied avenues of Beijing in spring 1989. The students at Tiananmen Square were driven by the spirit of serving their country. When they were crushed by tanks, it triggered a domino effect that led to the collapse of the Communist camp, but the 1989 generation nurses regret and hatred to this day. Ultimately it was Liu Xiaobo who represented their ideals and rebellion and entered the Nobel Hall. At a deeper level, it was not the living who chose Liu Xiaobo but rather those who fell on Chang'an Avenue. They wanted this former dark horse to represent them in order to tell the world that killing people isn't politics but only brutality, and killing in vengeance only compounds the brutality. China must fight for the day when people can talk reason.

*Translated by Stacy Mosher*

## NOTES

1. Li Zehou (b. 1930) is a Chinese scholar of philosophy and intellectual history credited with "emancipating a whole generation of young Chinese intellectuals from Communists ideology" (in the words of Princeton professor Yu Ying-shih). After criticizing the Chinese government's response to the 1989 Tiananmen protests, Li was placed under house arrest for three years, after which he went to live in the United States.—Trans.
2. Liu Xiaobo, "To the Seventeen-Year-Old" (in Chinese), Epoch Times, June 2, 2004, http://www.epochtimes.com/gb/4/6/2/n556102.htm.—Trans.
3. Ding and Jiang's seventeen-year-old son, Jiang Jielian, was killed on the night of June 3, 1989. They subsequently became leaders of the Tiananmen Mothers campaign.—Trans.
4. Liu Xiaobo, "Vibrations from the Tomb" (in Chinese), Epoch Times, April 5, 2004, http://www.epochtimes.com/gb/4/4/5/n501121.htm.—Trans.
5. Hannah Beach, Austin Ramzy, "China's Eyes on the Prize," *Time*, October 25, 2010, http://content.time.com/time/magazine/article/0,9171,2025569,00.html.—Trans.
6. Norwegian Nobel Committee, "The Nobel Peace Prize for 2010," herein.
7. The Uprising of Chen Sheng (?–208 BC) and Wu Guang (?–208 BC), also known as the Dazexiang Uprising (209 BC), was the first rebellion against Qin rule following the death of China's first emperor, Qin Shihuang. Chen and Wu were army officers who organized villagers to rebel against the government. The Xinhai Revolution was a popular rebellion in 1911 that overthrew China's last imperial dynasty, the Qing, and established the Republic of China.—Trans.

# A Formidable Personality

*Jean-Philippe Béja*

When I first heard that Liu Xiaobo had reached the final stage of liver cancer, I was in Hong Kong, hoping to hop on a plane to see him before he left this world. Unhappily, his "release" was very relative, and I soon learned that it would be impossible to say goodbye to an old friend that I hadn't seen for more than eight years.

After he died, I saw Liu Xia's face while she dispersed his ashes in the sea. I couldn't help from crying. But when I heard Liu Xiaoguang thank the party for the way it had treated his brother's cancer, I was terribly angry. Thanking the party? For what? For having done nothing to save the Nobel Prize laureate? For having imprisoned him for eleven years because he had dared express his ideas? July 13, 2017 was one of the saddest days in my life.

I couldn't help from remembering the last time I had seen him, in October 2008, when we joked about all our friends, especially the prodemocracy activists that he had introduced to me. On that day, Xiaobo was in a mood of nostalgia. He talked a lot about friendship that, he said, he valued more than everything, more than comradeship. It was a nostalgic evening, one of the rare times that I saw him with Liu Xia.

A few months before that night, he had insulted me: I was in Beijing and had tried to contact him as usual, but he was under house arrest. One day as I was going home, I got a phone call from him, and he told me to go to his place and wait for him. I did. His wife, Liu Xia, let me in and told me that Xiaobo had left so that the plainclothes officers who were watching him would follow him and allow me to enter his apartment so that I could wait for him. We had hardly started talking when a security guard knocked at the door and said to Liu Xia: "There is a foreigner here. Let him out or I shall call the police, who will take you." She refused, but when the guard left, I was worried. After a few minutes, there was another knock at the door, and this time, the guard almost pushed his way in. Liu Xia and I then decided that my presence was too dangerous for her, so I left. In the middle of the night, I received a call from Xiaobo, who called me a coward and said that Westerners were really too afraid of the Chinese police. I tried to explain that I left to protect Liu Xia, that I ran absolutely no risk, but he refused to listen. He was absolutely furious. I felt really bad, as I thought I had lost an excellent friend, but I still believed I had acted rightly. I went back to France, and a few months later, I got an email from Xiaobo telling me that Liu Xia was going to France and asking me if I could see her and help her. I was glad to meet her and she told me that Xiaobo had confessed that he had acted a little too rashly with me that night. When I saw him in October 2008, I said that I had been quite angry with him but that I knew it was part of his character. We had a good laugh and spent a very pleasant evening. Both Xiaobo and Liu Xia were then in kind of a nostalgic mood, and we spent a lot of time speaking of the importance of friendship. How could I know it was the last time I would see him? After his arrest, I often saw Liu Xia and admired (and still do) her incredible courage. Although she was not that interested in politics, she learned and did all she could to try to obtain Xiaobo's release. She has spent all these years under police surveillance but couldn't tell her husband what her situation was until April 2017. For almost a decade, she has been enduring terrible hardships and still is.

### The Dark Horse

The first time I heard about Liu Xiaobo, I was in Jinshan, Shanghai, taking part in a conference organized by the then–minister of culture Wang Meng to celebrate the New Period Literature in the 1980s.[1] Although not a specialist of literature, I had been interested in the literary works published (or made public on the democracy walls)[2] after Mao's death, as they described the sufferings of Chinese citizens under Mao. On the second day of the conference, a photocopy of an article published in the *Shenzhen Qingnian Bao* (*Shenzhen Youth Daily*) started to circulate among the participants, themselves famous writers who had played an important part in the scar literature movement.[3] This article had a huge echo, and soon enough, everybody was discussing the "radical" ideas that it carried. In effect, whereas they were still the target of attacks by conservatives and Maoists, these authors were shocked to be criticized by a young liberal literary critique. All the more so as Liu Xiaobo's writing was particularly acute: he vehemently denounced intellectuals' self-satisfaction and their tendency to assume the position of the counselor to the prince. From the day the article was circulated, Liu's article was at the center of all the conversations, and both conservative and liberal writers criticized it. Of course, it was never mentioned during the debates that were taking place on the stage.

I was particularly interested in this young intellectual, whose radicalism reminded me of his May 4 predecessors.

Liu didn't take into account the reformers' struggle against Maoism; he denounced what he considered wrong, whatever the consequences. His attacks against the new fashion of the "search for the roots," his denunciation of Chinese intellectuals who presented themselves as the main victims of Maoism whereas ordinary people had suffered a lot, were quite bold at the time.[4] Although I didn't meet him, I started to follow his writings. The more I read him, the more I realized he was not afraid of shocking his readers and was not, as were many of his colleagues, a tactician who supported one faction against the other in order to reach his goal.

His declaration to the *Emancipation Monthly* (later renamed *Open Magazine*) that if, in order to reach the present state, Hong Kong had to go through one hundred years of colonialism, then China would need three hundred years of the same, shocked most progressive Western intellectuals, me included. However, after reflection, I understood that it was a kind of provocation: at the time (1988) many Chinese thinkers, shocked by the excesses of Maoism, were convinced that China's closure to Western ideas was one of the reasons of the tragedy it had been through. Liu was then only pushing this reflection to the extreme. In fact, although at the time he was readily accused of "wholesale Westernization," he did not appreciate the way Westerners approached him. In an article he wrote during his stay in Norway, where he had been invited to spend three months, he criticized the ignorance of Western sinologists who did not understand his way of thinking.

Liu showed that he had China's future at heart when, during a stay at Columbia University (then the dream of many Chinese intellectuals) he decided to go back to Beijing to get involved in the prodemocracy movement which was shaking the country. I do not know of anyone else who followed this course. Xiaobo went directly to the Tiananmen Square, where he spent more than two weeks until the June 4 Massacre. His involvement in the movement did not prevent him from criticizing the antidemocratic behavior of the students who, despite this, continued to show their admiration for the man who had dared come back and stay among them.

After the massacre, although he had the possibility to escape, he stayed in Beijing and was arrested. The official press lashed out at the "black hand" behind the demonstrations. Xiaobo spent almost two years in jail.

## The Activist

It was at the end of June 1992 that I finally met him for the first time in Beijing. He was with Zhou Duo, also one of the Four Gentlemen of Tiananmen Square who had launched a hunger strike days before the massacre and who had helped negotiate the evacuation of the Square. Zhou had also been in jail, and both of them wanted to continue the struggle.

I was surprised by Xiaobo's attitude: whereas I was expecting to talk to an angry young man, having in mind the provocateur of the 1980s, I was faced with a rational intellectual who analyzed the general situation in detail. We talked about the 1989 Democracy Movement and of the prospective for democracy in China: "As to the part I played during the 1989 democratic movement, I understood that one cannot completely put one's theory in practice once involved in political action. . . . One has to simplify his ideas and learn how to compromise." I was quite surprised, but more was to come: "During the 1989 pro-democracy movement, I was against the criticism of Deng Xiaoping. . . . Of course he is a despot, but it was useless to attack him. He could have changed his mind if he hadn't felt threatened. . . . I think that the students should have stopped their movement once the dialogue had taken place. But they were too radical, they had no experience of compromise. And besides, they were absolutely unable to coordinate their actions with other social groups. The decisions of the United Conference were never followed." During this long night,

Liu Xiaobo told me he had faith in the role that the *lao sanjie* could play in China's change, as they were very open-minded.[5] He told me that many were favorable to democracy. He also told me that the Deng Xiaoping trip to the south (*nanxun*) had been a very bold move and that it could pave the way to democratization. He said that democrats should work with the reformers who supported the *nanxun*. Whereas Zhou Duo declared that he was interested in "neo-authoritarianism," Xiaobo said he opposed it as he thought that it wouldn't work in China. In sum, my first encounter with him was a huge surprise as he appeared as a calm, rational, and moderate intellectual. Later I was to understand that the June 4 Massacre had changed him and that his mission had become to fight for democracy in order to be able to face the lost souls of that night.

I met Xiaobo regularly from this time on. Every year I went to Beijing; I spent hours with him discussing the Chinese situation, talking about the role of intellectuals in the struggle for democracy. Xiaobo had become an activist, and he was appreciated by all the components of the prodemocracy movement. In 1993 he achieved the dream of most dissidents as he was allowed to go abroad. However, after a few months, he returned to China and started to launch numerous collective letters to defend those who had dared defy the regime. He became one of the best connected activists in the prodemocracy movement. A prolific writer, he published very sensible articles on the political situation in Hong Kong magazines *The Nineties*, *Zhengming*, and *Open* and in the dissident magazine *Democratic China*, published in the United States, that he eventually edited. Every time we met, he explained to me how the prodemocracy movement was developing, described its successes and failures, giving a very realistic picture of the situation. Despite the fact that he had a strong character, Xiaobo was always ready to put his ideas in question and was curious about what others thought of his positions. He took part in most of the actions in favor of democracy after he was released in 1992 until 1996. After three years of silence while serving his *laojiao* (RTL) sentence, he immediately became active in 1999 and organized innumerable petitions to obtain the release of those who had dared defy the party.

Although an opinionated person, he was able to compromise and to rally activists with very different backgrounds. In 2008 he was immensely respected by most actors of the prodemocracy movement, a remarkable feat in a group that appears terribly divided. Intellectuals inside and outside the system, workers, veterans of the Communist Party were all willing to relate to him and often asked for his advice.

These features explain why the party decided to arrest him in 2008. It has often been said that he was arrested because of Charter 08. Although he did take part in its elaboration, he cannot be considered its main writer. However, he spent a lot of energy convincing people with different backgrounds to sign it. Despite his skepticism about the efficiency of the Charter, he decided to assume the main responsibility of its writing.

For all these reasons, Liu Xiaobo's arrest represented a terrible blow to the prodemocracy movement. The respect he enjoyed in the prodemocracy movement explains why the party treated him rashly until the end, eventually forcing his widow, Liu Xia, to disperse his ashes in the ocean so that there would be no grave where people could rally to honor his memory in China. Despite this attempt, commemorations have taken place since his demise, and the tens of thousand miles of China's coastline have become places where his followers have gathered to honor him. The party has succeeded in getting rid of this formidable personality. However, those who continue to fight for democracy in the Middle Empire will keep paying their respects to an intellectual who has sacrificed his life to the cause.

## NOTES

1. Wang Meng (b. 1934) is a Chinese prolific author. In 1957 he was labeled a rightist for his controversial short story criticizing the bureaucracy within CCP, leading to his hardship of reeducation through labor in 1958–78 and his redress in 1979. He served as China's minister of culture from 1986 to 1989 and was dismissed for his excuse of sickness from greeting the martial law troops after the June Fourth Massacre in 1989.—Ed.

2. From November 1978 to December 1979, the Democracy Wall Movement was characterized by the walls in major cities of China where many people put up big-character posters about the political and social issues toward freedom and democracy, termed as the democracy walls.—Ed.

3. Scar literature, or literature of the wounded, was a late 1970s genre of Chinese literature that described the sufferings of the youth, cadres, and intellectuals during the Cultural Revolution (1966–76).—Ed.

4. The Xungen Movement ("search for the roots") was a Chinese cultural and literary movement starting in the late 1980s for the reconstruction of the pluralistic Chinese identity based on local cultures, which were damaged during the Cultural Revolution.—Ed.

5. The Old Three Grades (*lao sanjie*) were middle school or secondary school students when the Culture Revolution started in 1966 who graduated in 1966–68 as the "educated youth" for receiving reeducation in the rural areas.—Ed.

# Tiananmen Square and After

*No Enemies*

# In Memory of My "Best Friend," Liu Xiaobo

*Zhou Duo*

After nine years of torment, Liu Xiaobo finally left us. But he left in such a painful way that people were filled with grief and indignation, and the waves of protest this aroused throughout the world were only natural.

As Liu Xiaobo's "best friend"—as he introduced me to others—I feel compelled to step forward, even though I can't predict the consequences, except to be certain that it will not improve my situation.

In order to write this essay commemorating Liu Xiaobo, I pulled out a copy of his great work *The Monologues of a Doomsday's Survivor*, which I had pushed into the deepest recesses of my bookcase, and carefully read it once again. It shook my innermost being as much as it had the first time I read it. In my view, this book is the most authoritative, comprehensive, and in-depth material for understanding Liu Xiaobo as well as a rare case-observation study for understanding the 1989 protest movement (as Liu Xiaobo defined it) and anticipating the prospects for China's future democratization. Unfortunately, few people have read this important book, and I'd like to take this opportunity to recommend it in hopes that Taiwan's China Times Publishing Company will reprint it.

A person's character is tied to his ideas, but they cannot be considered one and the same. I must frankly admit that Liu Xiaobo was by no means perfect (is anyone on this earth?). Not only was he imperfect, but in fact he had many flaws. But that's not the point of this essay, in which I only wish to correct two current popular misconceptions, both of them one-sided: one embellishes him into a god, and the other vilifies him as a devil. If someone asked me to summarize Liu Xiaobo in one sentence, I would say, "This was a person within whom God and the devil were engaged in constant battle of incomparable intensity that rendered both sides bruised and bloodied." This is all I have to say on this subject for now.

The focus of this essay is to discuss Liu Xiaobo's standpoints and ideas and also to clarify the truth on certain matters.

### Why Did Liu Xiaobo Win the Nobel Peace Prize?

As an influential historical figure, what is truly important about Liu Xiaobo is not his character but rather his ideas and positions. Why did Liu Xiaobo win the Nobel Peace Prize? This question can be answered in a few words: because of his position and concept of "We have no enemies"—which brought him under attack from two sides as he put his principles of peace and nonviolence into practice. He suffered repeated persecution and incarceration under the Chinese Communist Party, guided by the ideology of Marxist radical revolution and its "enemy mentality" (an expression I heard the first time from Liu Xiaobo). He also suffered the invective, slander, and vilification of radical anticommunists who shared an almost identical thought pattern, knowledge structure, and mental foundation with the CCP and referred to Liu as a "no enemy faction," collaborationist, appeaser, capitulator, spineless, whitewasher, and so on. His situation was extremely difficult. Without Liu Xiaobo's superhumanly staunch beliefs and willpower, it would have been impossible for him to persist to the last day of his life. Chinese people with such staunch beliefs and willpower are as rare as unicorns these days. Awarding the Nobel Peace Prize to Liu Xiaobo was undoubtedly international mainstream society's robust affirmation and commendation of his stands and convictions, and this is something that no number of attacks or negations can obliterate.

It is no exaggeration to say that those of us in the moderate reformist faction, including Liu Xiaobo, who insist on "peace, reason and nonviolence" and "we have no enemies," and who advocate that China's modernization and democratization take the road of gradual reform rather than radical revolution, have chosen the hardest path. As the Bible says, we have entered by the narrow gate on the narrow path, and that path has been lined with thorns rather than flowers, with earthshaking curses rather than thundering applause, with sacrifice and martyrdom rather than honor and riches.[1] How many opportunists would accept such a losing proposition?

Only personal experience reveals what prison is like. Nine years behind iron bars was enough to make up for all of Liu Xiaobo's flaws—based on that alone, those living in comfort and security abroad have no reason to be overcritical of Liu Xiaobo.

In June and July 2017 alone, I was "sent on a forced vacation" three times, yet I have heard not a single protest from the overseas democracy movement. I can only understand this as being because 1) they cannot tolerate critical opinions, so my criticism of them has displeased them greatly (in fact, they not only refuse to accept any of my criticism but also do their utmost to defame me as a "traitor," "secret agent," "capitulationist," "whitewasher of the autocratic regime" and so on); and 2) they hope that suppression in China will become even more brutal and violent, leading to the emergence of even more martyrs and victims, enabling them to "arouse the masses," demonstrate that the Communist Party has made no progress, and prove the legitimacy of their empty revolutionary prattle.

That would be bad enough, but even more lamentable is that regardless of wishful thinking, the objective result of certain CCP policy makers initially sentencing Liu Xiaobo to eleven years in prison was to fully comply with extremists in the overseas democracy movement. Through barbarous, mentally defective and outmoded policies, they repeatedly showed the world that the radical revolutionary faction was correct and that people such as Liu Xiaobo and I were wrong! Comparatively speaking, the "soft autocracy" of "enforced vacations" inflicted on me and other dissidents seems much cannier and actually makes overseas protests virtually disappear![2]

Although our country has veered off onto the wrong path and is full of injustice, I refuse to become cynical, dispirited, and despairing because of that. Since I've taken this hardest of roads, I feel compelled to cast off cheap philosophy and have no illusions of rapid success but persevere in unrelenting and resilient struggle. I will not change my faith in gradual reform because of Liu Xiaobo's distressingly unjust treatment. Instead I steadfastly believe that this is the correct road, that it conforms best to the long-term and fundamental interests of the Chinese people and that there is no reason to change course. Only people who lack true faith will change their beliefs at the slightest setback. Regrettably, I don't have space in this essay to provide detailed arguments for our stands and ideas, but those who are interested are welcome to read my three books: *Collected Works on Gradual Democracy*, *More Collected Works on Gradual Democracy*, and *A Plan for a Vitalized China: Three People Discuss Modernization*.

As everyone knows, Liu Xiaobo was an extremely caustic critic who excelled at castigating people (what set him apart was that, as mentioned before, he "exposed" and criticized himself in the same way). I never became accustomed to that and in fact strongly disliked it. Yet I now sorrowfully acknowledge that when a sage is born among men, unless he leads the life of a recluse, he can have only two fates: to curse or be cursed by others. In the past I tolerated criticism and disdained to confess, confident that people were capable of drawing their own conclusions that the truth could not be faked and the false could not be turned into truth, and that truth would always come out. But as I've made my way in the world, this belief of mine has been destroyed, and I'm compelled with deep regret to declare, Ladies and gentlemen, that is not true. By no means continue in innocence and naivety: if you don't come out and defend the truth, no one will stand up for you.

For this reason, what follows is my clarification of some matters—not as criticism but to let the facts speak. Berating others has never been my strong point.

For some reason, having reached this point, a coarse expression of Liu Xiaobo's keeps lingering in my brain: He several times said, "It's not worth doing anything for the fucking Chinese." I now feel compelled to venture a further remark: There are a lot of Westerners who aren't worth much, either, and their good intentions are poor compensation for a great deal of selfishness, ignorance, and arrogance. They are not only completely out of their league over how to implement democracy in non-Western countries but are even half-ignorant about their own democracy and freedoms, and their capacity to destroy themselves along with others is truly shocking.

Revitalizing China (the "China Dream") must start with telling the truth.

I'll admit that compared with Western civilization, Chinese culture has the quality of putting moral virtue above all, "attempting to use morality to solve all problems" (in the words of Lin Yu-sheng) and not emphasizing the pursuit of truth.[3] We've become accustomed to cavalierly sacrificing truth for the sake of a treasured value objective. The most laudable quality that set Liu Xiaobo apart from the crowd was his demand for truth, to the point where he defamed himself, became muddle-headed, and entered dead alleys, which truly amazed me. Reading his *The Monologues of a Doomsday's Survivor*, it is impossible not to be shocked by his merciless self-analysis and self-flagellation, which is unique among Chinese. Even if the truth is not so one-sided—and as mentioned before, Liu Xiaobo was an extremely complex and contradictory mixture of qualities—I've never seen anyone up to now who has been able to reach this point.

For this reason, as Liu Xiaobo's "best friend," I feel compelled to continue this undertaking of seeking truth—and start by clarifying the matter of being his "best friend."

I first met Liu Xiaobo in 1987. That year, the Beijing Stone Group, where I was working, merged with a state-owned enterprise in Kunming.[4] Since the corporate culture of the state-owned enterprise was incompatible with Stone's, the Stone leadership decided to open a Stone Academy for Managers to train managers from the state-owned enterprise. I was assigned the initial organization work of choosing the courses and hiring the instructors. I decided to have a course in aesthetics—now, with everyone knowing the story of Steve Jobs, that may not seem at all strange, but back then it was considered an "earth-shattering" notion. I asked several friends who might teach this course, and someone recommended Liu Xiaobo. I invited him to Kunming to give a lecture, and that's how I came to know him.

Not long after that, Liu Xiaobo began telling everyone he met that I was his best friend, which continues to puzzle me to this day.

Everyone who is acquainted with both of us says that we "disagreed on almost everything." The famous writer and an old friend, Ma Jian, recently said this on WeChat, and in private I felt it was true, but was it possible for me to jump out and say "it's not true" that we were best friends? When he was still living a normal life, I had no reason to say it; when he was persecuted and imprisoned, I especially could not say it. Only now that he's dead and crowned with the laurels of a Nobel Peace Prize and countless people who knew him or never had any connection with him are attaching themselves to him, I have an opportunity to tell the truth.

I need to clarify a second fact. Liu Xiaobo in August and September 1989 came out in the Chinese government's official media and testified that "we didn't see anyone die" during the clearing of Tiananmen Square. This is something I suggested to the relevant government authorities while in custody. My motivation for doing this was first of all to save Liu Xiaobo's life. At that time it was generally believed that as the number 1 "black hand" on the government blacklist, Liu Xiaobo might well be executed. I therefore made it a condition of raising this suggestion that criminal charges would be dropped against Liu Xiaobo and the other three of us. To tell the truth, I had little confidence in this unprecedented and unheard-of trade-off between prisoners and the government, but the results completely exceeded my expectations: the government kept its promise in full. Liu Xiaobo told me that just before he was released, his interrogator told him that he was being exempted from prosecution because of the "meritorious service" he had performed during the clearing of Tiananmen Square (which of course referred to averting bloodshed by mobilizing the protesters to leave the square).

Besides, our testimony was absolutely true and factual. At that time, the whole world had been duped by the lie of a bloodbath at Tiananmen Square, and I firmly believed that this lie had no positive meaning from any perspective. For example, it would be preposterous for someone to say, "Only bloodshed can arouse the masses and overturn the Communist Party." First, it is impossible to rely on falsehood to overturn the Communist Party; even if it was actually overturned, the moral degeneration that would result would be extremely deplorable. Second, in fact at that time virtually the entire world believed there had been a bloodbath at Tiananmen Square, and our testimony to this day is still vilified as a lie by many people who would rather believe in the bloodbath, so please tell me how many of the masses have been aroused by this widely believed "fact" of a bloodbath? On the contrary, I've only seen collective silence and denial, and only a tiny number of people will even admit to what kind of behavior they took part in during June 4. Please don't misunderstand—I do not in any way oppose this group silence and denial from the standpoint of consistent humanitarianism. In a situation when the balance of forces is so skewed, choosing self-protection is the right thing to do. But what I utterly despise are those who close their eyes to the truth and who indulge in the absurd, cruel revolutionary logic that bloodshed (not their own blood, of course) will arouse the masses. In his book, Liu Xiaobo quoted me as saying, "Lying is the spiritual cancer of the Chinese," and that could not be more appropriate here.

If we ask further what the source of this "spiritual cancer" is, I can only say that it comes from the vast gulf that separates the magnificent ideals flaunted by the Stalinist model and its Marxist-Leninist ideology introduced from the Soviet Union and social reality. For example, the Constitution of the People's Republic of China, which was drafted on Stalin's insistence, clearly stipulates in black and white that "the National People's Congress is the highest organ of state power," but everyone knows what the truth is. The deplorable corruption resulting from this monstrous lie fabricated in the supreme law of the land cannot possibly be overemphasized.

Third, the reason Tiananmen Square was very fortunately spared major bloodshed was that as the clearing of the square reached a critical moment, the four of us risked our lives to negotiate with the martial law troops and energetically mobilized the students and residents to peacefully withdraw. That is the only way such a miraculous result could have occurred. If we didn't speak, who, including the many who were present, would stand up for justice on our behalf? On the contrary, countless of those involved and not involved continue to this day to wantonly spread the sheer nonsense of a massacre at Tiananmen Square. Where is the truth in their hearts? Instead there is only a bosom full of hatred toward the Communist Party, and the belief that anything is justified in thoroughly blackening the name of the Communist Party, regardless of the truth. But this is exactly what I absolutely disagree with because hatred will only poison rather than help establish democracy, and lies are a deadly poison that ruins democracy.

Therefore, fourth, at that time I had already begun considering, things being as they were, what should be our next step. How could we be extricated from the profound hatred created by the June Fourth Massacre? I steadfastly believe that violent revolution and overturning the Communist Party is both impossible and undesirable. Continuing to push gradual reforms aimed at comprehensive modernization is the only way out, and taking that road means making the effort to bring about reconciliation among all of China's people. A few years after I was released, I read two extremely important books: Andrew Rigby's *Justice and Reconciliation:*

*After the Violence* and South African Archbishop Desmond Tutu's *No Future without Forgiveness*, which strengthened my conviction.

Given space constraints, I cannot describe in detail the South African model of truth and reconciliation presented in these books but can only point out the three essential conditions for the success of this model, summarized in *No Future without Forgiveness*.

The first of these three conditions is Christian faith: "We were inspired not by political motives. No, we were fired by our biblical faith." Furthermore,

So frequently we in the (Truth and Reconciliation) commission were quite appalled at the depth of depravity to which human beings could sink and we would, most of us, say that those who committed such dastardly deeds were monsters because the deeds were monstrous. . . . We had to distinguish between the deed and the perpetrator, between the sinner and the sin, to hate and condemn the sin while being filled with compassion for the sinner. . . . Theology said they still, despite the awfulness of their deeds, remained children of God with the capacity to repent, to be able to change. . . . In this theology, we can never give up on anyone because our God was one who had a particularly soft spot for sinners. . . . Those who think this opens the door for moral laxity have obviously never been in love, for love is much more demanding than law. . . . Each of us has this capacity for the most awful evil— every one of us. None of us could predict that if we had been subjected to the same influences, the same conditioning, we would not have turned out like these perpetrators. This is not to condone or excuse what they did. It is to be filled more and more with the compassion of God, looking on and weeping that one of His beloved had come to such a sad pass. . . . Despite all the evidence that seems to be to the contrary, there is no way that evil and injustice and oppression and lies can have the last word.[5]

Every time I read these words, my soul is shaken anew, and I find myself repeatedly sighing with sadness over our pitiful people, long ago abandoned by God, our hearts clogged with hatred and only knowing how to engage in life-and-death struggle with others, with no self-reflection, mercy, or forgiveness.

Second is Ubuntu, the spirit of tribal unity among black South Africans:

Ubuntu . . . is to say, "My humanity is caught up, is inextricably bound up, in yours." We belong in a bundle of life. . . . Harmony, friendliness, community are great goods. . . . Anger, resentment, lust for revenge, even success through aggressive competitiveness, are corrosive of this good. To forgive is not just to be altruistic. It is the best form of self-interest. What dehumanizes you inexorably dehumanizes me. It gives people resilience, enabling them to survive and emerge still human despite all efforts to dehumanize them.

In a real sense we might add that even the supporters of apartheid were victims of the vicious system which they implemented and which they supported so enthusiastically. . . . It flows from our fundamental concept of ubuntu. . . . The humanity of the perpetrator of apartheid's atrocities was caught up and bound up in that of his victim whether he liked it or not. In the process of dehumanizing another, in inflicting untold harm and suffering, inexorably the perpetrator was being dehumanized as well.[6]

The third is the example of leaders: the souls of "truth and reconciliation" in South Africa were Nelson Mandela and Archbishop Desmond Tutu.[7] The 1984 Nobel Peace Prize laureate, Tutu embodies the Christian spirit, and he played the irreplaceable role of nucleus and leader as chairman of the Truth and Reconciliation Commission. As for Mandela, Tutu says:

Had F. W. de Klerk encountered in jail a man bristling with bitterness and a lust for retribution, it is highly unlikely that he would have gone ahead with announcing his initiatives. Mercifully for us, he encountered in prison a man who had developed into the prisoner of conscience par excellence. . . . He found a man regal in dignity, bubbling over with magnanimity and a desire to dedicate himself to the reconciliation of those whom apartheid and the injustice and pain of racism had alienated from one another. Nelson Mandela emerged from prison not spewing words of hatred and revenge. He amazed us all by his heroic embodiment of reconciliation and forgiveness.

The awarding of the Nobel Peace Prize to former president de Klerk and Nelson Mandela was fully deserved:

> Nothing will ever take away from F. W. de Klerk the enormous credit that belongs to him for what he said and did then. . . . I believe that, had he not done what he did then, we would have experienced the blood bath and disaster that so many were predicting would be South Africa's lot. It required a considerable degree of courage to try to persuade the white community that its best interests would be served by negotiating themselves out of exclusive control of political power. Very few constituencies are likely to take too kindly to candidates for political office who say their platform is to hand over power to their traditional adversaries.

It also helps to have wise leaders among radical organizations:

> There were other political organizations that sought to portray themselves as more radical than the ANC, and which opposed any thought of negotiating with the enemy as a sign of weakness. Mr. Mandela had to contend with that as well. It required a great deal of political courage and skill and authority to bring his organization along with him. We were fortunate that he and others in the leadership were convinced that that was the way to go. Mr. Mandela was aided and abetted by some of the more radical among the party hierarchy, who carried a lot of clout among the young and radical-minded. It was fortunate that the much-admired general secretary of the Communist Party, Joe Slovo, had shown himself committed to the entire process of negotiation and making concessions and accommodation.[8]

In comparison, China doesn't have a single one of these conditions at present. On the contrary, the historical legacy of our mutually alienating, mutually contrary and incompatible ultra-leftist radical party culture is so profound that its toxins have seeped into the blood and bone marrow of every Chinese.

I find myself continually asking, is there any hope left?

On further consideration, the suffering of South African blacks under apartheid rule was at least as great, if not greater, than ours. If our brothers in South Africa can do it, why can't we? Aren't we Chinese an ancient cultured race with many virtues? If the conditions don't exist now, can't we make an effort to create them?

The radical faction's black and white extremist party culture means that their judgment of any social phenomenon at any time will be that it is "completely black and without hope" and that nothing short of revolution can relieve the people from these dire straits. But at the risk of universal condemnation, I must ask them once again: What is so dark about today's China? Is China after reform and opening the darkest period in China's history? You may think it is, but how many ordinary Chinese people agree with your judgment? Have you carried out a scientific and comprehensive social survey? Who is it that you actually represent? Weren't the various abuses you hate so much left behind by the previous revolution? Won't another revolution make things even worse? Today's battle between China's reformist faction and revolutionary faction is a replay of the Xinhai Revolution of 1911. Looking back at history, an increasing amount of evidence shows that truth was on the side of Kang Youwei and Liang Qichao, and not on the side of Sun Yat-sen and Huang Xing.[9] If you say the current situation is different, I can only say that the success rate for revolution today is even lower, far lower than the success rate for reform. If you ask me to choose the most foresighted great man in modern Chinese history, that would undoubtedly be Liang Qichao.

Yes, the road Liang Qichao espoused back then is the road I want to take now.

I've stated in previous articles that China's situation is very complicated, but if the crux is grasped, it can be very simple. In domestic politics it's the rule of law and constitutional government, and in diplomacy it's Sino-American relations. The fourth plenum of the Eighteenth Central Committee resolved to "comprehensively push forward the construction of rule of law."[10] Didn't the information communicated at the Sino-American summit at Mar-a-Lago in April this year show that the CCP is in fact taking, or at least wants to take, this correct path, and is not committing "subversive error"?[11] Where does the complete lack of hope originate? Isn't it from the completely erroneous judgment resulting from your own radical standpoint? Was it Liu Xiaobo who ignored the truth in making the concession of defending the autocratic regime, or is it that your own brains have become so giddy and lacking in the most basic common sense that you intentionally misled the masses?

About two years ago, a newly appointed police department head asked me, Mr. Zhou, if you someday have space for free movement, where would you place yourself? I immediately said, "The position I've set for myself is very clear and has never changed. I am a bridge, a communication link between all kinds of mutually incompatible, life-and-death antagonistic political stands for gradually forming a consensus toward the objective and path of China's future reforms, allowing everyone to make a concerted effort toward achieving the great revitalization of the Chinese people."

Many friends say to me, your stand is very good and we agree with it, but can you succeed? Is your path of gradually improving democratization actually workable?

I can only answer in all honesty: I don't know. The future cannot be predicted, and none of us is God—not to mention that God is rolling the dice, and the cosmos we live in is governed by the laws of probability and not by the laws of determinism, and therefore perhaps not even God can predict the future. We can only do our best and leave the rest to God. "Better to light a candle than curse the darkness." This famous saying was my motto when I returned from the United States in 1994 and created Candlelight Project to help impoverished rural teachers. A candle has only a dim light, but it's enough to light one's path in the darkness. That's why I thoroughly despise those radical blabbermouths who can only curse the darkness but have never lit a candle.

Besides, even if I can't guarantee the success of my path, what other path is guaranteed success?

I believe, or I hope, that the path I've chosen is also the path Liu Xiaobo chose.

I therefore offer this essay in memory of my friend Liu Xiaobo. May his soul rest in peace in heaven.

*Translated by Stacy Mosher*

1. Matthew 7:13: "Enter by the narrow gate. For the gate is wide and the way is easy that leads to destruction, and those who enter by it are many. For the gate is narrow and the way is hard that leads to life, and those who find it are few."—Trans.

2. Of my three "forced vacations," the first was the usual outing connected with the twenty-eighth anniversary of June 4; the second occurred after I issued an appeal on June 29 asking the CCP to permit Liu Xiaobo to go to the United States for treatment on medical grounds (inexplicably, *Reuters* reported that "not one of the other three of the Four Gentlemen came out with statements"); and the third time was when Liu Xiaobo died.

3. Lin Yu-sheng (b. 1934) is a historian best known for his book *The Crisis of Chinese Consciousness: Radical Anti-traditionalism in the May Fourth Era* (Madison: University of Wisconsin Press, 1978).—Trans.

4. The Stone Group was a major computer company that ran afoul of the Chinese authorities for supporting the 1989 student movement. Its founder and president, Wan Runnan, fled China soon after the June 4 crackdown.—Trans.

5. Desmond Mpilo Tutu, *No Future without Forgiveness* (New York: Doubleday, 1999), 93, 83–86.

6. Tutu, *No Future without Forgiveness*, 35, 103.

7. Nelson Mandela (1918–2013) was an anti-apartheid revolutionary who was imprisoned for twenty-seven years. After his release in 1990, he served as president of the African National Congress Party from 1991 to 1997, and he served as South Africa's first black head of state as president from 1994 to 1999.—Trans.

8. Tutu, *No Future without Forgiveness*, 38–39, 37–38, 42.

9. Kang Youwei (1858–1927), Liang Qichao (1873–1929), and Tan Sitong (1865–98) were reformers of the late Qing period. After the failure of the Hundred Days' Reform of the imperial system they inspired in 1898, Liang was forced to flee the country for a time, and Tan was killed. Sun Yat-sen (1866–1925) and Huang Xing (1874–1916) were revolutionary leaders who founded the Kuomintang, which ruled China after the fall of the Qing dynasty.—Trans.

10. This plenary session was held from October 20 to 23, 2014.—Trans.

11. Chinese President Xi Jinping met with U.S. President Donald Trump at Trump's Mar-a-Lago estate on April 7–8, 2017.—Trans.

# Liu Xiaobo, Who Has Ascended the Altar
*Yi Ping*

## 1

More than twenty years after June 4, what Xiaobo found most distressing was that while in prison in 1990 he had "admitted his guilt and expressed repentance," and he could never forgive himself for that.

On this point, Xiaobo dissected and criticized himself mercilessly and at length in his book *The Monologues of a Doomsday's Survivor*. He wrote:

> I not only took responsibility for a crime, but also took the initiative to admit that I'd committed a criminal act, voluntarily wrote a "statement of repentance" and signed my name to an order for residential surveillance, detention warrant and arrest warrant. Thinking back on it now, my penitence was not against my will, but a sincere falsehood, bowing my head to lies, fraud and violence for the sake of self-preservation. No matter what I might have been thinking, my actions themselves were completely authentic. My display of penitence profaned and even raped honesty, truth, conscience and the victims of June 4th. Given a choice between self-preservation and adherence to truth, I chose the former and abandoned the latter.

In terms of modern Western morality and values, this is no great matter. When compelled by an imperious and ruthless regime, a person is justified in admitting guilt and repentance against his will as a necessary means of self-protection. When American soldiers are taken prisoner during a war, even when they appear on television "admitting their guilt" to the world, they're still regarded as heroes after they're released and return home. So why did Xiaobo interrogate himself so harshly?

It's because so many young lives ended that night and so much innocent blood was spilled. He reproached himself for those thousands of deaths that occurred around him. That is why he felt that "admitting guilt" to the killers betrayed and profaned those victims and their blood. Facing truth, death, and conscience, he was unable to forgive himself.

He recalled in *Monologues*:

I'd wanted to go to Tiananmen several times but dared not to; on two occasions I reached the vicinity of Xidan before turning back. I didn't dare face the Monument [to the People's Heroes] on my own, didn't dare revisit my scarred memories; I was agonized by these past events, so inextricably bound to me, and I constantly had to force back tears . . . I happened to be looking out the window when the bus reached Tiananmen Square, and I suddenly spotted the Monument. An immense pressure overwhelmed me, as if confronting a catastrophe, and I began trembling uncontrollably from head to toe, a pain wrenching the pit of my stomach. I wanted to bow my head, but I couldn't; my gaze was fixed on the Monument, as if its attractive force could suck me right out of the window of the bus. Tears trickled down my face. I suddenly broke down in sobs, trembling uncontrollably. . . .

After I'd calmed down somewhat, I felt disgusted, more disgusted than I'd ever felt toward myself. I'd taken part in June 4th, but I hadn't shed blood, and after being arrested and sent to Qincheng Prison, I was treated better than most people imprisoned for June 4th. Now I was still alive and had achieved a level of so-called fame, and had gained my freedom and the concern and protection of friends and strangers. But what of the dead and those still in prison? What of their friends and families? What had happened to the young man who stood with his arms spread wide in front of the tanks? Had all of your blood been shed in vain? Had your courage, conscience and spirit of self-sacrifice been turned into a joke? Some people manage to turn suffering into fame, and sacrifice becomes fodder for attaining status and wealth; the sorrow of our entire race may have merely enriched a handful of cowards and swindlers, myself among them. There was no way I could ever forgive myself until the day I was placed in a tomb, because I was able to sell out my conscience in exchange for freedom—repentance.

These words of Xiaobo's were sincere, straight from the heart, agonized, and blood-streaked. In his youth, Xiaobo had opposed tradition and morality—the May 4 tradition—but in fact he was idealistic, opposing tradition out of an even higher idealism with even higher and harsher moral expectations. In his self-reflection he quoted his former words:

Facing and understanding human weakness is a completely different thing from accommodating and excusing human weakness. Facing is not the same as accommodation, and understanding is not the same as excuse. In fact, it is because human weakness cannot be accommodated that it must be faced, and it is because human vileness cannot be excused that it must be understood. Starting out with accommodation and excuse leaves nothing to face and understand. It is essential to understand why human beings do evil, and at the same time never to excuse it. Even in Christianity, which emphasizes loving all people, including one's enemies, there are fires of purgatory for burning away human wickedness, and a hell waiting to punish the evil. God exists in order to punish humanity's wickedness.

This is already an absolute morality; it is God's moral law. Here we can see another side to the youthful fanatic Xiaobo and the ethical ideals deep within him. It's hard to imagine that on one hand he opposed tradition and professed the need to "put an extreme emphasis on money and flesh" while on the other hand he possessed an absolute ethical ideal in the depths of his heart. If we see the ethical demands deep in his heart, we can understand how at the critical moment he could risk his own life to help the students, why he refused to take refuge in an embassy, why he was so harshly critical of himself and the 1989 Democracy Movement, why he could hold fast in China, and why he ultimately gave his life for the cause. His sacred life values were identical to the absolute moral ideals in his heart; this was the force that motivated his life and led him step-by-step to the sacrificial altar.

Unfortunately, Xiaobo lived amid the ruins of China's contemporary civilization, which is what caused the contortion and arrogance of his youth. Otherwise there would have been a different Liu Xiaobo. But he was not buried in the ruins; he stood on top of them and finally found the starting point of civilization—sacrifice, the sacred meaning that rises from pools of blood. This was the mission God gave him.

After Xiaobo died, Xu Wenli revealed, "Liu Xiaobo once divulged to me that when he gave testimony against his will on television that time, it was because the authorities forced his father to lobby him to give in. He painfully recalled, 'Normally I could argue with my father and even fall out with him, but when my father knelt before me in that place, I fucking fell apart! . . . I've never told anyone about this before, and I wanted to tell you today. I still can't fucking excuse myself! Especially when I face the Tiananmen Mothers, there's no excuse, just shame, and I berate myself as such a despicable creature!'"[1]

## 2

Liu Xiaobo was arrested on June 6, 1989, and locked up in Qincheng Prison until January 1991. In January 1993 he was invited to visit Australia and the United States, but he refused friends' advice to seek asylum and returned to China in May that year. After drafting "Drawing from a Lesson Paid for in Blood and the Process of Promoting Democracy and Rule of Law: An Appeal on the Sixth Anniversary of June 4th" in May 1995, he was held under "residential surveillance" in the Beijing suburbs by the Beijing Public Security Bureau until January 1996. He spent three years in RTL starting in October 1996 for issuing the Double Ten Declaration with Wang Xizhe. In December 2008 he was arrested for taking part in Charter 08 and was sentenced to eleven years in prison and died while still in custody on July 13, 2017.

In the twenty-eight years after the June Fourth Incident, Xiaobo preferred to go to prison rather than leave China. In political terms, he did it to uphold his belief in freedom and democracy, to resist the CCP's totalitarian rule, and to promote China's institutional reform. This was Xiaobo's ideal and goal for China's politics.

In his essay "The Poverty of China's Popular Opposition: On the 13th Anniversary of June 4th," he wrote:

Aung San Suu Kyi, having lost her freedom, would rather go to prison than go into exile, and through various efforts issued a powerful voice of resistance. Inspired by her noble and dauntless character, the [Myanmar] National League for Democracy also maintained their resistance. It could be said that the dauntless spirit that filled the military junta's prison sustained the resistance of Myanmar's popular opposition party. It was this dauntless tenacity that provided the moral and organizational resources for the opposition party's own development and the support of the international community, and in 1991, Aung San Suu Kyi was awarded the Nobel Peace Prize. The government that deprived a Nobel Peace Prize laureate of her personal freedom was unable to bear the resulting heavy moral pressure. On May 6, 2002, Aung San Suu Kyi and the opposition party that she led finally welcomed the dawn of social harmony . . . But in China, although the massacre turned many reformists inside the system into dissidents. outside of the system, and although the popular opposition's sporadic challenges to the CCP regime never ended, they lacked an emblematic leader such as Aung San Suu Kyi or a fully formed popular opposition organization such as the National League for Democracy, added to which many of the leading figures of the 1989 democracy movement fled overseas. This deprived China's popular opposition movement of a cohesive moral core, not to mention an organized public mobilization force, and it could only exist in a dispersed and isolated form and become increasingly marginalized.

Here we can clearly see why Xiaobo held fast in China and sustained the popular resistance. Because others had retreated and the majority of dissident leaders had gone into exile overseas, leading to an outflow of moral resources, he resolved to be like Andrei Sakharov, Aung San Suu Kyi, Adam Michnik, and Vaclav Havel and stand with the Tiananmen Mothers in taking moral responsibility in China.

Xiaobo took on this responsibility because of the bloodshed on June 4 and his experience of that tragedy. He witnessed the killers' bullets and the death of so many people, and he felt a measure of responsibility for that tragedy because he'd fomented the radicalism of the students with his speeches and especially with his launch of a hunger strike by the Four Gentlemen. In his *Monologues* he wrote, "I felt I had gained my freedom at the expense of the suffering of others. My release was a betrayal of the dead and of those in prison. . . . While I had been deeply embroiled in the 1989 protest movement, I hadn't shared the evil consequences—suffering in prison. Wasn't that a crime in just another form . . . ?" With so many dead and so many still in prison, he felt he could not let them down, so he took on their mission to compensate for his errors and to console the dead.

## 3

As an individual, Xiaobo had two hidden reasons for holding fast in China: shame and "atonement."

For Xiaobo, his "statement of repentance" in prison was his greatest disgrace, and he could never wipe it away. There is an old Chinese phrase: "shamed into bravery." The sense of shame is a deep-seated ethical consciousness for Chinese people. One reason why General Zhang Zizhong (1891–1940) was so brave with outstanding battle achievements and ultimately gave his life for China during the War of Resistance against Japan was that he had been publicly branded a traitor when Beiping (as Beijing was then known) and Tianjin fell to the Japanese army in 1937, and he was ordered to stay behind as an acting chairman of the Hebei-Chahar political committee and mayor of Beiping. After that, General Zhang swore to purge his shame by dying bravely.

In his *Monologues* Xiaobo wrote, "Repentance is a fait accompli and cannot be retracted, and I will bear this stain for as long as I live." He castigated himself:

Everyone, open your eyes wide and look, this is the person everyone regarded as a fearless "dark horse." . . . The so-called brave man who, as the movement at the square began to falter under the white terror, came up with the idea of a hunger strike; this was the so-called spiritual leader of the student movement, the so-called conscience of China's intellectuals. . . . Someone as weak, despicable and shameless as this should be one of China's scenic attractions. And it is just this person who was once so filled with righteous indignation and constantly spouting off about the spinelessness of China's intellectuals. Good people, lost souls slumbering beneath the earth, don't you feel fooled? Don't you feel shocked and disappointed?

This shame was unforgettable to him. In his *Monologues*, Xiaobo quoted the Australian sinologist Geremie Barmé as saying, "All Chinese elites want to be a martyred Christ and become big heroes attracting worldwide attention, but they're unwilling to be eternally nailed to the cross. Instead, they want to be nailed for a short time and then taken down amidst the applause of others. This is the martyr descending the cross with Chinese characteristics." Xiaobo blamed himself for "being unwilling to pay the price but still wanting everything, as greedy as if the whole world was there just for me. Is that what's called democratic thinking? Is that what's called a hero? Go to hell! Having written this much, I've really started to lose confidence in myself. I've degenerated so far that I'm irredeemable."

Xiaobo's sense of shame was not only for his "repentance" but also for his desire to be a "great hero" and his haggling for fame and public image. He clearly saw himself as the "Christ descending the cross" Geremie Barmé described. He felt incomparably ashamed while facing the blood of victims and colleagues in prison.

This shame and disgrace were engraved in Xiaobo's heart, but he did it to himself. It didn't matter how other people regarded him; he could never forgive himself. That's why, in the second half of his life, he purposely took responsibility for the aftermath of June 4 and died for this cause as a way of redeeming his former disgrace. In 1999 he wrote a letter to Liao Yiwu, saying, "Living in disgrace, for the blood of the innocents, is the only reason I can find. The dawn of June 4th was the darkest and also the brightest day in my heart."

## 4

Xiaobo was more or less influenced by Saint Augustine when he wrote his *Monologues*. He once said, "In the 1980s, St. Augustine's *Confessions* was one of my favorite books. I read it several times, and it turned my impulse to follow in the footsteps of saints into a conscious desire for faith."[2] He wrote a poem to Liu Xia entitled "To St. Augustine," which included the lines,

> Why, after forsaking drunken debauchery
> did you choose to be a saint and not a gambler . . .
> I wonder if you really trembled in repentance

Is the road to atonement really so long?
In God's play
people perform solemn tribute.

Couldn't it be said that this was also Xiaobo making another choice in his life after self-reflection and repentance?

Xiaobo had a strong sense of religion. It's too bad that contemporary China lacks religion, or he might have become a devotee. In his essay "Moved behind Bars: Reading *On Being a Christian* in Prison," he wrote,

> Although I grew up in an atheistic culture with absolutely no religious background, I'm not incurable. Deep in my soul there is still religious piety, and that great and deep religious feeling always moves me intensely. . . . Perhaps I will never become a Christian or join an organized church, but Jesus Christ is my personal model. I know there's no way to match up to the character of a saint, but to be moved and shaken by this kind of book shows that I still have personal devotion and humility, and have not been swallowed up by the calamity of imprisonment or corrupted by the renown I once enjoyed. I can still be saved, and can still turn my life into a process toward becoming that kind of person.

Here we can see Xiaobo's religious feelings and ideals.

Objectively speaking, his criticism of himself in the *Monologues* is excessively harsh and beyond secular limits and could be considered religious in nature. For someone with no religious beliefs, this harsh exposure and criticism of himself caused great self-injury—his friends called it "self-abuse." Human beings have a sense of guilt (sin), and the more religious feeling a person has, the more intense this sense of guilt. In religion, exonerating sin is one of God's important functions, which is why Christianity has the rite of confession. As long as a person repents, God pardons him. Christ redeeming sinners is the core content of Christian faith. Regrettably, Xiaobo never became a Christian, but he was a humanist. He had a deep religious sense but no religious faith; he was conscious of his sin but not of God's forgiveness. For this reason, his conscience was not freed of guilt, and as long as he lived he had to bear his guilt and try to redeem himself.

In the *Monologues*, we can see Xiaobo's inner struggle and pain. He considered himself guilty but could not free himself from this guilt, and he lived with that pain from June 4 onward. In the *Monologues* he wrote,

> I have a faint unease, a sense of moral crime, and always feel that the people who died under the gun barrels of the martial law troops were related to the hunger strike I started. I'm always accompanied by the inescapable inference, when I was thrown into Qincheng Prison and when I obtained my freedom, and until I enter the grave: "If I hadn't launched the hunger strike, there wouldn't have been a new upsurge to the movement; if there hadn't been a new upsurge, the government might have waited for the students to disperse on their own rather than forcibly clearing the square; if the square hadn't been forcibly cleared, Beijing residents wouldn't have clashed with the troops, and perhaps there wouldn't have been the massacre." . . . Every time I think of it, I feel that I unconsciously joined with the Communist Party in engineering the June 4th massacre.

Why did Xiaobo refuse to leave China? Why maintain his dissident struggle? Why insist on his notions of freedom and democracy? Why insist on nonviolence? One reason was that this was his way of making atonement. He wanted to join with the Tiananmen Mothers in keeping watch over the lost souls, defending the honor of the dead, and holding up their spirit.

## 5

Xiaobo held up Christ as the best model for the sacred values and absolute morality he hoped for. Xiaobo wasn't a Christian, but from his secular vantage point he observed Christ's sacred meaning to civilization. The ultimate value of Christianity was in keeping faith and not hesitating to offer one's life; the entire history of Christianity was built on the spirit of martyrdom, symbolized to its ultimate degree by Christ's own ascent to the cross. This is the foundation of Christianity.

We have repeatedly stated that Chinese civilization was reduced to rubble after 1949. How can we rebuild civilization atop this rubble? Where do we start? Xiaobo wasn't a Christian, but based on his painful life experience and in-depth soul-searching, he established two base points on the cultural rubble of contemporary China: one was the pool of blood from June 4, and the other was the sacred meaning and absolute morality of which Christ was the model. The first provided a footing, and the second provided direction, and between the two would be established a moral spirit for today's China that could resist totalitarian rule, push China toward civilization, and complete the transformation to constitutional government.

In his essay "The Inspiration of the Tiananmen Mothers: On the 19th Anniversary of June 4th," he praised the Tiananmen Mothers as "a group that has regularly faced terror politics for 19 years without ever giving up the struggle or wavering in their standpoint":

> No matter how cold-blooded the dictators or how apathetic the masses, they have persistently sought redress for the dead, using motherly love to resolve hatred, using courage to defy brutality, using patience against endless waiting, using their unsparing inquiries to counter forced amnesia, using individual cases to expose the truth of the massacre and puncture a falsified existence. . . . In the steadfast efforts of the Tiananmen Mothers over the past 19 years, I see not only a courage that defies power and a persevering tenaciousness, but even more a sense of public spirit honed by suffering and that transcends personal suffering and vengeance for one's own flesh and blood—an ethics of responsibility forged from motherly love, tolerance, rationality, patience and tenacity.

For more than twenty years after June 4, Xiaobo stood with the Tiananmen Mothers in their unyielding struggle and raised suffering to the level of morality and justice. While in prison in 2010, Xiaobo told his lawyer, "I believe that what I'm doing is just, that China will someday become a free and democratic country where all people will live under the sun without fear, and to this end I have paid a price, but without resentment or regret. For an intellectual pursuing freedom in a dictatorship, prison is the first threshold toward freedom. I've already crossed this threshold, and freedom cannot be far off."

## 6

In a letter to Liao Yiwu nearly twenty years ago, Xiaobo wrote:

> It is natural to expect kindness and grit from people, not so natural to anticipate evil or cowardice. Every time a disaster occurs, I am surprised

when the evil and cowardice appear . . . One main reason for the silence and amnesia that enshrouded China in the years after the massacre is that no inspiring moral leader stepped forward to be a symbol.

Compared to people in other nations who have lived under the dreary pall of communism, we resisters in China have not measured up very well. Even after so many years of tremendous tragedies, we still don't have a moral leader like Vaclav Havel. It seems ironic that in order to win the right of ordinary people to pursue self-interest, a society needs a moral giant to make a selfless sacrifice. In order to secure "passive freedom"—freedom from state oppression—there needs to be a will to do active resistance. History is not fated. The appearance of a single martyr can fundamentally turn the spirit of a nation and strengthen its moral fiber. Gandhi was such a figure. So was Havel. So, even more, was that humble boy born in a manger two thousand years ago. Human progress is the result of the accident of birth of people such as these. We cannot expect a society's conscience to spring automatically out of ordinary life. A moral exemplar is needed to articulate principles of conscience so that these will catalyze the consciences of ordinary people. In China our need for this kind of exemplar is especially strong. For us the power of an ethical model could be immense; a single symbol could tap large reservoirs of moral sentiment.[3]

These words tell us that Xiaobo was most pained not only by China's totalitarianism but also by the way that following the destruction of its civilization, China's people had gone bad, its spirit had died, justice and morality had died, and conscience had died. That's why a moral giant was needed who would become a martyr and with his or her life reignite the light of justice and morality, awaken the souls of the Chinese people, and uplift their spiritual quality. In the darkness of a morally moribund China, the final direction and choice he gave himself was to stride forward as a moral giant and martyr and "sacrifice personal freedom for the sake of freedom for all." Xiaobo kept his promise and ultimately died for morality and justice.

In the decades of China's dissident movement, there have been many people of noble conduct, some who approached sainthood, such as Yang

Tianshui, Chen Xi, and Tang Jingling.[4] As an individual, Xiaobo had many flaws, but he had a strict spirit of self-reflection and high moral standards. Hu Ping wrote, "For more than 20 years, Xiaobo devoted himself to China, and his steadfast struggle and calm in the face of suffering gradually raised his spiritual outlook to a higher plane."

Xiaobo wasn't perfect, but he made a constant effort toward sacred meaning. As Hu Ping wrote, "Saints are sinners who go on trying. . . . No one is born perfect; perfection is embodied in the constant pursuit of perfection. Those who spend their lives pursuing perfection are perfect."[5]

*Translated by Stacy Mosher*

## NOTES

1. Xu Wenli (b. 1943) was a founder of the China Democracy Party who participated in the 1979 Democracy Wall Movement. He was arrested in 1981 and subsequently sentenced to fifteen years in prison. In 1998 he was arrested again and sentenced to thirteen years in prison. He was exiled to the United States on medical parole in December 2002.—Trans.

2. Liu Xiaobo, "Moved behind Bars: Reading *On Being a Christian* in Prison," *China Observer*, September 6, 2008. (*On Being a Christian* is a book by the Swiss theologian Hans Küng.—Trans.)

3. Liu Xiaobo, "A Letter to Liao Yiwu," trans. Perry Link, in *Liu Xiaobo: No Enemies, No Hatred*, ed. Perry Link, Tienchi Martin-Liao, and Liu Xia (Cambridge MA: The Belknap Press of Harvard University Press, 2012), 288.

4. Yang Tianshui (b. Yang Tongyan, 1961–2017) was a dissident writer who spent a total of twenty-one years in prison and died in November 2017 while being treated for an aggressive form of brain cancer after serving eleven years of a twelve-year prison sentence for "subversion of state power." Chen Xi (b. Chen Youcai, 1954) is a human rights activist who in December 2011 was sentenced to nine years in prison for incitement to subvert state power." Tang Jingling (b. 1971) is a rights defense lawyer who in January 2016 was sentenced to five years in prison for subversion.—Trans.

5. Hu Ping, "For Whom the Bell Tolls," herein.

# The Values of Peace and Reason Are Eternal

*Wu Zuolai*

Even now quite a few people still harbor prejudice toward Liu Xiaobo and misunderstand or look down on his political pursuit of peace and rationality. For example, his contention that he didn't see mass killings at Tiananmen Square on June 4, his assertion that he had "no enemies," and even his claim that he was treated well in prison have been criticized as "glamorizing the CCP's prisons."

We need further introspection and awareness in order to understand Liu Xiaobo's political pursuits and ideals.

## Starting with Liu Xiaobo's Smashing Guns at the Square

As I retreated from Chang'an Avenue to the square in the early hours of June 4, I saw many students with rods and stones preparing to ambush the armed troops who were entering the city, and along the way I advised them against this impulse, which would only bring useless sacrifice. As I entered the square, I saw students bleeding from the chest and back being carried onto the square in search of help, and I saw club-wielding students attacking and encircling soldiers on the square. When we tried to stop them, they berated us as traitors.

I understand the radical behavior of those young students even now.

Looking back, the situation Liu Xiaobo confronted when he smashed guns on the square was even more intense and severe.

He first knelt down before two citizens holding machine guns and begged them to toss away their weapons in order to guarantee that the protest at the square was peaceful and especially to prevent mass bloodshed. One can easily imagine, if soldiers entering the square had encountered machine-gun fire, some soldiers would have been killed or wounded, but far greater casualties would have been suffered by the peaceful group of students on the square.

Liu Xiaobo's rationality was based on this conjecture, so he later smashed a semiautomatic rifle with his own hands. It could be said that the incident at Tiananmen Square began with three students kneeling and submitting a petition at the eastern entrance to the Great Hall of the People and ended with Liu Xiaobo kneeling and begging gun-wielding citizens to put down their weapons, ultimately achieving the peaceful withdrawal of the vast majority of people from the square.

Chinese tradition is filled with examples of people kneeling on the ground and pleading to heaven or to their parents. During the protest at the square, there were two exceptional instances of kneeling by the students and Liu Xiaobo, begging the government to heed the voices of the people and begging society for nonviolent confrontation against a much more powerful tyranny.

In this process, Liu Xiaobo himself came under violent attack when agitated people regarded him as a traitor and wanted to violently eliminate him. Both the gun-wielding people who were determined to fight to the death and the crowd who vowed to remain on the square encountered the pacifist Liu Xiaobo at a time when rationality was lost and internal harm could begin. This was before the process of external fighting to the death had even started.

These people all gave the same two reasons for fighting. First, the soldiers initiated the massacre, so of course we should fight back with guns; second, you students and teachers have status that will allow you to retreat, but we ordinary citizens and workers can only fight to the death. By leading the students to peacefully withdraw, you're destroying our dreams of dying for a righteous cause.

Some said that if too few people died at the square, it wouldn't arouse the people to revolt, but this is a major error. It wasn't that there were too few casualties at the square but rather that there were too few rational adults, especially university professors and intellectuals. There were not even enough influential intellectuals who took part in the protest marches, and an even smaller number who directly participated and influenced the movement at the square, like the Four Gentlemen Liu Xiaobo, Hou Derchien, Zhou Duo, and Gao Xin.

We have to acknowledge that at the crucial moment, the peaceful rationality of the mature scholars was a decisive factor in the peaceful withdrawal.

Facing the countless casualties during the CCP's June Fourth Massacre, people denounced the violence and also regretted that more people didn't rise up, all of which is justified. But on the other hand, if the young students had recognized the nature of the democracy movement as peaceful petitioning, once the peaceful petitioning was brought to an end by violence, shouldn't their first priority have been to protect their own lives? Humanitarian rules require not making unnecessary sacrifice, and once tyranny becomes dyed with blood, its change or transformation may become even more difficult.

Looking back now on the Four Gentlemen advising the students to peacefully withdraw, and especially on their successful negotiation with the CCP armed forces, we see that it saved the lives of thousands of students at the square. In terms of Liu Xiaobo's life experience, it is this effort by Liu and his colleagues toward peace at the square that should be considered a more important factor in his being awarded the Nobel Peace Prize.

### The Bogus Issue of No One Dying "on the Square"

The Chinese government made Hou Derchien testify that he didn't see any people die on the square.

Liu Xiaobo struggled internally. He knew that if he said that no one died on the square, he would be corroborating the Chinese government's lies, but ultimately he convinced himself to state what he had seen, rationalizing that Hou Derchien had already done so.

Memoirs have made clear that Liu Xiaobo, Hou Derchien and the others devoted great effort to convincing students and other civilians to peacefully withdraw from the square. They were located near the Monument to the People's Heroes at the center of Tiananmen Square, an area that in fact remained calm and tranquil, but intense conflicts occurred at the periphery of the square, especially in front of Tiananmen after soldiers surrounded it. Some students burned military vehicles and tanks, resulting in casualties. Even rescuers were shot. Hou Derchien and Liu Xiaobo had no way of knowing this, and even I, walking through the square all this time and witnessing the whole process, had no way of knowing it.

Furthermore, what overseas media reported as occurring at Tiananmen Square also included Chang'an Avenue and the periphery of the square, while Liu Xiaobo and Hou Derchien referred to the area within the range of their eyesight that night.

We need to fully understand the testimony that Hou, Liu, and others gave against a background of no freedom and especially under severe persecution. They didn't give false testimony but merely expressed a partial truth, and in any case, the Chinese government used it to no effect because there were countless photos and video recordings proving that the Chinese government carried out an inhuman slaughter at Tiananmen.

Anyone using this to blame Liu Xiaobo and Hou Derchien lacks the proper sympathy and understanding.

### Understanding Liu Xiaobo's "I Have No Enemies"

Is "I have no enemies" a weaker version of Christianity's "Love your enemies"?

"Love your enemies" is a transcendence espoused by religion, while "I have no enemies" was Liu Xiaobo's political transcendence. Those who blame "No Enemies Liu" should reflect on Liu Xiaobo's reasons for saying this.

Liu Xiaobo smashed the gun at the square because he had no enemies. If he had regarded the soldiers as enemies, he would have fought them hand to hand, but was that what Liu Xiaobo was pursuing and what the peaceful democracy movement needed? Liu Xiaobo and others eventually drafted Charter 08 and launched a signature campaign, not in order to create enemies, but for the sake of China's progress toward constitutional government and democracy.

Critics may say, "But he was apprehended and persecuted by the dictators and their henchmen."

But these critics can trot out anyone they like, and Liu Xiaobo would not acknowledge that person as an enemy (or even an opponent) but rather as a victim of the system and a sick person in a dictatorship. Punishing the crimes of these henchmen would require a trial by law, and following a peaceful democratic transformation, the result of the trial might well be to forgive and pardon them. What Liu Xiaobo devoted himself to was ending the system that created the evil.

Few people have taken the trouble to understand what Liu Xiaobo wrote here:

> Hatred only eats away at a person's intelligence and conscience, and an enemy mentality can poison the spirit of an entire people. . . . It can lead to cruel and lethal internecine combat, can destroy tolerance and human feeling within a society, and can block the progress of a nation toward freedom and democracy. For these reasons I hope that I can rise above my personal fate and contribute to the progress of our country and to changes in our society. I hope that I can answer the regime's enmity with utmost benevolence, and can use love to dissipate hate.[1]

Changing people is a matter during a process of enlightenment and tutelage, while exterminating the direct creators of evil through revolution is a radical approach. In other words, although a revolutionary uprising is a naturally reasonable approach, what Liu Xiaobo pursued was a peaceful approach, another difficult path. All he hoped was that China would take the path to democratic constitutional government without that path being stained with blood and paved with human skulls. Proponents of democracy who pursue revolution might have their rationale, but that doesn't mean denying the rationale of Liu Xiaobo's political pursuit.

*Translated by Stacy Mosher*

NOTE

1. Liu Xiaobo, "I Have No Enemies: My Last Statement," trans. Perry Link, in *Liu Xiaobo: No Enemies, No Hatred*, ed. Perry Link, Tienchi Martin-Liao, and Liu Xia (Cambridge MA: The Belknap Press of Harvard University Press, 2012), 322–23.—Trans.

# Liu Xiaobo and His View of "No Enemies"

*Jin Zhong*

Exhausted after a trip to Hong Kong, I had just returned to New York when I got the call: Liu Xiaobo was gone. It had happened while I was still in flight. While I was in Hong Kong, friends had told me they felt he had only a few days left, but I was still devastated when the time came. I watched as the authorities handled the funeral and scattered the ashes in little more than a day, as if dealing with a mortal enemy, giving Xiaobo's friends no opportunity whatsoever to bid him farewell. Online, rage with the government rose like ocean billows against the cold palace walls of the Chinese Communist Party. It had been revealed that Beijing's top officials had decided that Xiaobo would not leave prison alive, and now their stability maintenance had scored a major achievement. But the American media still asked in puzzlement, "What are they afraid of?"

## The Hatred Mentality in the Public Security Ministry

Outsiders don't understand the convention in Chinese politics of "using the dead to oppress the living." Hadn't Hu Yaobang's death served as a catalyst for the 1989 student movement? The nightmare of 1989 is already forgotten by the younger generation, but it is certainly not forgotten in the Jiang-Hu-Xi power chain. The foremost objective of their stability maintenance efforts over the past twenty-eight years has been to absolutely forbid any non-official gatherings at Tiananmen Square. Liu Xiaobo was not only a representative figure of June 4 but an international celebrity who had been awarded the Nobel Peace Prize, so one can only imagine the anxiety at Zhongnanhai.[1] Xiaobo was fated to die without a final resting place. The facts bore out that any thought of Xiaobo leaving prison at the age of sixty-five was mere wishful thinking.

I recently read the memoirs of the famous rights defense lawyer Gao Zhisheng.[2] His vivid descriptions of torture in prison included one particularly horrifying record. After Liu Xiaobo won the Nobel Peace Prize, a Public Security Bureau department head, Yu Hongyuan, came to talk with Gao Zhisheng. Yu said, "They gave the Nobel Peace Prize to Liu Xiaobo, but so what? He gets a pile of cash, but he can't even spend it, stuck in his prison cell. They ordered the Communist Party to release him. What do we care? Has that changed the Communist Party? No. Who gives a shit about the Nobel Peace Prize?" He warned Gao, "Don't stick with your foolishness and keep refusing to listen to good advice. There aren't going to be any meat pies dropping from the sky, and even if there are, they won't be for you." He went on, "Let me state it clearly: If the Communist Party was going to become extinct tomorrow, I would kill you tonight. The moment it looks like the Communist Party is finished, the last thing I will do is liquidate you."[3] This naked language is like a footnote to Xiaobo's death. In fact, one of the main focuses of the CCP leaders and their departments of dictatorship since the June Fourth Incident and the collapse of the Soviet Union and Eastern Europe has been to eliminate leading figures with public influence. To this end, they are willing to use any method, and they plan well in advance. It can be certain the Liu Xiaobo was their top target.

### The Profound Implications of the "No Enemy" Discourse

What were they doing it for? Their objectives were the privilege of being the sole party and the enormous benefits of monopoly. But the impetus for their behavior required a spiritual prop—the hatred arising from tradition, discipline, and brainwashing. The aforementioned Director Yu is a prime example. What was Gao Zhisheng's crime? What was Liu Xiaobo's? Wasn't it that they belong to the leadership of a democratized China of the future? The nineteen recommendations of Charter 08 mean such a heavy duty project! Director Yu's words cannot be explained with any word but "hatred." As Xiaobo said,

> Hatred only eats away at a person's intelligence and conscience, and an enemy mentality can poison the spirit of an entire people. . . . It can lead to cruel and lethal internecine combat, can destroy tolerance and

human feeling within a society, and can block the progress of a nation toward freedom and democracy. For these reasons I hope that I can rise above my personal fate and contribute to the progress of our country and to changes in our society. I hope that I can answer the regime's enmity with utmost benevolence, and can use love to dissipate hate.[4]

This quote was the fundamental formulation of his final statement in court, "I have no enemies."

Reviewing this self-vindication today, I feel that the so-called No Enemy concept that Xiaobo put forward included his unique content and grievance, clearly from the lessons of (Mao era) history and from his prediction of a free and democratic China. A constitutional democracy makes no distinction between the "enemy and us"; this is where Liu Xiaobo transcended the mindset of his fellow citizens. His ideology of peaceful and nonviolent resistance had already taken shape before June 4, influenced by the nonviolent movements of great thinkers such as Mahatma Gandhi, Nelson Mandela, and others and also a practical reflection on China's twentieth-century Communist revolution. Essentially, this was not only his personal political belief but also his appeal to those in power: he pointed out that "the regime's enemy mentality has pushed me into the defendant's dock," but the even deeper meaning was "Life-and-death struggle has already caused rivers of bloodshed in our country. Put down your butcher's knives and don't be an enemy of the people." Or perhaps Xiaobo overestimated the CCP's post–Cultural Revolution moderation and tendencies and his personal treatment in prison, but his good intentions cannot be denied. Opposition movements can consider many strategies. Using softness to prevail against strength is not the same as "capitulationism." Isn't hatred and enmity the feature of Islamic terrorism?

In short, Xiaobo's "no enemy" discourse means, in the political sphere, setting oneself against the Communist Party's violent revolution that constantly calls for drawing a line between the enemy and us, and especially opposing the dictatorial system that regards the people's freedom with hostility in peacetime, and in the legal sphere, esteeming rule of law, opposing party rule, and placing constitutional principles above all else. Social conflicts should be resolved by law, distinguishing only between the guilty and the not guilty with no latitude for the concepts of "the enemy" and "us." On this foundation, the CCP must abandon the characteristics of a revolutionary party in order to establish its legitimacy and in order for society to benefit from genuine harmony and stability.

## A Scholarly Quality of Responsibility for the World

I came to know Xiaobo in winter 1988 and carried out the interview in which he shocked the world by talking of "300 years of colonialism," until I participated in revising and republishing a book of Charter 08 in 2009.[5] Xiaobo wrote ninety-nine articles for *Open Magazine*. In our twenty years of literary communication and spiritual communion, I feel he never displayed a politician's skills but rather had a profoundly scholarly quality of responsibility for the world, minus the pedantic nature of the literati of former times. His "Self-Defense" was a powerful rebuttal of "speech crime." It is absolutely true. His literary talent, courage and insight qualify him as a thinker advocating for peaceful nonviolent struggle in contemporary China and an outstanding commentator opposing totalitarianism. As an intellectual of independent character, he had the rare quality of constantly challenging and negating himself. His expectation of himself was "whether in conduct or in writing, to live sincerely, responsibly and with dignity." Without aspiring to perfection, he spent sixty-one years accompanied by controversy, and in our era sunken in the physical and material, he achieved a life of singular radiance.

*Translated by Stacy Mosher*

## NOTES

Edited from a speech given at a memorial ceremony for Liu Xiaobo in New York in July 2017, revised on November 6, 2017.

1. Zhongnanhai, a former imperial garden in Beijing, serves as the central headquarters for CCP and China's central government. It is often used as a metonym for the Chinese leadership at large, in a sense similar to the term "White House."

2. Gao Zhisheng, *Unwavering Convictions: Gao Phishing's Ten-Year Torture and Faith in China's Future* (Durham NC: American Bar Association and Carolina Academic Press, 2017).—Trans.

3. Zhisheng, *Unwavering Convictions*, 109.—Trans.

4. Liu Xiaobo, "I Have No Enemies," trans. Perry Link, in *Liu Xiaobo: No Enemies, No Hatred*, ed. Perry Link, Tienchi Martin-Liao, and Liu Xia (Cambridge MA: The Belknap Press of Harvard University Press, 2012), 322–23.—Trans.

5. Li Xiaobo and Zhang Zuhua, eds., Charter 08 (Hong Kong: Open Books, 2009).—Trans.

# Liu Xiaobo, an Eternal Monument

*Pan Yongzhong*

On July 13, 2017, Liu Xiaobo sorrowfully passed away. His passion and his splendid life disappeared from this world, and even his final grave does not exist. . . .

When a person leaves this world but still lives in the hearts of people around the world, then this is eternal life. The spirit of Liu Xiaobo, the soul of Liu Xiaobo, has left an eternal monument in the heart of a generation. This is a monument of the times.

I never actually met Liu Xiaobo, nor did I talk with him on the phone, nor did we have any contact through written correspondence or email. In terms of the five senses, I did not know him.

## Understanding Liu Xiaobo from the Clash in Public Opinion

Like many people, I gradually learned about Liu Xiaobo from the media and from public opinion. The Liu Xiaobo I knew was linked together with the 1989 Democracy Movement. At that time, the Four Gentlemen of the Square, Liu Xiaobo, Hou Derchien, Gao Xin, and Zhou Duo, had a resounding reputation. Liu Xiaobo seemed destined to be a figure at the heart of the struggle—where the winds and waves are fiercest.

I remembered that after the 1989 movement, Liu Xiaobo testified on China's state-run CCTV: he had not seen the CCP's army kill anyone in Tiananmen Square. In 1992 his *The Monologues of a Doomsday's Survivor* was published in Taiwan. In this book, Xiaobo expressed regret for testifying that no one was killed in Tiananmen Square, and at the same time he defended himself, which led to harsh criticism from the overseas prodemocracy circles. In early 1993 Liu Xiaobo traveled to Australia and the United States and published "We Were Knocked Out by Our 'Justice,'" a critical self-examination of the 1989 Democracy Movement, causing great controversy among dissidents at home and abroad.

I remember in August 1993, Zhou Duo came to Germany for a visit and spent a few days at my home. Naturally, our conversation topics touched on Liu Xiaobo. Mr. Zhou objectively discussed the controversy over Liu Xiaobo's statement, "I didn't see anyone killed on the Square." I've long since forgotten the specifics of what we discussed; I only remember that there were two aspects of his meaning: First, Xiaobo really had not seen anyone killed when the square was cleared. This was a fact, which must initially be recounted truthfully to respect history and as a record of history. Second, it was normal to conduct a critical introspection of the 1989 Democracy Movement. With no introspection and no review, the Chinese democratization movement would not grow nor mature. Frankly speaking, my initial understanding of Liu Xiaobo only started when I regarded him as a fighter in China's democracy movement.

### The Storm Caused by His "No Enemies" Statement

At the beginning of 2010, Liu Xiaobo's "I Have No Enemies: My Final Statement" was disseminated, once again causing a great uproar. For a time, in the overseas prodemocracy circles, many people harshly denounced this statement. Frankly, his "no enemies" position did not surprise me at all. The first time I heard "no enemies" was in a speech given by the Dalai Lama in 2009.

In August 2009 I participated in the Finding Common Ground International Sino-Tibetan Dialogue Conference, which was held in Geneva. In his speech, the Dalai Lama mentioned the leaders of the Chinese Communist Party but did not directly state their names as Hu and Wen, but instead, politely referred to them as Mr. Hu Jintao and Mr. Wen Jiabao. We know that the CCP's propaganda machine has always demonized the Dalai Lama, vilifying him as a "splittist" and calling him a "wolf in sheep's clothing." The Tibetans had deep-seated accumulated grievances and anger toward Hu Jintao. After the unrest in Tibet in 1988, Hu Jintao began serving as party secretary of the Tibet Autonomous Region and later became the general secretary of the CCP and president of the country. The Dalai Lama said that the Buddhist texts do not contain the notion of "enemy"; rather, they are our opponents, not our enemies. It is precisely the realm of Buddhism to use benevolence and truth to face people in the world and to care for them. Although I understand that Buddhism has always upheld benevolence, charity, and goodness, the contrast in the attitudes of the two sides is so great that I still wonder.

I can accept Liu Xiaobo's "no enemies" doctrine because the Dalai Lama has really influenced me and given me nourishment. I've come to realize that people with great wisdom and intelligence are often calm minded and even tempered; they treat people with courtesy, requite evil with virtue, use reason to convince people and emotion to move people. Liu Xiaobo should have already reached such a state, as his book *Aesthetics and Human Freedom* was a research study precisely about the perfect realm of human life.

### "No Enemies" Illuminates the Future World

In fact, with respect to the "no enemies" doctrine, I have a few other thoughts.

War and massacre have permeated every stage of the development of human society; the concept of "enemy" has always been a specter overhead, surrounding human society. The CCP's doctrine of struggle further elevated and strengthened the hostile sentiments and contradictions in the world. Mao Zedong put forward the "theory of class struggle" and pushed the mutual killing and slaughter of human society to the extreme. In the thirty years from 1949 to 1979, the number of unnatural deaths in China reached more than forty million. China has always faced the endless creation of new "enemies," and an endless new round of repression and slaughter.

Liu Xiaobo advocated Charter 08, emphasized the rule of law and established the authority of the constitution. In the future, a democratic society will inevitably ban the concept of "class enemies." A constitution resides at the core, foundation, and highest position in a country's legal framework and its system of laws. All laws and regulations must be based on the constitution and the constitution taken as the criterion. In this sense, citizens should obey the law. In such a society, at most "lawbreakers" will appear, but not enemies.

I have lived in Germany for nearly three decades. I have never heard anyone discuss who is an "enemy." Someone once wrote: ". . . it is because every citizen and every politician firmly establishes the idea of 'I have no enemies' in their hearts that there is fair competition in their political life! . . . In real democratic countries, the citizens and politicians don't have between them the notion of who is the 'enemy' of whom."

Some people insist on the doctrine of enemies, which I don't think is such a big deal. These people still live amid the theory of struggle and are immersed in the inertia of hot war and "Cold War" of human society. But I firmly believe that human society will gradually eliminate the concept of "enemy," and we'll have instead only violators of the UN Charter and constitutions, human rights abusers, and perpetrators of crimes against humanity, and so on.

Taiwan's social transformation also reflected the idea of "no enemies." The Kuomintang and the Democratic Progressive Party changed from being "enemies" to political opponents, conducted fair competition, lifted the ban on newspaper publications and political parties, and brought Taiwan's society in line with international democracies. As a result, Taiwan has entered the stage of modern political civilization.

For the mainland prodemocracy activists, the idea of "no enemies" will not affect our persistence in opposing the CCP's dictatorship or its trampling on human rights, nor will it affect our efforts to promote China's prodemocracy movement and the establishment of China's constitutional and legal system.

## The Keys for Social Transformation

Looking back on the past two decades, the social transformation in many countries had a key that started the change, that is, either a historical event or a world-class democratic figure. For example, the key to the social transformation of Hungary was the Hungary Nagy Incident; the key to the transformation of South Korean society was the Gwangju Incident; the key to the transformation of Taiwan's society was the February 28 Incident; the key to the transformation of Myanmar's society is a figure, Aung San Suu Kyi; the key to the transformation of Polish society was Lech Wałęsa; the key to social transformation in South Africa was Nelson Rolihlahla Mandela; and the key to the transformation of Czech society was Vaclav Havel, and so on.

Mandela was a famous anti-apartheid revolutionary, politician, and philanthropist in South Africa. He is also widely regarded as the founding father of South Africa. When Mandela led the anti-apartheid campaign, South African courts convicted him of "conspiracy to overthrow the government" and other criminal charges. Mandela served a total of twenty-six and a half years in prison. Aung San Suu Kyi is a Myanmar politician who has long insisted on promoting the political democracy movement in Myanmar and suffered long-term imprisonment. Havel was a Czech writer and playwright and one of the famous dissidents and thinkers in the Velvet Revolution.

The social transformation experience in these countries involved firmly grasping this key, maintaining publicity, and spreading the truth and facts about the actual state of affairs to the entire society. When most people in the society can recognize social constitutional democracy, social transformation is not that far away.

China similarly also has such keys for change. One of them is the June Fourth Incident; another is Liu Xiaobo. Therefore, publicity about Liu Xiaobo and the spread of Liu Xiaobo's spirit are one of the main indispensable parts of the Chinese democracy movement.

The activists of the Chinese democracy movement in Europe have realized the precious key of Liu Xiaobo, so we have organized many events, including conferences and demonstrations, to focus on Liu Xiaobo's thinking and actions. We also highlighted his imprisonment, of course, in order to attract public attention to exert continued pressure on the Chinese authorities. After Liu Xiaobo's death we held a memorial service for him. We've worked together with German human rights organizations and a German priest, Roland Kuehne, who is also a teacher at the Rhein-Maas Vocational College in Kempen city. From 2010 to 2017, each year, he organized nearly three hundred students and teachers to drive four hundred miles to protest in front of the Chinese embassy in Berlin to demand Liu Xiaobo's freedom. Tienchi Martin-Liao, the president of the Independent Chinese PEN Center since 2016, who also served an earlier term from 2009 to 2013, was always with us. In 2001 Liu Xiaobo and other colleagues founded ICPC, which Tienchi Martin-Liao described as Liu Xiaobo's legacy, and thus it was now more important than ever for its work to continue uninterrupted. Liu Xiaobo said that he hoped he would be the last victim of the literary inquisition in China. But this wishful thinking is currently unrealistic. As of May 2018 ICPC still had nine mainland members behind bars. The fight for freedom of expression in China, which Liu Xiaobo sacrificed his life for, must go on.

Everyone in the world knows the story of Jesus, but there is almost no mention made of the story of Jesus from birth until about the age of thirty. Just three and a half years after Jesus preached the word, Jesus was accused by the Jewish high priest Caiaphas and was sentenced to death by the prefect of Judea, Pontius Pilate, and was then crucified. In fact, that year very few people knew about the story of Jesus. During that year, Jesus's reputation was probably not as strong as Liu Xiaobo's today. But Jesus used the candle of life to light the spirit of human love and he lit the torch of human light. It was only after two thousand years of dissemination that humanity has the great Christian culture of today and today's beautiful and brilliant European culture and Western civilization.

Liu Xiaobo used the candle of life to light up the awakening of the Chinese. Only constitutional democracy can save China. We have the responsibility to lift this candle high and spread it to every corner of the world. One of the main parts of promoting the democratization movement in China is to praise Liu Xiaobo's spirit and spread Liu Xiaobo's thoughts.

### Let Liu Xiaobo's Life Candle Last Forever

Sandor Petofi's verse "I'll Sacrifice My Life" is reflected in Liu Xiaobo's sacrifice of his precious life for freedom.[1]

Liu Xiaobo believed in universal values throughout his life, carried out peaceful and rational struggles, promoted the country's constitutional democracy, and pursued social fairness. Charter 08 is the declaration and heroic movement of Liu Xiaobo and the democratic intellectual circles pursuing constitutional democracy. It promotes freedom, human rights, equality, republicanism, democracy, and constitutionalism. It is an important political document for Chinese democrats in raising political opinions and ideas.

Humans have only one life, but Liu Xiaobo dissolved his life into the pursuit of constitutional democracy. On July 13, 2017, Liu Xiaobo left; he lit the world with the candlelight of his life and fulfilled his ideal of coming into the world. His brave soul is immortal, and his spirit everlasting! He will forever live in the memory of the world, becoming the beacon of China's democratic cause and becoming a monument in the heart of the world, an eternal monument!

*Translated by Andréa Worden*

## NOTE

1. Sandor Petofi (1823–1949) was a Hungarian poet and revolutionary. One of his most famous poems is "Liberty and love / These two I must have. / For my love I'll sacrifice / My life. / For liberty I'll sacrifice / My love." trans. G. F. Cushing, in Zoltán Bodolai, *The Timeless Nation* (Sydney: Hungria, 1978), http://www.hungarianhistory.com/lib/timeless/chapter23.htm.—Trans.

# Poems

*Shi Tao*

*To Liu Xiaobo*

## The Enemy

There is my enemy
In a chair empty
Waiting for me
Not allowing me voice for help a bit of cry achy
There is my enemy
In a sickbed empty
Waiting for me
Not allowing me to leave here for any . . .

My enemy is just a simple word:
Free
It is in front of me, so close but not to be
Just one thing is its hostility
Smile icy
In this July sultry
Silently pulling me
Into a nightmare inky

    *Dali*

## Song of October

The last brief poem is like a tide of sound
Sharply ended
Momentary silence brings

The winter wind on rough and clumsy footsteps
Now
A triumphal procession like a poem is somewhere
Gathering
So many pairs of brave and nimble hands are
Flying over keyboards–
Song of the Earth, Song of Freedom
"Is it the rustling of wind through the lush mountain forests?
Or ominous thunder concealed behind the snowy mountain peak?"
The connotation of a drop of ink is
Bearing witness to the last drop of blood shed for victory
His eyes are grim
And people follow his gaze to the sky
October
Comes from afar, but is not the end
October
Will become a festival for all the unfortunate and their friends

*From Yinchuan Prison, Ningxia*
*Translated by Yu Zhang and edited by Stacy Mosher*

# Poems
*Xu Lin*

## Mourning Xiaobo

I thought the eleven-year
Is nothing but a little while
For a great practitioner
It is just a minor ordeal
But the devils were more aware
Their doomsday would not be far but near
And you would not need to stay until
Full eleven years to get out of jail
So someone had long put a dirty finger
To prevent your heroism to reappear
In the end you could not withstand their persecution to kill
When practicing to the eighth year
You have become a sage
You have said you have no enemies
That is because
In your noble realm of thought
There remains no trace of impurities

## How Can I Save You?

When you should go
You refused to go
Insisting on planting freedom
In this plot of soil
In spite of being charged for no reason
Into prison
You still created

Something immortal

When you should not go
You are about to go
That devotedly cultivated fruit
Is about to mature
In spite of your indomitable will
You cannot finally get through
You say you have no enemies
But they refuse to let you go

How can I
Save you
I have come all this way
But cannot catch you
How can I
Save you
With my hot blood
Or a heaven-shaking roar?

*Translated by Yu Zhang and edited by Stacy Mosher*

# The Well after Its Name Has Left

IN MEMORY OF A DEPARTED POET

*Zi Kang*


The martyr's name has departed prostrate
Vacating a windowless room
A room open wide at the top
A well of unplumbable depth

Nobody has heard the name in the well
If not heard at twenty years old
It can never again be heard or understood
That is a deafening silence

The person with no enemies has gone
The person regarded as an enemy has gone
He has turned into smoke floating from the well's mouth
And will not need to worry about that name anymore

He succeeded in his illegal crossing over the Pacific Ocean
And reached that empty chair
At the well's bottom another name will appear
A person without even a chair

*Translated by Yu Zhang and Stacy Mosher*

# Message to Liu Xiaobo and Liu Xia

*Tiananmen Mothers*

JULY 14, 2017

Tiananmen Mothers and Human Rights in China issues the group's message to Liu Xiaobo and Liu Xia:

**Xiaobo:** Although you lost your freedom and lost your life, you still possess the great love of the world, which no one on Earth can match. In our hearts, you live eternally.

**Liu Xia:** For Xiaobo, for yourself, and for all those in the world who truly love you, you must continue to live with strength and dignity! Love you! You are not alone; we are with you.

*Translation by Human Rights in China*

NOTE

Tiananmen Mothers, "To Liu Xiaobo and Liu Xia," Human Rights in China, July 14, 2017, http://www.hrichina.org/en/citizens-square/liu-xiaobo-and-liu-xia.

**1.** Liu Xiaobo, November 26, 2017. Photo by Hao Jian.

**2.** Liu Xiaobo on Tiananmen Square, June 3, 1989.

**3.** Opposite: ICPC's second award ceremony, Beijing, September 30, 2003. From left, around the front table: Bao Zhunxin, honorary director; Zhang Yihe, Freedom to Write winner; Liu Xiaobo, president; Wang Yi, deputy secretary-general; and Yu Jie, director.

**4.** Dinner party of the members of ICPC and two other PEN centers, Beijing, May 13, 2005. Back: Yu Zhang; Chip Rolly, Sydney PEN; Wang Yi Yu Shicun; Li Baiguang. Front: Liu Min, Yu Jie's wife; Kjell Holm, Swedish PEN; Liu Xiaobo; Nicholas Jose, Sydney PEN; Yu Jie; Liu Xia.

**5.** Liu Xia and Liu Xiaobo at Mount Lao in Qingdao, May 20, 2005.

**6.** Liu Xiaobo and Professor Sun Wenguang, ICPC honorary director, in Qingdao, May 21, 2005.

**7.** ICPC's third award ceremony, Beijing, January 2, 2006. From left: Mo Shaoping, lawyer; Yu Jie, vice president; Wu Si, Freedom to Write awardee; Liu Xiaobo, president; and Wang Yi, director and deputy secretary-general.

**8.** Visiting professors and ICPC honorary directors Ding Ziling and Jiang Peikun, with Liu Di, Zhao Dagong, and Liu Xiaobo (in back).

**9.** Liu Xiaobo at Yu Jianrong's farmyard in Beijing suburbs, August 30, 2007.

10. Liu Xiaobo, Beijing, September 13, 2007.

11. Liu Xiaobo at Bao Zunxin's funeral, Beijing, November 3, 2007.

**12.** Liu Xiaobo speaks at a weekend forum of Sanwei Book House, Beijing, May 18, 2008.

**13.** ICPC delegation meets Japan's Congressman Makino Seishu to support Liu Xiaobo, Tokyo, September 30, 2010. From left: Wang Jinzhong, ICPC vice president Patrick Poon, Makino Seishu, ICPC president Tienchi Martin-Liao, Li Jianhong, and Wu Yangwei.

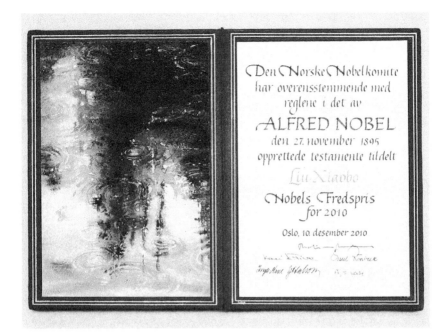

**14.** Nobel Peace Prize Certificate for Liu Xiaobo, Oslo, December 10, 2010.

**15.** Empty chair for Liu Xiuaobo at Nobel Peace Prize awarding ceremony, Oslo, December 10, 2010.

**16.** Honorary Director Cai Chu (left) and President Tienchi Martin-Liao at ICPC celebration demonstration in Oslo, December 10, 2010.

**17.** Demonstration in front of Chinese Embassy in Oslo, December 11, 2010. From left: Tsoi Wing-Mui, Wang Jinzhong, Patrick Poon, Yu Zhang, and U.S. Congressman Chris Smith.

**18.** Finding Room for Common Ground: No Enemies, No Hatred, International Conference of Four-PEN Platform, Malmö, August 30, 2017. From left: Yu Zhang, ICPC; Kaiser Abdurusul ÖzHun, Uyghur PEN; and with PEN International, Treasurer Jarkko Tontti, Vice President Hori Takeaki, and Vice President Joanne Leedom-Ackerman.

**19.** Liu Xiaobo Memorial Award to Dr. Shirin Ebadi, Malmö, August 29, 2017.

**20.** Liu Xia and her brother, Liu Hui, at Liu Xiaobo's funeral, Shenyang, July 15, 2017.

# Politics, People, and PEN

*Facing up to and Resisting Reality*

# Our Last Parting Unexpectedly Became Our Final Farewell

*Wang Debang*

## 1

On the morning of July 13, 2017, the local state security bureau called to catch up, and I took the opportunity to request permission to go to Shenyang to visit Liu Xiaobo, who at that time was critically ill. In order to win their approval, I agreed to be accompanied by one of their officers there and back. But within a few hours, the internet reported the sad news that Liu Xiaobo had passed away.

In my enormous grief, I decided to attend Liu Xiaobo's farewell service at all costs, and I contacted friends in Beijing to find out what arrangements had been made, only to learn that not one of them had any information. All of them were waiting to be notified by Liu Xiaobo's family or the authorities.

On July 15 photos were posted on the internet of Liu's farewell ceremony and the sea burial of his ashes. Unable to believe they were real, I read every news report I could find. Finally, in despair, I sat in front of my computer for a long time, my face covered with tears as I murmured to myself—Was that what had become of Liu Xiaobo? Was that really the end?

## 2

I first met Liu Xiaobo in 1988. He had just defended his PhD dissertation, "Aesthetics and Human Freedom," creating an uproar in the academic world. Some students in Beijing Normal University's Chinese Literature Department even copied off parts of Mr. Liu's dissertation and distributed it or read it out at the March 18 Memorial on campus.[1] In that time of rare ideological and academic invigoration in China, a "dark horse" in the literary and philosophical community had leaped out and was eagerly promoted by many young scholars. I remember how one night, as I was on my way to a self-study session, I passed by one of the university's lecture halls and saw a large number of students sitting on window ledges and crammed in the doorway while quite a few stood in the lawn outside the lecture hall to listen. Curious, I asked one of the students what was going on and learned that Liu Xiaobo was giving a lecture. I also wanted to push my way in for a look, but there were too many people, and I could only stand under a window and listen. The scratchy amplifier relayed a stammering but resonant and penetrating voice permeated with the tone of a cultural pathfinder who disdained the ways of the world and those in power and who believed he was making an irreplaceable contribution to the world of literature. Indeed, Liu Xiaobo's essays from that period communicate an intense expressiveness, pungency, and arrogant rebellion against orthodoxy. Hearing his lectures and reading his essays left me with the impression that Liu Xiaobo was proud, aloof, and unapproachable. Eventually one of the students sitting on the window ledge climbed down for a rest so, I replaced him and craned my neck to gain a glimpse of Liu sitting at the rostrum. The distance and the large number of people inside prevented me from forming a strong impression. During the 1989 patriotic anticorruption and prodemocracy movement, I was active in the university's dialogue delegation, and Liu was leading the resistance in front of Tiananmen, but still I had no opportunity for contact with him. As I result, when I finally met him more than ten years later, I didn't even recognize him.

One day in autumn 2002, Ren Bumei visited Beijing and was staying at a guesthouse near the zoo, and he telephoned me to come over and see him.[2] When I arrived at his room, I found quite a few people sitting in a circle in animated discussion with a slightly stammering man. Ren Bumei came over and told me that the man in the middle was Liu Xiaobo. I was quite startled, but looking more closely, I vaguely recognized his face. Going over to shake his hand, I said, "Mr. Liu, you were the idol of university students in the 1980s. I was in the class of 1985 studying philosophy at BNU, and I heard your lecture." Liu looked stupefied for a moment and paused the debate as if wanting to ask me something, but ultimately he didn't say anything.

While Liu was in graduate school, he was roommates with Yuan Guiren, who had taught epistemology to my philosophy class and then became minister of education, so he may have been moved by my saying I was a philosophy student at that time or wanted to ask me something. Even so, during my contacts with Liu over the next few years, I never heard him speak of his interaction with Yuan Guiren.

I remember that among the people surrounding and debating Liu Xiaobo that day was Wan Yanhai, as well as several people whose names I've forgotten.[3] Because I had an urgent matter to attend to that day, I took my leave when the others went to dinner. After that, I had the good fortune to encounter Liu at a number of dinner parties in Beijing, and we became better acquainted. I felt there was a vast difference between Liu and the proud, aloof image I'd formed of him in the 1980s.

Just before the spring festival in 2004, I ran into Mr. Liu at a dinner party, and while eating we talked about the Independent Chinese PEN Center. I expressed a willingness to join, and Liu, who was ICPC's president at the time, immediately agreed to refer me for membership. I sensed how sincerely and amiably Liu treated others.

I attended another dinner party arranged by Bao Zunxin for friends in Beijing, but there were too many people there for me to exchange more than a few words with Liu.[4] Even so, something he did at that dinner left a deep impression on me. A server came to clear the dishes and picked up a platter that still had a few vegetables on it. Before he could remove it, Mr. Liu took the platter from the server's hands, pushed the vegetables and their juices into his bowl, and ate them up. His frugality was amazing. During subsequent meals with Liu I noticed that he persistently maintained this practice of cleaning up all of the food.

One afternoon before the mid-autumn festival in 2004, I went to visit Liu at his home. At that time I was manager of a privately run school in Beijing, and he asked me in detail about the situation of such schools. As someone in that field, I was deeply concerned with the problem of investors being interested only in profits. After listening, he said, "Although privately-run schools have a lot of problems, aren't they still better than public schools?" There was no way to answer this question in a few brief sentences, so I just said that there was a difference between private schools under China's totalitarian system and private schools under a democratic society and market economy, and to a certain extent the disparity in the quality of education they offered was much greater. Later, Liu said that he would like to have an on-site look at a private school when it was convenient, but I left that school soon afterward, so my intention to invite him for a visit never came to fruition.

In summer 2005 my college classmate Zhu Jiuhu, who at that time was a lawyer representing well owners in the Northern Shaanxi oilfield case, was detained by the local authorities. The intellectual community launched a rescue campaign, and I wrote an essay entitled "The Stormy Road of Rights Defense: A Record of Lawyer Zhu Jiuhu's History of Rights Defense" to express my support. One night, I received a phone call from Liu Xiaobo. He said he had also written an essay on behalf of Zhu Jiuhu, and he wanted me to know that he had cited some of the material in my essay. I was happily surprised and deeply moved by Liu's strict approach to scholarly work. This also set an example for me in my own writing and made me less rash in quoting other material and evidence.

On November 3, 2007, a memorial ceremony was held at the Beijing Dongjiao Funeral Parlor for the sadly departed leader of China's modern democracy movement, Bao Zunxin. Obstruction by the police prevented the ceremony from being carried out at its appointed time that morning. When I hurried over, I saw Liu Xiaobo in tears of grief and indignation after an unsuccessful attempt to negotiate with the police. That was the only time I saw Liu Xiaobo cry. Of course, he was crying in grief over Bao's being so unjustly treated even after his death. Who would have guessed that a little more than ten years later, Liu Xiaobo would meet with even greater cruelty and injustice?

## 3

On the night of July 22, 2008, taking advantage of a brief gap before strict controls were imposed for the Beijing Olympics, the famous constitutional scholar Zhang Zuhua held a dinner party attended by Liu Xiaobo, Wang Lixiong, Woeser, Mo Shaoping, and me at a restaurant near the home of famous legal scholar Yu Haocheng.[5] The eighty-three-year-old Yu, accompanied by his daughter, drank liquor as he chatted, while Liu Xiaobo drank tea as always. We took photos together to commemorate the dinner. When it was my turn for a photo with Liu Xiaobo, I stood behind him and made him sit, but Liu Xiaobo adamantly refused and demanded that we either stand or sit together. I was once again struck by Liu Xiaobo's amiable and approachable character in such stark contrast to my impression of him as aloof and arrogant in the 1980s.

That night everyone talked enthusiastically and drank their fill, but I had an uneasy feeling that I couldn't pinpoint. On further reflection, I feel that Zhang Zuhua must have arranged this dinner party in anticipation of going to prison, because Charter 08 was about to be released, and the related work had reached a critical stage. To tell the truth, among the people in my acquaintance, it was Zhang Zuhua who was most aware of the risk involved in Charter 08, and as a result he had made full preparations to be imprisoned. Strangely, the authorities ultimately didn't imprison Zhang Zuhua but handed a heavy prison sentence to Liu Xiaobo. Clearly it could not be said that the authorities didn't fully grasp the situation because Zhang Zuhua openly stated to the police that he was the person responsible for Charter 08, but ultimately the authorities released him and imprisoned Liu Xiaobo.

Some people later interpreted this as an attempt to force Xiaobo to leave the country. I see a larger plan at work, however. The authorities were well aware of Charter 08's historic significance, so they intentionally shifted the focus of the international community from the political figure, Zhang Zuhua, to the literary figure, Liu Xiaobo, in order to dilute the subsequent impact of the Charter. This also put Liu Xiaobo under control in a tangible prison and Zhang Zuhua in an invisible prison. Of course, Liu Xiaobo's role in Charter 08 and his untiring support of China's human rights and democracy from 1989 onward fully qualified him for the Nobel Peace Prize. Not only that, China has another group of people, among them the Tiananmen Mothers, Zhang Zuhua, Liu Xianbin, Chen Xi, Guo Feixiong, Gao Zhisheng and Qin Yongmin, who for decades have untiringly and tenaciously fought for the progress of China's human rights and democracy and who also deserve the honor of a Nobel Peace Prize.[6]

That night, those who attended the dinner party knew very well that harsh controls imposed for the Beijing Olympics would prevent them from getting together for a time, but they never guessed it would mark their final parting from Liu.

## 4

On the night of December 8, 2008, I was browsing on my computer when I suddenly received the news that Zhang Zuhua and Liu Xiaobo had been taken away by the police and their homes had been ransacked. I realized that the authorities had begun cracking down on the impending release of Charter 08. Afterwards, Liu was put under criminal detention on suspicion of "inciting subversion of state power," and although this was subsequently changed to residential surveillance, he was subsequently arrested again. On Christmas Day 2009, he was sentenced to eleven years in prison.

On the night of January 10, 2009, the Beijing municipal state security bureau summoned me and ransacked my home. In his conversation with me at that time, StateSec (state security) division leader Ye told me that Mr. Liu Xiaobo said I had taken part in activities connected with Charter 08, and he wanted me to make a full accounting of this matter. I naturally knew that StateSec was using Xiaobo's name to deceive me, but keeping in mind that Liu Xiaobo had had no contact with the outside world since being detained, I wanted an opportunity to see him and gain an understanding of his situation. I therefore demanded that StateSec allow me to challenge Liu Xiaobo to his face. Of course StateSec didn't agree, and my wish to see Liu Xiaobo again was not realized. On the day Liu Xiaobo went on trial, I was kept under watch at home by Fangshan District StateSec and was unable to go to court. After the sentence was announced, I said with no little irony to the StateSec officers, "You're finally going to get a Chinese to win the Nobel Peace Prize!" I said bluntly, "Do you really think you can imprison Mr. Liu Xiaobo for eleven years?" I firmly believed that China had reached a juncture at which enormous change could happen at any moment, surely in less than eleven years, so Liu Xiaobo was sure to be released before completing his sentence.

But as the days, months, and years passed, China did not move toward civilization and instead regressed unto barbarity. After enduring nine years in prison and with his release within sight, Liu Xiaobo was suddenly diagnosed with terminal liver cancer on June 26, 2017, and reached the end of his earthly life soon afterward.

**5**

During the time when I was fortunate to have known Liu Xiaobo, from the 1980s when I believed he was arrogant and aloof, until I later had contact with him and personally experienced his temperate rationality and amiable approachability, he underwent the change that the calamities of the thousand-year drama of the Chinese people wreaks on an individual life. As Liu Xiaobo himself said, "June 1989 has been the major turning point in my life, which now is just over one half century in length."[7] But amid this evolving external appearance, Liu Xiaobo tenaciously held fast to an unchanging principle—I have no enemies!

There has been a great deal of controversy regarding this discourse of "I have no enemies." Anyone who wants to understand the deep meaning of Liu's discourse must look back at the process of its emergence and evolution.

On June 2, 1989, Liu Xiaobo carried out a hunger strike at Tiananmen Square with Hou Derchien, Zhou Duo, and Gao Xin and drafted "The June 2nd Hunger Strike Declaration," which states, "We have no enemies. We must not let hatred or violence poison our thinking or the progress of democratization in China."[8]

On December 25, 2009, Liu Xiaobo made his final statement, "I Have No Enemies," while on trial for inciting subversion of state power at the Beijing Municipal Intermediate Court. In it he once again declared: "I wish to underscore something that was in my 'June 2nd Hunger-Strike Declaration' of twenty years ago: I have no enemies and no hatred." He further explained:

> Hatred only eats away at a person's intelligence and conscience, and an enemy mentality can poison the spirit of an entire people. . . . It can lead to cruel and lethal internecine combat, it can destroy tolerance and human feeling within a society, and can block the progress of a nation toward freedom and democracy. For these reasons I hope that I can rise above my personal fate and contribute to the progress of our country and to changes in our society. I hope that I can answer the regime's enmity with utmost benevolence, and can use love to dissipate hate.[9]

From Mr. Liu Xiaobo's statement it can be seen that "I have no enemies" is a demand he made as his personal life standard. It was not a description of the actual situation in society, much less a denial of the existence of enemies of democracy and conscience because he clearly perceived the "regime's enmity." Much of the current controversy surrounding "I have no enemies" therefore departs from Xiaobo's original intention.

## 6

"I have no enemies" is the life precept Mr. Liu Xiaobo held fast to, but it dealt a fatal blow to the soft spot of post-totalitarian society. Its sociological, political, and philosophical significance and reach give it spiritual links to such great thinkers of Eastern Europe's transitional period as Vaclav Havel and Lech Wałęsa, and to a certain extent, it can be considered the Chinese expression of Eastern European transitional thought.

The truth is that post-totalitarian society needs enemies and has an enemy dependency that makes it constantly create enemies. This is because post-totalitarian society needs to constantly expose and criticize, forestall, suppress and negate the various ideological enemies of the proletarian dictatorship. Without these enemies, post-totalitarian society cannot demonstrate its steadfastness to its ideology, and this ideology of the "enemy and us" that is based on the fight between progressive and backward classes must constantly seek out enemies to fight in order to demonstrate its revolutionary nature. That is why the ideological scope of post-totalitarian society constantly launches campaigns to oppose and purge the enemy's bourgeois liberalism, spiritual pollution, universal values, and so on.

If a post-totalitarian system doesn't manufacture external enemies or seek out and designate as hostile the various internal forces that surmount the power system, then it cannot find the customary basis for carrying out systemic suppression, and the system's suppressive apparatus is threatened with foreclosure, fundamentally imperiling post-totalitarian rule. A post-totalitarian society therefore requires enemies to prolong its existence.

A post-totalitarian society facing problems of legitimacy continues to whitewash and boost itself by seeking enemy plots that terrify the public and alert and placate the ruling clique. Vested interests protect their own interests by obstructing social reform as much as possible.

The elite clique (vested interests) labels demands for reforms that affect vested interests as the most "hostile forces" intended to "subvert state power" or "Westernize" China. This escalates a social reform issue into an issue of ideology or state power with the result that the protection of personal interests is transformed into safeguarding the regime and defending ideology. This politicizes social reform issues and introduces a hostile element to the path to reform with the result that organizations and the state are held hostage in service to protecting personal interests. This method of using the created enemy as a pretext for protecting vested interests is extremely common and effective in post-totalitarian societies.

Post-totalitarian society's need for enemies demonstrates its crisis of legitimacy. As the world has become wary and obstructive of the dangers of totalitarianism and the general public has become increasingly aware of rule of law and human rights, instances of resistance have proliferated, causing panic to the ruling clique. The direct response to this panic has been harsh suppression of all challenge and resistance, and nipping in the bud all dissenting voices and actions. This requires unearthing and even creating enemies to suppress in order to intimidate the public and consolidate the ruling clique. Making enemies has consequently become a pillar on which post-totalitarian society relies for its existence. To fill the vacuum of legitimacy, the efforts of a post-totalitarian system to seek out social enemies become increasingly prevalent and violent. In its intense need for enemies to save itself, post-totalitarianism takes the initiative to create those enemies. In a certain sense, totalitarianism creates enemies by treating humanity as the enemy. Totalitarianism makes humanity's competition for limited resources into an ideological issue and on that elevated plane pronounces destruction on the "enemy" and the victory of "our side." It turns mutual competition into the historical and moral responsibility and mission of "our side" to exterminate the "enemy." This mission creates an institutional dependence on the enemy.

As long as post-totalitarian society requires and relies on enemies to prolong its existence, "I have no enemies" will continue to be a wrench in the works of the totalitarian system. That gives it value on both the practical and theoretical levels. In this respect, the CCP authorities' sentencing of Liu Xiaobo can be considered a reaction to his "I have no enemies" discourse hitting them in their most vulnerable spot.

Liu Xiaobo lives forever!

*Translated by Stacy Mosher*

## NOTES

Written October 21, 2017, the one-hundredth day after the death of Liu Xiaobo.

1. The March 18 Memorial commemorates the violent suppression of a protest against the Beiping government's concessions to foreign incursions on March 18, 1926. Forty-seven protesters were killed and more than two hundred were injured.—Trans.

2. Ren Bumei (b. 1967) is an independent writer and Christian thinker living in Canada.—Trans.

3. Rd. Wan Yanhai (b. 1963), who started his career in the Ministry of Health, became a prominent activist on AIDS issues.—Trans.

4. Bao Zunxin (1937–2007) was a Chinese historian and dissident intellectual who served three and a half years in prison for his participation in the 1989 Democracy Movement.—Trans.

5. Wang Lixiong (b. 1953) is an independent writer on environmental and Tibetan issues. Woeser, Wang's wife, is a Tibetan poet. Mo Shaping is a prominent rights defense lawyer. Yu Haoching (1925–2015), former editor of the Masses Publishing House, an organ of China's Ministry of Public Security, was subjected to imprisonment and house arrest for eighteen months after defending the 1989 Democracy Movement. Yu was allowed to leave China in 1994 and was granted political asylum in the United States in 1997 and became a founding member of ICPC in 2001 and later its honorary director. He returned to China in 2005 and was an early signatory of Charter 08.—Trans.

6. Liu Xianbin (b. 1968) is a Sichuan-based human rights activist, cofounder of the China Democracy Party and signatory of Charter 08. In 2011 he was sentenced to ten years in prison for inciting subversion of state power. Chen Xi (b. 1954), aka Chen Youcai, is a Guiyang-based rights defender who was also sentenced to ten years in prison in 2011 for inciting subversion of state power. Guo Feixiong (b. 1966), aka Yang Maodong, is a rights defense legal worker and activist, and has been detained and imprisoned multiple times, most recently in 2015, when he was handed a six-year sentence. Gao Zhisheng (b. 1964), a rights defense lawyer, has been subjected to repeated imprisonment and detention. Qin Yongmin (b. 1953) is a political commentator, human rights activist, and cofounder of the China Democracy Party and has been imprisoned multiple times, for more than twenty-six

years in total. He was detained in January 2015 and sentenced to thirteen years' imprisonment in July 2018.—Trans.

7. Liu Xiaobo, "I Have No Enemies: My Final Statement," trans. Perry Link, in *Liu Xiaobo: No Enemies, No Hatred*, ed. Perry Link, Tienchi Martin-Liao, and Liu Xia (Cambridge MA: The Belknap Press of Harvard University Press, 2012), 321.—Trans.

8. "The June 2nd Hunger Strike Declaration," trans. Perry Link, in Link et al., *Liu Xiaobo*, 282.—Trans.

9. Xiaobo, "I Have No Enemies," 322.—Trans.

# Missing My Good Friend Liu Xiaobo

*He Depu*

Liu Xiaobo and I met in 1999. It was He Xintong (wife of Xu Wenli, who was in prison at the time) who took me to Liu Xiaobo's home. Liu Xiaobo and Liu Xia were very happy to see He Xintong and me, and we chatted for a long time. Later, I talked with Xiaobo several times in the teahouse near Xiaobo's house; there were two meetings that left me with the deepest impression.

At the beginning of the year 2000, I brought a few friends to meet with Liu Xiaobo at the teahouse. At the turn of the century, I was responsible for the national work of the Democracy Party (July 1999 to November 2002). At the end of the twentieth century, I organized the drafting of the Declaration of the China Democracy Party Welcoming the New Century. After seeing Xiaobo, I gave him a printed copy of the declaration. As Xiaobo read it, he asked me, "Did you write this?" I said yes. At that gathering, we also talked about other things.

The other meeting was on December 7, 2001, in the afternoon, from 1 to 4 p.m. The location was still at the teahouse near Liu Xiaobo's home (and the last time we met). This time the two of us met alone, and we talked about a wide range of issues: for example, the policies of Western democratic countries on the difficult situation for human rights in China, the current status of Chinese intellectuals' pig philosophy, the launching of mutually supportive rights protection activities, the work of the Chinese prodemocracy movement, and our respective positions on imprisonment.[1] When we left the teahouse, a big snowstorm suddenly fell from the Beijing sky; that heavy snowfall brought Beijing's traffic to a complete standstill. Many Beijingers who got off from work that evening didn't get home until 3 the next morning.

I understood Liu Xiaobo in this way: he was really willing to help others, his behavior was low profile but very persistent. He was a tough guy with ideas who dared to act and take things on himself. Although we didn't have much contact, I always held him in deep respect. With his writing he defied the powerful and wealthy; he wrote with passion for the common people. His articles were basically all published in overseas newspapers and magazines. Each article, without exception, incisively drove its point home and gave the reader a feeling of passion, comfort, competence, and a sense that the style mirrored the man.

On November 4, 2002, I was detained by the Beijing domestic security police under the residential surveillance measure. I suffered all kinds of torture and eighty-five days later was officially arrested. On October 14, 2003, I was tried, and on November 17, Liu Xiaobo wrote "Protest CCP's Trial of He Depu" and accepted interviews with overseas media about my trial.

On November 6, 2003, the Beijing No. 1 Intermediate People's Court sentenced me to eight years in prison for inciting subversion of state power. After hearing the verdict in court, while my wife, Jia Jianying, was on her way home alone, she received a call from Liu Xiaobo inviting her to his home for dinner. The dinner was prepared by Liu Xia. With sincere emotions, Liu Xiaobo and Liu Xia always expressed their concern for the family members of political dissidents.

At the beginning of 2000, many families of political prisoners who had received heavy sentences received help from Liu Xiaobo. At the same time he used his pen and mouth to exercise his freedom of expression, Liu Xiaobo used various methods to care for and assist the families of political prisoners though the fees he received from his writing were too limited to help all of them.

In 2008 Liu Xiaobo organized the drafting of Charter 08. The Chinese government believed that Charter 08 was an event that involved both words and deeds, and that someone had to take responsibility for this offense. In an act of awe-inspiring righteousness, Liu Xiaobo shouldered the cross. After the Chinese authorities arrested him, he was sentenced to eleven years in prison.

In 2009, when Liu Xiaobo was being held at the detention center, the police informed his family that Liu Xiaobo wanted a cotton-padded mattress. After Liu Xia delivered the mattress to the detention center, the police returned it to her on the grounds that it didn't meet the required measurements. After learning about this, Jia Jianying bought cotton and cloth from the store. Based on the measurements (length 190 centimeters, width 85 centimeters) that I provided, since I was in prison at the time, my wife sewed a thick cotton-padded mattress for Liu Xiaobo, and Liu Xia took the thick mattress to the detention center.

On October 8, 2010, the Norwegian Nobel Committee awarded Liu Xiaobo that year's peace prize. After she learned that Xiaobo had won the award, Liu Xia was extremely happy and invited 143 colleagues and friends from China to participate in the Nobel Prize awards ceremony on December 10. Jia Jianying's name was also included on the list. But in order to prevent her from going to Norway to attend the awards ceremony, the police put her on the blacklist of those forbidden to leave the country; the exit prohibition was for one year.

On January 24, 2011, after I had served the full eight years and eighty-five days in prison, my release was quite a high-profile event. After I was released from prison, I learned that Liu Xiaobo, during his tenure as president for the first two terms in 2003–7 after ICPC was founded in 2001, exerted a great deal of effort to help me and other political prisoners in jail. Liu Xiaobo got my name put on PEN International's Case List and made me an honorary member of ICPC and Swiss French PEN, and they also provided support for me and my wife for our living expenses. At that time, I was in prison serving my sentence, and I needed about eight hundred yuan per month, mainly to pay off the prison guards to make things a bit easier. Consequently, in May 2008 my open letter to Juan Samaranch, the former president of the International Olympics Committee, was able to be sent from prison. On the eve of the opening ceremony in Beijing, the letter landed on Samaranch's desk in Beijing, and the bad conditions in China's prisons received a great deal of attention from the international media. I was in Beijing No. 2 Prison, where many political prisoners' manuscripts and letters home were able to fly smoothly over the prison's high wall and then be disseminated on the internet. None of this would have happened without the invaluable assistance of Liu Xiaobo.

On June 26, 2017, the news broke that Liu Xiaobo was suffering from end-stage liver cancer and that he had been transferred from Jinzhou Prison to the First Affiliated Hospital of China Medical University, Shenyang, for critical care. This news gained a high level of attention in the outside world. At the same time, the Beijing Public Security Bureau police quickly positioned themselves in front of the stairway to my home. Taking shifts, they monitored my wife and me day and night. In front of my home there were three sets of ultra-high-definition camera probes, police, guard posts, and police cars. The police clearly told us that we were not allowed to go to Shenyang to visit Liu Xiaobo and that when we left our home, we were required to ride in the police car.

On the morning of July 11, when the police who were on duty in front of our home were not paying attention, Jia Jianying and I snuck away to travel to the northeast where Liu Xiaobo was. The Beijing police called and threatened me, "You will definitely be taken into custody as soon as you arrive in Shenyang!" On July 14, my wife and I were in Harbin when we learned that Liu Xiaobo had died the day before. We made small white flowers and pinned them to our chest as we gradually approached Shenyang. On the morning of July 19, we arrived in Shenyang. It was the seventh day after Liu Xiaobo's death. Wearing our white flowers, the two of us stood in front of the First Affiliated Hospital of Shenyang's China Medical University to mourn the soul of Xiaobo. According to the explanation of the "seventh day" given by the Shenyang domestic security police officers: on the seventh day after a person dies, his soul would return to the places where he stayed while he was alive. His soul is able to see everyone who mourns him. After this day, Liu Xiaobo's soul would fly away. At noon that day, we were seized on the street by eight Shenyang domestic security police officers and taken to the Shenyang Case Processing Center for twenty-five hours. During my detention, the police beat me.

Liu Xiaobo's ashes are buried at sea. Every year on July 13, we will all go to the beach to remember this tough guy who dared to think and act, and we use our actions to comfort the spirit of a brave martyr. Liu Xiaobo's final wish will be achieved by us!

*Translated by Andréa Worden*

NOTE

1. Thomas Carlyle (1795–1881), a Scottish philosopher, described utilitarianism as "pig philosophy."—Trans.

# Mourning Little Brother Xiaobo

*Cary S. Hung*

Little Brother Xiaobo, we haven't met, but smooth communication enabled us to hold the same ideas of democracy and same viewpoints on the prodemocracy movement, and also over a long period of time, we confided in each other and promoted, hand in hand, one battle after another in the Chinese prodemocracy movement.

Shortly after *Democracy Forum* was founded in 1998, you had just finished your third stint in prison. As soon as you got out, you received a message that I had asked my Beijing friend to take to you, inviting you to contribute to the publication. You quickly became an important writer for *Democracy Forum*. Consequently, you received a substantial amount of payment for your articles, which enabled you to travel around and visit friends. You not only generously supported fellow sufferers in the prodemocracy movement but also widely recruited writers for *Democracy Forum*.

This led you, Tang Yuanzhang of Liaoning, and Wang Jinbo of Shandong to become the promoters and heroes of expanding the impact of the team of *Democracy Forum* writers, as well as their influence. The Chinese Communist Party is afraid of you; it put you into prison and finally murdered you with the trick of ignoring your cancer. The CCP is very wicked. However, this also undoubtedly proves that our prodemocracy movement is heading in the right direction, and we have given the CCP strong enough and big enough pressure, haven't we?

You have passed away. Not only are the Chinese people unwilling to accept it, but also the world opinion is much outraged by this injustice to you. The most interesting thing is that Tibetans and Uyghurs who are now being severely ruled, Hongkongers who are now being deceived by "one country, two systems," and Taiwanese who were once indifferent to

Chinese affairs and who are now being compelled to recognize that "Taiwan belongs to China"—they all stepped forward to mourn you. You were concerned about the well-being and aspirations of the people, not whether their homeland belonged to China; the democratic constitutionalism of your Charter 08 received widespread favor among these peoples; your recommendation on federation or confederation is a necessary precondition for these peoples to possibly accept China!

When all I could do was watch that you had no choice but to go, I felt utterly helpless. However, I believe that you know in your heart that I, who have devoted twenty years to the Chinese prodemocracy movement, will definitely continue to work hard for our common cause and make the dream of Charter 08 come true.

May Little Brother Xiaobo go in peace! Freedom for Liu Xia!

*Translated by Andréa Worden*

# Some Recollections of Liu Xiaobo

*Zhao Dagong*

My dear mentor and bosom friend Liu Xiaobo left us so suddenly and with the authorities so anxious during his critical phase. I sensed this because the relevant authorities frequently invited me to tea and gave me friendly warnings on certain matters requiring my attention.

I was born in the same year as Nobel laureate Liu Xiaobo, 1955, which also happens to be the birth year of Nobel laureate Mo Yan. I sometimes feel proud to have been born in the same year as two Nobel laureates and like to brag about it a little, as if their honors were also my own.

Not only were Liu Xiaobo and I born in the same year, but our family backgrounds were also similar. We were both the sons of Communist cadres, and our fathers were denounced during the Cultural Revolution. Our childhood memories are of hunger (as are Mo Yan's), and although born to such families, we were similarly rebellious.

## Getting to Know Liu Xiaobo

In the early 1990s, with the development of the internet, I regularly posted jottings, essays, and political commentaries on overseas forums and websites, always including my email address at the end.

Liu Xiaobo had been famous for a long time by then, while I was just a kid picking up seashells on the beach and never dreamed that I would get to know him or associate with him. One day in 2002, my Hotmail inbox received a message with Liu Xiaobo's name on it. The email said that he'd enjoyed some of my essays on the transformation of the former Soviet Union and Eastern Europe. I was pleasantly surprised and wondered if it was really Liu Xiaobo who had sent me an email. Of course, I knew that Liu Xiaobo had mistakenly attributed to me essays that had been written by a famous writer who also happened to be surnamed Zhao, and in my reply I explained this to him. That was the beginning of what became an increasingly close association.

Back then, Liu Xiaobo greatly admired an essay I had posted in May 2002 entitled "Ideology Still Decides World Patterns." In this essay I wrote, "Fascism is an ideology, Communism is an ideology, Islamic Fundamentalism is an ideology. All of them go against the democratic liberal ideology that represents the progress of human society, and for this reason, they have become historically inevitable." Liu Xiaobo said admiringly that this essay could be published in *Apple Daily*.

Liu Xiaobo liked to use internet voice chat tools (starting with the telephone) to read out his latest commentaries to me. Sometimes he sent essays directly to my email inbox. Although he modestly said he wanted me to look for problems and make corrections, I considered it a pleasure as well as an opportunity to learn from a master. Occasionally I would express an opinion, but very seldom; mostly I would ask him about points I didn't understand.

## Liu Xiaobo the Naughty Boy

On July 20, 2017, Hong Kong's *Apple Daily* published this description of the young Liu Xiaobo:

> Born to a scholarly family, he was smart and rebellious, often getting into fights and skipping class, and ganging up with neighbor boys to pick on a deserter from the Kuomintang army who lived in the village. Thinking back on his wild and bullying youth, he felt remorse: "Insulting the weak is the worst of human nature. The secret of dictatorial rule is to draw out this kind of vicious instinct." The Cultural Revolution broke out when he was 11 years old. Mao Zedong called for suspending courses to carry out revolution, and all of China's colleges and secondary and primary schools were obliged to respond. Liu Xiaobo's fourth grade studies were suspended for three months. On the day it was announced that courses would be suspended, he began the habit of smoking dozens of cigarettes a day: "My feelings toward cigarettes were those of curiosity, risk-taking and rebellion, and ultimately I became addicted." His first cigarette was

the superior grade Peony brand. In an interview, Liu admitted that in his wild youth, he supported his smoking habit by lying, deceiving his parents for money and stealing his father's cigarettes.[1]

Liu Xiaobo was a smoker but not a drinker. I only saw him sipping a glass of red wine at dinners, never hard liquor.

But I've found that many biographies of Liu Xiaobo have recounted none of the pranks he carried out while in primary school. His music teacher was a young woman who wore her hair in a single braid. As in my school, there was an organ at the front of the music classroom, and students sang to its accompaniment. Liu Xiaobo said that one time before class, the teacher was playing one of the songs she was going to teach. He silently snuck up behind her, grabbed a cotton string, and tied the teacher's braid to her chair, then silently crept away and hid off to the side to enjoy the show. The result was that the teacher, unaware of her impending doom, finished playing the song and then stood up to leave. At that moment, she and the chair fell over together. Liu Xiaobo and his classmates laughed their heads off while the young teacher lay on the floor sobbing. Later other teachers came over to discipline the naughty Liu Xiaobo, who dashed off with the teachers in hot pursuit. When he saw the teachers about to catch up with him, the nimble Liu Xiaobo climbed up a telephone pole, leaving the teachers standing helpless below.

## Liu Xiaobo the Soccer Fan

Before Liu Xiaobo was arrested in December 2008, we chatted nearly every night, and at least half of the time we spent talking about soccer. At first, before there was Skype, we talked about football over the phone, and it was always Liu Xiaobo who telephoned me. Later we used Skype for voice chats (in fact, MSN voice chat was available first, but I've never trusted MSN).

Although Skype made chatting much easier, Liu Xiaobo didn't find it enjoyable enough. He always asked complainingly why I didn't have a television in my study. Yes, I'd been to Liu Xiaobo's home several times, and his computer was in the living room, which was also where his study was, and the living room had a television. He could watch soccer on TV while chatting with me. It was different for me. I had a separate study without a television in it and had to go into the living room to watch soccer. When we chatted about soccer over Skype, he would watch as he talked, suddenly launching into a vivid discussion of the match while I remained in the dark and responded to his grandiloquence with vague agreement.

I never talked with Liu Xiaobo about Chinese soccer. Chinese don't like to talk about Chinese soccer, only about European and South American soccer, especially European. Liu Xiaobo and I were both night owls, going to bed in the morning and rising at noon. Europe was around six or seven hours behind China, so European soccer matches were usually played after midnight or in some cases didn't start until 5:30 a.m. Our favorite teams were the British Premier League's Manchester United, Chelsea, Liverpool, and Arsenal, and La Liga's Real Madrid and Barcelona. I hated Italian soccer matches. Although I knew that A.C. Milan, Inter Milan, Rome, and Juventus were all outstanding teams, I bore a grudge against them because of the cheating by Italian teams that had been exposed years ago. I was not at all interested in France Ligue 1 or Germany's Bundesliga.

Liu Xiaobo lived in Beijing and I in Shenzhen. I had better TV channels than Liu Xiaobo did because CCTV's Channel 5 (the sports channel) usually broadcast Bundesliga matches, while Guangdong and Shenzhen sports stations usually broadcast Premier League matches. Ironically, I sometimes had to tell Liu Xiaobo what was happening with Premier League games. Later, however, there was no real problem; Liu Xiaobo was able to watch matches on the internet without being limited by TV broadcasts.

Famous writer Sha Yexin remembered chatting with Liu Xiaobo:

I asked Liu Xiaobo, based on the behavior of those outside the apartment (plainclothes policemen), how did Shanghai compare with Beijing? Liu Xiaobo said Shanghai was harsher than Beijing. The climate for democracy and freedom was worse than in Beijing, and the police were also meaner than in Beijing. Then Liu Xiaobo began telling me stories about his contact with Beijing's State Security authorities over the last ten years or so, and they were so funny that we laughed out loud. He said he was very familiar with the StateSec officers who kept watch outside his building, and had practically become friends with them. Apart from some orders that they could not fail to execute, anything else was open for discussion, and both sides could make concessions. For example, one time, a particularly terrific foreign soccer match was going to be broadcast live, and the StateSec officers downstairs were big soccer fans. They telephoned Liu Xiaobo and asked if he could promise not to go out or do anything that night and give them a break to watch the game. Liu Xiaobo readily agreed.

The police officers "bargaining" with Liu Xiaobo over a soccer match must have known that Liu Xiaobo was a hardcore soccer fan.

I wonder if in the nearly nine years that Liu Xiaobo spent in prison, from December 2008 until his death in July 2017, the prison guards were ever lenient enough to let this Nobel laureate watch a soccer match.

*Translated by Stacy Mosher*

## NOTE

1. "Liu Xiaobo—Juvenile: Young Rebel Becomes a Literary Dark Horse," *Apple Daily* (Hong Kong), July 20, 2017, https://hk.lifestyle.appledaily.com/nextplus/magazine /article/20170720/2_530752_1/.—Trans.

# A Prisoner on His Road

*Ye Du*

## 1

It's been one hundred days since Xiaobo's death. For these hundred days, I didn't want to write anything for him at any point in time because whenever I raised my pen, I had nothing to say. There is no heaven in this world. In the bloody reality, language is so weak it can neither give the lost souls even a modicum of comfort nor make the living wake up and rise up.

However, in the end, I still have to say something.

His voice, his name have already become sensitive words in this land and thus disappeared; his body has also been destroyed. If I don't say something, how can I face the sacrifice of his life and pay homage to him?

## 2

It was because of the internet that I became acquainted with Xiaobo.

In the early days of the Chinese internet, the Democracy and Freedom website that I founded was blocked by the authorities forty-eight times, making it an internet legend. Xiaobo was a loyal netizen supporter of Democracy and Freedom. He said in an article, "Since the Internet entered mainland China, popular private websites, independent of the official position, have emerged. Among the private websites, most self-regulate while treading a fine line, and try hard to avoid current political issues, and there are only a few brave websites that hold fast to the belief in freedom of information. Among the small handful of the private websites that dare to break through the blockade on speech, the 'Democracy and Freedom' website administered by Ye Du is undoubtedly one of the boldest and most tenacious."[1]

From 1999, when he was released from prison, to 2003 when he became the president of the Independent Chinese PEN Center, Xiaobo was very lonely in Beijing. As a well-known dissident, under the harsh political atmosphere at that time, he was excluded from the mainstream institutional intellectual circles. There wasn't much social contact and so he had a lot of time to hang out on the internet. The Democracy and Freedom website I founded became the site he most liked to browse because it published sensitive political news and remarks by sensitive figures. He registered the screen name Shuipi Xiamei (which means "water's skin" [i.e., wave or *bo*] and "shrimp girl," a homonym of Liu Xia's nickname Xiamei, "Little Sister Xia" [i.e., "rosy clouds girl"]). With this screen name, Xiaobo posted on Democracy and Freedom and had exchanges with netizens. Amid the repeated closures of the website, Xiaobo and I gradually became familiar with each other, and then we became close friends who told each other everything.

I often recall each night that I spent together with Xiaobo, separated by a thousand miles but connected by a computer line.

At that time, after he finished writing an article, he liked to read it aloud once via Skype to either Zhao Dagong or me. While reading aloud, if he sensed some problem with a sentence, he stopped immediately to make a revision. Then he continued to read. At that time he did not stutter at all. So I was the first listener to many of his articles.

At that time, we both loved soccer, and whenever he mentioned the Barcelona team and Lionel Messi, he talked nonstop. Every weekend when there was a soccer game, we opened our chat software and watched the TV live broadcast while commenting on the game via our computers.

At that time, when he had spare time, he liked to talk about the people and things he had experienced. He brought up how Wang Shuo had helped him and mentioned Wang Xiaobo's past and in this way appraised others.[2]

At that time, Xiaobo paid very careful attention to my situation. When I was targeted, he immediately wrote an article in support titled, "Ye Du, Guardian of Popular Websites." When I needed money to buy a flat to live in order to extricate myself from the difficulties of being driven out of rental apartments by the authorities, Xiaobo stepped forward to raise money for me from many different parties. This enabled me finally to be able to settle down. When a member of my family was hospitalized, Xiaobo immediately called to offer me his sympathy. Even before he lost his freedom, he was still worried about my livelihood and asked other friends to find more ways for me to increase my income.

I often think of the scene on the winter day when we met for the first time. When I pressed his doorbell, he rushed down from upstairs to open the door and then stretched out his arms to embrace me.

I remembered that we chatted freely in his living room until six in the morning. From the moment I went to sleep on his couch in a daze and then woke up and saw that he had carefully covered me with a quilt and already prepared a meal—Xiaobo's was a warmth I have felt from that moment until now.

A few days before he was detained, we were still chatting about how cold it had been in Beijing since the onset of winter. He planned to travel south to Guangdong with Liu Xia to escape the cold. I was already arranging the itinerary for their arrival.

Unexpectedly, that was a journey never to be realized.

When he left, I lost a friend, a teacher, an elder brother.

This pain is the convulsion of the soul.


## 3

A few days before the news of Xiaobo's cancer spread, some of Xiaobo's friends and I met. As Xiaobo had already served eight years in prison and with less than three years to go until his release, we fervently discussed that after he came out—facing today's China in which the political ceiling is getting lower and lower—how would he be able to make up for the lost eleven years? How would he be able to observe and adapt to this even crueler era for dissidents? But I did not expect that something crueler than his loss of freedom had already befallen him.

During these past eight years, I saw him in my dreams countless times, with my hopes unceasing like dreams, feeling that there were still three years, and then I would be able to hear that familiar stuttering voice again and listen to the familiar "national curse" (*tamade*) mantra, just like yesterday. On Skype we could talk about the smooth gorgeous offense of Barcelona's team and discuss the growth of civil space in China. After eight years, our favorite Messi is still king of the soccer field, but hardships have quietly dyed his temples, declaring that his era is gradually coming to an end. After eight years, the Chinese people, who were looking forward to their gradual and moderate push for social transformation, have found their dream broken into pieces upon the iron curtain. The years are so mercilessly changing this world and changing people's hearts.

## 4

In this eight-year period, China moved from a post-totalitarian era to a new totalitarian power, and the free space that had been struggling to grow to maturity during the Jiang Zemin–Hu Jintao era was crushed by the iron fist of a comprehensive mop-up operation. Eight years ago, countless people were excited about the growth of civic space, longing for more freedom, and looking forward to the gradual transformation of society. Xiaobo's "I have no enemies" represented the hopes and dreams of that era. But in fact, the suppression of Charter 08 and the sentencing of Xiaobo already demonstrated the rigidity and toughness of the regime. At the same time it also heralded the arrival of an era of terror. However, the fact that Charter 08 spread so widely and had such an impact and Xiaobo was the only one arrested and subsequently won the Nobel Peace Prize led the joyous freedom camp to ignore the fact that the totalitarian power's malevolent fangs were getting closer and closer.

The suppression of Xiaobo and the Charter 08 group was a sign that the new totalitarianism, with a renewed strengthening of social control as its primary means, had become the regime's only stance. Limiting social self-organization and development, controlling social organizations' challenges to the regime, and persecuting human rights became the norm. The price paid by Xiaobo and Liu Xia is the cruelest among these victims. The suffering of this couple is conclusive proof that China is sinking into darkness.

Xiaobo, who was completely blocked from obtaining information in prison, did not know any of this. He did not even know about the hardships suffered by his beloved wife. This was completely different from his experience while in prison in the late 1990s totalitarian era. At that time, he could marry Liu Xia, with whom he shared a passionate love. Under the new totalitarian rule of today, he could only be forced to develop cancer by the authorities' actions, and his wife was forced to be clinically depressed, alive but not free. Even in death Xiaobo was not free.

**5**

But his soul is free. All those who knew Xiaobo later in life were amazed at his gentleness, tolerance, and humility—completely different from the literary "dark horse" of the 1980s, who was like a wild whirlwind. This spirit of forbearance comes from the sediment of life. It comes from the warmth of Liu Xia's love, and it is also inevitable from the relentless pursuit of freedom.

The radicalism of his earlier years and the tolerance of the later period were wonderfully united in Xiaobo. This is the broadmindedness that comes after a long river has cut through mountains to open a path that then merges into the ocean. A tolerance that has never fiercely struggled for freedom, by contrast, is nothing but a pool of dead water.

Therefore, Xiaobo was not only a man of words but also a man of action. This is unique among contemporary Chinese intellectuals. He used his articles to incisively reveal the absurdity and ridiculousness of what lay underneath the skin of "Flourishing China." Xiaobo never thought the party-state had the slightest possibility of reform. On the contrary, he believed that "the future of free China lies with the people" and that it would be created by the subjective will of the people. To this end, he not only used his pen as a flag but also encouraged protests, and he practiced what he preached. He was involved in the establishment and development of the Independent Chinese PEN Center.

**6**

One month before he was detained, the two of us talked about a common friend, Liu Lu, who at that time was applying for political asylum in the United States.

Xiaobo asked me what I thought about it. I said, "I respect everyone's choices, but I will never leave this country. My belief has always been: This is my motherland, and I want to make her free."

Then I asked him how he would decide whether or not to leave China. He said the only possibility under which he would choose to go abroad is if China had achieved democracy and freedom. Only then would he take Liu Xia on a trip abroad to see many different countries, to make up for what he owed her after so many years.

He chose this thorny road. He is worthy of the country, his friends, colleagues, and morality. The only debt he owes is to Liu Xia.

After he received the Nobel Peace Prize, whenever the media reported that in exchange for his freedom, Xiaobo would leave China, I always scoffed at such reports. I was clear about the firmness behind the words he had spoken to me that day.

But at the end of his life, he asked to go abroad with Liu Xia for treatment. His whole adult life, he was either in prison or on his way to prison. He already had done too much for his country, which was unworthy of him. In the end, he only wanted to use the contravention of his conviction in exchange for freedom from suffering for his beloved wife, to whom he owed so much.

## 7

Xiaobo had fought for freedom for thirty years. His being-toward-death struggle for freedom of life and freedom for the country will surely become a precious source of energy for China's freedom fighters. The light of his thoughts is even longer and more extensive than his life.

As a friend, I engraved in my memory "Prisoner of the Road"—a song performed by Sivert Høyem at the 2010 Nobel Peace Prize concert. I am thinking of all my memories related to Xiaobo, tears streaming down my face, and they stream every single day.

*Translated by Andréa Worden*

NOTES

1. Liu Xiaobo, "The Watchman of Popular Websites, Ye Du," *Democratic China*, January 14, 2006, accessible on the ICPC website: https://blog.boxun.com/hero/liuxb/492 _1.shtml.—Trans.
2. Wang Shuo is an author, director, and actor with whom Liu Xiaobo published a book of literary dialogues using a pseudonym. Wang Xiaobo (1952–97) was a renowned novelist and essayist.—Trans.

# Liu Xiaobo and I

*Liu Di*

The first time I met Liu Xiaobo in person was at the end of 2003, just after I left the detention center. I had heard that Liu Xiaobo had written many appeals on my behalf, and I was very grateful. A few days after I came out, ICPC's Zhao Dagong took me to Xiaobo's home, where I met him and Liu Xia for the first time. Liu Xia brought out a carton of Baixi Ice Cream, and I unapologetically gulped it down. After that, Liu Xiaobo told people, "The Rat is a funny little glutton." After Liu Xiaobo won the Nobel Peace Prize, Liu Xia lost contact with the outside world. One day friends saw Liu Xia appear on the social network, but they weren't sure if it was really her or StateSec (state security) agents masquerading as her and wanted to test her out. I suggested asking what I had eaten the first time I saw Liu Xia.[1]

Later I had many more meals with Liu Xiaobo and went on trips to the outskirts of Beijing with Cui Weiping, Hao Jian, and other friends.[2] I remember one time we all took group photos outside of Qincheng Prison. I said we were speculators coming to view property. After Liu Xiaobo was sent to prison, I and several other friends accompanied Liu Xia to Jinzhou Prison, but when we took photos outside of the prison, we were taken to the police station and a record was created. I recalled that no one had interfered with us when we had taken photos outside of Qincheng Prison before.

After news spread that Xiaobo had cancer, a Japanese reporter interviewed me. He wanted to know what we talked about at dinners with Xiaobo. I felt it was hard to answer this question because we talked about everything, not just freedom and democracy. I remember that Xiaobo most often talked about how badly his parents had treated him as a boy, and it made me feel that much of the opposition to the Communist Party originates in opposition to parents. Xiaobo didn't much resemble an opposition leader but was a very emotional person. He had a very strong personality and was never afraid to express his opinion. He didn't kiss up to anyone or try to make people love him. We felt we were his friends rather than his followers. We loved him rather than worshiped him. Among the "democracy warriors" were many who wanted to be leaders, and many who fit the mold, but none of them inspired the kind of love that Xiaobo did. Perhaps they were too conscious of the leader status to expose their true selves. Or perhaps those who don't resemble leaders are actually the best leaders.

When signatures were being collected for Charter 08, Liu Xiaobo contacted me by Skype to get my signature. I suggested changing the Charter to call for redrafting the constitution instead of amending it. Xiaobo said the Charter was written this way in order to attract as many signatures as possible, so I agreed to sign. After Xiaobo was arrested, StateSec asked me who had asked me to sign Charter 08, and I said it was Liu Lu in the United States.[3] One Sunday in October or November, Xiaobo went to an event at San Wei Bookstore, but I went to a different event and didn't see him. I thought it wouldn't matter, because I'd have other chances to see him. I never guessed that he would be arrested soon afterwards, much less that I would never see him again.

Xiaobo went to trial on Christmas Day 2009. I knew StateSec might send people to keep me under house arrest, so I left home early, before they could get there, and took the subway to the Beijing First Intermediate People's Court near Babaoshan. As soon as I left the train station, I was detained by StateSec police. Just as I was being loaded into the police vehicle, I saw a netizen named Hualuoqu pass alongside the vehicle. He was dressed like a soldier or police officer, probably hoping to infiltrate the enemy forces. I waved at him and asked to look at the newspaper he was carrying.

A few days before the trial, Liu Lu in the United States had voluntarily written a Declaration of Surrender in which I stated my wish to accompany Liu Xiaobo to prison. StateSec asked me about this while I was sitting in the police van, and I said I hadn't written it, but I acknowledged it. It was like how Xiaobo had not written the initial draft of Charter 08, but he took responsibility for it.

After I was taken to the police station and put on record, I was held at a nearby guesthouse for a few days until Liu Xiaobo's eleven-year sentence was announced.

In summer 2010 Liu Xiaobo was sent to Jinzhou Prison to serve his sentence. On the hottest day in Beijing that summer, Mo Zhixu, Wang Jinbo, Wang Zhongxia and I accompanied Liu Xia to the prison. Mo Zhixu had said earlier that he wanted to sell netizens the right to accompany Liu Xiao to the prison. This made me think of Tom Sawyer selling his friends the rights to whitewash the fence. Mo Zhixu, Wang Jinbo, Liu Xia, and I traveled together by train from Beijing to Jinzhou, while Wang Zhongxia drove from Huludao and met us in Jinzhou.

When we reached Jinzhou, we found that the prison was its only attraction. Everyone in town knew where the prison was, just as all Beijingers know where Tiananmen Square is. Near the prison was a vertical boulder with the words "Jinzhou Prison" written on it in beautiful script. We approached a barred side door to the prison on which the words "Jinzhou Prison" were written in traditional Chinese characters, giving it the appearance of a cultural site. We had brought several T-shirts emblazoned with the Charter 08 logo, and we wore them as we took a photo in front of the door and yelled out, "Liu Xiaobo!"

Next to the prison walls were several buildings, on one of which was written "1984," making us think of Orwell's novel. Wang Jinbo got out of the car to take a photo, but he spent too much time gesticulating at the building and was arrested by security guards. The security guards examined his camera and saw the photos of us wearing the Charter 08 T-shirts. Finally they called the police, and we were taken to the police station.

There a record was taken for each of us. I felt the Jinzhou police officers weren't very professional.

Q: What were you doing?
A: Visiting the prison.
Q: Visiting whom?
A: Liu Xiaobo.
Q: What crime did he commit?
A: Inciting subversion of state power.
Q: How do you write "subversion"?

A: Let me write it for you.

Q: How did you get here?

A: By train.

He even had trouble writing that properly.

They also threatened, "We're going to send them to Xinjiang and you to Tibet!"

We all said we didn't know who had brought the T-shirts, so they were unable to learn anything. I think they must have telephoned Beijing and asked for someone to come fetch us. But on such a hot day, StateSec couldn't be bothered to come (although Jinzhou was cooler), so they first released me, Liu Xia, and Wang Zhongxia (we all had Beijing household registrations), and then later released Mo Zhixu and Wang Jinbo.

By that time it was past visiting hours at the prison, so we had to spend the night in Jinzhou and go back to the prison the next day. When we went to the prison, only Liu Xia was able to see Xiaobo, while the rest of us sat in the reception lobby and waited. Thinking back, this was probably the closest I got to Xiaobo in those ten years.

In 2010 Liu Xiaobo was nominated for the Nobel Peace Prize. That year, China was at loggerheads with several major countries over various issues. Not long before the Nobel Peace Prize was announced, the chairman of the Norwegian Nobel Committee, Thorbjørn Jagland, publicly stated that China had put pressure on members of the committee. This indicated that there was a strong possibility that Liu Xiaobo would win the prize. In the period before the prize was announced, we looked at an overseas gambling website every day. At first the website gave 1:6 odds that Liu Xiaobo would win the Nobel Peace Prize, but then the odds improved to 1:3, 1:2, and then 4:5. Finally the betting site felt that the recipient of the peace prize had been leaked and continued taking bets on other contenders but not on Liu Xiaobo; too many people were betting on him, and the website was afraid of taking a loss.

On the night of October 7, some friends and I had dinner at the Fenghuangzhu Restaurant near the Bell Tower. We decided to split up the next day, with some people going to the entrance of Liu Xia's building on Yuyuantan South Road and others celebrating at the Fenghuangzhu Restaurant.

Afraid that the police would detain me at home, I again went out early the next day and hid out for a while at a friend's house in Yanjiao.[4] Around noon we went back into Beijing. At that time, Mo Zhixu wrote on Twitter that the police hadn't posted guards at the homes of "sensitive persons," so it appeared that Liu Xiaobo hadn't won the prize. I was strolling through the Beijing Book Building in Xidan around three or four o'clock, when I saw on the internet that police had started keeping watch on people's homes. (They had gotten the news too late—by then all of the "sensitive persons" had long ago left home to celebrate. We had gathered from the gambling website that Liu Xiaobo was highly likely to win, but the state security police hadn't made any advance preparations.) We grabbed a taxi to Liu Xia's home on Yuyuantan South Road.

By then the residential area where Liu Xia lived was packed with reporters carrying cameras with telephoto lenses. Mo Zhixu sat in a teahouse nearby, preparing to deliver a speech on Liu Xia's behalf. As news spread that Liu Xiaobo had won the prize, everyone was jubilant. Curious passersby asked what had happened, and we proudly told them that a Chinese had won the Nobel Peace Prize. Liu Xia was under house arrest, so Mo Zhixu delivered a speech on her behalf with Wang Zhongxia and another netizen, Li Rifei, sitting on each side of him. Mo Zhixu, wearing a borrowed mustard-colored suit, said it was his happiest day in twenty years, yet the three of them had pained expressions on their faces.

I later learned that other friends had been arrested for putting up banners celebrating Liu Xiaobo's Nobel Prize, and police had obstructed the celebratory feast at the Fenghuangzhu Restaurant. But because the entrance to Liu Xia's home was packed with media, the police didn't dare to make a move. When seven or eight of us left, a plainclothes police officer followed us. I told the person next to me a joke I'd read on the internet: "One day, two people went to take part in a gang fight, but when they reached the place they found they were hopelessly outnumbered, so they ran off. They ran so fast that their opponents couldn't catch them, but one was close on their heels and wouldn't give up. As the two of them ran, one said to the other, 'Why are we running?' 'We're being chased by a lot of people' 'There's only one behind us.' The other looked back and saw that in fact only one was still chasing them. So the two of them turned around and beat up that guy and then kept running." The man behind us must have heard me because he stopped following us. We found a restaurant and had a celebratory meal. When I went home that night, I found StateSec police waiting downstairs.

I was kept under house arrest for the next two months. When I had to go to the hospital (to remove a dark mole), an auxiliary police officer in a nurse's uniform accompanied me to the clinic. During this time, several netizens came to my home bringing meals and cake. Someone drafted a name list of people who could accept the Nobel Peace Prize for Liu Xiaobo, including me, but the list was just intended to put the authorities off the scent. It was impossible for anyone on the list to accept the prize, but it was meant as a cover for other people who could leave China to do so. This plot failed, however, because not only were those on the list forbidden to leave China but even marginal possibilities such as children and wives were put on the border control list. As a result, the only people able to attend the ceremony were some who were already overseas and not allowed to return to China. Australia-based Zhang Heci originally planned to fly to Beijing and see us and then fly to Oslo for the ceremony, but he was detained as soon as he reached Beijing. The Chinese authorities didn't even allow him to fly directly to Oslo from Beijing. He had to return to Australia and then fly to Oslo from there.

Before the Nobel Peace Prize ceremony, StateSec kept me under house arrest in a holiday villa in Guangying. Having nothing else to do, I read Liu Cixin's *Three-Body Problem*.[5] Two StateSec leaders talked to me. A female leader said she had seen Liu Xiaobo and that he refused to take advice and that she had gone to Beijing Normal University to learn more about me. Since Liu Xiaobo was also a graduate of the university, I wonder how the university administration felt about that.

After I got out, I heard that several young friends had gone to my building and shouted my name, including Wang Zhongxia. At that time, Wang Zhongxia was in hiding outside of Beijing, and the police wanted to put him under house arrest. When Wang and two others hailed a taxi to leave, the local police station sent seven or eight vehicles full of policemen to surround and arrest them as if they were bank robbers and took them to the Hujialou police station. The police asked why they had come, and a young man said they had come to discuss economics with me, while a young woman said she'd come to discuss science fiction novels with me. The police asked them what my political viewpoint was, and they answered, "Ultraliberal?" The police said they didn't understand. They answered, "Anarchist?" and the police again said they didn't understand: "Just say if she wants Western democracy or not." After the questioning, Wang Zhongxia was put under house arrest in a guesthouse, and the other two young people were taken to police stations near their homes and then released. The young woman said that the police telephoned her parents and said, "Your daughter was arrested while petitioning." Her parent asked, "What would she need to petition about?"

December 28 was Liu Xiaobo's birthday, and we held a birthday party for him in his absence. Dozens of people attended, but I was the only one who knew Liu Xiaobo. When the restaurant saw us bring a birthday cake, they gave us a free bowl of long life noodles, but we didn't know who should eat it. After dinner we went to a bar to hang out, and on my cell phone I saw that Wang Zhongxia was out.

After Liu Xiaobo won the Nobel Peace Prize, Liu Xia remained under house arrest, cut off from contact with the outside world. Following Liu Xiaobo's arrest, my task had been to share meals with Liu Xia, but now even that was impossible. In 2012 we decided that since it was impossible to restore contact with Liu Xia, we would do a lot of detective work around her home. Liu Xia's home at No. 9 Yuyuantan South Road was not far from the old CCTV tower, so we had a beautiful young woman posing as the mistress of a certain CCTV leader go to the complex with an agent from Lianjia Realty, saying she was interested in buying an apartment and wanted to look around. She learned that apartments there were quite expensive but that entering and leaving the complex was quite easy (the easiest way to sneak in was to carry vegetables from the market or a doggy bag from a restaurant, which looked less suspicious), so we often went there to carry out our investigation. Even during Beijing's massive rainstorm on July 21, 2012, when someone drowned in the street, we were investigating around Liu Xia's home. Hu Jia, Hao Jian, Cui Weiping, and others also took part in the operation. There was a cot in the corridor outside of Liu Xia's home, probably for the security officer watching her. Across from her unit was a white shack fitted with a one-way mirror that prevented anyone seeing who was inside, but security officers sometimes came out of it. Once when the security officer downstairs didn't notice, one of our young friends sat in the security guard's chair and took a photo. Another time we discovered that a security guard watching Liu Xia was raising a large goose. Hao Jian had an interesting idea. In front of passersby he said loudly that we should be like the revolutionary party in the movies and pretend to be lovers and kiss. We felt that as a professor at the film academy, he had watched too many movies.

We came up with the idea of communicating with Liu Xia with a laser pen. We flashed the laser pen on her window (the security officers watching her home usually waited in the corridor and on the other side of the building and didn't see us), and if Liu Xia was at home, she would open the window and talk with us. On December 7 an AP journalist succeeded in entering Liu Xia's home. The next day, we discovered a row of cars parked with their engines running on the road beside the Yuyuantan Canal behind her home and worked out that it was police officers rather than journalists in the cars.

On the night of December 28, Liu Xiaobo's birthday, I had dinner with Xu Youyu, Hao Jian, Hu Jia, and some other friends at a restaurant near Liu Xia's home. After dinner, we all went to Liu Xia's building and from beneath her window persuaded her to turn on the access control system so we could come up to see her. There was a heavy snowfall that day, and only one security guard was stationed in Liu Xia's corridor. We easily pushed past the security guard and rushed upstairs. One friend was responsible for tying up the guard downstairs, but I felt he was missing out by having to stay downstairs with the guard, so I stayed with him. Liu Xia tossed a piece of chocolate to me from the window.

After the rest of the group came down, security reinforcements also arrived, and we confronted each other downstairs. The head of the security guards wouldn't let us leave, saying he was going to call the police. Xu Youyu said, "Go ahead and call them if you're not afraid of being on CNN tomorrow." The security head said he wasn't even afraid of the United Nations. I said, "Don't count on support from your leaders. The moment something happens, you're just temporary workers." The security head probably realized I was right, because when Xu Youyu said we wanted to leave, they no longer tried to stop us. We split up and went home. Our group was made up of men and women, old and young, tall and short, fat and thin, and once we split up we didn't have any distinctive features. I guess they still called the police, but when the police vehicle drove up to me I just kept walking, and it didn't stop.

The next day, two municipal StateSec officers came over and asked if we'd gone out drinking the day before. I think the eight of us drank a total of two bottles of beer, which was a lot (in fact, both bottles had been drunk by one person, and the rest of us only had soft drinks).

I later heard that Liu Xia was being allowed to see some friends and could make telephone calls, so we didn't make another attempt.

In a WeChat group on June 26, 2017, I was shocked to read that Liu Xiaobo had terminal liver cancer. A young companion and I took the train to Shenyang two days later. Reading *Global Times* on the train, I rolled my eyes at chief editor Hu Xijin's editorial "My Humble Opinion on Medical Parole for Liu Xiaobo, Suffering from Liver Cancer."

We arrived at Shenyang around noon. It was only around two kilometers from the Shenyang Train Station and our hotel to the First Affiliated Hospital of China Medical University, where Liu Xiaobo had been admitted. After lunch we went to the hospital, which as the largest hospital in the three eastern provinces was packed with people.[6] On the internet it was reported that Liu Xiaobo was in an open ward on the twenty-third floor of Block 1, but that ward could easily be accessed with a door card. No one was guarding it so it seemed unlikely that Liu Xiaobo was there. On the other hand, the lobby of Block 3 was full of security officers, and even the elevated corridors of Block 3 and Block 4 had security guards sitting in them. It was said that Block 3 had an elevator that went straight to the rooms for senior officials. I thought Liu Xiaobo was likely to be there, but we had no way of getting to him. That was probably the closest I came to him during those ten years (unless it was that time at Jinzhou Prison).

While we were eating dinner that night, StateSec telephoned and said they didn't want to come and pick me up so I should return on my own the next day. We returned to Beijing late the next night after first visiting the Liaoning Provincial Museum and the Science and Technology Hall.

A few more days passed, and Zeng Jinyan, who had just returned from Hong Kong, wanted people to accompany her to Shenyang.[7] StateSec wouldn't allow me to go to Shenyang again, so I found Wu Qiang and someone else to go with her.[8] On July 12 they rented a car and drove from Beijing to Shenyang.

When we had been in Shenyang two weeks earlier, the hotels had been empty. Now all of the hotel rooms facing the hospital had been rented by the authorities and were no doubt occupied by police. The three eastern provinces had been suffering from economic collapse for years, and Shenyang's hotels had probably not been so fully occupied for a long time. Everyone there was either a policeman or a journalist, and soon as Zeng Jinyan and Wu Qiang arrived, they were mobbed by journalists wanting interviews. They also heard the hotel's front desk call staff to prevent journalists from entering the rooms and photographing the hospital. In order to evade plainclothes police officers, Zeng and Wu switched hotels several times.

Shenyang's streets had also become a battlefield with the streets near the hospital full of police vehicles. A major hospital like the First Affiliated Hospital of China Medical University could not possibly close its doors to the ill. Due to the economic collapse, only civil servants had jobs in the eastern provinces, so a lot of idle people roamed the streets. Added to that, such a spectacle had probably never been seen here before, and the police probably didn't know how to deal with it. As a result, mobs of people gathered to stand around and watch. It is said that people were indiscriminately arrested in Shenyang's streets on the night of July 13.

After being besieged by journalists, Zeng Jinyan and Wu Qiang were afraid to stay in Shenyang much longer, and they left on the night of July 13. Their other friend stayed behind. That night, the Shenyang municipal government website that everyone had been glued to reported that Liu Xiaobo had died. The First Affiliated Hospital of China Medical University held a news conference. Someone observed a hearse driving away from the hospital. It was raining heavily in Shenyang at the time, and Zeng Jinyan and Wu Qiang, still on their way back to Beijing, were obliged to stop over in Huludao.

At the same time, there was thunder and lightning in Beijing but not a drop of rain. In low spirits, I met up with young companions in a restaurant that stayed open until 3 a.m. After the restaurant closed, we went to a 7-Eleven and bought some cigarettes, vodka, and Coke (Liu Xiaobo smoked, but he preferred Coke to alcohol), and we held a ceremony for Xiaobo on a street corner.

After Xiaobo died, our greatest concern was whether Liu Xia could regain her freedom. At one point we heard that the Chinese authorities had promised to allow Liu Xia to leave China after the dual sessions of the National People's Congress and Chinese People's Consultative Conference in March, but there was no further news. Finally, on July 10 we learned through the WeChat community of Liu Xia's younger brother, Liu Hui, that Liu Xia would leave China for Germany. Just the day before, I had been discussing with friends over dinner when Liu Xia would be able to leave China.

I hope she will enjoy freedom and happiness overseas.

*Translated by Stacy Mosher*

NOTES

1. It was confirmed. See "Twofold Grievous News, Nothing Can Top It," by Wang Jinbo, herein.—Trans.
2. Cui Weiping and Hao Jian are professors at the Beijing Film Academy.—Trans.
3. Liu Lu is the pseudonym of Li Jianqiang, a rights defense lawyer who went into exile in the United States after the Chinese authorities rescinded his license.—Trans.
4. A town east of Beijing.—Trans.
5. This is the first volume of Liu Cixin's highly regarded science fiction trilogy, *Remembrance of Earth's Past.*—Trans.
6. Referring to Heilongjiang, Jilin, and Liaoning.—Trans.
7. Zeng Jinyan is a feminist blogger and activist and the ex-wife of Hu Jia.—Trans.
8. Wu Qiang, a dissident intellectual, formerly lectured in politics at Tsinghua University.—Trans.

# The Most Forgiving Opposition

*Zheng Yi*

We've come here today to commemorate our comrade-in-arms on Tiananmen Square, the former president of our Independent Chinese PEN Center, Liu Xiaobo. I felt Su Xiaokang's eulogy just now was great; he spoke out many of the feelings in my heart. Liu Xiaobo's bravery and determination, the way he devoted himself to his ideals, these things he did remarkably well, but this was not his unique quality alone. Many of our colleagues present here and in Mainland China, who've struggled for democracy and freedom, have all upheld such a spirit and will.

The deepest impression Liu Xiaobo gave me was his gentleness. He and Liu Binyan and several others of us established ICPC together. After that, we had more interactions among ICPC members than we had had before, except for our contacts on Tiananmen Square. At that time, my sense was that Xiaobo was not an angry warrior. Within ICPC, everyone thought that he was an old lady. Why? We all know that it is not easy for Chinese people to do one thing together; there are many contradictions and all kinds of various opinions. But when Xiaobo was president of ICPC, he stayed in front of his computer night and day and spent almost all of his time discussing issues with ICPC members around the globe. In fact, this was in order to mediate everyone's differing opinions and conflicts, including the personal relationships between individuals. He spent too much of his energy on this. After he stepped down from his position as president, ICPC would never again find such a gentle, patient, and caring president.

Xiaokang just now said that he was very sad in his heart and deeply worried about China's future. In fact, this is what I also wanted to say. Liu Xiaobo was unquestionably murdered. It is hard to imagine that a government went so far as to brutally murder the most moderate leader in the opposition. I agree with this kind of judgment: in fact, the government is closing the door to a peaceful transition. It has accumulated too much hatred, and the blood debt it owes is too deep. Originally, Liu Xiaobo, as the most moderate, rational, and forgiving person in the opposition, could have participated in and led China's peaceful transition. However, the last opportunity for this was thoroughly buried by the devils. Therefore, I am deeply worried about the future of China. I think the future may be an era in which rivers of blood will flow. Of course, as Liu Xiaobo's colleagues and his comrades-in-arms, we should carry on his legacy and mission. We will do our best to turn China, peacefully, without bloodshed, or with as little bloodshed as possible, toward constitutional democracy and freedom. We will all miss him forever!

*Translated by Andréa Worden*

## NOTE

Zheng Yi delivered this speech at the public memorial service for Liu Xiaobo in front of the Victims of Communism Memorial in Washington DC.

# The Liu Xiaobo I Knew

*Cai Chu*

Xiaobo and I were acquainted with each other on the internet. In the preface he wrote at his home in Beijing on July 4, 2008, "Poetry Spanning Half a Century—Preface for the Selected Poems of Cai Chu," for my collection of poetry *Wherever There Is Freedom, That Is My Home,* Liu Xiaobo wrote:

> The last poem in Cai Chu's collection, "Fluttering Heart—for the Independent Chinese PEN Center (ICPC) Online Conference," written on October 5, 2007, led me to recall my friendship with Cai Chu. Without the ICPC, we probably wouldn't have had a chance to become friends. From the time ICPC was established, through some bumpy times over almost seven years of ICPC's history, all these years, all of my interactions with Cai Chu have been on the Internet. To this day, we still have not had the opportunity to meet in person.

The Independent Chinese PEN Center was established in July of 2001. In November of that same year, at the PEN International's Sixty-Seventh Congress, ICPC was voted into PEN International by an overwhelming majority. Xiaobo and I were two of the thirty-one founding members of ICPC. It was remarkable that he lived in Mainland China but was not afraid of the Chinese Communist Party. In its multiple crackdowns, he stepped forward bravely to spread the spirit of freedom and to protect writers' right to write and the spiritual freedom of writers around the globe. I volunteered at ICPC in 2002 as editor of the website. Xiaobo and I worked together. He wanted us to register ICPC as a nonprofit in the United States. In 2004 ICPC volunteers Li Jie and Jennifer Salen were able to fulfill his wish.

On February 8, 2003, Liu Xiaobo suggested some revisions to the letter

I had drafted, titled "Greetings from ICPC Writer Friends to ICPC Chair Mr. Liu Binyan for His Speedy Recovery." He thought that the ending of the letter was a little dramatic and unnatural and wanted me to delete the verse of Shelley's poetry I had included. After I made the change, Liu Xiaobo added his signature to the letter. Altogether four ICPC members signed: Liu Xiaobo, Cai Chu, Mo Lihua, Fu Zhengming.

In August 2003 I started an ICPC group on MSN, and we began to discuss, and then subsequently passed, the charter of ICPC. In October 2003 we also held the first congress of the ICPC membership assembly, elected and established a board of directors, and adopted the ICPC Charter. Xiaobo was elected president of ICPC; Chen Maiping and myself were elected vice presidents. Those made the foundation for ICPC to become registered as a nonprofit organization in the United States and then in 2004 obtained the support of the National Endowment for Democracy. Xiaobo served two terms as president, until October 2007. During the period when Xiaobo was president, the ICPC Freedom to Write Award ceremony was held twice in Beijing—first on October 30, 2004, and then again on January 2, 2006. During the second event in 2006, ICPC also presented the inaugural Lin Zhao Memorial Award. Moreover, ICPC held a symposium in Chengdu in the afternoon of April 23, 2005, to pay tribute to Liu Binyan and all those who were in exile overseas. At that time, ICPC members in Beijing, Chengdu, Nanjing, Guiyang, and elsewhere in China, under the guise of book reading groups, promoted constitutionalism and human rights and revealed the CCP's lies. Those activities caused serious concern among the Beijing authorities. Consequently, the Beijing police not only monitored Xiaobo but also summoned him and took him into custody several times.

Also worth mentioning is that on September 19, 2005, Xiaobo received a phone call from the wife of ICPC member Yang Chunguang. His wife, Cai, called from Panjin City, Liaoning Province, and said Yang Chunguang had suffered a sudden cerebral hemorrhage and died at three o'clock that morning. Because I was responsible for the collected works of Yang Chunguang, I knew about him. Xiaobo and I discussed on Skype what we should do. I suggested that ICPC should announce his death and commemorate Yang Chunguang. It never occurred to me that on that same day Xiaobo would take the train to Panjin City to visit Yang Chunguang's family. Because

Xiaobo was not familiar with the area, it was very late at night before Xiaobo finally located Yang Chunguang's home. After Xiaobo bid farewell to Yang Chunguang's body and offered condolences to his widow, Cai Dongmei mentioned that they had some financial difficulties. Xiaobo immediately took some money from his pocket and gave it to Cai Dongmei, and then quickly left. Later, I called her from the United States, and she told me that Xiaobo privately gave her a thousand renminbi. And Xiaobo never mentioned this to anyone, which illustrates the sincerity and generosity with which he treated others.

In October 2006 Su Xiaokang retired as editor in chief of *Democratic China*. Liu Xiaobo, Zhang Zuhua, and I registered Democratic China as a nonprofit organization to continue the *Democratic China* electronic journal in Alabama. The journal is devoted to the democratic forces who will participate in the future process of democratic transition in China. This includes negotiations and the drawing up of a constitution. The journal provides necessary knowledge, theory, and talent reserves with a view to developing citizen power and toppling the autocratic iron wall so that in the future China will become a free and democratic country with a constitutional government. At that time, Liu Xiaobo served as president and editor in chief of *Democratic China* electronic journal, I served as executive director and editor, and Zhang Zuhua served as a director and China managing editor. *Democratic China* electronic journal is the only periodical in China or abroad that exclusively researches and explores China's democratic transition. Since the journal's inception, it has adhered to the founding purpose captured in ten characters: "Freedom, Democracy, Human Rights, Rule of Law, Constitutionalism." It has devoted itself to the in-depth exploration of how to advance and realize China's democratic transition, foster civil society, and promote the establishment of rule of law. In addition, it serves as a platform for the study and discussion of democratic theory, focuses on changes in the current political situation, and sums up democratic practice and the experience of the citizens' rights defense movement, all with the purpose of making theoretical and experiential contributions to promote China's democratic transition.

At that time, we set up a chat group on Skype in order to convene the board of directors and discuss editorial matters. Xiaobo was responsible for planning and external outreach; Zhang Zuhua was responsible for the initial review of manuscripts and for composing work summaries. I was responsible for finalizing and uploading manuscripts as well as issuing payments for articles, contacting the writers, and other daily affairs. From the time *Democratic China* electronic journal was first established, Li Jie served as a volunteer, providing long-term assistance on many different matters, including translating documents and applying for the journal to be registered as a nonprofit organization.

In the course of handling daily matters, Xiaobo contacted me almost every day. From deciding which topics to solicit articles on for the year, to modifying the layout of columns, to contacting authors and adjusting the table of contents—no matter how small the task, he took responsibility. One thing especially worth mentioning is that because of the time difference, in order to communicate with me during the daytime in the United States, he adjusted his working hours to the middle of the night so that I was able to work during the day and sleep at night. His spirit of putting others before himself moved me deeply.

From the inception of the new *Democratic China* electronic journal, in order not to jeopardize the safety of Xiaobo, Zhang Zuhua, and other mainland authors, we decided not to use Xiaobo and Zhang Zuhua's names on the masthead of the journal and instead used He Lu ("Where is China headed?") as a pen name for them. Later, Charter 08 stated: "Where is China headed in the 21st century? Will it continue with 'modernization' under authoritarian rule, or will it embrace universal human values, join the main-stream of civilized nations, and build a democratic system? There can be no avoiding these questions."[1]

Xiaobo also suggested that members of the editorial team of *Democratic China*, without exception, should not receive payment for articles they publish in the journal. The board of directors approved this decision, and to this day, members of the editorial team still strictly observe this rule. After Xiaobo was sentenced, the *Democratic China* electronic journal also launched humanitarian assistance activities for mainland prisoners of conscience and their families. Zhang Zuhua often recommended some members of vulnerable and marginalized groups to receive assistance.

Xiaobo was a genuine man of feeling. Although his essays coldly expressed his views on freedom, as a person, he had hot blood, deep feeling, aesthetic sense, and constant loyal affection. His disposition manifested itself in his poetry. Xiaobo's poetry reminds people to squarely face June 4. An excerpt from one of Liu Xiaobo's poems reads:

> Fifteen years ago
> Massacre
> Completed before a dawn
> I died
> And was reborn. . . .
> Fifteen years ago
> Every nightmare I have contains the souls of the dead
> I see
> Everything is blood-stained
> The things I write
> Every sentence
> Every pen-stroke
> Are subsequent
> Talks with the graves.

He wrote in the poem "Shouldering: For My Suffering Wife,"

> Before you enter your grave
> Do not forget to write me with your ashes
> Do not forget to leave your address in the netherworld.

Xiaobo first was a writer, poet, and literary critic. He was compelled by the suppression he suffered at the hands of the Chinese regime to become a political commentator; this was his method of resistance—to use his pen against the gun. On June 4, 2008, he told me on Skype that he felt he had let down the lost souls of June 4. If the June 4 issue were resolved, he would emigrate to the United States. At that time, many friends who were gathered at my home heard his sobbing, and they were all moved by the man who could not forget the lost souls of June 4. Later, upon receiving the news of his Nobel Peace Prize, I felt very sorry for him, and felt that the desire he had his entire life, his thirst for freedom, would unlikely be realized. I have a poem as proof!

"For Liu Xiaobo"
by Cai Chu:

I heard the news of your award in the autumn rain, and my tears
   flowed like rain
Like hearing once again the big stutter we were accustomed to—
Every June 4th, you say on Skype that you apologize to the lost souls
   of June 4th
Crying intermittently like this autumn rain stretching out our
   concern
Some people say you are soft like rain and not strong enough
Some people say that your persistent efforts have already
   transformed
I said not to raise you up on an altar
Liu Xia is calling you home

*October 2010.*

On December 10, 2008, 303 people from all walks of life in Mainland
China, including Liu Xiaobo and Zhang Zuhua, jointly issued Charter 08.
Subsequently, many signatures from people in China and abroad were
added; to date, there are thirty-five groups of signatories, totaling more
than fourteen thousand people. Charter 08 states:

> The Chinese people, who have endured human rights disasters and
> uncountable struggles [over a long period of time], now include many
> who see clearly that freedom, equality, and human rights are uni-
> versal values of humankind and that democracy and constitutional
> government are the fundamental framework for protecting these
> values. By departing from these values, the Chinese government's
> approach to "modernization" has proven disastrous. It has stripped
> people of their rights, destroyed their dignity, and corrupted normal
> human intercourse. So we ask: Where is China headed in the 21st
> century? Will it continue with "modernization" under authoritarian
> rule, or will it embrace universal human values, join the main-stream
> of civilized nations, and build a democratic system? There can be no
> avoiding these questions. . . . Accordingly, we dare to put civic spirit

into practice by announcing *Charter 08*. We hope that our fellow citizens who feel a similar sense of crisis, responsibility, and mission, whether they are inside the government or not, and regardless of their social status, will set aside small differences to embrace the broad goals of this citizens' movement. Together we can work for major changes in Chinese society and for the rapid establishment of a free, democratic, and constitutional country. We can bring to reality the goals and ideals that our people have incessantly been seeking for more than a hundred years, and can bring a brilliant new chapter to Chinese civilization.

Combing through the history of China's democracy movements, those of the largest scale and greatest impact include 1989 Democracy Movement and the Charter 08 constitutionalism movement. Charter 08 positions the demands of the democracy movement onto the foundation of a "resistance struggle, citizens' movement" and "building a country that is free and democratic, with a constitutional government." The Charter 08 constitutionalism movement is not past tense, but is progressive present tense. The Charter 08 movement will not cease until a free, constitutional government has been realized and perfected.

Before Charter 08 was made public, on December 6, 2008, at 10:16 a.m., Xiaobo sent the document to me via email: "Greetings from Xiaobo: next week's manuscript, reply upon receipt!" That evening, via Skype, he sent me the first batch of names of three hundred people who signed Charter 08 and wanted me to publish it on December 10, World Human Rights Day. The next night, he also chatted with me via video on Skype; because he could not go abroad, he wanted to meet me in the mainland. Innocent Xiaobo did not foresee that the next day he would be taken into custody by Beijing public security officers (*guobao*). That night, Zhang Zuhua was also taken away and his home searched. Fortunately, Zuhua had already sent the final version of "Chinese Individuals from All Walks of Life Jointly Issue Charter 08" with the first batch of 303 signatories to an overseas organization for release, so there was no delay in publishing Charter 08 one day ahead of schedule. To this day, the Democratic China website retains signature information for all who signed Charter 08 after it was first published. The Charter 08 Forum also publishes this information, and there is also a link to the Charter 08 Information Network on the Democratic China website—these three websites have become the platform for discussing and revising Charter 08.

In November 2008 Xiaobo sent me some photographs; he said his favorite photo that Liu Xia took of him was one taken in Ding Zilin's home, which had as a background Liu Xia's photograph "Cloth Dolls." After Xiaobo was imprisoned, I continued to report information and news, and every year I traveled around to participate in meetings to express support for and help prisoners of conscience in the mainland.

I have maintained contact with Liu Xia. But Liu Xia's phone is difficult to get through to; sometimes even if I dialed her number several times, it still wouldn't work. In late April of 2017, I managed to speak with Liu Xia and asked her the status of Xiaobo's health. She told me his health was better than hers. She also said, however, that the authorities gave Xiaobo a physical examination but afterwards did not tell Xiaobo and her the results. Consequently, she was still worried. I asked her to convey my good wishes to him when she visited him in prison. She said that with a window separating them, and police surveillance, there was no way she could mention the names of other people. If she did there would be no more visits. However, according to recent media reports, the authorities already knew the status of Xiaobo's actual health condition in April but did not disclose it and instead delayed. This political delay was the slow murder of Liu Xiaobo.

In June 2017 Chinese authorities disclosed that Xiaobo had late-stage liver cancer. On the night of July 5, I again saw a photo of Liu Xiaobo and his wife and heard that Xiaobo was critically ill; I could not help but let the tears flow freely from my aged eyes. Amid grief and indignation, I wrote, the husband and wife who are mere skin and bones use the ashes of the dead to express their love:

Tonight there is brighter light in this place,
The clear moon, less than full, not yet worn away.
The candles are shedding tears when departing.
Thousands of joss sticks and candles light up the galaxy.

Over the years, Xiaobo had always insisted that he would rather sit in prison for the rest of his life than go abroad. But this time, he told the doctors from Germany and the United States who had come to China to consult about his case that he was willing to go to the West for medical treatment, and that if was going to die, he would prefer to die in the West. He also wanted Liu Xia and her younger brother, Liu Hui, to accompany him abroad. Liu Xiaobo long ago gave his life to the souls of June 4 and thereby achieved redemption for his own soul. This time, he used his last breath to fight for freedom for Liu Xia. This kind of love truly is "rare to hear of in the world of mortals."

Liu Xiaobo did three big things in his life: he became a "black hand" for supporting the students on June 4; he founded ICPC and strengthened *Democratic China* electronic journal; and he used his own imprisonment to promote Charter 08. He wanted to live as a free man and die as a free soul: his love was moved by passion, passion from his soul. This was Xiaobo's lifelong pursuit.

*Translated by Andréa Worden*

## NOTES

Originally published in *Democratic China*.

1. This and other quotations from Charter 08 are taken from Perry Link's translation in the *New York Review of Books* 56, no. 1 (January 15, 2009).—Trans.

# Xiaobo, Tonight I Light a Cigarette for You

*Emily Wu*

I became acquainted with Liu Xiaobo in 2006. At that time, Xiaobo was the president of the Independent Chinese PEN Center. I was an alternate director and treasurer. At the end of 2007, when the terms for the officers of ICPC were up, he became a director, and I became the vice president. He was in China and I was in the United States. We often connected using email and web-based calling.

In the beginning, we just talked about some ICPC matters. Gradually, we became close friends talking about everything. Whatever was bothering me, whether it involved work or a private matter, I liked to seek him out to discuss.

Almost every day, Xiaobo was stuck inside at home; he spent his days under house arrest, day and night inverted—writing articles, watching TV, and making phone calls.

For a period of time, I was in a very bad mood after losing my job. Daytime in the United States is nighttime in China. We often met on the internet. I went on and on, complaining to him. He always listened so patiently to me and slowly, with a slight stutter, gave me advice.

There was a time when my children, during their adolescent years, were rebellious and causing trouble and as a result made me so angry I almost lost my mind. Xiaobo told me about the pain in his heart because he could not accompany his only son. He urged me to cherish my time with my children.

I have lived in the United States for more than twenty years. When I write articles in Chinese, I'm afraid that my use of words and syntax may be inappropriate. Every time I finished an article, I always first sent it to Xiaobo, and asked him if he could help me see if there were any language problems. He helped me revise, word by word, the Chinese version of my autobiography, *Feather in the Storm: A Childhood Lost in Chaos*.[1]

Xiaobo could write thousands of words of wonderful text each day. I was often his first reader. I couldn't suggest any changes to his articles. But because he typed so fast, sometimes he'd make errors, so I specialized in pointing out his typos.

Xiaobo was lucky to have Liu Xia as his companion during his house arrest; otherwise, who knows how hard it would have been. Xiaobo liked smoking; I once scolded him, "Don't smoke anymore; you're not afraid of death, but think of Liu Xia, and live a few years longer."

"Afraid of what?" Xiaobo chuckled in response, "She smokes with me."

I laughed, and said, "You win. When we see each other, I'll also have a cigarette with you."

There were times when, because I was writing articles or, more often, because I was afraid that I might disturb Xiaobo's writing, I would just stay on the internet phone but not utter a word. I quietly listened to him pounding his computer keyboard, striking a match, smoking, and sipping tea; it seemed as if he was sitting just across from me. There was an inexplicable tranquility in my heart.

One day, he was particularly pleased to tell me, "The braised fish my wife made today was so delicious."

I said, "It's making my mouth water."

He said, "When you come to Beijing, let my wife cook it for you."

In early 2009, a few months after Xiaobo was "disappeared" because of Charter 08, a friend was going to Beijing. I thought for a moment about asking him to take some cigarettes to Xiaobo for me. I oppose smoking, but the damage to his body of an imprisoned life is definitely worse than smoking. What's more, this was just a token of my regard and to show that I was thinking about him. He might not receive it in the end. When I went to the store to buy cigarettes, I was flabbergasted, so many different brands to choose from; I had no idea what kind of cigarettes Xiaobo liked. When I was young and bought cigarettes for my father, I remember he just exhorted, "Buy the Big Iron Bridge brand for one mao four fen; don't buy the East Sea brand for two mao eight fen." After looking for a long time,

I finally picked the most expensive brand, hoping that if he was able to smoke them, he would like them.

This morning I was shocked by the sad news of Xiaobo's death.

Xiaobo, what you are most worried about is probably Liu Xia. I am looking forward to eating her braised fish in the near future.

Xiaobo, because of you, on Sina Weibo, all candle emojis are blocked.

Xiaobo, tonight, let me light a cigarette for you, as a heartfelt memorial.

*Translated by Andréa Worden*

NOTE

1. English edition: Emily Wu and Larry Engelmann, *Feather in the Storm: A Childhood Lost in Chaos* (New York: Pantheon, 2006).—Trans.

# Liu Xiaobo, Me, and Independent Chinese PEN Center

*Qi Jiazhen*

1

In late August 1987 I arrived in Australia still traumatized from my time in Mainland China. It was only in late January 2005, after I had been in Australia for seventeen and a half years, that I cast off my terror and lifted my head, saying what I wanted to say and do what I wanted to do. Since then, I've been able to stand up as a full person.

The Independent Chinese PEN Center entered my life just at this time.

After Tsoi Wing-mui, Yu Jie, and other famous writers attended the Asia-Pacific Writers Conference in Melbourne in early November 2005, Ah Mu hosted them at his home in Melbourne. Through their spirited introduction, we were happily surprised to learn of an Independent Chinese PEN Center that included mainland and overseas writers. Liu Xiaobo was one of the founders and was president at that time. Everyone was very excited and felt they had found a family. I and four other Melbourne-based writers, Ah Mu, Ah Sen, Lao Daiwei, and Zi Xuan, immediately signed up. None of us had ever joined an organization before. After that, the prominent bilingual writer Chen Biao also joined, and several more writers joined later.

Liu Xiaobo managed the household affairs of our family, and we loved it. After I joined ICPC, Liu Xiaobo always looked after me and encouraged me and assisted me in various ways.

We chatted several times over Skype. He always spoke in a low voice for fear of disturbing Liu Xia's sleep. We spoke of everyday life and of writing. I told him of my ten years in prison, my book *Tears of Goddess of Liberty* and another book, *Red Dog*, which was nearing completion. Xiaobo's conversation was amiable and natural, with no pretenses, and I sensed his friendliness and sincerity.

In September 2007, Xiaobo entrusted me with going to Sydney on his behalf to accept the Courage of Conscience Award from New Zealand's Asia-Pacific Human Rights Foundation and to read out his acceptance speech. Melbourne-based ICPC members Lao Daiwei, Ah Mu, and I, and a good friend named Tom, drove ten hours to attend the ceremony. We all felt that accepting the award for Liu Xiaobo was a great honor as well as an encouragement and spur to action.

Liu Xiaobo declared that he was donating all of the award money to the Tiananmen Mothers. In his acceptance speech, entitled "Courage Does Not Necessarily Represent Conscience," he said:

> Today, as I accept this "Courage of Conscience" award, I feel more guilty than honored. . . .
>
> If this award represents an honor, I can only be a conduit for this honor in commemorating the lost souls. . . .
>
> Resisting dictatorship does not automatically make a saint of the resister. Resistance to evil is not invariably by the righteous; in some cases evil may oppose evil. . . . Those who resist dictatorial regimes do not lack courage, but courage is not the same as responsibility, just as the ethics of morality is no substitute for the ethics of responsibility. In other words, putting conscience into practice requires not only the courage to resist, but even more it requires rational and responsible public participation . . . Tenacity and sobriety, rationality and responsibility, confidence and optimism are far more precious than fleeting righteous indignation. . . .
>
> It is only by humbly seeking guidance from the souls in heaven that I learned the heavy responsibility of surviving. It is only by tenaciously resisting terror, lies and subornment that we can shoulder, to a greater or lesser degree, our responsibility as survivors.

ICPC member Jian Zhaohui evaluated Liu Xiaobo's acceptance speech in this way:

> I really like Liu Xiaobo's speech. I really like a "hero who can see through the hero mystique." Truly, more than courage, a "revolution" needs to emphasize responsibility and ethical principles. I have never believed that a person can use despicable means toward a legitimate end. . . . I'm

a seeker who believes in truth, but I don't believe those who proclaim that they've found the truth. "Revolution" isn't a pursuit of the "heroes' arena" and even less is it to gain prestige and power for oneself. A mature civil society has no need for "opinion leaders" or "revolutionary leaders."

The person in ICPC who influenced me most was Liu Xiaobo. Early on, Xiaobo encouraged me to run for the ICPC board. This was something I had never dreamed of, and I accepted his suggestion with trepidation. I knew little about the internet, but Xiaobo taught me how to join the ICPC community and begin expressing myself there so members would begin to understand who I was. When I joined the board as an alternate member in 2007, I told Xiaobo I was moved to tears. He replied, "This was the result of your own hard effort." I've served on the board for ten years since then, including as the ICPC's secretary-general and as vice president for two terms.

I love the ICPC. Love is something you give rather than take.

All of our members in Melbourne take pride in being associated with the ICPC. We all admire the ICPC's aim of defending freedom of expression to the greatest extent possible, and we've become powerful agents of change in Australia through path-breaking programs in recent years. We joined with the Falun Gong spiritual movement in presenting a lecture series by Yu Jie and Wang Yi, during which Yu Jie spoke on "Dismantling China's Yasakuni Shrine: The Mausoleum of Mao Zedong" and Wang Yi said, "China's rights defense movement is now on the rise, but the rights defense movement has not yet been launched among overseas Chinese." We hosted a lecture by the famous Taiwanese author Lung Ying-tai on "Understanding and Misunderstanding the Chinese World," attended by some 350 Chinese from Mainland China, Taiwan, Hong Kong, Vietnam, Malaysia, Indonesia, and Singapore. We hosted Dai Qing's lecture on "The 'Peaceful Liberation' of Beiping—Starting from a Horizontal Scroll" and a showing of Hu Jie's documentary *In Search of the Soul of Lin Zhao* at a symposium on the fortieth anniversary of the Cultural Revolution. At another symposium, the biographical writer Ye Yonglie spoke on the fiftieth anniversary of the Anti-Rightist Campaign.

As ICPC's fame spread, its name inspired deep respect among Melbourne residents and pride among its Melbourne-based members. Events we organized were almost always standing room only. Speakers took the initiative to address daring topics, and the audience responded enthusiastically. Opposing views were incisively argued on the basis of reason, with neither side conceding ground and the guest of honor interacting with vigor. At that point, we could almost be considered the ICPC's Melbourne branch.

With the support, encouragement, and help of president Xiaobo and other board members, I represented the ICPC at a literary conference in Fiji. Apart from writing a report on the conference, I managed to score a speaking slot during which I explained that we exposed the CCP's darkness in order to pursue the light. I attended a conference in Hong Kong, hosted by Asia-Pacific Writers and the ICPC, and gave a speech in which I emphasized the need for writers to have a social conscience and sense of mission. I attended PEN International's annual congress in Senegal and wrote two reports, one of which was entitled "Supporting African Women Is Supporting Ourselves."

I especially remember attending the London Book Fair in April 2012. ICPC president Tienchi Martin-Liao, UK-based ICPC member Zhang Pu, and I smuggled banners into a grand banquet for hundreds of people hosted at immense expense by CCP tycoons. My fellow "guerrilla combatants" and I unfurled slogans in Chinese and English stating "We want free speech," "End the literary inquisition," and "Free Liu Xiaobo and all other writers in prison" like spring flowers blooming in a field. It was a glorious battle without bullets but thick with the gunpowder haze of freedom of thought.

As a timid person who had kept her head down overseas for more than seventeen years, I suddenly realized what the world had to offer. The human mind didn't have to passively accept what was poured into it but could operate independently. I realized that a person's thinking should break through its confines and advance deep into forbidden territory to explore solutions and present unusual and surprising opinions. I learned that it was impossible to be an exceptional person by "fearing neither heaven nor earth, but only the CCP." Reversing the situation required making the dictatorial political party and dictatorial regime fear the people!

It's true that I now have Australia's backing, but I cannot deny the following facts:

Would the rain and dew of knowledge have poured into my empty head without the contributions of ICPC founders such as Liu Xiaobo and Zheng Yi, the ICPC's first president Liu Binyan, and so many ICPC members behind the scenes, these model thinkers and beacon-like literary warriors whose moral glamour and practical abilities led me to open my eyes and mount a platform; without the attentive and tenacious help that combined to open my blocked-off soul and narrow thinking and illuminate and dispel my cognitive blind spots and misconceptions; without the superior and unique conditions of the ICPC that taught me the ABCs of democracy and led me to courageously pursue free speech; without the ICPC's fostering, encouraging, and supporting me and choosing me to take part in so many stirring battles that tempered my willpower and bolstered my knowledge? Could I have transformed my slave mentality into a rebel mentality in the activities that ICPC arranged for me to participate in, where I was like a blind person viewing a beautiful scene, or a deaf person listening to a celestial chorus? Without ICPC, would I have been able to ignore all else and summon all my courage to speak the truth and act in truth? Would I have been able to change from a timid person afraid of her own shadow and an ostrich with its head in the sand into a fledgling bird of freedom who dared to spread my wings and fly?

I eventually established Qi's Cultural Foundation. I owe this to the previous ideological padding and years of developing my abilities through participating in the ICPC's practical affairs, as well as the wholehearted assistance of Ah Mu in Melbourne and the support of Jian Zhaohui and other friends. Without soil there are no flowers, without parents there are no children, and without so many benefactors Qi's Cultural Foundation would never have been born. There is no excuse for ingratitude toward those who have helped us.

2

After Liu Xiaobo was released from prison in 1991, he wrote in his June 1 poem "To the Seventeen-Year-Old Jiang Jielian":

When you fell carrying the flag
You were only 17

But I survived
And now I'm 36.
Facing your departed soul,
Living is a crime,
And writing a poem to you is a disgrace.
The living must shut up
And listen to the grave.
I am unworthy
To write a poem for you.
At 17 you surpassed all language and man-made creation.

This was Xiaobo's admission of guilt and repentance for the error of his "on-air testimony" and declaring that "no one was killed in Tiananmen Square." He even felt that "living is a crime, and writing a poem for you is a disgrace" and that he was "unworthy"! In his acceptance speech for the New Zealand Asia-Pacific Human Rights Foundation's Courage of Conscience Award, Liu Xiaobo said, "Rather than saying I'm honored, I should say I feel deeply guilty. I feel guilty before the lost souls of June 4th who still cannot rest in peace, and especially before those who gave their lives saving others." Xiaobo clearly took to heart his admission of guilt and repentance and on-air testimony more than a decade earlier and took the opportunity to once again express his repentance and acknowledge his error at a public occasion. I admire those who have the courage to admit their errors and faults and even more serious problems; I admire people who have the spirit of self-interrogation, self-examination, and self-rebuke. As the proverb says, "No melon is completely round and no person is perfect." Under exceptional circumstances, the human weakness to seek gain and avoid harm frequently comes uninvited, and "external pressure and inner struggle" may turn "me" into "not me" and cause us to commit errors that shock even ourselves. What matters is that we understand this: "Denying a mistake is like committing it twice." Knowing and admitting one's error and repenting of it, requesting forgiveness and pardon and seeking peace of mind is the best way out for those who make mistakes.

We praise and respect a person not because he or she is perfect but because that person acknowledges imperfection, constantly scouring the filth from his soul and cleansing the dirt from the bottom of her heart to become clean again and draw ever nearer to perfection.

For all his life, Liu Xiaobo deeply and absolutely loathed himself for the error of allowing himself to be used in his admission of guilt and repentance and on-air testimony. Not everyone can attain this degree of morality and character. He "longed to use resistance and imprisonment to atone for my crime, and achieve my personal convictions, ideals and character."[1] He longed to redeem himself through the interrogation of justice and punishment of prison, and in this way Liu Xiaobo approached self-redemption.

On December 8, 2008, Xiaobo was arrested because he had helped draft Charter 08 and had actively collected signatures for it. The next year, the CCP made a point of choosing Christmas Day to sentence Xiaobo to eleven years in prison for inciting subversion of state power. Liu Xiaobo, once a formidable "dark horse" who had become a pioneer of democratic constitutional thought, was reborn in prison on Christmas Day. He sought and obtained benevolence, lent luster to his humble surroundings, and lived in a way that would bring him no more shame.

On October 8, 2010, the news that Liu Xiaobo had won the Nobel Peace Prize swept across the world. I received repeated phone calls from Melbourne-based ICPC members at my mobile home in the countryside. The next day, Ah Mu invited more than forty friends to a celebration at his home, and I rushed to Melbourne to take charge. People were in a state of extreme excitement. Liu Xiaobo's spirit of self-sacrifice in saying "If I don't go to hell, who will?" and the stark disparity between the immense wisdom, love, and courage of his "I have no enemies and no hatred" and the CCP's "Everyone is an enemy, and we hate all of them" highlighted the repulsiveness, brutality, and anti-humanitarianism of the Communist autocracy.[2] Liu Xiaobo's Nobel Peace Prize was the inevitable result.

On December 10 of that year, ICPC president Tienchi Martin-Liao, Executive Secretary Yu Zhang, and ICPC staff Tsoi Wing-mui, Xiao Qiao, Wang Jinzhong, and others, as well as myself and two other Australia-based ICPC members, Ah Mu and Ah Sen, went to Norway to attend the Nobel Peace Prize ceremony. It was the solemn, elegant, and glorious experience of a lifetime! The Chinese government refused to allow the imprisoned Xiaobo or any of his family members to attend the ceremony, so Xiaobo was represented by an empty chair on the stage of the auditorium. Due to the absence of ICPC's honorary president (and Liu Xia's subsequent loss of her freedom), the Nobel Committee gave us a larger quota of people to attend the ceremony, which is how we enjoyed this honor that we will never forget as long as we live. Remembering how this came about, we are deeply grateful to Xiaobo and his long-suffering wife, Liu Xia.

The Nobel Peace Prize ceremony also arranged for a path-breaking performance by a children's chorus that was all the more moving because Xiaobo and Liu Xia loved children but had decided not to have their own child. When I was asked to give a speech in a small rural town on Australia's National Day, January 26, 2011, I told everyone the story of the Nobel laureate Liu Xiaobo and of Liu Xia being kept under house arrest all this time. I said, "When your children shoulder their backpacks and go dashing off to school, you probably can't imagine how impossible it is for the children of political prisoners in Mainland China to escape unfair treatment like bias, surveillance and harassment. That's why Liu Xiaobo and Liu Xia decided not to have children. It's such a pity!"

**3**

We eagerly awaited the return of our honorary president Liu Xiaobo, patiently waited for Liu Xiaobo to finish his sentence and return home, his freedom restored, and formally resume leadership of a healthy, functional, and intact ICPC.

In a bolt from the blue, our ICPC cofounder, former president, and now honorary president Liu Xiaobo was diagnosed with terminal liver cancer and left us on July 13, 2017. The victim of a slow death at the hands of the CCP, Nobel laureate Liu Xiaobo didn't share the fate of the Nobel laureate held in a Nazi prison, Carl von Ossietzky; on November 23, 1936, the Nobel Committee went to the hospital where the seriously ill von Ossietzky had been released on medical parole and gave him the prize. Liu Xiaobo is the only laureate who was not allowed to receive the prize either in person or through a family member.

In the prime of life, Liu Xiaobo suddenly left us!

We were enraged, grieved, disheartened, and powerless to do anything about it.

On the morning of August 26, the Melbourne Literary Festival organized a special performance commemorating Liu Xiaobo's life and death. As ICPC vice president, I introduced the ICPC and Liu Xiaobo and told everyone, "The beautiful dream that we ICPC members had of Liu Xiaobo leaving prison and coming back to serve as president has been shattered, completely shattered." Someone told me that hearing these words made her weep.

Our tears won't bring Xiaobo back. Only sixty-one years old, he has gone far, far away, carrying with him his erudition and ideas and concepts of democratic transition, his hope that he would be "the last victim of China's endless literary inquisition," his endless guilt that "while I sit in centralism's tangible prison, those I love sit in the invisible prison of the heart that I built for them," and his profound guilt toward his beloved wife, Liu Xia.[3]

When I joined ICPC, I was sixty-five years old. Now, at seventy-seven, I don't have the strength to keep on, much as I want to. Looking for a path ahead, I'm at a loss.

Among the ICPC's members, I'm probably the least young. There are hundreds who are younger, much younger than me. I hope you will self-lessly and fearlessly step forward in the name of Liu Xiaobo, who lives on in spirit, and take up the banner of the world's largest Chinese writers' human rights organization, the ICPC, for the sake of our colleagues imprisoned for speech crimes and for freedom of speech for our compatriots in China. The ICPC's existence and growth requires your continued effort!

*Translated by Stacy Mosher*

NOTES

Remarks on Liu Xiaobo's Nobel Peace Prize, delivered at an award ceremony in Sydney.

1. Liu Xiaobo, "Vibrations from the Tomb: On the 11th Anniversary of June 4th," *Epoch Times*, April 5, 2000, http://www.epochtimes.com/b5/4/4/5/n501121.htm.—Trans.
2. Kṣitigarbha Bodhisattva (Dizhang Pusa) quoted in Han Xin, *Well-Known Temples of China* (Shanghai: Eastern Publishing, 2006). See "Ksitigarbha," Wikipedia, https://en.wikipedia.org/wiki/ K%E1%B9%A3itigarbha.—Trans.
3. Xiaobo, "Vibrations from the Tomb."—Trans.

# Being-toward-Death

REMEMBERING XIAOBO

*Xiao Qiao*

It has been one hundred days since Liu Xiaobo left us, in what feels like a blink of an eye. For several months, I was immersed in unspeakable sorrow, and I did not know how I could express the grief I felt for my mentor. You "have no enemies," but those who regarded you as an enemy nonetheless held you captive until your life's last breath! You left this ice-cold world in confinement and accompanying you at your last moment were only your true love, Big Sister Xia (Liu Xia) and a handful of relatives. Friends who have been worrying about you day and night, who have been forcibly separated from you for nine years already, were able neither to say good-bye to you for the last time nor to see you off. Authorities who stripped you of your liberty did not even allow a normal funeral after you died. On the third day after you left, they rushed to throw your ashes into the sea. Citizens across China who publicly mourned you were taken into custody and jailed on unwarranted charges. Even though you have left this world, they are still scared to the bone of you!

You were my respected mentor and close friend. My earliest acquaintance with you was in the spring of 2003. You took a trip south with your beloved wife, Big Sister Xia. That day, our friend in Hangzhou, Wen Kejian, drove you and Liu Xia to Shanghai. That was the first time I met you, but before this, I had long been familiar with you through your writings and regarded you as my spiritual mentor. You went from the literary "dark horse" with universally shocking essays during my student days to the one who suddenly interrupted his visit abroad to return to China at that unforgettable turn from spring to summer. You, who at the bloody dawn had a close brush with death and calmly led the withdrawal of thousands of students from the deadly square, were then condemned as a "black hand."

After undergoing twenty months of imprisonment, an outstanding teacher who was popular among students lost his podium, and a brilliant writer was blocked in his own country and disappeared from the view of readers. This kind of legendary experience made my heart yearn to meet you. Before our first meeting I thought that such a towering figure could only be seen from a distance as one beholds a high mountain in awe. However, the technological advancement of the internet has greatly shortened the distance between people, and it has also broken through the information blockade of the tyrants. How lucky am I that we could become acquainted, and I could get to know you! It was only after I had close contact with you that I discovered that beneath your inspiring texts and wildly unrestrained behavior, this literary talent was actually a very gentle person in private.

Perhaps it was the grindstone of life that had long ago already tempered you into steel. Time removed quite a few youthful frivolities from the arrogant "dark horse." Through valuable experience you accumulated a bit of steadiness, magnanimity, and calm. You were very considerate of your friends and were an energetic man of action. However, you never forced your own ideas on people, nor did you use a high ethical standard to censure others. You even treated gently and amicably the fellows from the "relevant departments" who had been monitoring you for years. As a liberal with respect to both positive liberty and negative liberty, your ideas and actions can be said to be perfect in my eyes.

Those few years when I was homeless and adrift were the heavy price I paid for frankly expressing myself online. You were in your own difficult situation but nevertheless never forgot to give friends and colleagues warmhearted help. Just like many other people who received your selfless help, I also got a lot of encouragement and help from you. Mainly out of admiration for your character and your literary talent, I applied to join the Independent Chinese PEN Center (ICPC), led by you, and also took the liberty to ask you to be my recommender.

My relationship with the Shanghai domestic security police had become more tense by the day. My parents and friends were anxious and alarmed about this! Under your care and with the direct help of ICPC, in early 2008 I received an opportunity from an international aid agency. The Culture

Department of Stockholm City invited me to visit Sweden for one year. After I received the invitation, I started a difficult negotiation with Shanghai's domestic security police. This period of complications and humiliation caused me on one occasion to want to give up the opportunity to go abroad! When one of my close friends told you that an intense conflict had erupted between the domestic security police and me, my friend later told me that you expressed concern about me in a blaming tone: How will she be able to go if it's like this? My friend told me that you were worried about my situation and afraid that if I continued to stay in Shanghai it wouldn't be safe for me. When I finally could no longer bear it, I went online and poured out my grievances and depression to you. You patiently talked me around and urged me to try my best to exercise patience and strive for the journey as much as possible; otherwise many friends' efforts in the preceding period would have been in vain. Finally, under police escort, while my parents were both reluctant to let me go and also relieved they would no longer have to worry that their daughter would become a prisoner of the state, I left the country.[1] I originally thought I was just leaving for a year or two. I thought this was just a brief farewell. Who would have imagined that life was so unpredictable? After I left, I lost my beloved mother, as well as you, the most important mentor and older brother–like friend in my life.

Less than a year later, you were jailed for Charter 08. Although we jointly signed an open letter, "Liu Xiaobo Is Indivisible from Us," although I also went from Sweden to the front gate of the Liaison Office in Hong Kong and raised a placard seeking to return to China for the same crime as you, it is you and Big Sister Xia who really suffered the most. We couldn't be a substitute for you, nor could we share even a fraction of your burden! All I could do was worry and think about you and Big Sister Xia during sleepless nights in a remote, foreign land of Sweden.

Your suffering also achieved your glory. In Oslo friends and I shared grief and joy. We witnessed and shared your glory. The sadness was that you were suffering for all of us. Even your wife, Big Sister Xia, was forcibly isolated from the world after the Nobel Peace Prize announcement. The happiness was that the international community saw your contribution and gave unprecedented attention and encouragement to the cause of human rights and democracy in China.

At the end of 2013, after repeated weighing and planning, I decided to take a roundabout route through Vietnam to get over the wall with my body and return home. After New Year's Day in 2014, I successfully entered Yunnan from Vietnam and returned to my motherland. At that time, you had already spent more than five years in prison and served nearly half of your eleven-year sentence. Although I held almost no hope that you would step across purgatory in advance, I previously never doubted that you would survive these eleven years and that you would come back and meet together with us! I looked forward to our early reunion.

However, reality is so cruel! When I learned the news that you were ill, it was as if I had been struck by lightning! During those several days, I was distracted and extremely worried. During night after night of insomnia, when I got online and tracked the daily notification of the patient's condition on the official website of Shenyang's China Medical University First Affiliated Hospital and online news and rumors that maybe were true or maybe were false, tears streamed down my face! The few previous brief meetings I was fated to have with you and our online exchanges also constantly flashbacked before my eyes. I remember the last time I saw you was in Beijing on the eve of my departure from China nine years ago. In my memory, you were always so optimistic and determined and had such tenacious vitality! Could it be that this was our final meeting? Before you were taken into custody, during our last online chat, you suggested that I consult with the Swedish entity that invited me to see if I could extend my visit in Sweden by six months in order to avoid the twentieth anniversary of the "sensitive period" (the Tiananmen massacre on June 4, 1989) and return home afterward. Perhaps the resistance would be less, and the days after my return would also maybe be a bit better. In considering the interests of your friends, you always put yourself in their place, but now, upon learning that you're on the verge of death, there is absolutely nothing I can do!

Ten days after your condition was publicized, I finally disregarded the relevant departments who advised against it and quietly went to Shenyang one weekend. Although I knew there was no hope of seeing you, this was the only thing I could do for you. That morning, I woke up in a hotel room in the city where you were located in the northern part of the country, thinking that you were in a hospital just a few hundred meters away from me, tossing about in a hospital bed suffering from the pain of your illness. There was nowhere I could send my thoughts of you, only a tear-stained towel! Sadness engulfed me like a tide!

My hands clasped beautiful lilies, which were carefully selected for you to wish you peace, but there was no way they could be delivered to you! I was in the China Medical University First Affiliated Hospital pacing back and forth and expecting to hear "No such person was found." I showed people photos of you and Big Sister Xia on my mobile phone, and I asked in all possible places if anyone had seen you, but in the end, I came up with nothing.

I feel your life is passing away little by little! Xiaobo, where are you? Can you sense that I've come to see you? Can you sense the care and concern of countless friends, known and unknown, outside? This is the closest I've been to you in nine years, I'm doing my best, but I still can't see you. . . . Xiaobo, don't leave us! There is so much unfinished business awaiting you. . . . The sky is drizzling, could it be that the firmament is also shedding tears of sadness for you? I was heartbreakingly aware that this would be our final farewell in this life.

Just on the fourth day after my return from Shenyang, the news of your death came. From the time the authorities had to disclose your medical condition, in no more than a short period of three weeks, your life came to an end. I thought of an elegiac couplet written by Tang Hualong for Song Jiaoren (after he was assassinated) during the early years of the Republic of China.[2] You are like Song Jiaoren; you are a martyr who died for an ideal. How can heaven bear it? Every critical juncture in history has given China the worst choice! Could it be that this land is actually cursed?

After you left, my heart sank into a huge black hole! Since my return to China these past several years, in order not to agitate my octogenarian father, I have lived in emptiness and forbearance, but I sought to "do what I could to survive in an age of chaos." But as long as Xiaobo existed, my heart would have hope. But now under the watchful eyes of the whole world, you were deliberately murdered, and there's no trace of you! Extreme grief and indignation! You treated people kindly, had affection and loyalty, and lived up to expectations. In a country that has been immersed in struggle philosophy and an enemy mentality for seven decades, you had Sisyphean perseverance and bravery and gave up opportunities to pursue your personal freedom and happiness, and you did not regret being a prisoner half of your life because it was to seek freedom for your fellow countrymen and for the future of the nation. It is an infinite sadness that there are so many compatriots who don't understand why you died and who don't even know about your existence. You "have no enemies," but you were attacked from all sides by mediocre people. The selfish and muddle-headed authorities banned you, suppressed you, imprisoned you, and killed you. "Young Chinese cyber-nationalists" whose minds have been hoodwinked by enslaving education cursed you as a "traitor." Arrogant and ignorant radicals and careerists at home and abroad slandered and defamed you. In the last nine years of your life, you were frozen in ice, and there was almost no information transmitted to the outside world. One hundred days after your death, almost no one can contact your beloved wife, Big Sister Xia, who has been kept isolated in lonely darkness. This world owes you too much!

"Live well!" An elder brother in a foreign land who has been unable to return to China for many years exhorted me from a remote end of the network. Yes, we should all live well. Heidegger said "being-toward-death." Death is the limit of physical life, and it is a future that no one can avoid. However, it is precisely because of the existence of death that our limited life is rendered more meaningful. Over the years, you urged yourself on, having been entrusted by the "dead souls" to live for the sake of those departed spirits who fell on that bloody dawn. You eventually ignited yourself as a torch—offering yourself as a sacrifice for your ideals—and dispersed the boundless darkness of this mundane world. You made your life blossom with dazzling splendor. Now that your soul has returned to the sea, you've returned to the source of the beginning of life. Xiaobo, rest in peace! You have completed your mission on earth. Those who are to join you later will move forward with higher spirits, and continue to walk your unfinished road.

Xiaobo, we love you!

Xiaobo, we miss you!

*Translated by Andréa Worden*

1. Xiao Qiao writes of her experience leaving China in "ETA Unknown," collected in *In the Shadow of the Rising Dragon*, trans. Stacy Mosher (New York: Palgrave Macmillan, 2013).—Trans.

2. Song Jiaoren (1882–1913) was a Chinese revolutionary, constitutionalist, and one of the founding members of the Kuomindang. After leading the Kuomindang to a landslide victory in China's first democratic election of parliament in 1912, Song was assassinated. Many believed that Yuan Shikai, the provisional president, was responsible for Song's murder, though he was never officially implicated or charged. Although only thirty years old, it was thought that Song would become China's premier. Tang Hualong (1874–1918) was a prominent member of the Progressive Party, interior minister in the republic, and a friend of but political rival to Song Jiaoren. In 1918 Tang was also assassinated.—Trans.

# China's Free Spirit

*Qin Geng*

Eighteen days! It was only eighteen days from the day the news of your illness broke to your sudden death, only eighteen days! After reading the hospital's routine medical report of July 12, I realized that the day you and I would be forever parted would probably be July 13.

During these eighteen days, the eyes of the whole world have been focused on you. Everywhere on earth, people are calling out and praying for you. Many friends made great efforts to rush over the numerous barriers on the bumpy roads to Shenyang and search every corner of the hospital looking for you. I uncharacteristically posted a number of WeChat messages every day; each WeChat message expressed the same words: grief and indignation! During these eighteen days, although I was far away, my heart was being tightly pulled into that hospital ward, the precise location of which was not clear.

In these unusual eighteen days that made me and other friends sorrowful and angry, from beginning to end you had been isolated in a corner, bundled up tight, bayonets, iron nets, and high walls forcing you to be separated from your family and friends, even though this was the last eighteen days of your life. The love of beloved ones was blocked, and the friendship of friends was cut off, which lets the loneliness and illness torment you in turns. You were imprisoned just because you were an innocent person!

I read your last words before you died. You wrote that you lost your freedom eight years ago, and now you were about to lose time as you neared the end of your life. But you had no fear! Yes, you fearlessly lost your freedom eight years ago. Today, you fearlessly lost your life because your heart is full of freedom and your ideas will never die! God said in Matthew 10:28, "Do not be afraid of those who kill the body."[1]

Now you are gone; you've used your death to finally defeat their prison! You're free!

When people were used to using MSN, your MSN name was llx. That's the abbreviation of Liu Laoxia (Old Warrior). I never asked you, but I figured that Laoxia relates to Liu Xia, because she is Xiaoxia ("Little Glow"). Subsequently you taught me how to use Skype to communicate with friends. You personally guided me through the entire process of downloading and installing Skype over the phone. Afterwards, in those days, you were the person I most frequently talked with on Skype. Even now, as long as I log onto Skype, I can still see your thin but energetic avatar. Your phone number is 135 5297 2115; up to now it still exists in my address book. All the text messages between us are still on my retired Nokia phone. When people began to use smart phones and WeChat, I still foolishly waited for you to get out of jail, install WeChat on a new mobile phone, and go to your friends' circle every day and like their posts. Now, as long as I enter "xiao" on the keyboard of my Samsung mobile phone, the words that the system automatically selects are "xiaobo" . . . but I have lost you forever! Regardless of whether it's through Skype or China Mobile, there is no way I can hear you again; I can no longer hear your deep and stuttering voice.

In 2006 I participated in a low-profile manner in the grassroots elections for the local People's Congress. At the last moment, the organization that controlled the election process ordered one of the candidates to withdraw, intentionally making the number of candidates less than the statutory minimum, then at midnight urgently announced the suspension of elections in my election district. They used this "legal" method to prevent me from being elected. Afterwards, you said to me, just short a half step for your sneak attack to be successful! Because in that election year, more than two hundred high-profile independent candidates across the country were strangled at the initial stage. It's only because I adopted a low-profile approach under your guidance that I got to the final moment of the announcement of the official candidates list; the next step was the formal vote. You also said laughingly, "I had mentioned when I would go to Hainan that a representative of the People's Congress would be accompanying me."

That year you learned that I was going to get married; you appeared to be even happier than I was! Because you hoped that love in the world would be perfectly satisfactory and that each of your friends and their families would be happy. You said to me that routinely wherever you went, you had seven or eight people tailing you, and with such an excessive number of troops, wherever you went you would just bring trouble to your friends there and cause your friends to lose in the future the kind of tranquil life they had in the past. You referred to your long-term, year-round, tightly controlled monitoring as a travel inconvenience and so did your best to minimize travel. Therefore, you specifically entrusted a good mutual friend, like an envoy, to travel thousands of kilometers for the special trip to Hainan to congratulate me.

One night in Beijing that year, we were in a taxi, and you said to me that someday you might be locked up again, so you were writing as much as you could, and you wanted to save the greatest amount of author's fees possible for Liu Xia when the time came. I know your thoughts very well. You never wanted to see anyone go to jail for publishing opinions and always urged every one of your friends not to be radical or impetuous and to use a rational and gentle tone when speaking. You always lamented anyone—regardless whether or not you knew them—who was imprisoned for their speech, and you were the first person to stand up and rush around relentlessly campaigning for them. However, you calmly faced your own imprisonment, which could come at any time. In 2008 you were in jail. Each time you met with a lawyer, the first question you asked was, who else was implicated? I learned that, in the end, the highest order was to be as "hard as it should be, and soft as it should be," and I and others were not affected. A thousand crimes would be borne by you alone, and your heart was at peace.

According to my understanding of you, during the interrogations you took charge and took everything onto yourself, and there's also that big brother style, wanting to provide cover for a group of younger brothers. It was also on this night when we were on the road to Qixian Village that you shook hands with me after you got out of the taxi. Even now, this scene is still vivid in my mind. During the following year, I went to Beijing for business, but because I knew your daily routine, I didn't drop by to visit you. Because of that momentary slip the previous year, our shaking hands at midnight became the last time we saw each other.

You are gone, free! Leave the endless sorrow to us and also leave the hardships of the future with us. In the future, there won't be anyone like you, who took on the role of acting like a big brother to us. With your body, you shielded us in the safest possible place. But no matter how difficult the road ahead is, we must move forward with determination. Although you withdrew in this way that none of us were prepared for, you will always live in the hearts of everyone who longs for freedom. You have already become the spirit of freedom for this country and this nation!

A thousand-word essay of course cannot express my grief and boundless thoughts and memories. What I can do is to pray to God. I firmly believe that God already has a perfect plan for salvation that will surely lead us toward what you exhausted your life in pursuit of: freedom!

May your spirit reach the kingdom of the Lord and enjoy eternal rest! May the shackles that once bound your flesh no longer bind the living ones. May God care for this country and nation you left behind, and may God save us! May God be gracious!

Xiaobo, my dear brother, when I was young, you were my idol, and in my middle age, you were a good teacher and helpful friend; farewell forever! May your soul be with God and enjoy freedom forever!

*Translated by Andréa Worden*

NOTE

1. The verse ends with the phrase "but cannot kill the soul."—Trans.

# The Final Farewell

*Yu Jianrong*

I really did not want to write this essay. This is because over the years, with the exception of writing such words for my mother, many relatives and friends have also passed away, such as Chen Ziming, Cai Dingjian, Gao Hua, and others, for whom I've never expressed how I felt about being parted from them forever. It's not that I didn't love and respect them, but they had many friends. Since everyone else was expressing the sorrow I wanted to pour out, it was fine for me to just become a member of the audience. Of course, you have more friends. You will soon depart, and this has already caused shock and sadness throughout the world. I've nevertheless decided that since you are terminally ill, I should give you a formal farewell.

We met at a lecture organized by the Sanwei Bookstore. That was more than ten years ago. That day I was the keynote speaker. I was invited to talk to an audience of several dozen about peasants' anti-tax rights defense actions, and I also called for the abolition of agricultural taxes. You sat quietly in a corner, listening, taking notes, thinking, but never said a word. It was only after I had finished speaking and was about to leave that you came over and told me that you were that black hand in the square. We shook hands and laughed; I suppose that's when we considered we had become acquainted at last.

Afterward, we went to a small restaurant nearby along the road, ordered a few side dishes, chose tea instead of alcohol, and began to drink together. I remember you humorously told that young security guy you always had around you: "We are two PhDs having a meal and chatting. There's no need for you to join in." That guy blushed and walked out of the restaurant. We talked for a long time about everything under the sun. Many views were expressed with a smile to each other, and nothing more needed to be said.

After that, we called each other several times and chatted about some things, but not in any depth at all—just a few words touching on the issues.

In the summer of 2007, you gave me a call and said you'd like to come to my little farmyard at Songzhuang town in the Beijing suburbs for a few days to discuss some important issues. Of course I welcomed you. However, I hoped that you wouldn't come in the evening but rather openly in the daylight. You said: "If they find out, it will be detrimental to you." Laughing, I told you, if you come at night, they'd know anyway.

You came to Songzhuang together with Zhang Yaojie. Of course it was during the day; moreover, I swaggeringly drove you to my place. You stayed in the guest room on the west side of my east study. At that time, you were thinking about drafting the document that would later become your indictment. You urgently needed to talk with friends who were far away. You mysteriously told me that there was a software application in which conversations were not monitored, and so it could be used without concern. I was very surprised by your lack of sophistication, that you even believed there was such magical technology. Of course, to be polite, I nonetheless let you install this magical software on my computer, and also let you use it to chat with friends remotely. But as soon as you left the east study, I deleted the software.

In your days in the east study, besides reading and writing, you chatted. Although stuttering, your words were full of passion. You stated systematically and clearly your observations and thoughts on the reality and future of Chinese society. I should say that in principle, I agreed with your basic viewpoints. But one point that I repeatedly expressed was that I didn't like those kinds of lofty words, underneath which the living conditions of individuals—particularly the current most vulnerable groups—had been ignored. Or in other words, I have never agreed with the view of those people who hope that those who are oppressed suffer even greater persecution such that in the end they will rise up and revolt. You listened very seriously and thought about it.

Shortly after you left the east study, that document was published to bring you one more round of the calamity of imprisonment. Although I basically agreed with the views expressed in your text, I nevertheless held fast to my decision not to sign it or participate in it.

Afterward, you once again completely lost your freedom. At that time, I thought we would still have opportunities to see each other again. Until one day I came to another conclusion. That was the day you won the prize. At that time, I was having a meal with famous American scholar Minxin Pei at a restaurant next to the Chinese Academy of Social Sciences. He learned about the news of your winning the prize online, and, shifting from his usual calm and gentle style, he banged the table hard and said: "Great! Great! He will finally have a chance to come out." But I was so sad that tears streamed down my face. I said to the surprised and puzzled Professor Pei: "We will never see him again."

I think it will be hard for us to see each other again in this life. This is true regardless of whether you are able to overcome your critical condition. In fact, whether or not we are to meet again is not such an important issue. After turning fifty years old, when one has achieved a deeper understanding of the evil of human nature, people and things in this world are taken more lightly. Everyone must die. No matter whether they are emperors or poor people, all inevitably disappear from this world. This actually is not horrible. But for you, there are many things you haven't done, and you also bear the expectations of many people. This perhaps is a painful thing. What makes friends more sad and angry is that they ignore your final fundamental freedom. And in my opinion, no matter how they treat you, nothing should be a surprise. I've said before that you are a lofty mountain; no matter how many people tread on you, no one can damage your dignity and majesty.

However, as far as we're concerned, although we were acquainted once, there's no hope for us to meet again in this life. And since I don't believe in an afterlife, then here is a final farewell.

*Translated by Andréa Worden*

NOTE

Originally published on *Boxun*, July 13, 2017.

# Profound Memories to Be Cherished Forever

*Yan Jiawei*

A poet once wrote, "Some live but have already died; some are dead, yet have been still alive."[1] Liu Xiaobo fits in the latter category. Although he was persecuted to death by the totalitarian authorities, he lives forever in the hearts of all people who hope for China to implement democratic constitutional government in China. A Chinese saying goes: "A dead Zhuge can repulse a living Zhongda." In other words, a likeness of the deceased Zhuge Liang could send the troops of Sima Yi (courtesy name Sima Zhongda) scattering in terror.[2] Similarly, the mainland authorities are scared to death of any memorials to Liu Xiaobo and have outdone Sima Yi's disgraceful performance by arresting and imprisoning people commemorating Liu Xiaobo along the seashore. This shows that Xiaobo also lives in the hearts of these evildoers and keeps them in a state of terror. Seven days after Xiaobo's passing, some paid hacks of the Celestial Empire overseas even concocted rumors that an internet personality surnamed Cao had read a newspaper report in Taiwan exposing Liu Xiaobo as a rapist. That selfsame Mr. Cao sternly refuted the rumor as baseless the next day. This and similar incidents prove that Liu Xiaobo lives not only in the hearts of those who ardently love democracy and freedom but also in the hearts of those who spare no effort to safeguard the vested interests of the totalitarian autocracy and that he has become a nightmare that they cannot dispel from their hearts.

I turned eighty this year and am a survivor of the Anti-Rightist Movement, a political catastrophe created by Mao Zedong in 1957. Although I can't claim to have been an intimate friend of Xiaobo, my brief contact with him led me to perceive him as an upright and outstanding scholar. I wrote this text to share with readers in commemoration of the one-hundredth day after his death.

In spring 2007 I had just started using computers and the internet, and I'm sorry to say that I was as awkward as Cao Xueqin's Granny Liu visiting Grand View Garden (Daguanyuan).³ But I've always been plagued with curiosity and a determination to explore what I least understand, combined with a propensity for word-mongering, which is how I came to be labeled a rightist in my youth, landing in prison and almost losing my life. Decades later, I still hadn't learned my lesson. At this time, an old friend from prison, Mr. Huang, came to Sichuan from Beijing, and while we were drinking tea and chatting, Mr. Huang began enthusiastically lauding overseas free media electronic magazines as marvels of "letting a hundred flowers bloom and a hundred schools of thought contend."⁴ With no little self-satisfaction, he produced an article of his that had been published in the overseas free media. My interest sparked. I spent my last penny on a secondhand computer and began a new career as an online freelance writer.

At that time, even my wife and children thought I was wasting my time. Wasn't it crazy for someone in his seventies to write articles? I was determined to ignore the ridicule of others, but my experience with submitting articles on the mainland had taught me that it was difficult for a nobody like me to catch the eye of an editor, and I had no reason to believe it would be any different overseas. I requested advice from Mr. L, an instructor at a certain university in Shandong who had been publishing freelance articles online for some time. Mr. L enthusiastically recommended people and told me to send them my work. One was the chief editor of the *Democracy Forum* website, Cary Hung, and the other was Liu Xiaobo. I should mention that editor Hung later gave me a good deal of advice and help, but I will say no more, as it is unrelated to this essay. I am only talking here about Xiaobo.

At the end of March 2007, I sent Mr. Liu Xiaobo an essay entitled "The Story of Moving a Bolder." It was about how after the Cultural Revolution ended, various places began taking down the many statues of Mao scattered all over the country. At that time I was "employed" in a prison, and the article described what I saw, heard, thought, and felt when sent to take down the Mao statue at the prison. I didn't really expect Liu Xiaobo to think much of my article but very politely asked "Teacher Liu" to give me his corrections and instructions. In less than forty-eight hours I received a reply email that surprised me with its enthusiasm and modesty.

*Democratic China* (at that time Cai Chu was the editor in charge) eventually published the article in its April issue under the title "'Class Enemies' Smashed Mao's Statue in Prison."[5] Liu Xiaobo later also published my essays "The Death of 'Political Lunatic' Li Jingxiao" and "To Hell with Lies" on *Democratic China*. He told me about the situation with Cai Chu, Chen Kuide, Yang Lili, Yi Ping, Zhang Weiguo, and other people in charge of overseas media, as well as the websites *Observe China* (*Guancha*), *China E-Weekly* (*Yibao*), *Humanity and Human Rights* (*Ren yu Renquan*), and others and gave me their email addresses. I had never had even a chance encounter with Xiaobo, and his personal situation was so difficult, yet he was so helpful and showed me nothing but consideration and kindness. Ultimately I felt too embarrassed to bother him anymore. In Sichuan we have a saying, "Teachers open the door; you enter by yourself." Xiaobo was the teacher who brought me in the door of online writing, and after that it was up to me to practice.

There was a minor episode during this time: One day in 2007, an email from an "uninvited guest" arrived in my inbox. The sender was p_knowledge, p_knowledge@126.com. The text consisted of one line in large text: THIS MESSAGE HAS BEEN INSPECTED.

Not wishing to cause him further trouble, I sent no more email to Xiaobo except for holiday greetings.

In autumn 2008 I set off for Beijing to visit friends and see the sites, and when I passed through Chengdu, several fellow "rightists" invited me to drink tea in the park and have dinner. Some of them knew I was going to Beijing and said I must visit Liu Xiaobo. Zhu Guogan even showed me a letter Xiaobo had written with his own hand, modestly addressing Zhu as his elder and hoping that the large amounts of valuable material on the Anti-Rightist Movement would be preserved. Zhu Guogan wrote a letter and asked me to deliver it personally to Xiaobo. In fact, I had long formed a deep desire to make Xiaobo's acquaintance.

I arrived in Beijing well after the Olympic Games, but an atmosphere of "struggle with the enemy" was still pervasive. On October 2 I took a turn around Tiananmen and saw nothing but police vehicles and a forest of police officers patrolling, blowing their whistles, and glaring about as if countless Bin Ladens or suicide bombers were interspersed among the tourists. Even an old man like me attracted their notice. I was carrying a plastic bag that contained several poems, essays, business cards, and a small camera, weighing a total of at most one kilogram, almost flat and not bulging, and it was clear at a glance that it couldn't possibly contain a time bomb or Mr. Yang Jia's sharp knife. A "people's" police officer whose "revolutionary vigilance" was aroused strode over and peremptorily demanded to inspect my bag. I politely asked him to produce a search warrant, which he very rudely refused to do, saying, "This is Tiananmen Square; we're acting under orders and don't need to produce any kind of search warrant." Without waiting for my permission, he rummaged through my bag. This really opened my eyes: it turned out that it was a routine practice to carry out unlawful searches at Tiananmen Square!

When I went back and told my friend what had happened, he advised me, "If you still want to visit Liu Xiaobo, beware of being hauled into a police car before you've even seen him. The authorities regard him and Yu Jie as the most dangerous people in town. The only reason they don't arrest them is to make a show to foreigners that China still has human rights." I felt that my friend was talking sense, and that I'd have to adopt a strategy to avoid the displeasure of the "people's" police. I went to see another friend, Mr. Z, who was a scholar of history, and with his help and maneuvering, I took the subway to Gongzhufen Station with Mr. Z on the night of October 20, 2008. After leaving the station, we took a taxi to a restaurant where Xiaobo was to meet us. Along the way, Mr. Z told me, "Xiaobo's been especially busy lately, and it was very difficult for him to make time today. We need to keep this as short as possible, because he's really very busy." I said, "I don't have anything major to discuss with him. I just want to pay my respects and see him in person. And several old rightists from back home asked me to pass on their respects to him."

When we reached the restaurant, I saw a big man in the doorway holding a cell phone and looking around. Having seen his photo on the internet, I blurted out happily to Mr. Z, "Hey, isn't that Liu Xiaobo?" It was only after Mr. Z shushed me and said, "Why are you shouting?" that I blamed myself for saying this "sensitive name" so loudly.

People say that "a man resembles his writing." Xiaobo of course had a beautiful writing style, but he wasn't a smooth talker and he stammered slightly. Even so, his unaffected, humble, and poetic sincerity was contagious on first contact. When I passed on the greetings from the elderly Chengdu Rightists and gave him Mr. Zhu Guogan's letter, Mr. Z said mockingly off to the side, "Aiya, look at that, even the old Chengdu Rightists consider you Lord Bao!"[6] Xiaobo said, "I have no power or influence. I'm just a poor scholar with nothing but a pen, so there's no way I can be any kind of Lord!" I said, "Shaoxing is famous for its brushes, referred to as 'priceless,' and Mr. Xiaobo's pen is priceless for its truth and justice." He quickly objected, "I can't claim any virtue or ability and don't deserve your praise!"

At that time I noticed a middle-aged man who didn't look like a restaurant employee or a customer walking around near us. He didn't greet the servers, and the servers also ignored him. Some things in China are understood by everyone and can't be spoken of. In any case, we were just meeting up and exchanging respects and regards and had nothing to hide, so he was welcome to listen if he wanted to. But I also sensed that Xiaobo was preoccupied, so we kept our meeting to half an hour. Now that I think back on it, this must have been at the time that Charter 08 was being finalized, but he didn't mention a word about it, and that's understandable.

As I watched his tall frame slowly disappear into the darkness, I silently wished him peace while feeling convinced that this man would become an important historical figure. My mood at the time echoed that of a student at Beijing Normal University, who said, "I feel proud of Liu Xiaobo!" The student said this because Liu Xiaobo was from his alma mater, but I say it because I feel that Liu Xiaobo was my friend as well as my guide who directed me onto the path of speaking out for China's democratic transformation.

*Translated by Stacy Mosher*

NOTES

1. A variation of the poem by Zang Kejia, "Some People," written to commemorate the thirteenth anniversary of the death of the great modern Chinese writer Lu Xun (1881–1936).—Trans.

2. The Battle of Wuzhang Plains was fought in 234 during the Three Kingdoms period between the military leaders Zhuge Liang and Sima Yi. After Zhuge Liang died of illness during the campaign, his troops created a wooden statue of his image (or,

according to another version, another commander disguised himself as Zhuge Liang), which was successfully used to scare off Sima Yi.—Trans.

3. In Cao Xueqin's classic *Dream of the Red Chamber*, Granny Liu is an elderly and rustic distant relative to a noble family who provides comic relief in the novel. This phrase, referring to Granny Liu's awkward visits to the family's luxurious estate, is used in modern parlance to describe an unsophisticated person overwhelmed by new experiences.—Trans.

4. Mao Zedong borrowed this line from a classical poem to encourage people to speak out in 1957. Those who criticized the party at the time were then labeled rightists and persecuted.—Trans.

5. Liu Xiaobo was actually editor in chief at this time, but Yan Jiawei was not aware of that.—Trans.

6. Bao Zheng (999–1062), known as Lord Bao, was a Song dynasty magistrate who is still held up as the epitome of a just and righteous Chinese official.—Trans.

# Twofold Grievous News, Nothing Can Top It

*Wang Jinbo*

The first time I met Liu Xiaobo was in July 2007. He and some friends held a welcoming dinner for Gao Hongming, who had just been released from prison. There were nine people at the dinner, including Jiang Qisheng, Li Hai, Yang Kuanxing, Mo Zhixu, Xue Ye, and Liu Di. During the meal, Yang Kuanxing took some photos of the eight of us and left me with the only photo taken of Liu Xiaobo and me together. Later I saw Liu Xiaobo several more times, but not many, a total of about five times. One occasion was on February 23, 2008, when I went to the Wansheng Bookstore to listen to a talk given by Ah Cheng. After the lecture, Liu Xiaobo, Yang Kuanxing, and Wen Kejian also arrived, and we also ran into Ma Jian from England. The last contact I had with Liu Xiaobo was on November 10, 2008. I asked him on Skype to help me revise an article. Two days later I returned to my hometown in Shandong to accompany my father for medical treatment. At the end of December, when I returned to Beijing, he had already been detained.

In less than a year and a half, there were three months during which I had fairly frequent contact with Liu Xiaobo. We'd often leave messages and talk via Skype. During this period of interaction with Xiaobo, I profoundly felt his deep awareness of the equal dignity of all people when he came into contact with others, and he understood why he had so many good friends in different circles. Moreover, I personally saw him call for signatures of an appeal for Hu Jia, who had just been imprisoned. He also appealed for migrant workers who were discriminated against under the dual system of urban and rural household registration (*hukou*). Moreover, Xiaobo called for support for Tibetans, who were severely suppressed after the March 14 incident. On March 29, 2008, I was summoned by three levels of the Beijing police apparatus jointly—the Beijing Municipal Public Security Bureau, the bureau's branch office, and the local police station. After being summoned, I was compelled to reduce my contact with Liu Xiaobo. However, I didn't feel that because of this Liu Xiaobo was dissatisfied or distant from me. On the contrary, he actively helped me to apply for funding from the Yahoo Human Rights Fund and clearly stated to me: "This money is for people just like you, and it's natural and right for you to receive this financial assistance."

The first time I met Liu Xia was at a dinner party. She and Liu Xiaobo were both there. After that, I had little contact with Liu Xia. But in February 2010 I began to have more interaction with Liu Xia until eight months later, when Liu Xiaobo was awarded the Nobel Peace Prize. My deepest impression from closely observing Liu Xiaobo and Liu Xia's affection for each other was the time when Liu Di, Mo Zhixu, Wang Zhongxia, and I accompanied Liu Xia to Jinzhou Prison to see Liu Xiaobo. I used this lament from Wang Zhongxia as an epigraph at the beginning of my article describing the visit: "As you get closer to Liu Xia's family, you cannot see democracy, but filling your eyes is a love so magnificent as to be breath-taking."

In 2008 my wife and I registered for our marriage certificate. In 2009 we held wedding ceremonies first in my hometown and then in her hometown. But there was no ceremony in Beijing, the city where we usually live. In fact, I originally planned to hold a wedding ceremony in Beijing and intended to invite Liu Xiaobo to preside over it. In 2010 Liu Xia and I talked about this regret. Liu Xia said that in the future when Liu Xiaobo is released from prison, he would make up for it.

On October 6, 2010, Liu Xia and I met alone and talked about the Nobel Peace Prize that would be announced in two days. She said that regardless of whether or not he won the prize, there might be some interviews with journalists. If she could see a reporter, it would, of course, be easy to handle. But if she couldn't see any journalist, it would be best to have someone come forward and express thanks on her behalf. She asked me to return home and think about who the right person might be. After I got home that evening, I thought hard about it but couldn't come up with a suitable candidate because I'd only had limited contact with them and was not familiar with their interpersonal circle. Later, on Twitter, I saw that Mo Zhixu was getting ready to fly back to Beijing from Sichuan and so recommended him to Liu Xia. Liu Xia agreed. Accordingly, I asked Mo Zhixu to meet the following day. On the evening of October 7, Mo Zhixu, who had just flown back to Beijing, met with me. I told him about the situation. He was very happy and agreed to meet me in front of the gate to Liu Xia's neighborhood the next afternoon.

On the afternoon of October 8, 2010, I, along with Mo Zhixu, Liu Di, Li Hai, Wang Zhongxia, Du Guanyu, Zhang Jialong, and others witnessed this historic moment at the gate of No. 9 South Yuyuantan Road, the compound where Liu Xia's residence is located. Liu Xia lost contact with the outside world that same night. On October 10 I published "Moved and Encouraged—Written after Xiaobo Was Awarded [Nobel Peace Prize]." That night Liu Xia's Twitter account began to speak. The whole world was paying attention to Liu Xia's movements, so everyone was wondering if it was she herself tweeting or whether her account was taken over. I figured out a way to directly talk with Liu Xia on the phone and confirmed that she sent out the tweet and announced for herself Liu Xiaobo's reaction to the award: "Xiaobo told Liu Xia: 'This Prize is for the lost souls of June 4th.' Xiaobo cried."

My direct contact with Liu Xia continued until October 18, after which it was completely broken off. In an unprecedented move, the authorities posted a guard outside my home for sixty-two days. With the award ceremony approaching, the monitoring of my wife also reached an unimaginable degree, simply because she had once studied abroad and has always held a valid passport.

On December 6, 2012, the Associated Press reported its "surprise" interview with Liu Xia. The scene of Liu Xia's aggrieved cries was deeply fixed in my mind. A few days later some officers from the Beijing Municipal Public Security Bureau branch office's domestic security unit (guobao) came to visit me. I said, now it's been confirmed that Liu Xia has been illegally detained by you all along. How can you deny it? The guobao asked, how do you know that the report is true? I said it's easy to confirm, how about you take me to Liu Xia's home to have a look? The guobao did not respond.

On the evening of December 28, 2012, after a dinner for Liu Xiaobo's fifty-seventh birthday, Xu Youyu, Hao Jian, Hu Jia, Liu Di and I, and some other people, went to Liu Xia's home. Seeing Liu Xia in the window from afar, I shouted: "Big Sister Xia, I am Wang Jinbo!" Liu Xia responded with both joy and restraint. Xu Youyu and others broke through the security line and rushed up. I stayed behind the security guards until Xu Youyu and the others came down. Although I didn't go upstairs to see Liu Xia, I didn't regret it. This was a new breakthrough after the Associated Press journalists had made a surprise visit to Liu Xia twenty-two days before. Thinking about it now, the action that night was very exciting because we hadn't expected it. Until today, whenever I hear the Henan dialect being spoken—that alarmed security guard who shook his head in panic, ignorantly and foolishly, claiming, "Liu Xia? No, it's impossible"—the twofold memories of sight and sound come to my eyes and ears.

After Liu Xia's phone line was opened up again in early 2014, I could contact her directly. In November of that year, I returned to my hometown in Shandong to accompany my father for medical treatment. After that, I didn't call Liu Xia for a period of time. Later, there was a time when I called to discuss something with her, and she asked, "You went back to your hometown and stayed with your father in the hospital, right?" I said yes. Later I heard that her father was also seriously ill. So each time we spoke on the phone we asked each other, "How is your father?" However, I didn't call her very often, especially after her birthday on April 1, 2016. It wasn't until April 2017, after her mother died, that I called her to offer a few words of consolation. I also told her I was still in my hometown staying with my father.

On June 26, 2017, three hours before my father's death, news of Liu Xiaobo's cancer shocked the world. My phone and WeChat received constant inquiries. In those three hours, my feelings were complicated, and until today, I haven't been able to describe them. I'm afraid I will never be able to describe them. In this world, there's probably no one else who would be able to understand.

On July 13, 2017, Liu Xiaobo left us forever. Liu Xiaobo's first seventh day after death is precisely my father's fifth seventh day.[1] My father's one-hundredth day is this year's mid-autumn festival. Liu Xiaobo's father, Liu Ye, died on the mid-autumn festival in 2011.

Many people have shed tears for Liu Xiaobo. But I did not cry for Liu

Xiaobo. This is because I cannot think of Liu Xiaobo's death alone. For me, Liu Xiaobo's cancer and death and the death of my father are intertwined and inseparable. I'm already numb, numb beyond measure.

*Translated by Andréa Worden*

## NOTES

1. In my hometown, in the initial period after a person dies, the memorial service, which includes a visit to the grave, is only the third day (that is, the funeral procession is the third day after death) and the fifth seventh day. (The fifth seventh day is not the thirty-fifth day but based on the situation of the children of the deceased, the day is calculated based on the Yanggong Day and the 10 Heavenly Stems and 12 Earthly Branches, which usually varies from around twenty days to approximately thirty days after the death. In addition, there are usually two or three dates for this day, and the family members can choose one of them.) Regarding the one-hundredth day after death and similar markers, the first seventh and ending seventh that are highly valued in many places don't exist in my hometown. There were two dates for my father's fifth seventh" I chose June 29, which was the earlier date.

# Charter 08

*No Hatred*

# Liu Xiaobo's Self-Cultivation in Suffering

*Xu Youyu*

I look forward to the day when I will be the last victim of China's relentless literary inquisition.

—Liu Xiaobo

## On Reading Liu Xiaobo's Reading Notes from Prison

Liu Xiaobo was detained by the Beijing police on October 8, 1996, and soon afterwards was ordered to serve three years of reeducation through labor. Xiaobo was then transferred to the Dalian RTL Camp where he stayed until the conclusion of his term on October 7, 1999, when he was released. Yu Jie collected some of the reading notes Xiaobo had written during those three years that he lost his personal liberty, from October 1996 to October 1999. Yu Jie compiled them into the third volume of Liu Xiaobo's collected works, which has been published in Taiwan. Those of us who are immersed in grief and indignation, as well as in a yearning mood, are glad to read Xiaobo's collected works.

During other periods, Xiaobo also wrote a large number of manuscripts, but the police seized most of them. Thus, his reading notes from this three-year period are far from sufficient to reflect his reading, thinking, and writing in the 1990s but nonetheless are rare material for us to glimpse the threads of his thinking and more or less to understand the evolution of his thinking from the 1980s to the 1990s. This is a transformation from unruly to restrained, from sharp to tolerant, from surprise victory to skillful ease; this transformation is reflected not just in the style of his writing but even more so in the content of what he wrote.

For determined people with lofty aspirations, jail is just another kind of university. Those who serve their sentences, whether three years or five years or even eight or ten years, come out different people. Just as the ancients said, "After even just three days' absence, a scholar must be regarded with new eyes."[1] The traces of misery and abuse remain on their faces and in their bodily movements, while the elevation of knowledge and self-cultivation manifests itself in the quality of their speech, writing, and bearing. Liu Xiaobo is an example. Chen Ziming is another example.[2] A little further back, Yang Xiguang (Yang Xiaokai), who spent ten years in prison during the Cultural Revolution for writing a big-character poster titled "Whither China?" (*Zhongguo xiang he chu qu?*), is another example. They transformed their careers behind bars into a period of time for diligent study and deep thinking, which clearly enabled them to increase their knowledge, broaden their view, and develop their thinking. Those who are familiar with Xiaobo's writings from the 1980s can easily compare his earlier vehement and lofty tone with his later calmness and broad-mindedness.

The range of Xiaobo's reading during this period was quite wide. He read everything, including religion, philosophy, history, literature and art, biography, memoir, and so on. His reading was not cursory. From his reading notes, it's clear that he studied with intentionality and purpose—conscientiously studying, thinking, and researching—rather than just skimming books he was interested in. As an undergraduate, Xiaobo studied Chinese literature and was also a member of the student poetry club; his master's and doctorate degrees were in Chinese literature. His specialty was literary and art theory. Although in the mid-1980s his popularity soared, having become an instant hit for his essay titled "Crisis! The Literature of the New Age Is Facing Crisis," no matter how famous he became, in essence, he was still a literary youth. Throwing himself into the prodemocracy movement and actively becoming involved in giving speeches about public affairs prompted Xiaobo to expand and shift his professional interests and knowledge perspective, which led to richer ideological resources and a more solid theoretical basis with which to better understand the real situation in China and reflect on China's future.

In the mid-1990s, a so-called shift in political philosophy took place within intellectual circles in Mainland China. Some humanities scholars who had originally specialized in philosophy, literature, aesthetics, and religion turned their interest and attention to political philosophy, political theory, and other social sciences and humanities disciplines. There are two reasons for this shift. First, some humanities scholars with a sense of social responsibility—the influential figures of the culture fever (*wenhua re*) of the 1980s—lost their voice in the social unrest in 1989. This caused them to keenly feel that when confronted with social unrest and social problems, in the end, the specialties they were interested in and cared about were of no practical use. The second reason is that the wave of market reforms and commercialization that began in the early 1990s caused the upholding of a moral position to pale in comparison with the theoretical analysis. Of course, most socially responsible intellectuals were still dealing with the relationship between professional and public discourse in the manner of Albert Einstein and Bertrand Russell. That is, there was a clear distinction in the two statuses—there were experts in a field and there were social critics; the line between the two was not to be crossed. However, a small number of people changed professional direction to integrate their social roles with their professional accomplishments, each complementing the other, and in this way, during the period of social transition, they were better able to retain the right to speak on public affairs.

Xiaobo was excluded from the intellectual community early on. During this shift in political philosophy, he was neither observing nor following the academic fashion, but rather, alone in difficult circumstances, he relied on intuition and instinct, or observation and judgment, to complete the transformation of his knowledge structure. Here, we have no choice but to admire Xiaobo's sensitivity to the trend of the times and his experience and observation of the pulse of the times. Although excluded from the intellectual world by political power, Xiaobo did not fall behind but stood in the front row of the trend. It was not easy to do this, and Xiaobo's manuscripts left the mark of his efforts at self-renewal. It is easy to see that when he discussed Zhuang Zhou, Friedrich Nietzsche, Fyodor Dostoevsky, and others—those topics he was familiar with—his writing is smooth and easy, facile, and spirited, but when he read works of political philosophy, especially the works of contemporary masters of liberalism, the attitude he manifested was one of learning, understanding, and exploration. In Xiaobo's article "The Origin of Freedom: Humanity, Culture and Systems— Reading Hayek's *The Constitution of Liberty* in Prison," he wrote at the very beginning: "Having read Peter Schumpeter's *Capitalism, Socialism and Democracy*, and then reading Hayek's *The Constitution of Liberty*, I felt a sense of excitement and respect I hadn't felt for a long time." He reflected, "I knew little about 20th century liberalism; it was only in the 1990s that I began to read in detail Mises, Hayek, Rawls, Nozick, Berlin, Constant, Friedman, Buchanan, and Schumpeter, and books about institutional economics."

During the 1989 Democracy Movement, Xiaobo was primarily focused on resistance to the evils of the dictatorship, the liberation of the people, and the development of humanity in pursuit of democracy. Morality and humanitarianism were his main driving forces. By the mid- to late 1990s, Xiaobo's thinking on democracy was proceeding in the historical dimension, focusing on the level of institutions. He remarked in one of his reading notes,

> The key to a good system is not to encourage people to be more proactively charitable and kind, but rather to effectively prevent people, especially those in power, from doing evil as they please, and minimize to the greatest extent possible, the opportunities and possibilities for them to do evil. On the other hand, a bad system is one that persistently advocates in high-sounding words that morality calls for people to do good deeds, but the result is that the biggest "do-gooders" are those that do the most evil. It is precisely because a liberal system is morally low-key that it is able to cherish humanity and enable the maximum creativity of human beings. Such a system does not use methods involving cruel sacrifices, nor does it aim at creating saints, but rather most deeply values this priceless life, and fully respects the modest desires of ordinary people, and takes adherence to rules and obeying the law as the common measure of what it means to conduct oneself with integrity.[3]

During that period, Xiaobo devoted his efforts to the issue of religion, which not only demonstrated how his knowledge and interests had expanded, but to an even greater extent manifested his post-1989 soul-searching, repentance, and new understanding of the meaning of life. His reading notes do not display much discussion of differences in religious doctrines, but they are full of religious feeling. In "Moved Behind Bars—On Reading *On Being a Christian* in Prison," he wrote:

> Perhaps I will never become a Christian, nor join an organized church, but Jesus Christ is my model for character and human dignity. I know that in this life his saintly character is unattainable, but to be so shaken and moved by this kind of book means I still have a human being's piety and humility, and that I have not been engulfed by the adversity of prison, nor corrupted by my earlier sudden fame. There's still hope for me, and I can still change the course of my life to make great efforts to approach this kind of moral character.[4]

The passage among Xiaobo's reading notes that has moved and enlightened me the most is this:

> Humankind must have a dream, and this dream requires us to seek love and equality amid our difficult situation filled with hatred and discrimination. It is precisely because of desperation that there is hope for us. Even if the earth were set to be destroyed tomorrow morning, we nonetheless would plant a tree of hope tonight. In this sense, when faith is rooted in our souls, we have the courage and determination to fight for the impossible even though we know there is nothing that can be done.

This is the clear self-expression of Xiaobo's thought as it moved toward maturation.

## Liu Xiaobo and Charter 08

Charter 08 directly led to Liu Xiaobo's arrest by the Chinese Communist Party (CCP) regime, as well as his heavy sentence. Charter 08 was also an important reason why Liu Xiaobo won the 2010 Nobel Peace Prize. Indeed, Liu Xiaobo didn't draft the original text of Charter 08, but the formation of the final text of Charter 08, the signatures of so many people, and its recognition and support from so many prominent jurists, scholars, social activists, and public figures from all walks of life were all closely related to Liu Xiaobo's leadership and organization of signature activities.

Regarding the relationship between Liu Xiaobo and Charter 08, we need to recognize and evaluate two different aspects. On the one hand, the publication of Charter 08 formed a massive and continuous movement among Chinese at home and abroad for constitutional democracy and human rights, in which Liu Xiaobo played a spiritual role. On the other hand, constitutional democracy became the central goal for China's future social and political construction and development. It attracted the broadest consensus among the majority of Chinese citizens in China who strived for and defended their own rights.

This is the result of diligent exploration and study by Chinese (both Mainland and overseas), including intellectuals, academics, the press, and others after the June Fourth Incident in 1989. It was not the product of the individual thinking of Liu Xiaobo or Zhang Zuhua, or flashes of brilliance. Rather, Charter 08 is a manifestation that China's overall social and political pursuit. Understanding had reached a certain high level. It will not discontinue or lose power because of the departure of Liu Xiaobo.

I remember on November 15, 2008, when Xiaobo, Bao Tong and I were dining at a restaurant not far from where Xiaobo and Bao Tong lived. Xiaobo handed me the text of Charter 08 and asked me to sign it. I told Xiaobo that I fully agreed with the text's point of view, but I had reservations about publishing such a Charter at that time. I was not afraid of the anticipated suppression by the regime following the publication of Charter 08; the problem wasn't that. In my opinion, people with independent or different political views in Chinese society should follow the principle of "as few as possible" when they issue protest, appeal, and other kinds of open letters. They should adopt a posture of issuing such letters only when the situation demands that you speak out and stand up for what's right. If speaking out becomes conventional and routine, on the contrary, such efforts won't be able to attract concern and attention.

In 2008 a number of public appeals (some of which Xiaobo initiated and several of which I also signed) had already been published. In 2009 there were definitely going to be many statements and sign-on letters because that year there were big anniversaries of the French Revolution, the May Fourth Movement, and the anniversary of the founding of the People's Republic of China. We should avoid the situation of "statements flying around everywhere, and so many open letters that people are overwhelmed and can't take them all in." Each utterance or statement should be a serious and major political event.

Xiaobo clearly was trying to persuade me. He said that the publication of Charter 08 had its necessary and special significance. Our usual appeals all target a specific social incident. The Charter expresses our basic aspirations; it's a platform, a plan of action. Moreover, 2008 was the sixtieth anniversary of the adoption of the Universal Declaration of Human Rights and the tenth anniversary of the Chinese government's signing of the International Covenant on Civil and Political Rights. We should declare our position, stating clearly that regarding the values and norms recognized by human civilization, Chinese people recognize these and are not an exception. I told him I would carefully consider it and take the text of the Charter back home to study.

On November 18 I saw Xiaobo again. I told him that I agreed to sign it. I also proposed a few revisions to the Charter's text. My opinion had two aspects. One was to revise some formulations to make them more precise in terms of political science and jurisprudence; the other was to change certain wording to make it more restrained and moderate in order to gain more recognition for the text of the Charter. I still hoped that friends who were more politically risk-averse would also be willing to sign.

A few days later, at another gathering, I saw Xiaobo ask Cui Weiping and Hao Jian to sign the Charter.[5] They readily agreed and, at the same time, also proposed some revisions to the text. Xiaobo also gave me a new text, saying that he had passed my proposed revisions along to Zhang Zuhua. After discussion, they incorporated my suggestions into the new text.

On November 29 a leader of my work unit called and grilled me about the process of my signing Charter 08 and demanded that I make a public statement withdrawing my signature. Of course, I strongly refused and scoffed at his argument that I had "been deceived and exploited by someone." A while later the police officer who was assigned to monitor me came to the door. In fact, he fully knew my position; it was only a formality.

It's evident from my signature process that the success and smoothness of the collection of signatures had a great deal to do with Liu Xiaobo's personal charisma and warmth. Moreover, he treated the various proposed revisions with full respect and good judgment. I have also initiated many sign-on open letters, so I know quite well how difficult it is to strike a balance between respecting everyone's opinions and avoiding getting caught in the trap of suiting everyone's taste. The task of coordinating Charter 08 was much more difficult because of the large number of signatories, many of whom had strong views and personalities and were also serious about the written language.

In hindsight, the final text of Charter 08 still has some places that could be given further scrutiny and improved. However, under the close monitoring of the police, it was already not easy to obtain such a text that involved soliciting the views of many parties and repeated revisions. If there is a need and opportunity, I'm willing to spare no effort to perfect the text of Charter 08. But since the day it was published until today, I have always emphasized that Charter 08's propositions, examined from the perspective of constitutionality and legality, are all unassailable. The various civil rights and demands reiterated and advocated for in Charter 08 conform with the current constitution and laws of the PRC, as well as the United Nations charter, declarations, and treaties signed by the Chinese government. To use Charter 08 as "evidence of a crime" to convict Liu Xiaobo is illegal and ridiculous.

Charter 08 is not a thesis in which a few scholars or thinkers expressed their innovative ideas; rather, it is an expression of society's consensus of its own demands and its own direction and goals for development and construction. Taking the demand for China's political modernization and democratization and refining it from a general and vague concept of democracy to a more concrete and focused goal of constitutional democracy is the result of the hard work of Chinese intellectuals to study, think, and explore.

Beginning in the 1980s, China reinitiated the process of pursuing modernization, accompanied by a frenzied ideological liberation movement and cultural enlightenment movement. However, due to the monopoly position of Marxism and the long-term isolation from Western academic and ideological resources, the specific goals pursued by China's progressive intellectuals for political modernization were superficial and vague. There was basically a lack of consideration of the arrangements in the form of government and the ways power would be enforced in a future China.

There's a famous saying in the *Communist Manifesto* by Karl Marx and Friedrich Engels: "In place of the old bourgeois society, with its class and class antagonisms, we shall have an association, in which the free development of each is the condition for the free development of all." This ambiguous idea of "an association of free people," which can be interpreted in various ways, was basically the highest goal and ideal state for progressive intellectuals who lack expertise in political theory. Combined with its history and traditions, the Chinese Communist Party has not even able to distinguish true democracy from the "democracy" represented by the December 9 Democracy Movement.[6]

After the bloody crackdown on June 4, 1989, enveloped under a shroud of desolation and misery, Chinese intellectuals undertook earnest and serious learning and thinking. One of the most important questions was "What exactly is democracy, and how does democracy manifest itself in the arrangement of the nation's political system?" Reference to resources of Western academic thought was once again initiated. One example was Beijing Joint Publishing's publication of the *Collection of Translations on Constitutionalism*, a series comprised of eleven books edited by Liang Zhiping and He Weifang, which gave rise to a popular upsurge in reading and commentary.[7]

A group of outstanding public intellectuals who emerged in the 1980s shifted their academic interests and expertise from literature, philosophy, religion, and other humanities subjects to political science and other social sciences in order to continue their own public speaking at a more professional level. Li Zehou summarized this phenomenon as "the shift of political philosophy" that occurred in Chinese intellectual circles at the turn of the century. Xiaobo also clearly experienced this shift.

Reading Xiaobo's post-1989 works, we can see that he was already skilled and facile with language. The literary criticism that brought him great renown shifted to China's political and social issues. This was not just a shift in topics; it was also supported by a change in his entire reading and academic resources. Under difficult conditions in prison, he read Hayek's *The Constitution of Liberty* as well as works by Ludwig von Mises, John Rawls, Robert Nozick, Isaiah Berlin, Benjamin Constant, Milton Friedman, James McGill Buchanan, Joseph Schumpeter, and others. At the same time,

Xiaobo's thoughts, ethos, and expression also transformed from unrestrained to reserved, from pointed to tolerant, from sharp to profound.

Charter 08, of course, is not Xiaobo's personal work. It can be said to be a collective work of Chinese intellectuals in pursuit of freedom and democracy. After the June Fourth Massacre, it was the response they submitted in the face of history, and it also reflected Xiaobo's personal effort, shift, and improvement.

Charter 08 is, in essence, a product of history and the times. If we expand our horizons outward from China, we can also say that Charter 08 is the product of a world trend. After the June Fourth Incident in 1989, dramatic changes in the Soviet Union and Eastern Europe followed. The experience and history of democratization in those places entered into the horizon of the Chinese people. Among them, Charter 77 in Czechoslovakia was remarkable. On March 10, 2009, in Prague, after Mo Shaoping, Cui Weiping, and I received a human rights award on behalf of Liu Xiaobo and the signatories of Charter 08 from the hands of President Vaclav Havel, we explained in our thank-you speech the relationship between Charter 08 and Charter 77. In our words expressing our thanks, we said,

> People have noticed the common fundamental spirit of Charter 08 and Charter 77. Yes, we were motivated and inspired by the Czechoslovak Charter 77 movement in the 1970s as well as by the works of Vaclav Havel and other writers. The consistency of the two charters stems from the fact that [at the time the charters were written] the two countries were under the same type of arbitrary power and ideological rule, and a similar atmosphere of social life and moral conditions—not telling the truth and not pursuing justice—and the consistency also comes from the same obligation and pressure to implement international conventions and protect human rights.

Since time will not stop the pace of progress, and history will not come to a standstill, the effect of Charter 08 will not disappear because of the departure of Xiaobo.

The day after Xiaobo's death, a French news outlet asked me whether the principles of rationality and nonviolent resistance proclaimed by Charter 08 and embodied by Liu Xiaobo would come to an end because the authorities paid no attention to the appeals for peace and because Liu Xiaobo died in such a tragic way? I firmly answered: definitely not.

Immediately after the interview, I received from Zha Jianguo in Beijing an appeal he reposted in which he insisted on the principle of nonviolent struggle; this was reposted specifically in light of Xiaobo's death.[8] I was glad and encouraged by this. After Xiaobo's death, some people thought nonviolent struggle had been declared "a dead end road." Twenty-three political prisoners and thought criminals who had been released from CCP jails and were represented by Zha Jianguo made a loud appeal to all citizens of Mainland China: nonviolence is still our unshakable principle. I think that since these people, who've suffered the greatest persecution and devastation, can adhere to nonviolence, other people can certainly do the same.

Xiaobo's spirit is immortal, and the principles described in Charter 08 will eventually become a reality in China.

*Translated by Andréa Worden*

## NOTES

1. Quote from "The Biography of Lü Meng," in Chen Shou (233–97), *Records of the Three Kingdoms* (220–80) (Beijing: Beijing Publishing House, 2007).—Trans.
2. Chen Ziming (1952–2014) was a dissident and democracy advocate who spent ten years in detention and house arrest for his participation in the 1989 Democracy Movement.—Trans.
3. Liu Xiaobo, *Freedom behind Iron Bars: Liu Xiaobo's Collected Works*, Vol. 3 (New Taipei City: Lordway Publishing, 2017).—Trans.
4. *On Being Christian* is a book by the Swiss Catholic theologian Hans Küng (b. 1928).—Trans.
5. Hao Jian (b. 1954) is a Beijing-based film studies professor and human rights defender.—Trans.
6. This refers to a mass protest led by students in Beiping (present-day Beijing) on December 9, 1935, to demand that the Chinese government actively resist Japanese aggression.—Trans.
7. Liang Zhiping (b. 1959) and He Weifang (b. 1960) are prominent legal scholars in China.—Trans.
8. Zha Jianguo (b. 1953), a dissident and cofounder of the China Democracy Party, served nine years in prison on the charge of subversion and joined Independent Chinese PEN Center after his release.—Trans.

# Deeply Concerned for Liu Xiaobo, on the Verge of Death
*Jiang Qisheng*

In the afternoon of June 26, the news was posted on WeChat: "Liu Xiaobo is being treated at a hospital for terminal liver cancer." The news was hard to believe, or I didn't want to believe it, so I immediately scaled the Great Firewall to access the Democratic China website, and in one glance saw the exact same shocking and heart-wrenching news! The news was disclosed by lawyer Shang Baojun. Immediately I sent him a WeChat message: "Hi, Baojun, Xiaobo is too unfortunate! Please send my regards to Liu Xia." Baojun replied: "Hello Mr. Jiang, the news is too bad! If I have the opportunity, I will definitely send your greetings."

"Xiaobo is too unfortunate!" contains two meanings: first, that he actually was so unfortunate to have been stricken with horrid liver cancer, and second, that he, in fact, had liver cancer and that unexpectedly, and even more unfortunately, it was not discovered and treated earlier, and now it's too late!

On the morning of June 27, Jiang Danwen circulated "Urgent Appeal: Return Liu Xiaobo's Complete Freedom (Draft for Comments)." After I offered two suggested revisions, I immediately signed my name. At noon that day, I arrived at Chegongzhuang Chongyang Restaurant; the gathering was hosted by Xie Xiaoling, and also attending the "old people's party" were Bao Tong, Jiang Yanyong, Wu Qing, and Zha Jianguo. I said I was extremely worried about Xiaobo's condition, and I condemned in no uncertain terms the fact that he was only hospitalized when his condition became critical.

Everyone can understand this: a human being who was in perfectly good condition, imprisoned unjustly by the authorities and isolated from the world for eight and a half years, and then suddenly the exceptionally bad news spread that he had already entered the final countdown of his life's journey—how could people, especially friends who know him well, not speak out, question, appeal? On June 26 Chen Ping, Zha Jianguo, He Depu, Huang Dadi, Zhao Cheng, Zhang Xianling, and Fu Guoyong one after another entrusted me to sign their names on the "Urgent Appeal." From June 26 to the present, every corner of the globe, regardless of skin color or ethnicity, has spoken with the universal voice of humanity. They are all imploring the Chinese authorities to respect and satisfy Liu Xiaobo's last wish: to release him to Germany or the United States to receive medical treatment.

But will the authorities release him? On the afternoon of June 29, a Hong Kong reporter called out to Xi Jinping from a close distance, and asked him when he would release Liu Xiaobo, but Xi did not respond. A few hours after this incident occurred, a Hong Kong friend asked me on WeChat: "Will Xi Jinping release Liu Xiaobo?" I replied: "I reckon Xi won't release Liu Xiaobo unless Trump makes a kickass move." In my opinion, the main reason Xi Jinping won't release Liu Xiaobo, who has been silenced for more than eight years, is that Xiaobo cannot be given the opportunity to make a final, free statement to the world. Because Xiaobo's final voice would inevitably be a political nuclear explosion, it would surely create a huge global sensation and impact, and his words would leave a moving and magnificent, indelible page in the history of China and the world. Xi is absolutely not willing to see this happen.

From June 29 until now, U.S. President Donald Trump has not only failed to make a fierce move, but he hasn't even made a strong condemnation (or demand). In this appeasement posture that renders people speechless, why would Xi Jinping consider releasing Liu Xiaobo? Xi has made up his mind now, and his decision is not to release Liu. Regardless of whether one tries to persuade him with reason or with an emotional appeal, whether one flatters and praises him for "becoming a world leader" or berates him as "inhumane," he won't respond to any of these efforts. Letting Liu Xiaobo go abroad was nonnegotiable. Xiaobo couldn't even use his mobile phone from his sickbed to let the outside world hear his last utterance of "kind words when death is near."

Several days ago, the government broadcast some scenes that I could not bear to watch: the energetic Xiaobo, who eight and a half years ago lived only a few hundred meters from my home and often invited me to play badminton, was already seriously ill, emaciated, and near the end of his life! The Xiaobo of eight and half years ago was working together with friends night and day, nailing down the final version of Charter 08 and collecting signatures of our fellow countrymen without pausing to rest. Now it seems doing this was the last important activity he would do in his life. He knew clearly that he faced an extremely high risk of imprisonment. At that time, Xiaobo said to me several times: "Qisheng, next year is the twentieth anniversary of June 4th, and I must make preparations for a long-term imprisonment. However, we are now doing this Charter 08 and we also must be prepared to be arrested." Around 5 p.m. on December 8, 2008, Xiaobo called me on Skype and then asked me: "Qisheng, are there police officers on duty there? Many have come here." I answered: "None were at my place this morning. I don't know if there are any now. Wait a moment, and I'll go out and take a look." Six hours after this call, Xiaobo was taken away from his home by domestic security police (*guobao*) officers from the Beijing Public Security Bureau.

On December 25, 2009, the authorities gave Xiaobo a heavy sentence, eleven years in prison. Although Xiaobo and I have had no communication since then, I firmly believed that Xiaobo would serve out his prison term. Moreover, I have always held the personal wish of looking forward to seeing Xiaobo after he got out of prison on June 22, 2020, to tell him in person: I read his "My Self-Defense" delivered in the courtroom, which greatly resonated with me, and I enjoyed reading it. But when I read his "My Final Statement" given in court, it put me in an uncomfortable mood that I haven't been able to shake off.[1] I even had a plan to clutch this statement and challenge him on it for a month.

However, no matter how much I might clutch and how much I might challenge, I absolutely would not give him such labels as a "pro-democracy flower vase" or a possible Kundera-style "cooperation faction" or a "harmonious ambassador" who was about "to be dispatched from prison" by the Communist Party.[2] Just as when Charter 08 was announced in December 2008, I similarly could never agree with the accusation that Charter 08's "coming out" was a Chinese Communist Party "conspiracy." The imprisoned Xiaobo knew nothing of these labels and accusations. Now, there is absolutely no need for him to know. Today, facing Xiaobo, who is quickly losing his vitality by the minute, facing this loyal martyr for universal values, facing the unyielding martyr for the concepts of constitutionalism and democracy, these labels and accusations have come to nothing.

Since June 26 I have been deeply mourning Xiaobo, who is already on the verge of death. The hospital's announcement today about his condition is heartbreaking. I can't read it. I understand that I will not be able to see him one last time before he dies. I won't be able to tell him that Charter 08, which he spared no effort to introduce before his imprisonment, has already been signed by thirty-five batches of fellow Chinese, for a total of more than 13,400 individuals. My current wish is to go to Shenyang to send him off on his final journey. Last night my friends had to painfully discuss Xiaobo's funeral affairs. Soon, Danwen sent my five-point preliminary suggestion to Xiaobo's family members: 1) family members firmly request that a certain number of friends be invited to participate in the ceremony to pay last respects to Xiaobo's remains; 2) it is recommended that the list of friends be drafted by Jiang Danwen and Mo Zhixu and selected by Xiaobo's family members; 3) once the list is confirmed, the family members will immediately transmit it to the authorities; 4) at the same time, each of the friends on the list should take this up with domestic security police (*guobao*) and express their wish, even suggesting that *guobao* go with them; 5) the wreaths and flower baskets sent by friends will be handled by members of the family who are already in Shenyang.

My desire for farewell follows nature's course and conforms to humanity. If anyone still will obstruct me from realizing this minimum desire, what will I regard him as, if not an enemy?

*Translated by Andréa Worden*

## NOTES

1. "My Self-Defense," trans. Perry Link, in *Liu Xiaobo: No Enemies, No Hatred*, ed. Perry Link, Tienchi Martin-Liao, and Liu Xia (Cambridge MA: The Belknap Press of Harvard University Press, 2012), 313–20; "I Have No Enemies: My Final Statement," trans. Perry Link, in Link et al., *Liu Xiaobo*, 321–26.—Eds.

2. In 2008 a document written by the Czech Communist police identified the prominent Czech author Milan Kundera (b. 1929) as a collaborator who informed on others. Kundera has denied the accusation. See "Milan Kundera Denies Being Communist Informant," *New York Times*, October 13, 2008.—Trans.

# On One of Liu Xiaobo's Ideological Legacies

*Pei Yiran*

While I was in Shanghai on January 4, 2010, Ding Dong in Beijing forwarded me a group message from Cui Weiping, which invited a response from dozens of intellectuals inside and outside of China regarding Liu Xiaobo's being sentenced to eleven years in prison. I immediately typed out a paragraph of text and sent it back, and after Cui Weiping went through the selection and editing, she tweeted:

> Pei Yiran's view: I am in complete agreement with Mr. Yu Ying-shih's viewpoint; of course Xiaobo has been imprisoned for the democratic cause. For Xiaobo, it may be said that the misery of the state is the luck of Xiaobo! His honor is increased each time! [Tan] Sitong has got a successor! Our only comfort is that so many people outside are "accompanying" Xiaobo.[1]

Cai Chu asked me to analyze Liu Xiaobo's ideological legacy, and limited by word count, I cannot comprehensively discuss Liu Xiaobo's thinking but can only give a brief analysis of his controversial statement delivered at his trial—"I Have No Enemies"—and then sketch the value of Xiaobo's ideological legacy.

After Xiaobo delivered "I Have No Enemies" in court on December 23, 2009, there were reactions in China and abroad. I was unable to read them online in China (being too stupid to know how to leap over the firewall) and could only resort to Hong Kong magazines "produced for export but sold in the home market." At first, I was also quite perplexed. How could he say "I have no enemies"? If there were no enemies, who was opposing China's democracy movement? Why was it necessary to struggle? In particular Zhongnanhai, the fountainhead of terrorist tyranny: Mao Zedong, Deng

Xiaoping, Li Peng . . . all those people who opened fire on students and ordinary citizens on June 4, who owed such a massive blood debt, weren't they the enemies of the people? Furthermore, when the underdog forgives the overlord and proffers unreciprocated love, isn't that just adopting an Ah Q mentality?[2] Does Zhongnanhai care anything for your forgiveness?

## The Jiang Faction's View of Xiaobo

On August 8, 2010, at the invitation of Zhou Zhixing, the publisher and chief editor of *Leader* magazine and the website Gongshiwang, I attended a dinner in Shanghai also attended by the scholars Liu Ji, Zhang Rulun, and Xiao Gongqin.[3] Liu Ji had been an aide to Jiang Zemin and was one of the drafters of Jiang's theory of "Three Represents," and he expressed comments that represented the Jiang faction's view of Liu Xiaobo. The rightists and leftists are a single faction, and the rightists helped the leftists. We can't talk about class struggle; it doesn't exist. The leftists criticize Liu Xiaobo, saying, "How can it be that class struggle has been extinguished?" For this reason, in this sense, both left and right are impossible; it's just one interdependent faction. In this sense, I feel that it would be nothing to execute Liu Xiaobo.

Did you hear that? Jiang Zeming, who from the present standpoint seems fairly open-minded, regard's Liu Xiaobo's "historical function" in terms of "execution" and appraises your "historical status" as "even death will not expiate all guilt." From the perspective of mutual reciprocity, Xiaobo's "I have no enemies" is in fact unbalanced and tantamount to "casting pearls before swine." But hold on, didn't Xiaobo know that he was the deadly foe of Zhongnanhai? Didn't he know that others considered him the kind of person who would defile their graves? Didn't he understand that for all his "I have no enemies," the other side still regarded him as Enemy No. 1? I feel this is exactly Xiaobo's shrewdness. He understood it all and also understood the "publicity value" of playing this card—the greater the contrast, the wider it would be disseminated.

## Understanding Xiaobo

Liu Xiaobo was in fact deeply influenced by Christianity, and "I Have No Enemies" distinctly reflects Christ's love for humanity, which forgives all evil and all enemies. Since it was impossible to argue the point in court, we have no way of learning why Xiaobo chose the formulation of "I have no enemies" as the grounds for his argument. But based on the spirit of Christ, I have gradually come to understand the deep implications of Xiaobo's "I have no enemies." Apart from powerfully advocating Christ's concept of universal love, it may also contain a threefold political function: 1) To place a stern emphasis on nonviolence directed at the democracy movement. Since there are no enemies, there is also no need for violent opposition. 2) To reduce the CCP's hostility as much as possible and diminish Zhongnanhai's terror of the democracy movement, thereby reducing the human factor in the process of democratic transformation. 3) To inspire the CCP and the rest of the world through an elevated Christ-like posture or perhaps use absolute love as an antithesis to Zhongnanhai's bloody brutality.

Regardless, the way that "I Have No Enemies" confronted hatred with love highlighted the moderation and inclusion of Xiaobo's thinking to the greatest possible degree. In the political sense, it can be seen as the extreme united front—uniting all possible forces to the greatest possible extent, bringing the government and public into a consensus in hopes of joint effort toward a democratic transformation.

Even more important, Xiaobo had the freedom to choose how to express his meaning, even if it was a statement under the butcher's knife. In terms of general orientation, condensed into Charter 08 were Xiaobo's main thinking and values, which of course were to end the CCP's one-party autocracy and achieve China's democratic transformation. Ultimately, "I Have No Enemies" was only a strategy aimed at highlighting nonviolent struggle. If perceived in the long term, all that China has left from nearly a century of class struggle is hatred, and generations of Chinese have spent their lives rolling in the mire of hatred—the Anti-Rightist Movement, the Cultural Revolution, June 4, weren't they all inciting the masses against the masses? It has reached the point where the Chinese spend their lives packed with hatred and perceive the streets filled with enemies. In Xiaobo's "I Have No Enemies," a harshly sentenced political prisoner who should hate the CCP more than anyone forgives all his "enemies" and espouses Christian universal love, objectively taking on the role of rectifying the ills of our times. Ultimately, the general orientation of exchanging hatred for love is correct.

## Xiaobo's Value

Although Xiaobo has passed away, his radiance is eternal. For a considerable period of time, his name will continue to have rallying power as a dazzling banner for the Chinese democracy movement, and the CCP will continue to dread him. We must naturally take pains to carry on and enhance his ideological legacy.

The Nobel Peace Prize was awarded to Xiaobo in honor of Charter 08 and the benchmarks Liu Xiaobo and his comrades established for the Chinese democracy movement—freedom and democracy, rule of law and constitutional government, equality and human rights, and nonviolent struggle. Xiaobo reciprocated this international recognition with his own life by loyally and steadfastly defending the great honor of the Nobel Peace Prize.

Of course, Charter 08 is a product of its times. The drafting process was obliged to incorporate various compromises, keeping demands within reason to make it easier for Zhongnanhai to accept—for example, not touching on the soul of the CCP regime and the most troublesome ideological obstruction, Marxism, and instead directly expressing various political demands. The CCP regime is irretrievably bound up with Marxism, and its legitimacy is rooted in that Red heresy, so hanging an inverted flag would imply surrendering that legitimacy. That is why Xi Jinping had been tightening the ideological valve and proclaiming strident reminders to "never forget why you started."

However, China and its 1.4 billion people are not the private property of the Chinese Communist Party. The CCP cannot be the sole director and actor in history of the CCP and of Mainland China. We must draw lessons from the past, apply them to the present and use them to anticipate the future. Marxism-Leninism is so preposterous, the International Communist Movement so flagrantly evil, and the CCP regime so vile and brutal, that I believe the vast majority of Chinese are silently asking, "How long can the red banner keep flying?" and secretly hoping, "When will China cast off the historical baggage of the CCP?" I believe that behind the red walls of Zhongnanhai, Politburo elders have also been long disenchanted with communism and have worked out their own plans of retreat.

The only way forward for China is toward the universal values of democracy and freedom. Is it even conceivable that China would not use the successful Euro-American model of constitutional governance but would instead persist with the dictatorship of the proletariat that failed in the Soviet Union and Eastern Europe? Even if the CCP insists that the "red banner will flutter for ten thousand generations," time is merciless, and history's natural selection will ultimately eliminate the crime-ridden and blood-spattered Marxist-Leninist model. For now, the CCP regime can only preserve the status quo through tyranny as Mao's portrait at Tiananmen Square crumbles. Is it possible for the CCP tyranny to continue for ten thousand years? It won't even last one hundred! Although we dissidents have been driven out, our comrades are everywhere in Mainland China, a "fifth column" for the democracy movement against which state security and domestic security are defenseless.

Xiaobo is not far away; his voice rings in our ears. Freedom will have its successor, and China's democracy movement continues on its road to a democratic China.

*Translated by Stacy Mosher*

NOTES

1. An allusion to a line from a poem by the Qing dynasty poet Zhao Yi (1727–1814). The original, as translated by Yan Zhou and Bob Black, is "The misery of a country is the luck of a poet." Tan Sitong (1865–98) was a Qing dynasty reformist thinker who was executed when his reform movement failed.—Trans.
2. Lu Xun's (1881–1936) *The True Story of Ah Q* depicts a man who deceives himself into believing that he is successful even in the face of abject failure.—Trans.
3. Gongshiwang is an outspoken Chinese website that specialized in wide-ranging political and economic analysis, which was forced to close down in October 2016. Liu Ji (b. 1935) is former deputy director of CASS, Zhang Rulun (b. 1953) is a professor of philosophy at Fudan University, and Xiao Gongqin (b. 1946) is a professor of history at Shanghai Normal University.—Trans.

# Mourning Liu Xiaobo

*Sun Wenguang*

The year Liu Xiaobo assisted in the drafting of Charter 08 and collected signatures, he was taken into custody, and he was sentenced to eleven years in 2009. In 2010 he won the Nobel Peace Prize.

He had spent almost nine years in prison. Everyone hoped that Xiaobo would return soon. No one expected that in June 2017, he would already have terminal liver cancer, be hospitalized for medical treatment, and in less than twenty days would pass away. When the shocking news broke, everyone cried in pain.

We had originally hoped that after he served his sentence and was released from jail, he would run for the presidency of China. We never expected this—an ending in which he was so hated that his bones would be ground to dust and tossed away. Under totalitarian China, Liu Xiaobo was the great standard-bearer of the prodemocracy movement and a torch in the darkness. He illuminated the way forward and warmed the hearts of the miserable.

In Mainland China Liu Xiaobo was our hope and enjoyed popular confidence. For more than two decades, he continuously published commentaries, wrote books advocating his theories, criticized totalitarianism, and promoted freedom and democracy in China. His was a bugle call that inspired common people and shook the high-level rulers. He served two terms as the president of the Independent Chinese PEN Center. Xiaobo often contacted representatives from all walks of life, and hosted and convened various meetings. He was a thinker, an inspirer, and an organizer—an organizer of actions.

Charter 08 is a typical example of his power of thought and executive skill. To this end, Xiaobo collected opinions from all sides. Not only did he seek opinions himself, but he also sent people to various places in China, draft in hand, to solicit opinions. In the end, he obtained signatures from more than three hundred people, including me. The signatories were not only figures from Beijing and Shanghai, but also people from Sichuan, Shandong, Guangdong, and other places; among them included many writers, scholars, and representatives from all walks of life. We signed Charter 08 not only because of our appreciation of its content, but also because of our respect for Liu Xiaobo.

Rest in peace, Xiaobo. The Chinese people will certainly remember you. Your words, deeds, and writings have left the world with precious spiritual wealth. The radiance of your spirit will illuminate the winding path leading to freedom and democracy. Your spiritual heat will warm the souls of many suffering people.

High-level authorities believed that by throwing your ashes into the sea they could prevent people from finding a gathering place to commemorate you. They were wrong. A great image will be deeply buried in the hearts of the people and will never fade away. Every year on or around July 13, people all around the country, in cities and villages, will gather to commemorate Liu Xiaobo. Charter 08 already has more than ten thousand signatures. More people will sign in the future.

Rest in peace, Xiaobo, your spirit will be immortal.

*Translated by Andréa Worden*

# What Liu Xiaobo Means to Hong Kong

*Albert Ho Chun-yan*

Before the 1989 Democracy Movement, Liu Xiaobo was already a famous young writer and literary critic. In the mind of the Hong Kong public, however, his image as a public intellectual was established shortly before the June 4 crackdown, when he and three other men from the arts and scholarly community, Zhou Duo, Gao Xin, and Hou Derchien, went on hunger strike at Tiananmen Square and remained there until all of the students had withdrawn. The spirit and courage of the Four Gentlemen left a deep impression on students and other Hongkongers who enthusiastically embraced the 1989 Democracy Movement.

After that Liu Xiaobo was repeatedly detained and imprisoned for maintaining his ideals. In May 1995 he joined with several other intellectuals, including Bao Zunxin, Wang Dan, and Liu Nianchun, in issuing a statement on the sixth anniversary of June 4 entitled "Drawing from a Lesson Paid for in Blood and the Process of Promoting Democracy and Rule of Law: An Appeal on the Sixth Anniversary of June 4th," for which he was taken into custody for more than a year. This drew concern and support from human rights organizations such as the Hong Kong Alliance in Support of Patriotic Democratic Movements of China. Several years after that, Liu Xiaobo was elected president of the Independent Chinese PEN Center and went on to publish a collection of poems by his wife, Liu Xia, as well as several volumes of political commentaries, including *A Nation That Lies to Conscience*. He focused his thinking and actions mainly on influencing the cultural and intellectual communities. Restrictions on communications and activities greatly limited Liu Xiaobo's exchanges with intellectuals and activists overseas and in Hong Kong.

Xiaobo was nevertheless able to leverage his astonishing drive and personal credibility to push forward the drafting of Charter 08, even to the point of arranging for it to be signed by 303 prominent mainland intellectuals, scholars, and professionals. Charter 08 caused a sensation when it was published on the internet on December 9, 2008.

The universal values of democracy, freedom, human rights, rule of law, and constitutional government that Charter 08 demands are no different from those in the Universal Declaration of Human Rights and the International Covenant on Civil and Political Rights. Its significance is as a political movement demonstrating that the humanitarian spirit has not been extinguished under autocracy and in reflecting the persistent struggle for reform and the people's idealistic desire for freedom and liberation. This is exactly what China's dictators have always feared the most, including Mao Zedong during the 1957 Anti-Rightist Campaign and Deng Xiaoping during the 1989 Democracy Movement. Liu Xiaobo and the other activists promoting Charter 08, including Zhang Zuhua and Jiang Qisheng, were taken into custody, but many others in the world's free societies, including the relatively free Chinese special administrative region of Hong Kong, also joined the signature campaign. During the second and third rounds, the number of signatories grew to more than ten thousand, many of them from Hong Kong's intellectual, political, and social activist circles.

Hongkongers had three main reasons for their deep feelings and enthusiastic response. First, Charter 08's ideals, objectives, and blueprint have also been embraced and pursued in Hong Kong. Hongkongers sense that under the one-country-two-systems concept, if Mainland China persists with a single-party dictatorship, Hong Kong will never have genuine democracy. Hongkongers therefore hoped that Beijing would accept Charter 08's universal values, endorsing the development of democracy and gradually implementing reforms toward a democratic constitutional government in Mainland China. This environment would give Hong Kong the conditions needed to implement full democracy without interference and obstruction from the central government.

Second, although Hongkongers are used to a free living environment, they know that mainlanders who demand freedom of speech and fight for reform are usually treated as antagonists or even subversives by the autocratic government. Liu Xiaobo paid the heaviest possible price for this. Even in this high-pressure political environment, we saw 303 mainlanders make a stand for justice and sign Charter 08 under their own names. Hongkongers have the greatest and most heartfelt respect for their sincerity and courage.

Third, the political arrangements for a special administrative region of China allow Hongkongers to enjoy relative freedom. When we see people just across the Shenzhen River being handed heavy prison sentences for "inciting subversion of the government" for nothing more than proposing reforms that we take for granted here in Hong Kong, Hongkongers feel extremely indignant and angry. When citizens are suppressed for taking part in protests against the CCP out of patriotism, love of their fellow citizens, or a sense of justice, some people feel it is essential to speak out so Hong Kong won't share a similar fate in the future.

After Liu Xiaobo was arrested and sentenced to prison, he was awarded the Nobel Peace Prize in 2010, but his wife, Liu Xia, was dragged down with him and placed under house arrest. For this reason, Hong Kong's human rights organizations, including the Hong Kong Alliance, Amnesty International, ICPC, the Justice and Peace Commission of the Hong Kong Catholic Diocese, and various democratic parties began staging joint protests in Hong Kong every year at Christmas, demanding "release of Liu Xiaobo and the restoration of Liu Xia's freedom." In the years since, this slogan has been regularly heard in Hong Kong. Liu Xiaobo and his wife became heroes of democracy whom Hongkongers knew, admired, and cared about.

Liu Xiaobo and Liu Xia were absent from the Nobel Peace Prize ceremony in December 2010, and the Nobel Committee placed an empty chair on the stage. From then on, the image of the empty chair became a symbol of silent protest against Liu Xiaobo's imprisonment.

In June 2017 the outside world learned that Xiaobo had terminal cancer and was receiving treatment in a hospital in Shenyang and that Liu Xia had been reunited with him. Hongkongers and Hong Kong civil society organizations were concerned about Xiaobo's health. When they later heard from Liu Xia's good friend, the Germany-based writer Liao Yiwu, that Xiaobo was willing to leave China with his wife to receive medical treatment overseas, Hongkongers issued public appeals for Beijing to immediately release Xiaobo on medical parole and allow him to leave China with his wife. In July, when the G20 Summit was about to be held in Germany, the Hong Kong Alliance went to the consulates of Germany, the United States, the UK, France, Holland, Japan, and other countries, urging their heads of state to ask Xi Jinping to release Liu Xiaobo and allow him to leave China with his wife for medical treatment.

Yet there was no progress after Xi returned to China. As Xiaobo's health became critical, supporters staged a round-the-clock sit-in outside of the Central Liaison Office under the Hong Kong Alliance banner and said they would not leave until Xiaobo's freedom was restored. Ultimately, however, they received the tragic news of Xiaobo's demise, which at least allowed his soul to enjoy eternal freedom.

The news of Xiaobo's death reached Hong Kong at ten o'clock at night, and we immediately appealed for a gathering outside of the Central Liaison Office in the early hours of the next morning. We placed a photograph of Xiaobo and a floral wreath on an altar that had been prepared in advance, and prepared fresh flowers that members of the public could lay at the altar. That night, more than one hundred people attended a public memorial ceremony, probably the first ceremony paying respects to Xiaobo anywhere in the world.

On the Saturday evening after Xiaobo's death, the Hong Kong Alliance held a candlelight vigil and protest march. More than one thousand people marched in the rain from Chater Garden in the Central District to the Central Liaison Office in Western District, where they once again paid respects before Xiaobo's portrait. The drizzling rain seemed like tears of mourning that made the silent protesters feel even more distressed.

On the seventh day after Xiaobo's death, the Hong Kong Alliance held a memorial ceremony at Admiralty's Tamar Park. Although Xiaobo was not allowed a grave, scattering his ashes in the ocean made the vast and endless sea his burial place, and people can make offerings to him anywhere along the coast. We scattered fresh flowers in the harbor to express Hongkongers' thoughts of Xiaobo.

At this year's candlelight vigil in Victoria Park marking the twenty-ninth anniversary of the June Fourth Massacre, pictures and statues commemorating Xiaobo were placed on the stage. After that, a bronze statue of Xiaobo in a chair was placed outside of Times Square in Causeway Bay for people to offer flowers from June 12 onward. The plan is to display the statue at Tamar Garden every year when the Hong Kong Alliance holds a memorial ceremony for Liu Xiaobo on the anniversary of his death.

While Hongkongers mourn Xiaobo, they especially recall the wish he expressed to his wife, Liu Xia, shortly before his death: "Live well." Hong Kong organizations and individuals who were concerned about Xiaobo will continue to devote their efforts to fighting for Liu Xia to be allowed to leave China and obtain genuine freedom as soon as possible. The Hong Kong Alliance has launched a global signature campaign demanding that the Chinese government allow Liu Xia to leave China before the first anniversary of Xiaobo's death. We believe that only when Liu Xia's freedom is restored will Xiaobo's soul genuinely rest in peace.

With the ideals and romanticism of a poet and the conscience and courage of a public intellectual, Liu Xiaobo spent his life exploring a future and pursuing a breakthrough for the Chinese people. With his indomitable spirit and audacity, he forged ahead on a thorny path, using his life to zealously promote the epoch-making Charter 08 as a blueprint for China's hoped-for democracy and freedom.

From hot-blooded Gentleman of Tiananmen Square to Nobel Peace Prize laureate, Liu Xiaobo, that champion of justice, made prison his final home. This reflects the true evil and injustice of China's autocratic rule. Having no way to hide their fear of him, China's rulers locked him up in prison while he was alive and denied him a grave when he died, blocking news and prohibiting mourning in hopes that the world would forget Liu Xiaobo. But for Hongkongers and concerned people overseas who know the truth, the heroic spirit of Xiaobo has joined with those who sacrificed their lives on June 4 in a vital energy that flows among the people and encourages the forces of freedom and democracy in Hong Kong and Mainland China in their march toward civilization.

*Translated by Stacy Mosher*

# Why I Follow Liu Xiaobo
*Lu Yang*

Liu Xiaobo is the person I revere the most, and he is also my spiritual mentor—my guide on the path of liberal democratic thought.

I love to write poetry. By chance, I once read an article Liu Xiaobo (I was young at the time and didn't know that he was a so-called June 4 black hand), which both startled and delighted me. What surprised me was that among Chinese writers, there was a writer who wrote like this—someone who actually dared to tell the truth. What delighted me was that this writer was in China. At the time, in my heart I cried out: Write like Liu Xiaobo!

So I then went through various channels feverishly collecting Mr. Xiaobo's works. I can now boast: in today's world I am the person who has the most comprehensive collection of Mr. Xiaobo's works! I discovered that the e-collection of Liu Xiaobo's works currently circulating on foreign websites was mostly compiled and organized by me some years ago. During the four years from 2006 to 2009, I took one night each week to send emails to the friends who had requested the e-collection of Liu Xiaobo's works.

What most satisfied my vanity, and to this day still makes me feel most self-satisfied, is that Mr. Xiaobo once personally wrote to me to ask me for his works. What he wanted was his own early works. He didn't have electronic versions of these works, and he asked me if I had them. Xiaobo's wife, Liu Xia, also went through the independent writer Wang Jinbo to ask me for the electronic version of Liu Xiaobo's collected works.

Flaunting these stories, I liked to tell my friends that I was a 100 percent Xiaobo fan and a fanatical worshiper of Liu Xiaobo. At that time, Mr. Liu Xiaobo had not yet won the Nobel Prize and wasn't famous. Why had I become so obsessed with him?

As a person wanting to become a writer and who has ambition in the field of human thought, I have read and studied many works of great men and sages. I have found that there are only three kinds of thought able to remain in the world throughout the ages: great love, great compassion, and great humanity.

Jesus's great love caused hundreds of millions of people to persistently follow him. The Buddha's great compassion has shone brightly in all directions for thousands of years. The great humanity of Confucius, from our Shandong, made him "resurrect" hundreds of years later, creating a Chinese civilization that has influenced the entire Eastern world.

By reading Liu Xiaobo and studying his thought, I discovered Liu Xiaobo is a thinker who combines—in one person—great love, great compassion, and great humanity. Here I can quip: Liu Xiaobo is a great saint in contemporary China. I quote from Liu Xiaobo so everyone will understand why I am no longer going to take any action against those old people who encircled me and beat me up in Jinan.[1]

Hatred only eats away at a person's intelligence and conscience, and an enemy mentality can poison the spirit of an entire people. It can lead cruel and lethal internecine combat, can destroy tolerance and human feeling within a society, and can block the progress of a nation toward freedom and democracy. For these reasons I hope that I can rise above my personal fate and contribute to the progress of our country to changes in our society. I hope that I can answer the regime's enmity with utmost benevolence, and can use love to dissipate hate.[2]

My friends know that not only after the event I declared I was not going to take any action against those old people who beat me up, but also that while I was being beaten, I held my arms tightly behind my back and let them beat me. My firm belief in such nonviolent resistance as a resolve to not strike back even if beaten to death was also due to the influence of Liu Xiaobo's thought of great love, great compassion, and great humanity.

Read this excerpt, taken from an essay I published abroad after I signed Charter 08 and after Mr. Xiaobo had been detained for a few days:

As everyone knows, Mr. Liu Xiaobo is an independent writer who has long insisted on the principles of peace and rationality, and has devoted great efforts to promote the realization of freedom of expression, freedom of press, and other basic human rights in China. He is also a freethinker who opposes any form of violence and advocates the use of peaceful methods to advance China's democratization process.

As an independent writer, he always uses his own voice to immediately address major incidents in the country as soon as they happen. His words are always in line with the conscience of a Chinese intellectual, reminding and warning people. There are many times he ignored slanderous and malicious personal attacks on his reputation and insisted on expressing his views in his unique voice.

For example, after the Sichuan Earthquake in May of this year, many people viewed the catastrophe as a punishment for the tyranny of the ccp, and posted some "rejoicing in other people's misfortune" comments on the Internet. Mr. Liu Xiaobo immediately posted: "In the midst of disaster, any joy in the misfortune of others is shameful! May 14, 2008."

After the violent Yang Jia Incident occurred, in the face of an increasingly cruel and fierce atmosphere in Chinese society and the fanatical support that some people in freethinking circles gave to Yang Jia for killing the police officers, he again wrote: "Yang Jia type violent revenge is only 'primitive justice.' September 1, 2008."

As a liberal thinker with great foresight, Mr. Xiaobo's speeches and writings do not take the position of a certain faction, nor do they serve a particular "political group" or "pro-democracy organization." Rather, standing at the height of humanity, he speaks from the standpoint of the country's and nation's progress. However, it is just such a writer consistently opposing all violence with a peaceful approach to defend the Chinese people's freedom of expression, freedom of thought, and freedom to write, who has now lost his freedom—because of "a crime" he has been criminally detained. We have to ask the question, who actually is committing a crime?[3]

At this point, I believe that my friends should understand why I didn't raise a hand when I was beaten up and why I forgave the attackers afterwards. If my dream at the outset was to become a writer like Liu Xiaobo, my ideal now is to become a liberal thinker whose heart, like Liu Xiaobo's, is full of great love, great compassion, and great humanity to oppose any form of violence, and to advocate for the advancement of China's democratization in a peaceful way!

*Translated by Andréa Worden*

## NOTES

1. Lu Yang and other rights activists were encircled and attacked by Maoists in January 2017 while protesting on behalf of Deng Xiangchao (b. 1955), a professor fired by Shandong Jianzhu University for criticizing Mao Zedong.—Trans.
2. Liu Xiaobo, "I Have No Enemies: My Final Statement," trans. Perry Link, in *Liu Xiaobo: No Enemies, No Hatred*, ed. Perry Link, Tienchi Martin-Liao, and Liu Xia (Cambridge MA: The Belknap Press of Harvard University Press, 2012), 322–23.—Trans.
3. Lu Yang, "Protest Beijing Police's Criminal Detention of Liberal Thinker and Writer Mr. Liu Xiaobo" (in Chinese), *Boxun*, December 10, 2008, https://www.boxun.com /news/gb/pubvp/2008/12/200812101705.shtml.

# Liu Xiaobo Is a Hero to Hongkongers

*Tsoi Wing-Mui*

I knew Xiaobo for more than ten years but never met him in person. At first it was because he wrote articles for *Open Magazine*, where I was an editor. We regularly spoke on the phone, discussing his articles and the current political situation, and we got along very well. Later, as president of the Independent Chinese PEN Center, he recommended me as a member, and this brought me even more work contact and friendly conversations with him. But I'm not going to discuss my personal feelings for Xiaobo here; rather, I will take this opportunity to describe the deep feelings of Hongkongers (not the pro-Communists, of course, but the democrats and ordinary people) toward Liu Xiaobo, their understanding of his thinking, and their unremitting appeals on his behalf following his arrest.

Many people have heard of Liu Xiaobo's two most controversial remarks. One was that China needed three hundred years of colonialism for which he was criticized mainly by pro-Communist leftists and nationalists. The other was his claim "I have no enemies," for which he was criticized by the anticommunists (right wing). But in Hong Kong, apart from pro-CCP leftists, Liu Xiaobo had no enemies or even critics. Even extreme localists, who declare themselves completely cut off from China, approved of Liu Xiaobo because they admired his criticism of Chinese traditional culture and endorsement of the British colonial Hong Kong of the past and because he wasn't one of the detested "Greater China morons."[1]

Liu Xiaobo's remark about three hundred years of colonialism was mainly pointing out that China's modernization, hampered by tradition, would be a long, slow process and would require a lengthy initiation into universal values. It was just that Liu Xiaobo, at that time something of a literary angry youth, used literary language as well as exaggeration intended to shock. A former deputy editor in chief of the pro-Beijing newspaper *Wen Hui Po*, Ching Cheong, wrote an article explaining that Xiaobo made his remark at a time when Mainland China's cultural and intellectual circles were eager to shake off the fetters of tradition and march toward the future.[2] He pointed out that Liu Xiaobo's argument was correct.

Liu Xiaobo's pronouncement "I have no enemies" gave rise to a great deal of criticism in overseas Chinese democracy movement circles, but from the time Liu Xiaobo was arrested, in conversations with friends in Hong Kong on the internet and in public remarks, I never heard or saw anyone hold a critical stance. On the contrary, this expression garnered great respect in Hong Kong's democratic circles. Local democrats felt that "no enemies and no hatred" was the ultimate spiritual outlook for humanity and that it was absolutely amazing for someone to reach this plane after spending most of the last half of his life in prison or under surveillance, experiencing political persecution, and in general being fully justified to hate his enemies. Once at a gathering I ran into Tang Yuen-ching, an assistant to the firebrand "Long Hair" Leung Kwok-hung and an active member of the League of Social Democrats, a local democratic party that regularly uses radical protest methods. I noticed she was wearing a T-shirt printed with Liu Xiaobo's head and the words "I have no enemies and no hatred." She told me that Liu Xiaobo's no enemies mentality was awesome. A Catholic priest in Hong Kong even said at a memorial gathering that Liu Xiaobo was a saint sent by God.

Some people say that Hong Kong is the most anti-Communist place in the world. The CCP has also labeled Hong Kong an anti-Communist base, but Hongkongers themselves understand that they are opposing the CCP in a safe place, and no matter how radical their words or actions, they are generally just "cannon mouths" who bear no personal risk. Hongkongers are even more aware of the genuine risk of carrying out an opposition movement under CCP rule. They have been shocked by the horrendous price Li Wangyang and Liu Xiaobo paid for this.[3] What has shocked them even more is that both of these martyrs continued to pursue justice while well aware of the risk. Liu Xiaobo was sixty-one years old at the time of his death, but he had spent the last twenty-eight years fully immersed in this extremely dangerous opposition movement, including a total of fourteen years in four prison stints and constant surveillance and harassment when not in custody.

I'd like to point out that in the 1990s, when internet communications technology was not yet widespread, involvement in an opposition movement in China was not only dangerous but also very lonely. Given that I was a journalist, plus the fact that Liu Xiaobo wrote articles for *Open Magazine*, I know something of Liu Xiaobo's isolation in the 1990s when he was silenced, excluded from society, unable to publish, shunned by many of his friends, and only able to associate with a small number of similarly situated dissidents. Xiaobo and other dissidents lived a very down-and-out existence, but Xiaobo could take the loneliness and cold-shouldering, and he toughed it out.

Most importantly, he could have chosen not to live that way. While in the United States in 1989 he bought a one-way ticket back to China, like a moth flying into the flame. He left China again for a brief trip in 1993, and he could have stayed out, but he returned against the advice of his friends. In the long years of the last half of his life, he was under unrelenting pressure from the authorities to go into exile, but he would not be moved. Many Hong Kong oppositionists admired Liu Xiaobo and Li Wangyang as men of iron.

Hong Kong's most famous street protester, Leung Kwok-hung, has two idols whose portraits emblazon the T-shirts he always wears. One is Che Guevara, and the other is Liu Xiaobo.

Another thing I'd like to say is that Hongkongers have been unceasing in their support for Liu Xiaobo and Liu Xia. When the rest of the world had forgotten Liu Xiaobo, Hongkongers kept making appeals on his behalf.

Liu Xiaobo's arrest was followed by wave after wave of support for him by Hongkongers. News of Liu Xiaobo's heavy prison sentence at Christmas in 2009 shook Hongkongers, and many local groups immediately staged protests at the liaison office of the Central People's Government in Hong Kong. Some outraged protesters burst into the building and clashed with police. That night, young people burned the CCP flag outside of the building while a young woman shouted about the murderous regime. Afterward, twenty-one young people who had signed Charter 08 turned themselves in, binding their own arms and wearing placards stating "Guilty of signing

Charter 08" as they tried to cross the border at the Lowu Bridge. Several were led away by Chinese border police even before they crossed. Provoked by the heavy sentence handed to Liu Xiaobo, local democrats launched a protest march to the liaison office on New Year's Day with thirty thousand people taking part.

Once Liu Xiaobo was in prison, Hongkongers continued to call for his release as he fell off the world's radar and also expressed deep concern for Liu Xia, who remained under house arrest. They launched many related activities, such as performance art supporting Liu Xia, with ten Hongkongers (three of them women) publicly shaving off their hair and demanding Liu Xia's freedom. On International Human Rights Day in December 2016, the Hong Kong Alliance in Support of Patriotic Democratic Movements in China launched a photo campaign calling for Liu Xiaobo's release. On Liu Xia's birthday on April 1, 2017, the Hong Kong Alliance held a birthday party for her at Causeway Bay's bustling Times Square, using photo bricks to create a group photo of Liu Xiaobo and Liu Xia.

The news that Xiaobo had been diagnosed with terminal cancer caused shock and grief in Hong Kong and was followed by a sit-in outside the liaison office around the clock in blazing heat during which protesters demanded that the Chinese government allow Liu Xiaobo to leave China with his wife for medical treatment. When Xiaobo succumbed to his illness and the authorities dumped his ashes into the sea, Hongkongers dressed in black and held a candlelight vigil in a rain storm, silently and tearfully marching from Admiralty to a memorial altar for Liu Xiaobo outside the liaison office. Memorial gatherings continued to be held for the next seven nights at Tamar Park along Victoria Harbor. As a participant, I intensely experienced the profound sorrow and anger that ordinary Hongkongers felt over Liu Xiaobo's tragic fate.

Liu Xiaobo was a hero to Hongkongers, and they will never forget him.

*Translated by Stacy Mosher*

## NOTES

This text was delivered as a speech at a memorial and discussion meeting for Liu Xiaobo on July 30, 2017.

1. *Dazhonghua jiao* is a term used in Hong Kong for Hongkongers who support the integration of Hong Kong and Mainland China.—Trans.
2. Ching Cheong resigned from *Wen Hui Po* in protest over the June Fourth Massacre. He later spent more than a thousand days in a PRC prison from 2005 to 2008 on accusations of spying for Taiwan.—Trans.
3. Li Wangyang (1950–2012), a labor rights activist, was imprisoned for twenty-one years for his role in the Tiananmen Square protests. On June 6, 2012, one year after his release from prison, and a few days after a television interview in which he continued to call for vindication of the Tiananmen Square protests, Li was found hanged in a hospital room in Shaoyang. The authorities initially claimed suicide as the cause of death, but after an autopsy his death was ruled "accidental."—Trans.

# Salute Liu Xiaobo!

*Zhao Changqing*

On the afternoon of June 26, I learned on the internet that Mr. Liu Xiaobo, who had already served eight years in prison, had been admitted to the hospital because he had terminal liver cancer. Immediately thereafter, the Liaoning Provincial Prison Administration Bureau posted on its own website the news that Liu Xiaobo had been given medical parole due to illness. The news said, "Liu Xiaobo, who is serving a prison sentence at Jinzhou Prison, Liaoning Province, was recently diagnosed with liver cancer. Recently, the Liaoning Provincial Prison Administration approved Liu Xiaobo for medical parole. The First Affiliated Hospital of China Medical University has already formed a medical treatment team of eight renowned domestic oncologists, who have developed a treatment plan, and Liu Xiaobo is receiving medical treatment according to the medical plan." Shortly after that, I saw a mobile phone video from Liu Xiaobo's wife, Liu Xia, who, through her tears, said his cancer was "unable to be operated on, unable to be treated with radiation, unable to be treated with chemotherapy." These pieces of news zipping by immediately shocked people from all walks of life, and people of conscience, such as Teng Biao, Gao Yu, Gao Zhisheng, Ai Xiaoming, Zhou Duo, Hu Jia, Yang Jianli, Wang Dan, and others, who, one after another, took action and appealed to the Chinese government to "Give Liu Xiaobo Back His Complete Freedom" and permit him to go abroad for medical treatment.

Like most prodemocracy activists, when I heard the tragic news that Xiaobo was suffering terminal liver cancer, my heart was very heavy—so heavy that I felt it was difficult to breathe. This was because I have been filled with a kind of heartfelt esteem for Mr. Xiaobo since my university days. In many respects, Xiaobo had a great influence on me personally in my youth. Because I had earlier read Li Zehou's books, such as *The History of Modern Chinese Thought* and *Critique of Critical Philosophy*, he once occupied the absolutely dominant position in my spiritual temple. But after reading the works of Xiaobo, such as *Aesthetics and Human Freedom* and *Criticism of the Choice*, Li Zehou's reigning status in my heart began to collapse. Xiaobo's critique and subversion of Li Zehou's theory of aesthetics, and his praise and glorification of sensibility and the Dionysian spirit all declared his praise and yearning for freedom. Reading Xiaobo's aforementioned works gives people a youthful, passionate, and emotional experience of life. There is a kind of quixotic bravery and fearlessness as well as a Faustian surmounting of limits and conquest.

Of course, Xiaobo's personal influence on me is not mainly the influence of his thought on aesthetics but his determined struggle and sacrifice after he left the academic ivory tower and moved toward the democracy square. In June 1988, after Xiaobo was awarded a PhD in literature from Beijing Normal University, he was invited to visit the University of Oslo, University of Hawaii, and Columbia University as a visiting scholar. It should be said that his future prospects as a scholar were bright. However, Xiaobo was not a scholar who would be content in the academic ivory tower; his heart had a higher and more sacred mission, that is, he cared about and felt compassionate about reality. He had an unforgettable understanding and experience of the systemic tragedies of this country. Transforming the system to enable Chinese society to democratize and thereby bestow upon one billion compatriots human rights, dignity, and freedom became his biggest lifelong subject. It was with just such a spiritual background that in April 1989, following the death of Hu Yaobang, when student groups launched a nationwide prodemocracy movement that Xiaobo resolutely suspended his scheduled visit to Columbia University, returned early to China, and plunged headlong into Tiananmen Square. He devoted himself to guiding the students' prodemocracy movement. In the end, he was labeled a "black hand" who manipulated the student movement and was sent to Qincheng Prison.

Since then, Xiaobo's life and destiny have been closely integrated with the cause of China's democracy, for which he has paid a very heavy price. He not only lost a good job and was constantly watched and subjected to residential surveillance, but also, in the late 1990s, because of his dissident views and criticisms of the government, he was given a three-year term of reeducation through labor. In December 2009, because he helped to draft Charter 08 and gathered signatures for it, Xiaobo was sentenced to eleven years imprisonment for "inciting subversion" and sentenced to two years of deprivation of political rights.

It can thus be seen that Mr. Xiaobo was not only an outstanding literary theorist and political theorist, but more importantly he was an excellent practitioner of the Chinese democracy cause and a man of action. He not only honestly put forward his own theory and thought on democracy but also faithfully put them into practice, for which he was repeatedly jailed. His personal integrity and demeanor of courage to practice and sacrifice deeply influenced me, not only winning my eternal respect but also deeply inspiring me to bravely advance in the same direction!

It was precisely because of this heartfelt respect that after Mr. Xiaobo was formally arrested by the authorities on June 23, 2009, I sent out an article titled "Each of Us Who Signed Is Liu Xiaobo" to *Boxun* on June 29. (Note: When *Boxun* published the article, the editor changed my original title, "Each of Us Who Signed Is Liu Xiaobo," to "I Am Charter 08's Drafter and Reviser.") In this article, I strongly condemned the arrest of Liu Xiaobo by the ruling authorities, and because I personally participated in the partial drafting and revision of Charter 08 and was in the first group of signatories, I publicized my own phone number and expressed my willingness to share the same fate as Xiaobo. At the same time, I called on all the signatories of the Charter "to ask to go to jail" and shoulder the responsibility that we should bear. On July 1 of that same year, *Democratic China* published an urgent appeal I wrote to the CCP Central Committee asking the ruling party to immediately and unconditionally release Liu Xiaobo: "Return to Mr. Liu Xiaobo all the rights and freedom accorded to him as a Chinese citizen." Although these words did not have any substantive significance, my respect and concern for Xiaobo nonetheless is still evident from them.

Xiaobo's heavy sentence for Charter 08 caused great concern and repercussions in the international community. Many prominent figures at home and abroad, such as His Holiness the Dalai Lama, former Czech president Vaclav Havel, South African Archbishop Desmond Tutu, and others began to circulate a joint letter to recommend Xiaobo as a candidate for the 2010 Nobel Peace Prize. For the cause of Chinese democracy, this was a good thing to strive for. However, in early January 2010, twenty overseas writers and dissidents, including Wu Fan, sent an open letter to the Norwegian Nobel Committee, Havel, and others, stating that they believed not only that Xiaobo had serious historical problems and that he "whitewashed and beautified the current regime" in court but also that he was "suspected of being a Communist spy," and therefore they opposed awarding the peace prize to Xiaobo. I thought it was quite unreasonable to censure Xiaobo when he was sentenced to eleven years in prison. In mid-March 2010, I published the article "Defending Liu Xiaobo" in *Democratic China* and systematically criticized Wu Fan and the others for the four accusations they made against Liu Xiaobo and called for the 2010 Nobel Peace Prize to be awarded to Liu Xiaobo. In September of the same year, I also contacted Xu Zhiyong, Teng Biao, and Fan Yafeng in Beijing, and several dozens of people publicly signed a letter in support of the awarding of the Nobel Peace Prize to the imprisoned Xiaobo. Thank God, the Norwegian Nobel Committee on October 8 of that year announced that the peace prize would be awarded to Xiaobo. Although The Butcher (Wu Gan), Big Sister Wang Lihong, and I were given administrative detention for gathering to celebrate Xiaobo's award, we were glad in our hearts. This award was both a recognition and tribute by the international community to Xiaobo for his decades of sacrifice and also an international recognition of the righteousness of China's democratic cause. Xiaobo thus became, in a certain sense, a symbol of the cause of China's democratic transition. His existence had irreplaceable significance both for the pursuit of our ideal and for the actual struggle.

But now Mr. Xiaobo unexpectedly has been struck down by illness. Given my experience of several imprisonments, prisoners able to obtain medical parole generally had strong connections and family backgrounds. They were either the wealthy using money to forge a way out or the powerful using their official relations to solve the problem. It is very difficult for prisoners at the lowest level of society to have the opportunity for medical parole. Even though there were rare cases of medical parole, those prisoners were already beyond cure, and it was difficult for them to achieve a new lease on life. As for imprisoned prodemocracy activists, obtaining medical parole is even more difficult. For example, Zhang Jianhong (also known as Li Hong), a Zhejiang writer imprisoned for "inciting subversion," was diagnosed with a serious illness as early as 2007. His family repeatedly applied for his medical parole, but the authorities rejected all applications. It was only in June 2010, when Li Hong was completely paralyzed, unable to speak or breathe on his own, relying on a respirator and IV drips to keep him alive, that he was finally granted medical parole. But at that point there was no way his life could be saved, and a few months later Li Hong sadly passed away.

Now, the same fate is once again being duplicated for Liu Xiaobo. Although the authorities had already granted him medical parole, from Liu Xia's cry, "unable to be operated on, unable to be treated with radiation, unable to be treated with chemotherapy," the rumor that Xiaobo had terminal liver cancer already was an indisputable fact. I was deeply indignant about this. Even though information on the internet that Xiaobo was "gradually murdered" by prison authorities has yet to be verified, the ruling authorities nonetheless had an unshirkable responsibility for Xiaobo's illness. There is no doubt that after falling ill with liver cancer, Xiaobo should have been given medical parole at the early stage. However, the ruling authority's arrogance of power and its contempt for basic humanity—even to the extent that their dark minds looked forward to Xiaobo's early death—made them prefer that Xiaobo endure the suffering of liver cancer in prison, letting the disease develop malignantly rather than releasing Xiaobo on medical parole at an earlier point. As a result, Xiaobo's condition has been pulled toward an abyss from which there is almost no turning back.

During the week since June 26, when the news of Xiaobo's severe illness was disclosed, until today, the international community has also attached great importance to the news. The new U.S. ambassador to China, Terry Edward Branstad, the U.S. Congress, the French government, the German government, and 154 Nobel Prize winners have all publicly called on the Chinese government to allow Liu Xiaobo to go abroad for medical treatment as soon as possible. The Norwegian Nobel Committee also publicly invited Xiaobo to go to Norway to receive his peace prize. Regrettably, as of now, regardless of whether the appeals are from Chinese or non-Chinese communities, the Chinese government is still, as before, indifferent, and it turns a deaf ear to the appeals. Leaders of the ruling party actually did not respond to any relevant questions asked by reporters at the Hong Kong Airport. This must be criticized! It must also be condemned!

I believe that with respect to Mr. Xiaobo, as the renowned recipient of the peace prize both at home and abroad, it can be said that for decades he left no stone unturned and spared no effort in the pursuit of the democratic transition of Chinese society. The path he promoted was one of peaceful, rational, nonviolent struggle. His "no enemies" goodwill, his high promotion of freedom, human rights, equality, democracy, republicanism, and constitutional rule as the fundamental principles of Charter 08, was the path with the smallest price, the healthiest and most desirable path to correctly guide Chinese society's great transition. This path is not only the safest for the Chinese people, but it is also the safest for the ruling party. It can effectively avoid a popular revolt and the ensuing retaliatory punishments against the ruling party and bureaucratic elite groups and a destructive mop-up operation. It can give the ruling party a safe, soft landing amid the increasingly antagonistic social crisis, as the Kuomintang did in Taiwan in the 1980s and 1990s. Therefore, the ruling oligarchs should be able to see the goodwill and brilliance of Liu Xiaobo, and they should see the enormous effort he made to avoid a great crisis for Chinese society. Amid the predicament of the current economic stagnation and anticorruption quagmire, we should waste no time seeking the path of peaceful transition and democratic constitutionalism promoted by Xiaobo.

Of course, the transition is not the focus of this article. As a citizen of this country who deeply respects Mr. Xiaobo, I urge the ruling party and the central government to sincerely listen to opinions and suggestions from the people of this country and the international community and quickly arrange for Mr. Xiaobo and his wife, Liu Xia, to go to the United States or Germany for medical treatment, and thus demonstrate the constitutional commitment of the Chinese government to "respect and protect human rights." I believe that if Mr. Xiaobo goes to the United States he will receive more appropriate and effective treatment. This is the best option for saving Xiaobo's life. If the ruling party refuses the proposal to send him abroad for treatment and insists that Mr. Xiaobo remain in the country for treatment, it should quickly arrange for a liver transplant. I believe that China's existing medical technology and related resources are sufficient for a successful implementation of Mr. Xiaobo's liver transplant surgery. Through prompt treatment and making an effort to save Mr. Xiaobo's life, the face and honor of the ruling party and the Chinese government can also be saved to some extent and will let the people regain some hope and confidence in the ruling party and the central government.

Finally, I would like to say that since the first awarding of the Nobel Peace Prize in 1901, a total of 104 prominent individuals have received this distinction. Almost all of the laureates, for example, Martin Luther King, Willy Brandt, Andrei Sakharov, Mother Teresa, Lech Wałęsa, Bishop Desmond Tutu, Kim Dae-jung, His Holiness the Dalai Lama, Aung San Suu Kyi, Mikhail Gorbachev, Nelson Mandela, and so on are not only highly respected by the people of the countries in which they live, but they also are respected by all of humanity. Regardless whether during their lifetime or after their death, the contributions made by these peace prize laureates to the righteous cause of humankind will be the wealth of all humanity. Similarly, for Liu Xiaobo's efforts and sacrifices to resolve the predicament of China's existing system and for the peaceful transition of Chinese society, he has not only won the universal respect of Chinese democracy activists at home and abroad but also garnered the respect of people who care about democracy and justice around the world. Liu Xiaobo is becoming a symbol of the cause of democracy and human rights in China in the future, regardless of whether he lives or dies, Liu Xiaobo and his major work, Charter 08, will be the pride of the Chinese people and the glory of mankind!

*Translated by Andréa Worden*

# Nobel Peace Prize

*Empty Chair*

# The Nobel Peace Prize for 2010

*Norwegian Nobel Committee*

The Norwegian Nobel Committee has decided to award the Nobel Peace Prize for 2010 to Liu Xiaobo for his long and nonviolent struggle for fundamental human rights in China. The Norwegian Nobel Committee has long believed that there is a close connection between human rights and peace. Such rights are a prerequisite for the "fraternity between nations" of which Alfred Nobel wrote in his will.

Over the past decades, China has achieved economic advances to which history can hardly show any equal. The country now has the world's second-largest economy; hundreds of millions of people have been lifted out of poverty. Scope for political participation has also broadened.

China's new status must entail increased responsibility. China is in breach of several international agreements to which it is a signatory, as well as of its own provisions concerning political rights. Article 35 of China's constitution lays down that "Citizens of the People's Republic of China enjoy freedom of speech, of the press, of assembly, of association, of procession and of demonstration." In practice, these freedoms have proved to be distinctly curtailed for China's citizens.

For more than two decades, Liu Xiaobo has been a strong spokesman for the application of fundamental human rights also in China. He took part in the Tiananmen protests in 1989; he was a leading author behind Charter 08, the manifesto of such rights in China which was published on the sixtieth anniversary of the United Nations' Universal Declaration of Human Rights, December 10, 2008. The following year, Liu was sentenced to eleven years in prison and two years' deprivation of political rights for "inciting subversion of state power." Liu has consistently maintained that the sentence violates both China's own constitution and fundamental human rights.

The campaign to establish universal human rights in China is being waged by many Chinese, both in China itself and abroad. Through the severe punishment meted out to him, Liu has become the foremost symbol of this wide-ranging struggle for human rights in China.

NOTE

Announcement of the 2010 Nobel Peace Prize to Liu Xiaobo, Oslo, October 8, 2010. Norwegian Nobel Committee, "The Nobel Peace Prize for 2010," The Nobel Prize, October 8, 2010, https://www.nobelprize.org/nobel_prizes/peace/laureates/2010/press.html.

# A Good Choice of Nobel Prize for Xiaobo

*Sha Yexin*

## 1. My First Meeting with Liu Xiaobo, in Shanghai

On the morning of November 3, 2006, I unexpectedly received a text message from Xiaobo: "Brother Sha: Hi! I'll arrive in Shanghai tonight; when you're free, let's meet and have a chat. Xiaobo." I was surprised by his text because I had never met him before nor communicated with him by any other means. In the past, there was another "sensitive" person from Beijing who wanted to see me but was obstructed from doing so by state security officers. They had even disallowed his request just to leave a gift for me outside the gate of my community. Xiaobo's level of sensitivity was much higher than that person's. Would he be blocked? Would he encounter trouble? I didn't think much about it and replied immediately: "Welcome!"

That evening, Xiaobo arrived in Shanghai. He was staying in the Qingyu Villa on Hengshan Road. I went to see him at nine o'clock the following morning. I originally thought he was an aggressive person who was eager to fight, based on my impressions of him when he returned to China without hesitation before the June Fourth Massacre in 1989 and also by his sharp essays on current politics. In fact, he was not a fierce and angry person. At first glance, his looks were ordinary, and his speech was not astonishing. Instead, the slight stutter and stammer when he spoke made me feel that he was sincere and honest, even a bit clumsy. Although I can't say we felt like old friends at our first meeting, I had quite a good impression of him.

I chatted with him for a while and then went with him to visit Wang Yuanhua, who also lives in the same villa. Wang Yuanhua served on Xiaobo's PhD dissertation committee in the 1980s, and they had kept a teacher-student friendship. At first I thought that with such a "big umbrella" as Wang Yuanhua, at least during Xiaobo's time in Shanghai, Xiaobo might be "desensitized," but that was not the case. The next day at noon, when

Xiaobo, I, and some Shanghai friends had a meal together at a Hunanese restaurant near my home, state security officers still followed and monitored us. We had a total of nine people in a reserved room. There were three state security officers, two men and one woman, sitting right outside our room on double row seats. Through the glass door and windows, both sides could clearly see everything the other side was doing.

I asked Xiaobo, looking at the situation outside the room, how does Shanghai compare to Beijing? Xiaobo said that Shanghai is tighter than Beijing. The atmosphere of democracy and freedom is not as good as that of Beijing, and the police are fiercer than those in Beijing. Then Xiaobo told a story about how he had dealt with state security officers for more than ten years, and everyone laughed heartily. He said he was on familiar terms with all the officers who had monitored him downstairs outside his home. They had almost become "friends." As long as it was not an order that they had no choice but to execute, other matters could be negotiated flexibly. Both sides could even make concessions. For example, once there was a live broadcast of an exciting international soccer game. The state security officers downstairs were soccer fans, so they called Xiaobo and asked him not to go out that night. They didn't want any mishaps and asked him to give them some time off so they could watch the soccer game. Xiaobo readily agreed.

Friends listened, and all said that such things could never happen in Shanghai. I thought it was precisely because of this that Shanghai experienced the vicious incident in which Yang Jia killed six public security officers, and the famous scandal involving "fishing" by the Shanghai Public Security Bureau hurt both sides.[1]

I also think it was because Xiaobo did not regard state security police as enemies that he had received a certain degree of humane treatment in prison. I believe that Xiaobo did not tell lies, nor did he whitewash the darkness of the Chinese Communist Party's prisons. What he talked about was the real situation he encountered in prison. As for why it was able to be like that for him while Gao Zhisheng was subjected to extremely brutal persecution, there were likely various reasons. It's too difficult to generalize. For example, the two places, Beijing and Xi'an, differ to some extent. Also there was a disparity in the influence of Liu Xiaobo and Gao Zhisheng, and so on. However, the concept "I have no enemies" that Xiaobo always adhered to may have been one of the reasons why his circumstances in prison were relatively good, though it was not necessarily the most important reason. Moreover, when Xiaobo said he was treated better in a Beijing prison, he was only talking about his own situation and about a particular Beijing prison. He wasn't extending this to say that all the prisons in the country were like that and that all political prisoners were treated similarly, so we can't excoriate Xiaobo.

## 2. Liu Xiaobo and Charter 08

At 3 p.m. on November 27, 2008, Zhao Dagong and his wife came for a visit from Shenzhen. They came to check in on how I was doing after a recent surgery. At that time I was recovering from a serious illness. The other reason is that they had been entrusted by Xiaobo to solicit opinions and signatures for the initial draft of Charter 08. That evening, Dagong and his wife invited me to dine at a home-style restaurant on South Lianhua Road, along with two other Shanghai friends. When I arrived at the entrance to the restaurant, I saw a tall, middle-aged man dressed in a black leather jacket, holding a mobile phone. At a glance, he appeared to be a state security officer. He stared at me and I stared at him; we stared at each other for a long time.

We had booked a reserved room on the second floor of the restaurant and looked downstairs through the window to see the state security officer near his original spot walking around playing on his mobile phone. I jokingly said to Dagong that the officer must be tired from his hard work, and it's cold outside, so we might as well ask the officer to come eat with us.

Dagong said that it might have been possible if it had been in Shenzhen. He and Shenzhen's state security police were in frequent contact, as if they were friends. An officer Dagong was familiar with once said to him: "As long as you don't rebuke Shenzhen in the articles you write, you're okay. You can curse other places as you wish—scold Beijing, scold Shanghai—we don't care. We're just a dog. Regardless of which dynasty it is, they will all be able to use this kind of dog. If you hold power in the future, you'll also have a need for us; we are also your dogs."

Every time there's a "sensitive period," state security police will not let Dagong leave Shenzhen, and he can't travel to Beijing at all. On one occasion, they even offered him ten thousand renminbi to take a trip to his hometown in Hebei and to buy some gifts for his father. Of course, Dagong didn't accept the money. He said this was a bottom line. If he had accepted the money, it would have meant he had been bought. Dagong also said that the money was used by state security police exclusively for the expenses relating to his "stability maintenance." He had also heard that Shanghai had funds specially for my "stability maintenance" as well.

I had never come into contact with state security police in Shanghai, except once, more than ten years ago, when I wasn't that "sensitive" and still relatively "stable." Two deputy chiefs of the Shanghai State Security Bureau invited me in succession to dine, wanting to make friends with me. But at that time they weren't called state security; I don't remember what they were called. As a mere scholar, I went from being a friend in the old days to becoming a target of "stability maintenance" today. It really makes one sigh deeply.

During the dinner, Xiaobo called from Beijing and asked me and the two Shanghai friends for our thoughts on the first draft of Charter 08. The two Shanghai friends thought that the purpose of the Charter was not confrontation but dialogue. They also believed it shouldn't be similar to a petition or a general statement of recommendations but rather should become a common political proposition for all people. Therefore, they thought it shouldn't be too focused on the organs of power but rather should focus on civil society. I agreed with the opinions of the two Shanghai friends and added only a few words: I said that the Charter must be rational and constructive with good faith consultation and without hostile emotion.

The next day, November 28, Xiaobo sent a text message; it was long. He said: "In my mind, and in the minds of many friends in Beijing, you are exceptional in the cynical world of Shanghai intellectuals. You long ago withdrew from utilitarian circles, and concentrated on your spiritual world and putting your conscience into practice. I have great faith in you, as a spiritual friend of mine for a long time, and I hope that I can have your support." Of course I supported him, and I agreed to sign Charter 08.

Later on, Xiaobo also used the Yahoo! Messenger chat website to discuss with me revisions to the Charter one more time. He was serious and modest, though I couldn't provide any particularly valuable suggestions.

Some people now deny that Xiaobo was a drafter of the Charter. I don't know the inside story of the drafting and writing of the Charter 08, but I can at least prove that, from his contacts with me, he was an important initiator and organizer of the Charter. His contributions were indispensable, though he didn't care about getting credit. The impression he left me with was that he was rational. His thoughts, speech, conduct, and temperament were moderate, very different from in the earlier days when he had written essays as a "dark horse" in literary circles. He was now therefore more easily accepted by all parties, which was an important quality to have as an initiator and organizer.

### 3. Liu Xiaobo and the Nobel Peace Prize

On October 8, 2010, at 5:17 p.m. Beijing time, I scaled the Great Firewall and went to Google's Hong Kong website, where I saw the news headlines and learned that Xiaobo had won that year's Nobel Peace Prize. In closed Mainland China, I think I was relatively early to know this good news. Of course I was happy for Xiaobo, for my fellow countrymen, and for the cause of democracy in China.

Awarding the prize to him has been somewhat controversial. The disputers are almost all Chinese, in China and abroad. They are all people who, like Xiaobo, have engaged in democratic activities and made outstanding contributions. Just as I feel toward Xiaobo, I am full of respect for them. Therefore, I don't think that their opposition to Xiaobo's award is an "internal strife" or a manifestation of a deep-rooted bad habit of the Chinese people. Because they share the same ultimate goal as Xiaobo and just have different approaches and methods, this should absolutely be a matter of seeking common ground while putting aside differences. Based on mutual respect, they gradually eliminate differences so that, on the whole, a general agreement can be achieved.

Last year when I went to Europe, I had some contact with overseas democracy activists. I greatly admired their uncompromising persistence and perseverance, and I was very sympathetic to their long-term plight of being shut outside of China's door, their loneliness and anger of having family they cannot return to. For this, I also shed tears. Therefore, I fully understand their slightly higher pitched remarks and the slightly more aggressive manner of their actions. I think if I were also in their current situation, I would be like them or even surpass them.

However, the principle of the Nobel Peace Prize is of great importance. It is not a matter of an individual; rather it is related to the overall situation of the future of China's democratic cause. The prize was decided by a review committee. Naturally they gave careful consideration to the matter and had sufficient reasons for their choice. We should respect their selection.

We should also be like athletes. During a match I will never give in to you, and a winner and loser must be decided. But once the outcome is established, I must also sincerely congratulate the winner. Therefore, after the decision was made that Xiaobo should receive this prize, we should also sincerely congratulate Xiaobo and let go of the earlier disputes and even forgive Xiaobo's shortcomings and mistakes of the past. Xiaobo, after all, is just a few years past half a century. There is still a long road ahead. We are looking forward to his future growth.

Xiaobo's peace prize signifies that he is already included in history, but whether or not he can create history, we can only wait and see. Because China is too big with too many variables, the power-holders are extremely strong and their tricks are very crafty. It's also hard to say how long Xiaobo will be able to hold this flag in his hands. We do not want to expect too much of Xiaobo as long as he does his best, for he should know his historical responsibility. China's road is still very long and needs him, you, me, everyone—perhaps a generation or even several generations of people to seek common ground.

When Xiaobo was sentenced to eleven years, I wrote a quatrain:

The royal prisoner is sentenced to jail eleven-year,
While there is always injustice in China every day.
As inside and outside the walls all prisons lay,
One must be detained here if not over there.

When Xiaobo won the prize, a poem had to be written, so I improvised a quatrain:

God finally opened his eyes for a good selection

For Xiaobo to win Nobel Prize as its champion.

As a history will begin its departure from today,

Hope you will make efforts to write a new play.

*Translated by Andréa Worden*

This piece was written on October 21, 2010, after Liu Xiaobo's Nobel Peace Prize was announced.

1. In an effort to eradicate unlicensed taxis, plainclothes police officers posing as customers "fished" for drivers of private cars to take them as passengers. One driver caught in the campaign posted a protest on the internet, after which more such cases surfaced, causing a public outcry and forcing the authorities to apologize.—Trans.

# The Spirit of Liu Xiaobo's "No Enemies" Will Exist Forever in Japan

*Makino Seishu and Wang Jinzhong*

We have been following closely the progress of economic prosperity in China and China's human rights issues. We fully support China's democratization and actively promote peaceful engagement between China and Japan. Consequently, we admire and endorse the spirit of peace and fraternity that Liu Xiaobo adhered to over the past few decades—"I have no enemies and no hatred"—and we regarded him as the hope for progress of the development of civilization in Japan and the world.

Ever since Liu Xiaobo received a heavy sentence from the Chinese authorities, he has garnered increasing attention from the media, and the public, in Japan. On October 8, 2010, after the Norwegian Nobel Committee announced it would award the Nobel Peace Prize that year to Liu Xiaobo, the major Japanese press reported the news immediately and gave it front-page coverage. This is the only time since the 1980s—when former CCP general secretary Hu Yaobang advocated "China and Japan should be friends for generations to come"—that a Chinese person has received this distinction. On December 31, 2010, those in charge of reporting and editorials at Japan's Kyodo News Agency and affiliated newspapers, radio, and TV stations selected, from a view on the frontline of journalism, that year's top ten news stories in Japan and abroad, and Liu Xiaobo's receipt of the Nobel Peace Prize was chosen as one of the top ten news items of 2010 for both Japan and the world.

## Supporting China's Democratization

Our concern, admiration, and support for Liu Xiaobo came before his award. Wang Jinzhong joined the Independent Chinese PEN Center in 2005 and soon thereafter was appointed by Liu Xiaobo, then president of ICPC, to be a member of the Writers in Prison Committee and the Translation and Linguistic Rights Committee, as well as ICPC's Japan representative; needless to say, Wang Jinzhong supported Liu Xiaobo. Makino Seishu was born on May 4, 1945, in northeastern China, in what was then called Manchuria. After the war, he returned to Japan with his family. Starting at the age of twenty-five, he was elected, for successive terms, to the Shizuoka City Assembly and the Shizuoka Prefectural Assembly. From the age of forty-eight, Makino Seishu was elected to be a member of the House of Representatives of the National Diet of Japan for four consecutive terms. The following year, Makino Seishu took up the post of vice minister of judicial affairs in the Tsutomu Hata Cabinet. In 2011 Makino became the vice minister of economy, trade, and industry in the Yoshihiko Noda Cabinet, and in 2012 he served as the vice chairman of the Democratic Party of Japan. Because we were both concerned about the democratization of China and the cooperation of the international democratic forces, in May 2006 we attended the inaugural meeting of the Forum for a Democratic China and Asia, which was held in Berlin. Makino Seishu was elected vice chairman, and Wang Jinzhong, a director. In Tokyo, on December 10—International Human Rights Day—of the same year, we held the inaugural meeting of Supporting Asia and China Democratization. Makino was elected chair, and Wang Jinzhong, a director. The editor in chief of *Criminal Defense Quarterly*, Kitai Daisaku, took up the position of executive director.

### Supporting Liu Xiaobo for the Nobel Peace Prize

In September 2009 PEN International held its Seventy-Sixth Congress in Tokyo. Attending from ICPC were the president of ICPC, Tienchi Martin-Liao, and vice president Patrick Poon, director Ma Jian, PEN International board member Yang Lian, Internet Work Committee coordinator Ye Du, assistant coordinator Li Jianhong of the Writers in Prison Committee, and Wang Jinzhong, along with ten members of ICPC. Wang Jinzhong was entrusted by ICPC to coordinate and arrange other activities in Tokyo. On September 25, one day before the opening of the PEN Congress, ICPC, Amnesty International Japan, and PEN America jointly held a symposium titled Solidarity with Liu Xiaobo and Other Writers in China. The symposium began at 6 pm that evening and was held in the Freedom Room at the Waseda Hoshien Kaikan Hall, near Waseda University. The host was Amnesty International Japan's representative, Kitai Daisaku, Tienchi Martin-Liao gave an introduction, and Patrick Poon, Ma Jian, Yang Lian, and Ye Du gave speeches. More than seventy people were invited to attend, including delegates and guests from all over the world who arrived early to the PEN International Congress and local audience and journalists, including the chair of the PEN International Writers in Prison Committee, Marian Botsford Fraser; PEN International's board members Kristin Schnider and Hori Takeaki; Uyghur PEN president Kaiser ÖzHun; Japan PEN Secretary-General Ide Tsutomu; and representatives from other centers, including South Korean PEN, Czech PEN, Danish PEN, PEN Canada, Belgian PEN, and Swiss German PEN.

The congress concluded on the morning of September 30. In the afternoon, Wang Jinzhong made arrangements for a five-person delegation from ICPC—Tienchi Martin-Liao, Patrick Poon, Ye Du, Li Jianhong, and himself—to go to the First Members' Office Building of the House of Representatives of the National Diet to meet with Representative Makino Seishu, the acting chairman of the ruling Democratic Party's Parliament Strategy Committee. The ICPC delegation thanked him for his long-term concern for freedom of expression in China and China's democratization and hoped that he would call on all circles in Japan to support Liu Xiaobo for the Nobel Peace Prize and urge that Liu Xiaobo be released early. Makino Seishu said on the spot, "I will soon issue a statement demanding the Chinese government release Liu Xiaobo and call on people from all walks of life to support Liu Xiaobo for the Nobel Peace Prize."

Eight days later, after the Norwegian Nobel Committee announced that Liu Xiaobo had been awarded the peace prize, Makino Seishu issued a statement that same night, "I warmly congratulate Liu Xiaobo on being awarded the 2010 Nobel Peace Prize and demand that the Chinese government immediately and unconditionally release Liu Xiaobo and other imprisoned ICPC members." Since he called on the members of the National Diet to organize a coalition, Japanese Parliament Members Supporting Liu Xiaobo, an inaugural meeting was held in the afternoon of October 21 in the First Parliament Members' Office Building of the Japanese Diet, and Makino chaired the meeting. Nearly one hundred people attended the meeting, including eleven members from both houses of the Diet, the representatives of ten other parliament members, and the heads or representatives of various human rights groups. It was the first time Japanese parliament members held activities to support Chinese dissidents. The meeting was chaired by Azuma Konno, the secretary-general of the coalition and a Democratic Party member of the House of Councilors.

Makino Seishu first offered some remarks: "Sentencing Liu Xiaobo to prison is unacceptable from a human rights perspective. We demand that the Chinese government immediately release Liu Xiaobo, remove the house arrest measures imposed on Liu Xia in their Beijing home, and guarantee freedom of expression. We will give our resolution to the Japanese Ministry of Foreign Affairs to forward to the Chinese government." Kitai Daisaku, the executive director of Japan's Supporting Asia and China Democratization Forum; Wang Jinzhong, ICPC representative; Fujita Mariko, chair of the board of Amnesty International Japan; and Kazuko Ito, a prominent human rights lawyer all delivered speeches. Shortly thereafter, letters of thanks from Liu Xiaobo's wife, Liu Xia, *Beijing Spring* editor in chief Hu Ping, and ICPC president Tienchi Martin-Liao were read aloud.

Before the meeting concluded, the Resolution Demanding the Immediate Release of Liu Xiaobo and the Democratization of China was read out, congratulating Liu Xiaobo on winning the prize and expressed respect for the Norwegian Nobel Committee that awarded him the peace prize. The resolution recognized that the Nobel Committee commended Liu Xiaobo for using a nonviolent approach in his activities in the struggle for basic human rights and stated that the Chinese government could not be allowed to violate the UN International Covenant on Civil and Political Rights, which China had already signed, by persecuting Liu Xiaobo. The resolution strongly urged the Chinese authorities to immediately release Liu Xiaobo and other Chinese democracy and human rights activists, restore Liu Xia's freedom, and guarantee basic human rights and related peaceful activities.

In December Makino Seishu, Wang Jinzhong, and Kitai Daisaku were invited to attend the Nobel Peace Prize Award ceremony in Oslo, Norway, on December 10. There we met up with other members of the Independent Chinese PEN Center, including President Tienchi Martin-Liao, vice presidents Patrick Poon and Qi Jiazhen, former vice president Cai Chu, and Chen Kuide. During this period, we also participated in other related activities, such as demonstrating in front of the Chinese embassy in Norway, held by ICPC and PEN International, Amnesty International, and representatives of the Hong Kong Alliance in Support of Patriotic Democratic Movements of China, and other groups.

## Concern for Liu Xiaobo's Illness, Treatment, and Death

On June 26, 2017, Liu Xiaobo was diagnosed with terminal liver cancer and released on medical parole for treatment at a Shenyang hospital. As the news spread, there was an uproar in public opinion in Japan, and people from all walks of life held a rally in the evening of June 30, at the meeting hall of the Bunkyo Ward Office in Tokyo. Nearly one hundred people attended the gathering, including representatives and participants from the Supporting Asia and China Democratization Forum, Amnesty International Japan, ICPC, Chinese prodemocracy groups based in Japan, and Japanese academics and politicians.

Makino Seishu said at the rally: "The Tiananmen Square Incident has great significance for the democratization of China. . . . I am unable to accept Liu Xiaobo's sentence, and I demand that the Chinese government release Liu Xiaobo and permit him to go abroad for medical treatment. My request will be transmitted to the Chinese government via the Japanese Ministry of Foreign Affairs."

On July 4 we went to the office of the prime minister to deliver a personal, handwritten letter to Prime Minister Shinzo Abe. The letter proposed that while Abe was in Hamburg on July 7 for the G20 Summit, during his talks with China's President Xi Jinping, he should raise the issue of letting Liu Xiaobo go abroad for treatment. When Seishu Makino met with the reception official at the office of the prime minister, he also submitted a copy of an open letter to Xi Jinping jointly issued by 154 Nobel Prize winners worldwide demanding that the Chinese government release Liu Xiaobo and his wife, Liu Xia, as soon as possible on humanitarian grounds and that they should be permitted to travel to the United States for medical treatment. Prime Minister Abe reportedly did in fact mention his concern for Liu Xiaobo during the talks.

The day after July 13, when Liu Xiaobo died from his illness, we issued an open letter expressing our deep condolences over Liu Xiaobo's death and requesting that Liu Xia be released. The letter stated that we would continue the work to finish Liu Xiaobo's unfulfilled aspirations—that we would continue to work hard to realize freedom, democracy, and peace in China.

At 7 p.m. on July 21, people from all walks of life in Tokyo, Shizuoka, Osaka, Fukuoka, Sendai, and many other cities, in a coordinated fashion, began memorial services for Liu Xiaobo and also demanded the release of Liu Xia. The memorial service in Tokyo was presided over by Japanese human rights activist Fumie Furukawa, Japan's ruling Liberal Democratic Party legislator Takashi Nagao issued a statement, and ICPC alternate director Wang Jinzhong also spoke at the meeting. Makino Seisho presided over the memorial service at the Hachiman Shrine in Shizuoka.

In the evening of August 4, people from all walks of life rallied in Minato City, Tokyo, and demanded that the Chinese government permit Liu Xia, the widow of Liu Xiaobo, and her younger brother, Liu Hui, to freely leave China. Upon our arrival, we also delivered remarks. At the gathering, Makino Seishu said, "I attended the ceremony of the Nobel Peace Prize for Liu Xiaobo in Oslo, and I strongly support China's democratization. . . . I demand that the Chinese government release Liu Xiaobo's wife, Liu Xia, as soon as possible on humanitarian grounds, and permit her to go abroad."

From August 28 to 30, 2017, the First International Conference of the Four-PEN Platform was held in the southern Swedish city of Malmö. The conference was jointly organized by the Swedish PEN, Independent Chinese PEN Center, Uyghur PEN, and Tibetan Writers Abroad PEN. The main theme was Finding Room for Common Ground: No Enemies, No Hatred. Makino Seishu and Kitai Daisaku received special invitations and attended as special guests. On the morning of the August 29, the opening ceremony was held in the meeting hall at Malmö City Hall. ICPC president Tienchi Martin-Liao, as co-chair, delivered welcome remarks and introduced the special guests, stating,

For many years, Mr. Makino has been a friend and a supporter of the Chinese democracy movement. In September 2010, when PEN held the Congress in Tokyo, I met Mr. Makino for the first time, and we discussed how Liu Xiaobo was sentenced to eleven years during the preceding year. Mr. Makino immediately initiated and founded a parliamentary alliance in Japan to support Xiaobo in the following years. Under his efforts as president, he has continuously appealed for Xiaobo's release from prison. Three months later in December of that year, Mr. Makino and I were invited to participate in the Oslo ceremony when the Nobel Peace Prize should have been handed to the new laureate, Liu Xiaobo. As you all know, the award was put on an empty chair while the awardee was ten thousand kilometers away in a Chinese prison.

On the evening of the September 30, Joanne Leedom-Ackerman, vice president of PEN International, presided over the closing ceremony of the conference, which was held in the Malmö Library Conference Hall. In conclusion, she stated that the Four-PEN Platform provides writers of all nationalities with a valuable platform for interaction and is a new and creative mode of communication for the large PEN International family. After thanking the Four-PEN Platform for organizing the event, she stated that PEN International would add to its agenda taking action to rescue Liu Xia and Ilham Tohti.[1]

We expressed our strong agreement with this statement. Finally, on behalf of the organizers of the conference and ICPC, Tienchi Martin-Liao announced that the Liu Xiaobo Memorial Award would be given to Joanne Leedom-Ackerman and Makino Seishu to thank them for their long-standing concern for human rights in China and long-term support for Liu Xiaobo. Tienchi Martin-Liao said: "In 2010, when Mr. Makino founded the Japan Parliamentary Alliance in Support of Liu Xiaobo as its chairman, this was the first and only international parliamentary group to directly support Liu Xiaobo. It takes both courage and unyielding integrity to direct this kind of action. Mr. Makino has both. He is a true friend to the Chinese people; and he deserves to receive the Liu Xiaobo Memorial Award." Soon afterward, Yu Zhang, a member of the conference secretariat and the coordinator of ICPC's Press and Translation Committee, presented the awards to the two winners—a bronze bust of Liu Xiaobo. Makino Seishu felt very honored, and Wang Jinzhong also shared his pleasure in the honor, though being far away in Tokyo and unable to attend the meeting.

We all agree that although Liu Xiaobo has departed from the world, his spirit will live forever in China, Japan, and the rest of the world, and it represents the direction and hope that we will continue to work hard to achieve!

*Translated by Andréa Worden*

1. Ilham Tohti (b. 1969) is an Uyghur economist from Xinjiang serving a life sentence on separatism-related charges.—Trans.

# China Will Face a Dilemma and Inconsistency between the Nobel Prizes for Literature and Peace

ONE THOUGHT AFTER THE DEATH OF LIU XIAOBO

*Hori Takeaki*

After having been engaged in PEN International's activities for years, I have become acquainted with many Nobel Prize laureates for literature through PEN events. But only a few PEN members have won the Nobel Peace Prize. One of these was Liu Xiaobo, who won the award in 2010 but was not allowed to attend the ceremony because he was in a Chinese prison. The contrast of the Chinese government's reaction to a Chinese citizen winning each of these awards is noteworthy.

Because I am engaged with PEN and with international writers, when October arrives almost every year, I am chased by Japanese journalists working for major newspapers. They are looking for a scoop for their readers, especially in the hope that the winner of the Nobel Prize in Literature might be their compatriot.

I face a dilemma between pain and pleasure almost every year. It is a painful job to keep my eyes wide open for the winner. To prepare a list of possible finalists, I often ask my colleagues at PEN International. I also ask the most established publishers as well as literary critics. I suggest only a few of the final candidates among many. Then the betting game begins. Japanese critics and journalists start calling me one after another. It doesn't matter how much or little I know about world literature; those who are chasing the same rabbit are everywhere and share almost the same information.

A few reasons for this can be pointed out. Firstly, the selecting criteria of the Swedish Academy (the institution entrusted with the task of choosing a winner for the Nobel Prize in Literature) has never been announced publicly.

I would dare to say that even the academy would face difficulty in defining the criteria clearly. They have to reflect the expectation of a global community through different periods of time. There are also so many processes involved. The final assessment will be governed by the discussion of eighteen members of the Swedish Academy. The academy used to be a gentlemen's institute, but now thanks to structural change, no less than a third of its membership must be women. In addition, earlier selection committee members with expertise in literature had to deal with the hardest works, the background of each candidate, the application of formal rules for the nomination of candidates, the choice of literature, the clarification of various recommendations, and so on. There is no possibility of leaking the criteria assessment or principles as a whole to the outside world.

It will be safe to guess that the judging process is similar to a weather forecast, which is always based upon a certain degree of prediction even in this super-computer world. Therefore, every literary critic can easily say, "It would have been such a result as I predicted," after the official announcement was made.

In those circumstances there was one special case that I precisely predicted. Japanese literary journalists did not believe me even though they came over to see me to hear my prediction. It was the 2012 Nobel Prize in Literature. Among many strong candidates I focused on one Chinese writer, but no one actually believed that he would win.

I predicted, and the academy announced Chinese writer Mo Yan as the Nobel Prize winner for the year 2012. From 2009 to 2012 I had concentrated on the trajectory and behavior of Mo Yan and the Chinese government. While chasing him from place to place, I finally reached my own conclusion. Most of my observations were learned through the various events of PEN International.

It is now accepted worldwide that China has made a great leap forward socioeconomically and is turning into a superpower state in line with the United States and Russia. It is therefore no wonder that we talk about her greatness appealing to the world mainly in economics and politics; however, her influence in the cultural and literary worlds is also increasing.

In 2009 China was the guest of honor at the Frankfurt Book Fair, the world's biggest book fair. China sent a large delegation. Many German writers complained and protested against the invitation, noting that in China the restrictions on freedom of speech and arguing that it was inappropriate to honor a country where all publications, including media, were under the tight grip of government censorship. The organizers argued that keeping engaged in ongoing long-lasting yet patient negotiations would lead to a change in Chinese society. They claimed that this particular decision was a part of that expectation. The organizers tried to get China to accept Chinese and Tibetan writers in exile or dissidents such as Bei Ling, Yang Lian, Dai Qing and Gao Xingjian (nationalized French, but born in China) as participants on the same symposium. China sought to stop their participation.

European powers including France and Germany began to look at China as the biggest and most promising market for economic growth. In 2012 the British Council invited China as the market focus to the London Book Fair. British intellectuals, including English PEN, openly protested the decision, criticizing the lack of freedom of expression in China, censorship, and the monopoly of the state over publications. However, the British Council defended their China position with similar reasoning as Frankfurt.

At the London Book Fair, to the best of my knowledge, more than 180 Chinese publishers—some placed the number as high as 600—and 57 artists participated. Besides, interpreters, public relations, administrative officers, executives of the Communist Party, and others were on the delegation team and saw the Chinese delegation as the largest delegation of the fair.

Thanks to the success of the London Book Fair, the Chinese government was encouraged and decided to move further in the literary and publication areas. It officially joined the International Publishers Association, following the call from China's General Administration of Press and Publication.

Among the participants at the London Book Fair, I saw Mo Yan. At the later Beijing and Shanghai Book Fairs, Mo Yan was also in the limelight. I had the chance to speak with him briefly. Earlier, Japan PEN had invited him as the main guest speaker to its event Natural Disaster and Literature, organized to celebrate the seventieth anniversary of Japan PEN.

Mo Yan was with the secretary-general of China PEN Center but was obviously dispatched from the Communist Party. He was confident and eloquent, but he did not take this opportunity to talk about the membership problems of Chinese PEN centers on the mainland. Chinese PEN centers on the mainland had walked away from activities of PEN International after the Tiananmen massacre in 1989. I emphasized my ideas for the members to return without arguing political matters. Instead, I stressed that at PEN there is room for all of us to talk about literature in a friendly atmosphere, with one condition. PEN's International Assembly is an open place for anybody who firmly believes freedom of expression is a fundamental human right, thus China must share the same floor with Tibetans and Uyghurs in exile, Taiwan and Chinese poets, and writers based overseas. It was an intense and tough talk, but he was patient.

In October 2012 the Nobel Prize in Literature was announced for Mo Yan. The Chinese government proudly declared that China had now become a great power even in the literary world. The Chinese people were also excited by this news. It was exactly the award that the Chinese government wanted so badly.

But when Liu Xiaobo was awarded the Nobel Peace Prize two years earlier, there was almost no mention of the award in the Chinese media.

I clearly remember the behavior of Mo Yan when I met him at a symposium held in Tokyo after the award. Based upon my observations (I may be wrong), I guessed that Mo Yan himself evaluated positively the significance of the Nobel Prize in Literature. He continued to live in China. He must know the benefit of the prize both economically and politically.

At the same time, some questions arose in my mind as to the decision of the Swedish Academy. I presume that the decision can be seen as a compromise of the Swedish Academy given the standing of China in the future world. The Swedish Academy must have reevaluated the impact and merit of these two Nobel prizes given to Chinese citizens, though the 2010 Nobel Peace Prize was awarded to Liu Xiaobo, founder of Independent Chinese PEN Center, by the Norwegian Nobel Committee. The only other living Chinese writer to receive the Nobel Prize in Literature is Gao Xingjian, who lives in France and was awarded the prize in 2000.

Mo Yan and Gao Xinjian met in Tokyo for a literary event. Both were decent and very quiet men. After this event, I visited Beijing wishing to invite Mo Yan as the guest speaker for the PEN International Congress to be held in Tokyo. However, the Chinese authorities gave me an excuse on his behalf. They said he returned to his hometown to take care of his daughter, who was due to give birth anytime, and this was his immediate priority. This conversation made me conclude that the Chinese authorities must be guarding him for their own reasons.

In June 2017 Liu Xiaobo, who was in prison serving an eleven-year sentence when he received the Nobel Peace Prize, was released from jail. The authorities explained that he was released because he was suffering from terminal liver cancer and needed to receive specialist medical treatment outside of prison (but he remained in custody).

The world soon came to know that his health condition was serious and deteriorating quickly. Liu Xiaobo and his wife, Liu Xia, expressed their wish to receive the best treatment possible in Western Europe, particularly in Germany. The German government responded quickly and expressed their willingness to accept them. At the same time, European human right activists, PEN International, Amnesty International, and many others started massive campaigns and asked for the release of Liu Xiaobo and Liu Xia.

Many noted that the Chinese government's actions and final refusal was exactly the same as a death penalty. Supporters couldn't understand how his liver cancer had deteriorated in such a short time and declared that Chinese authorities had a responsibility to explain why his cancer progressed so quickly to the terminal stage.

The shocking news followed a few weeks later that Liu Xiaobo had died in a Chinese hospital.

Immediately, the Chinese authorities stated it was "the wishes of his family, that the body be immediately cremated and his ashes scattered in the sea." Their final comment stated, "It was the hope of himself."

The death of Liu Xiaobo symbolizes the serious suppression by the Chinese government against democracy, freedom of expression, and human rights. The Chinese government ignited the voice of protest from all over the world and a series of memorial events have been taking place everywhere and are still continuing.

After the protest movement of the students involved in the 1989 Tiananmen Incident, a major crackdown followed in China, and many Chinese students and writers were forced to escape abroad and to live in exile. Exposed to democratic societies in the West, writers strengthened criticism against China through various means of expression, thus leading to the establishment of the Independent Chinese PEN Center in 2001 with Liu

Xiaobo as one of its founding members and then as its second president in 2003.

I have tried to offer an overview of the situation and to contrast how China dealt with the recent Nobel Prizes for Peace and Literature.

Finally, but not least, I would like to add one more special remark about the death of Liu Xiaobo. His death created a new page for the future history of China. It will never ever be wiped out, no matter how long the single-party dictatorship regime lasts or whether democratized China takes its place.

We can say that Liu Xiaobo's death set up the concrete measures to face the "solid, yet invincible truth." To the contrary, the Chinese government has been bogged down by so-called unfaithful facts.

We should remember another Nobel Prize in Literature awarded for writings about China almost eighty years ago. Pearl Buck, author of *The Good Earth*, won the Nobel Prize in Literature in 1938. She painted China's landscape with the colorful life of farmers on the agrarian soil. Most outstanding Chinese literatures have been created under dictatorship or autocratic regimes.

It is no doubt that the loss of Liu Xiaobo's life for "the realization of democratic open society" will be inherited by the next generation worldwide, along with the words "no enemies and no hatred."

The Nobel Prize laureates from China after the revolution are Liu Xiaobo for peace and Mo Yan for literature. However, there exists a major difference in the decision-making process between the two as far as the Chinese government is concerned. Still, in the Nobel Museum in Stockholm, there is no discrimination at all between the two laureates as far as their exhibit presentation is concerned.

However, China appreciated only the literary prize. The government issued an official statement proudly showing its confidence and saying, "Modern Chinese literature has proved itself to be at the top level in the world," whereas China neglected Liu Xiaobo with respect to his peace prize. To the contrary, his life was destroyed in prison as a living tree is broken into pieces.

Personally I have a rather good experience and memory about China. Whenever I visit China, I always try to meet as many people as possible, regardless of whether they are apparatchik of the Communist Party or ordinary citizens on the street. The Chinese people are generally kind and warmhearted. That is why I dare to say that the fundamental problem China has been facing comes from the one-party system with strong partisan mentality.

The party monopolizes the whole social system and tends to ignore all kinds of social contradictions. Society thus functions as a prison with a cold-blooded face. But it is still possible to find some free space untouched by anyone. The government can only destroy a man physically. Literature can remain and be sustainable forever as it is in pursuit of human dignity.

# Being-toward-Death

*Torch in the Darkness*

# Xiaobo and His Era

*Yu Jie*

Liu Xiaobo is dead, and one of the most precious parts of my life has died with him.

On the night of July 13, 2017, I was at Taipei's Tonsan Bookstore holding a book party for *Take Out a Rib and Use It as a Torch*. The last thing I said was, "The literary quotation 'Take out a rib and use it as a torch,' used by both Socrates and Gu Zhun, was something that Liu Xiaobo put into practice throughout his life. Liu Xiaobo was someone who used his rib as a torch to light the darkness of China after the June 4th massacre."[1] After saying this, I had a strange feeling.

When I turned on my cell phone after the book party, I was struck by a bolt from the blue: "Xiaobo has passed away." They were the words I had least wanted to read, and I almost passed out on the stairs of the Tonsan Bookstore. I supported myself with the handrail as tears poured down my face. I felt as if I were in a nightmare.

The authorities arranged for Liu Xiaobo's eldest brother, Liu Xiaoguang, to appear at a carefully scripted news conference, where he mechanically delivered the bizarre words, "I thank the party and the government for their humane arrangements, which were perfect and considerate." Liu Xiaoguang said that as the eldest brother, he spoke for the family. This showed his complete ignorance of the law. Shouldn't Liu Xia, as Liu Xiaobo's wife, be the one who should speak for him? How could someone who had severed all relations with Liu Xiaobo for nearly thirty years, a petty bureaucrat who at one point had tried to take a share of Liu Xiaobo's Nobel Prize money and who was deeply despised by Liu Xia for his devastation at learning that she had donated all of it to charity, claim the right to replace Liu Xia as the immediate family member? No wonder Lu Xun once said that a person's greatest enemy might be a family member.[2] Could Xiaobo, who had declared he had no enemies, have foreseen his brother's shameful performance? Apart from sharing the same blood, Liu Xiaobo and Liu Xiaoguang had nothing in common.

Liu Xiaobo was not like Zhou Enlai and Deng Xiaoping, who had both chosen sea burial and had polluted the ocean with their ashes. Both of them were butchers who killed people like flies, and they were afraid that if they were buried in the earth, future generations might desecrate their graves, nor were they willing to be air-dried into "old bacon" like Mao Zedong.

Liu Xiaobo was liver cancered and sea buried. This "neo-Nazi" or "super-Nazi" regime mutilated Liu Xiaobo in life and then destroyed his remains. For the incomparable apparatus of violence they wielded, nothing could be easier. In this episode, the Communist Party demonstrated its paramount belief in materialism through a policy of obliterating every last trace of Liu Xiaobo. The party could only feel truly at ease once Liu Xiaobo had completely disappeared in the physical sense; the lack of a place where friends and future generations could memorialize him would lead to a boundless amnesia.

Years ago, the family of Cultural Revolution victim Lin Zhao had dedicated a small gravesite to her, which became like an open wound as endless streams of people went to pay their respects and homage. The authorities were compelled to install a video camera in a tree next to the grave and assigned police officers to patrol around the clock to scare off admirers from all over the country. This instance taught the authorities a lesson for preventing possible problems in the future: without a grave, Liu Xiaobo would not continue to be a headache for the party-state as Lin Zhao was.

Yet the Communist Party, with its belief in materialism, never imagined how great the power of spirit and thought could be. Liu Xiaobo lived through his words, and his words cannot be vanquished or eradicated. These words contain the secret code of freedom, like a key or an antidote or wings that can help the lost find their way home, revive people from a deep sleep, or let the fallen fly. Every word is a grain of wheat, and just as a grain of wheat dropped to the ground dies and then produces many more grains, the words are printed into books that can never all be burned.

Every book of Liu Xiaobo's words emits an intense light that drives out the rats frolicking in darkness.

For a writer like Liu Xiaobo, the role of text is not entertainment but rather salvation—self-rescue and teaching others to save themselves are not mutually exclusive. I am one of the readers saved by Liu Xiaobo's words. If not for Liu Xiaobo's writing, how could I have removed myself from the debased existence in the sewer where Chinese have lived for thousands of years? If not for Liu Xiaobo's words, how could I resolutely abandon the deceiving and self-deceiving imperial Confucianism, "going naked toward God"?

The first time I read Liu Xiaobo's writing was in the somber atmosphere after the June Fourth Massacre. As a secondary school student in Sichuan, I couldn't bear how my head teacher reviled the "black hands of the pro-democracy movement" during political studies. By chance, at the Xinhua Bookstore I was able to buy a copy of *Liu Xiaobo: The Man and His Deeds*, published by China Youth Press, its blue cover emblazoned with a paper silhouette that bore a striking resemblance to Liu Xiaobo. This was a collection of essays in which the government's hired scholars expended full effort and their special talent for insult in criticizing Liu Xiaobo, but in the appendix the editors had painstakingly reprinted many of Liu Xiaobo's "most reactionary" essays, including the one declaring the need for three hundred years of colonialism. I became transfixed by the book and filled the margins with dense notes. I wanted to underline key sentences but found that each sentence was an aphorism. That book is now a treasured object in the bookcase of my new home on the U.S. East Coast. I brought it with me across the Pacific Ocean and then across the American continent, and it has become part of my mental structure.

The first telephone conversation I had with Liu Xiaobo was on a freezing cold winter's day in 1999. I was on my way to give a talk at a university when I suddenly received a call from an unknown number. The person on the other end of the line stammered out his introduction, "I—I'm Liu Xiaobo," and after confirming that I was Yu Jie, he launched into a nonstop stream of criticism that lasted for nearly half an hour. It turned out that while Liu Xiaobo was in prison the third time from 1996 to 1999, Liu Xia had brought him a copy of my first book, *Fire and Ice*, published in 1998, hoping that after reading it Liu Xiaobo would feel he had a successor. Instead, Liu Xiaobo discovered in it a great deal of youthful narcissism and opportunism and unsparingly criticized me from beginning to end in our first telephone conversation. I decided that he remained a "literary dark horse," unbearably lacking in courtesy or tact.

The first time I met Liu Xiaobo in person was in the home of a mutual friend, Zhou Zhongling (known to us as Zhongzhong). During that conversation, I found that our opinions on many people and matters were extremely similar; we were what Yu Ying-shih subsequently quoted Chen Yinke as calling "similar gas," or "kindred spirits."[3] We stammered at each other, which made us both stammer even more. Liu Xia, standing to one side, laughed and said, "It's exhausting listening to you two stuttering," and she turned and started talking to my wife, a conversation that made the two of them even more intimate friends than Liu Xiaobo and I. Zhongzhong had a Sichuanese housekeeper who was an excellent cook, and the chili chicken she prepared that night was outstanding. I remember Xiaobo wolfing down his food and guzzling Coke without restraint. I loved eating with Xiaobo—he had a hearty appetite, as did his companions, who fought with him over food. This first meeting was the beginning of a close relationship that I enjoyed with Liu Xiaobo over the next ten years, regarding him as both mentor and friend, right up until he was arrested on December 8, 2008.

If not for Liu Xiaobo's influence and guidance, I would not have gone so far on the road to freedom, a hard and glorious road few have taken.

While the vast majority of Chinese choose to live like grass, wavering and bending in whichever direction the wind blows, Liu Xiaobo stood ramrod straight, and that's what made him a staff gauge for his era. From June 4, 1989, to 2008 and then to 2017, he was like a moth that kept flying into the flame, until finally he was burned but not destroyed.

This era will not be defined by the monster-baby visages of Deng Xiaoping, Jiang Zemin, Hu Jintao, and Xi Jinping but by the emaciated prophet's visage of Liu Xiaobo. Without Liu Xiaobo, the China of this era would be as abominable as the biblical Sodom. With Liu Xiaobo, God has struck China from his extermination list for the time being. Liu Xiaobo has won China a reprieve to acknowledge her sins and repent. Whether or not China actually will repent is beyond Liu Xiaobo's reach.

Living in an upright position seems to be a hard choice. In this perverse era, living implies bending over, kneeling down, closing one's eyes, and blocking one's ears. Liu Xiaobo chose to live for the young victims of June 4. He felt he was unworthy to be their teacher and that for them to have died while their teachers survived was an enormous disgrace. The intellectual community, having lost all sense of shame, was insensible to this and danced with the wolves, but Liu Xiaobo, embracing an attitude of atonement, began the struggle that guided the remainder of his life. Some consider resistance a means of seizing power or the moral high ground, but Liu Xiaobo treated resistance as the most ordinary occupation and vocation.

During those years, my wife and I went on several excursions to the outskirts of Beijing with Liu Xiaobo and Liu Xia. Under the shadow-like surveillance of police officers, we always found a tiny crevice of time. Whenever Liu Xiaobo and Liu Xia saw trees in the countryside, they would sigh, "How beautiful!" Liu Xia loved to draw pictures of the trees, especially those that seemed to be thrusting their way from the earth into the sky. Liu Xiaobo so admired Liu Xia's drawings of trees that he couldn't bear to part with a single one.

One time they invited us to their home, and as we sat in their cramped living room, Liu Xiaobo, his face dripping with sweat, hauled out Liu Xia's drawings to show us. The normally bold and forthright Liu Xia looked embarrassed and said to Liu Xiaobo, "Those aren't your drawings, why are you showing them off?" When we praised Liu Xia's drawings, Liu Xiaobo seemed happier than when we praised his essays, laughing like a child.

Years later, in 2014, my third year in exile in the United States, Liu Xia's elder brother came to the United States and looked me up. I asked him if there was anything we could do for Liu Xia, who had been under long-term house arrest, and he said Liu Xia had repeatedly urged him to take photos of American trees for her. Long deprived of her freedom to venture outside, Liu Xia, as an artist, had to abandon *plein air* for drawing from photographs.

I took Liu Xia's brother to the largest national park on the East Coast, Shenandoah, and we drove and hiked for several hours among the overwhelming beauty of the Blue Ridge Mountains, photographing trees that towered into the clouds. Here not only people but even trees were free, with none of the malaise that Gong Zizhen described in his essay "My Plum Tree Infirmary."[4] Liu Xiaobo loved the United States, and it would have thrilled him to walk on winged feet through this forest and burst into song beneath those towering trees.

I don't know if Liu Xia created any new works from those photographs or if she was able to take photos of her new drawings to show to Liu Xiaobo in prison.

Memories are sweet but also a source of misery so human beings have learned to forget.

Xiaobo was imprisoned and became a Nobel laureate, maybe the most obscure peace prize recipient in history. His very existence was an embarrassment to the world: he was in prison, Liu Xia was under house arrest, and the world could do nothing. So people pretended he didn't exist.

After years of China's economic sanctions, the Norwegian government felt obliged to privately apologize to the Chinese authorities for the decision of the Nobel Committee, which had nothing to do with the government. Only then were top-level officials allowed to visit China. It seemed that China had returned to the "flourishing age" of the Qing dynasty's Qianlong era, when "ten thousand nations came to pay tribute." Who would dare to offend China for the sake of an undistinguished man like Liu Xiaobo? As Nobel laureates of all stripes signed joint letters calling on the Chinese government to release Liu Xiaobo, President Barack Obama's name never appeared, even after he left the White House. When the U.S. Congress passed a resolution to rename the street running past the Chinese Embassy in Washington Liu Xiaobo Plaza, Obama threatened to veto it.[5] Both were Nobel laureates, but what a difference in quality!

All that people knew about Xiaobo was that he was an intellectual leader during the 1989 Democracy Movement and that he was a key drafter and organizer of Charter 08. Xiaobo as a thinker and "spiritual warrior" was largely unknown.[6]

The day after Xiaobo died, someone from his circle of friends, the dissident writer Mo Zhixu, sent me a message through Facebook soliciting my opinion on a eulogy he had drafted for Xiaobo in the name of the Free Xiaobo Work Group.

I was very dissatisfied with it. First of all, the last two paragraphs were packed with trite literary platitudes, like a mandate issued by the emperor. Xiaobo flat-out rejected two thousand years of autocratic cultural traditions to become a dark horse among Chinese intellectuals. If he had any way of knowing about this pedantic memorial, there's no way he would have accepted it.

Second, I suggested adding in Xiaobo's important ideological contributions, however controversial: that China would need three hundred years of colonialism in order to become democratic and open, that unification meant slavery, that human rights should rank above state sovereignty, that inhabitants had the right to self-determination, and that we must oppose not only killing by the government but also Yang Jia–like revenge-killing by members of the general public. I felt that without this part, what was presented wasn't the complete and genuine Xiaobo.

Mo Zhixu agreed with me, but after he had a long discussion with the writer or decision makers behind the text, they ultimately rejected my suggestions, saying they wanted to "avoid controversy."

Xiaobo's life was full of controversy, so why avoid controversy now? Xiaobo had been abused to death by the government and reduced to ashes, and now so-called civil society and colleagues were distorting and rewriting him with a "tall (lofty), big (noble) and complete (perfect)" image that was exactly the opposite of what he wanted.[7] Xiaobo throughout his life targeted hypocrites and pretense, never guessing that ultimately his spiritual legacy would be blotted out and revised by his hypocritical and pretentious countrymen.

To some extent, Liu Xiaobo could be considered a betrayed prophet.

Over the course of nearly ten years, I met with Xiaobo more than five hundred times and had one-on-one conversations with him dozens of times. As Xiaobo talked endlessly, I took a large quantity of notes and also kept a record in my journal. Xiaobo and I exchanged at least one hundred email messages, lengthy and brief, discussing public affairs, sharing our personal lives, and even arguing heatedly over ICPC matters. These materials became the primary source for my *Liu Xiaobo: A Biography*, but even that book didn't contain all of these precious materials.

After Xiaobo was imprisoned for the fourth time in 2008, Liu Xia entrusted me with editing a collection of Xiaobo's essays entitled *The Fall of a Great Power*. That book was published in Taiwan the following year and became the best-selling collection of Liu Xiaobo's writings to date. Xiaobo was virtually "one man against a country," taking on the official discourse of a "rising great power" to present to the world "the fall of a great power," and foiling the Chinese government's strategy of tens of billions spent on "grand external propaganda" every year.[8]

After Xiaobo won the Nobel Peace Prize in 2010, the Communist regime placed me under unlawful house arrest as his accomplice. I was abducted with a black hood pulled over my head and tortured nearly to death before I fled into exile in the United States. In the study of the home where I resettled in the United States, I immediately set about editing ten volumes of Liu Xiaobo's writings. Several volumes of Liu Xiaobo's works have been published, but millions of words scattered throughout various websites had yet to be compiled and edited. I planned to publish two volumes every year, for a total of ten volumes in five years, by which time Liu Xiaobo would have completed his sentence and been released. These ten volumes would be my best gift to him.

This wish came to nothing with Xiaobo's sudden death, but after overcoming my sorrow and despair, I am determined to complete this enormous and arduous project.

At the same time, in my various writings over the past fifteen years, hundreds of thousands of words relate to Xiaobo. Some reveal unknown details about Xiaobo's participation in human rights activities, as well as analysis of Xiaobo's thinking and spirit. I think this content can help the wider world better understand Xiaobo and bring his blurry image into focus. Of course, the Xiaobo I perceived or interpreted may not be the whole story and may even deviate from reality, but at least I can give one perspective; it is in the cacophonous recollection and interpretation of the crowd that Xiaobo is "being-toward-death."[9]

Tao Yuanming once said, "My relatives may have further grief; the others for their part are already singing. When a man has gone in death, what more to say? They have given his body to become one with the hillside."[10] Human indifference, isolation, and amnesia are part of our insurmountably sinful nature. When Xiaobo died, the world's media reported it, and the world's political leaders issued statements, but after that everything inevitably progressed toward cold silence, and people kept going to Beijing to pay tribute to China's prosperity. This is the reality of abject callousness.

Yet Xiaobo wouldn't even mind. He's under the blazing Mediterranean sun, striding toward us with his arms spread in embrace.

I believe that in the course of China's future democratization, Xiaobo's thinking and spirit will blossom as proudly as the black narcissus that Liu Xia gave us. In this way, Xiaobo will always be with us.

As long as love and justice prevail, Xiaobo will live on in the hearts of those who love him.

*Translated by Stacy Mosher*

## NOTES

Author's preface to *Free Man in an Unfree Country* (2017). Written on a trip from Yilan to Taipei and Taipei to Taichung, around the thirtieth anniversary of the end of martial law in Taiwan, July 15 to 16, 2017.

1. Gu Zhun (1915–74) was a Chinese intellectual, economist, and pioneer of post-Marxist Chinese liberalism.—Trans.
2. Lu Xun (1881–1936) was one of modern China's greatest writers.—Trans.
3. Yu Ying-shih (b. 1930), a professor at Princeton, is an expert on Chinese history and philosophy. Chen Yinke (1890–1969) was considered one of the most creative historians of twentieth-century China.—Trans.
4. Translated by Yang Xianyi and Gladys Yang. Gong Zizhen (Kung Tzu-chen, 1792–1841) was a poet, calligrapher, and intellectual whose works both foreshadowed and influenced the modernization movements of the late Qing dynasty. Gong's essay describes the mutilation of plum trees to produce bonsai plants, and having bought several and seeing them fail to flourish, he removed them from their restrictive pots and planted them in the earth in hopes that they would return to health.—Trans.
5. Austin Ramzy, "Veto Likely to Block Renaming of Chinese Embassy's Street after Liu Xiaobo," *New York Times*, February 17, 2016, https://www.nytimes.com/2016 /02/18/world/asia/obama-veto-china-embassy-liu-xiaobo.html.—Trans.
6. Chinese writer Lu Xun (1881–1936) applied the term "spiritual warrior" to himself and refused to accept inaction and inoffensiveness.—Trans.

7. The heroic model in artworks promoted during the Cultural Revolution.—Trans.

8. "China's major media players initiated the conglomeration reform to collectively promote the 'grand external propaganda (*Dawaixuan*),' the CCP's plan to disseminate propaganda themes abroad. In 2008, the central government invested RMB 45 billion in beefing up four major Chinese media flagships, namely Xinhua News Agency, CRI, CCTV, and *People's Daily*" (X. Zhang, H. Wasserman, W. Mano, eds., *China's Media and Soft Power in Africa: Promotion and Perceptions* [New York: Palgrave Macmillan, 2016], 55).—Trans.

9. A concept generated by German philosopher Martin Heidegger (1889–1976).—Trans.

10. Tao Yuanming (365–427) was a scholar famous for his distaste for official position and depiction of a utopian Peach Blossom Spring. The quote is from Song 3 of "In Imitation of Coffin Puller's Songs," translated by Albert Richard Davis, *T'ao Yüan-ming, AD 365–421, His Works and Their Meaning* (Cambridge: Cambridge University Press, 1983).—Trans.

# A Life like a Symphonic Poem

FAREWELL TO LIU XIAOBO

*Tienchi Martin-Liao*


Deeply saddened, we bid farewell to our dear friend Liu Xiaobo, the former and honorary president of the Independent Chinese PEN Center. Xiaobo, a pacifist, was an advocate for human rights, democracy, and freedom of expression in China. After eight years of imprisonment, his health was ruined, and his severe illness was covered up by the authorities. He was moved from prison to a hospital for medical parole because a Nobel Prize laureate dying in prison would have harmed the image of the Communist Party. Xiaobo's last wish—to leave the country together with his wife— was not granted and will never come true. In the last two weeks of life, he was still surrounded by security police, and even the doctors might have been in the services of the party. We are not sure whether Xiaobo ever had a chance to speak unmonitored to his beloved wife, Liu Xia.

Xiaobo had always been a forerunner in his time. In the 1980s, as a young man in his early thirties, his critical articles on traditional Chinese culture and thought made an immense mark on intellectual circles. Consequently, he was able to convince the members of the examining board of his dissertation to unanimously grant him his doctoral degree. He became a popular teacher at Beijing Normal University. His role during the 1989 Democratic Movement might have been controversial, but there is no doubt that due to his negotiations between the students and the soldiers, larger casualties were prevented.

As a founding member of the Independent Chinese PEN Center, Xiaobo wanted to set up an institution to protect his writing colleagues in China. Many years later, in 2009, when he was giving his statement of self-defense in court, he said, "I look forward to the day when our country will be a land of free expression: a country where the words of each citizen will get equal respect." He knew too well that hundreds and thousands of other people before him had been punished for their words. He pled, "I hope that I will be the last victim in China's long record of treating words as crimes."[1] This noble wish was a gentle whisper in the darkness of the wasteland that is totalitarianism. For freedom of expression, Xiaobo had to pay with his personal freedom, his health, and finally his life.

During the last nine years of his life, Xiaobo was surrounded by prison guards, by other prisoners, by security police, by personnel of the Justice Department, and so on. No friends or family members were admitted to see him. His wife was allowed to visit once a month. They were not able to touch each other. A thick glass wall stood between them. The only way they could talk was through a phone on the wall, while every word was recorded by the prison authorities. The prison doctors were the ones to determine whether he was ill or not. In this instance, they reached their conclusion very late: his cancer of the liver had already metastasized. They granted him medical treatment in a hospital. Two weeks later he died. Was it a stage-managed intrigue or a cold-blooded act of murder?

The international community, world political leaders, and 154 Nobel Prize laureates pled for Liu Xiaobo's release and for his wish be granted to go abroad with his wife and her brother. Not only did this appeal fall on deaf ears with the Xi regime, but the authorities went on to cut off all the connections between Liu's family and the outside world. No one was able to communicate with the patient and his wife. Once again, both were left in total isolation. Why did the regime have such paralyzing fear of a dying man? As a prisoner, Liu received no information from the outside world. For nine years, he was allowed only to read the party newspaper and books the prison authorities selected for him. He had no access to the internet; he was not allowed paper and pen for writing—how could he be dangerous? And yet he must have posed an imminent threat to the government for it to decide to eliminate him. Liu Xiaobo has become a hero, a legend, an icon, thanks to the Communist regime. Physically he is gone, yet his spirit, his longing for freedom, democracy, and human dignity will be everlasting. It will linger over China, just as Marx and Engels proclaimed in 1848 that the specter of communism was haunting Europe—Xiaobo's specter will be a constant nightmare for the Chinese totalitarian regime.

"Single truths, drop by drop, can form a flood that washes away tyranny," Xiaobo said in his 2003 article "Using Truth to Undermine a System Built on Lies." He has now paid with his life by speaking the truth to the powerful. He also saw himself and his friend Liao Yiwu as fools. But fools they are not. Xiaobo was the wisest and most consequent person I have ever known. Tyranny continues ruling in Xiaobo's home country, a tyranny that did not allow his beloved wife to build a tomb for him. The regime's fear is so overwhelming that it doesn't even care to cover up its own lies. In the Chinese official language, Xiaobo is still a "criminal," a bad guy, who wanted to "incite subversion of the state's power." But let us ignore the ugliness of the Communist Party's mouthpiece. Let us cherish what Xiaobo was so convinced of—"Language gets its beauty from making truth glow in the darkness; beauty is concentrated truth."

Single truths, drop by drop, can form a flood that washes away tyranny.

Farewell, Xiaobo. Your life was as versatile and magnificent as a symphonic poem. For now, you have no tomb in China, but people who love you will set up an altar for you in their hearts.

NOTE

1. Liu Xiaobo, "I Have No Enemies: My Final Statement," trans. Perry Link, in *Liu Xiaobo: No Enemies, No Hatred*, ed. Perry Link, Tienchi Martin-Liao, and Liu Xia (Cambridge MA: The Belknap Press of Harvard University Press, 2012), 325, 326.—Trans.

# Liu Xiaobo Had a Dream

*Kaiser Abdurusul ÖzHun*

On July 13, 2017, Nobel Peace Prize laureate Liu Xiaobo died at age sixty-one in a hospital in the northern Chinese city of Shenyang under close guard by security agents after he was denied permission to leave China for treatment for late-stage liver cancer.

Liu Xiaobo played a significant role in the Tiananmen Square student protests of June 1989, which ended in bloodshed when they were quashed by government troops. He was imprisoned for a year and half afterward for his participation. In 1996 Liu's campaign for the victims during the Tiananmen Square protests landed him in a labor camp in northeastern China for three more years. There he was permitted to marry poet Liu Xia and released in 1999.

During his life Liu Xiaobo had a dream. He believed the implementation of democracy could lead everyone in China to have freedom and dignity. He campaigned for democracy in China, but in 2009 he was handed an eleven-year jail term after he compiled with other intellectuals Charter 08, a manifesto calling for an end to one-party rule and the introduction of multi-party democracy. In a statement at his trial in December 2009, he stated:

> I have no enemies and no hatred. None of the police who monitored, arrested, and interrogated me, none of the prosecutors who indicted me, and none of the judges who judged me are my enemies. . . .
>
> Hatred can rot away at a person's intelligence and conscience. Enemy mentality will poison the spirit of a nation, incite cruel mortal struggles, destroy a society's tolerance and humanity, and hinder a nation's progress toward freedom and democracy.

... That is why I hope to be able to transcend my personal experiences as I look upon our nation's development and social change, to counter the regime's hostility with utmost goodwill, and to dispel hatred with love.[1]

From September 25 to 30 the following year, the Seventy-Sixth PEN International Congress was hosted by Japan PEN in Tokyo where delegates from more than ninety PEN centers advocated on behalf of writers imprisoned, threatened or killed for the expression of their ideas, in particular Liu Xiaobo and Uyghur writer Nurmuhammet Yasin, author of "Wild Pigeon." Yasin had been arrested in 2004 after his publication of "Wild Pigeon" in the *Kashgar Literature Journal*. In this fable, a political allegory, a princely bird is captured by humans and caged. He longed for freedom and, in the end, preferred to die rather than live in captivity. The issue of the journal in which the story appeared was pulled out of circulation, and "Wild Pigeon" remains banned in China. After a closed trial in February 2005 in which he was not permitted to hire a lawyer, Yasin was sentenced by the Maralbeshi County People's Court to ten years in jail for inciting Uyghur separatism.

At the Tokyo PEN Congress delegates, including me, proposed that PEN stand behind Liu Xiaobo for the Nobel Peace Prize for his great contribution to democratic reform in China. Together with Tienchi Martin-Liao, Wang Jinzhong, and other colleagues of Independent Chinese PEN Center, we suggested PEN International march to the Chinse embassy in Tokyo with PEN's statement to free Liu Xiaobo signed by all the participants of the congress.

Although his dream has yet come true, Liu Xiaobo's legacy of "no enemies and no hatred" has been shared in our hearts.

In early 2017 Yu Zhang of ICPC and I agreed to call an international conference dedicated to Liu Xiaobo and Uyghur writer Ilham Tohti, who was jailed in 2014. On August 28–30, 2017, the Finding Room for Common Ground: No Enemies, No Hatred conference was held in Malmö, Sweden. The conference was organized by the Four-PEN Platform, which was established jointly by four centers of PEN International, namely the Independent Chinese PEN, Uyghur PEN, Tibetan Writers Abroad PEN, and Swedish PEN centers. The Four-PEN Platform is dedicated to the democratic and peaceful solutions to the problems among ethnic groups in China, particularly concerned with the basic human rights issues for the intellectuals of Han Chinese, Uyghurs, Tibetans, and Mongols among others, including writers, journalists, translators, scholars, publishers, teachers, artists, and other cultural workers in their home regions and abroad.

To our common knowledge and value, dialogue is the only way forward in cases of ethnic tension. More sixty guests participated in the conference, including 2003 Nobel Peace Prize laureate and Iranian human rights lawyer Shirin Ebadi, former Swedish Parliament member Göran Lindblad, former Japanese Parliament Members Supporting Liu Xiaobo president Makino Seishu, and Swedish Academy member Klas Östergre, and four leading figures of PEN International: vice presidents Joanne Leedom-Ackerman and Hori Takeaki, treasurer and former president of Finnish PEN Jarkko Tontti, and chair of Writers for Peace Committee and former president of Slovenian PEN Marjan Strojan. During the conference, Liu Xiaobo Memorial Awards were given to Shirin Ebadi, Makino Seishu, and Joanne Leedom-Ackerman for their longtime support of campaigns on his behalf.

In the work of encouraging peace and national understanding, Ilham Tohti's friendship and Liu Xiaobo's insistence on "no enemies" can be used to build bridges in the most unlikely places. Ilham Tohti argued that during this period there existed a relative "equality among ethnic groups" and a more "relaxed political atmosphere." His ideas of peaceful ethnic coexistence and good governance require values and institutions that are rejected by the Chinese government. He envisioned these ideas as a platform for cultural and social exchange between the Han and Uyghur peoples. According to Ilham Tohti, we "should not fear disputes and disagreements, but rather the silence and suspicion that exist within hatred."

Ilham Tohti has condemned counterproductive policies causing instability in the Xinjiang Uyghur Autonomous Region. As a result, he was sentenced to life imprisonment for alleged separatism. Considering the similarity of ideas between Ilham Tohti and Liu Xiaobo, many people fear that Ilham Tohti might be treated by the Chinese authorities as the Uyghur Liu Xiaobo and be destroyed.

The failure to adequately protect religious, linguistic, and cultural freedoms not only hurts Uyghur and other Central Asian minorities but also threatens the very stability and legitimacy of the Chinese Communist Party. If the government truly wants to stand up for the truth and correct mistakes, then it must listen to the voices of the people and heed their words well.

Dialogue is the only way forward in cases of ethnic tension. In the past century ethnic groups within China, including Uyghurs, Tibetans, Mongols, and Han Chinese, can hardly live in peace because of the lack of mutual understanding. More and more of us have been forced to leave our homes and become displaced somewhere else or in exile. The government has neglected this problem, and the situation is now worse than ever. People must understand each other in order to live in peace.

Liu Xiaobo's "no enemies and no hatred" is his legacy for us to find the common ground for peace. Although he has passed away, the Chinese regime cannot wipe out his spirit.

NOTE

1. Liu Xiaobo, "I Have No Enemies: My Final Statement," trans. Perry Link, in *Liu Xiaobo: No Enemies, No Hatred*, ed. Perry Link, Tienchi Martin-Liao, and Liu Xia (Cambridge MA: The Belknap Press of Harvard University Press, 2012),322.—Trans.

# Ascending the Altar

MOURNING LIU XIAOBO

*Chen Kuide*

The events that took place in a hospital ward in Shenyang, China, during the eighteen days from June 26, 2017, to July 13, 2017, were the public's concern in China and also an important spiritual occasion. The event will be included in the annals of Chinese history.

This is the martyrdom of Liu Xiaobo under the gaze of the whole world and his extremely disturbing and moving journey toward the altar.

Relying on the authorities' arbitrariness and careful control, our friend and the state's prisoner Liu Xiaobo, under thousands of staring eyes, step after step, day after day, became so emaciated, as if the flesh were being scraped off his bones, until all that was left were skin and bones. With the support of his mentally and physically exhausted, loving wife, while he was still alive, he walked toward the sacrificial altar. Witnesses from all over the world personally experienced this human tragedy as it was acted out in broad daylight. We were helpless and powerless to reverse this desperate situation. It was heart-wrenching, and we were overwhelmed with grief.

Xiaobo passed away like this!

Mysteriously, I seemed to hear Xiaobo's sigh and seemed to hear his call and his cry. In the dim annals of a history that's lasted for ages, one can't help but ask heaven, "Xiaobo: where are you now?"

I know, you have already quickly risen to heaven and have met together with eyes tearing the lost souls of Tiananmen, who haven't ever been able to close their eyes contentedly.

People once said that the tragedy of the June Fourth Massacre in China twenty-eight years ago hadn't produced a symbolic martyr. Today, Liu Xiaobo's great tragedy has come. With his status as a rescuer of lives when he negotiated the withdrawal from Tiananmen Square that bloody night, with his great tragic weight of being murdered by the tyranny, and with his heavy moral image as a sacrifice calmly striding toward the altar, he has indisputably been cast into a symbol of this Tiananmen martyr.

Seven years ago, when Liu Xiaobo won the Nobel Peace Prize, I wrote, "A true laurel is woven with thistles and thorns. The Nobel Peace Prize crowning Liu Xiaobo's head is a 'freedom laurel.'" This prediction was unfortunately honored. The boundless totalitarian thorn bush was eventually woven into a laurel of death. Xiaobo's eighteen-day crucifixion under the focus of the world was an incomparable symphonic movement and the most glorious dying passion music in his whole life. It has already been built into an immortal cross. With his virtuous achievements, Liu Xiaobo's magnificent life on the thorny path tread for freedom has finally come to a successful conclusion and reached its final destination.

In essence, the sufferings of the Chinese people twenty-eight years ago and those during the past sixty-eight years were dramatically concentrated in Liu Xiaobo's eighteen-day dying torment. His struggle during his last days is a microcosm of the sufferings of the Chinese people. This scene of a tragic historical drama has condensed how many songs, cries, lives, and deaths of contemporary Chinese people!

Liu Xiaobo passed away. He performed deeds of merit in uniting knowledge and practice, opposing tyranny, negotiating the withdrawal from the square on Tiananmen's bloody night, and establishing the Independent Chinese PEN Center. He expounded his ideas in writings by sharply criticizing the totalitarian regime and by participating in the drafting of Charter 08. He exemplified virtues by laying down his life for a just cause, going calmly to prison, and meeting death with generosity. In this way, he has reached the three immortal realms of merit, writing, and virtue.

As a contemporary symbol of free China, as a spokesman for civil society, as a martyr of the constitutional government of China, and as the first citizen of a democratic China, Liu Xiaobo has already entered the Hall of Fame for Virtuous People in China and even in the world.

Liu Xiaobo passed away. But, as in Matthew 4:16, "the people dwelling in darkness have seen a great light, and for those dwelling in the region and shadow of death, on them a light has dawned."

July 13, 2017, is not only the day of Liu Xiaobo's death but also the Passion Day of contemporary Chinese people. Liu Xiaobo passed away on behalf of China.

After the Passion Day, the day of resurrection is not far away.

*Translated by Andréa Worden*

# Two or Three Things about Liu Xiaobo

*Ai Weiwei*

When I first encountered Liu Xiaobo in 1989, he had come to New York as a visiting scholar at Columbia University and planned to stay for a while. One time, I arranged a get-together near Lincoln Center with him and a film director who was my classmate at the Beijing Film Academy and who had come to New York to participate in a film festival. I remember the first thing Liu Xiaobo said upon seeing him: "Does that movie you made count as a movie?" he blurted out, stammering. My director classmate was stunned, and not knowing how to respond, he simply replied, "Who are you? Do I know you?"

That spring, Beijing students went to Tiananmen Square. Liu Xiaobo said he'd be leaving soon and ended his residency at Columbia, which he had not completed. China was experiencing a period of intellectual thaw in the 1980s, and Liu Xiaobo was very excited before he left. He didn't want to miss this historic moment. He was a lecturer at the Beijing Normal University at the time, and many of his students had gone to Tiananmen Square.

What happened next I heard from friends or read in news reports. There was the inspiring student movement at Tiananmen Square and the outcry against corruption that spread throughout the country, followed by soldiers and tanks moving in, the students evacuating, and the regret and pain left behind by the corpses on Chang'an Boulevard and in the hospitals. Liu Xiaobo's role at the square drew attention, and he went to prison.

In the early 1990s, I returned to the home I'd left twelve years earlier. Beijing's intellectual climate was bleak. Those in power had intensified ideological censorship and control while relaxing economic policies to attract foreign capital, and economic opening had reached a stage of frenzied development. For a period of time I had nothing to do. Cities had more roads and taller buildings, but Beijing was still a wasteland. This wasteland in which devastation filled the eye could compare with any wasteland of twentieth-century human existence. There was no space for ideological or cultural discussion, no inspiring vision, and no voice to rouse the spirit; not to mention there were not any like-minded people.

In the early 1990s, I edited several underground art publications—the *Black Cover Book*, *White Cover Book*, and *Gray Cover Book*. At the end of 1997, I opened an art space called China Art Archives and Warehouse. I remember that at that time a book appeared that recorded a dialogue between Liu Xiaobo, following his release from prison, and the writer Wang Shuo. Liu Xiaobo used a pseudonym, but it would have been the same with or without a name, no one cared; it could be said that no one had a name. That dialogue showed that prison life had not affected him.

In speaking of Liu Xiaobo, it is impossible not to mention what happened during the student movement in 1989, a movement that accumulated the efforts and hopes of a generation or several generations but that in the end was violently suppressed and swept away as if by a windstorm. Afterward it seemed as if nothing had happened. Workers repaired the bullet holes in the Monument to the People's Heroes and replaced the granite slabs that had cracked under the rolling tanks. All information regarding the incident at the square was blocked, to the extent that young people today don't know that this violent, blood-soaked incident that horrified the world ever happened, don't know that a generation of young people sacrificed themselves in this way. To this day, no one is allowed to allude to people or matters related to Tiananmen Square; discussing Tiananmen Square is followed by arrest and imprisonment. The honor and glory of a generation is not recorded at the square; all that remains is shame and regret. To this day there is not a comprehensive list of the number and names of victims.

I next saw Liu Xiaobo not long after the completion of my art exhibition space in Longzhuashu, near Beijing's Third Ring Road. Liu Xiaobo introduced me to his young wife, Liu Xia, and bluntly said he hoped I'd hold an exhibition of Liu Xia's work. Liu Xia's square photographs, taken with a Hasselblad, were mostly of dolls placed on bookshelves or other places around their home. Emptiness, anger, and terror accompanied grief. It was longing for someone forcibly imprisoned, a silent testament to abduction and lost time. I agreed to exhibit Liu Xia's work, and this was the first and also the last photo exhibition that Liu Xia held in Beijing.

We didn't meet again for many years after that. One time, Liu Xiaobo said he wanted to see me for a chat, and we arranged to meet at a restaurant that I'd opened with friends in Liangmaqiao called Go Where? He arrived in a police vehicle that night. As usual, Go Where? was full of people drinking themselves to oblivion. At every Beijing dining table, people forgot everything around them, and we likewise forgot the two public security officers waiting in the police van outside, forgot the past ten years and what Liu Xiaobo and a wave of people like him had been through. Perhaps nothing at all had happened, and all that remained was each day and the next, each month and the next, each year and the next without anything really changing. During those years, sales of Beijing's erguotou liquor went through the roof. It was 2003 and already a new century.

Eventually I began to go online, and blogs really took off and created a major stir. The autocratic government was not yet fully prepared to deal with the Information Age. One time, Liu Xiaobo told me he liked my blog essays. During that liveliest period, however, Liu Xiaobo was not active. I knew he often published articles in overseas magazines, but his voice was seldom heard inside China. China was basically cut off from the outside world, and people and discussion related to the democracy movement were thoroughly banished.

Later on, Liu Xiaobo asked me to read a document, an early draft of Charter 08. Some paragraphs retained red revision tracking intended to solicit opinions. At that time I was on a trip overseas, and I didn't plan to sign it because I had reservations regarding the content. I wasn't in further contact with him about the Charter. It wasn't until I heard that he'd gone to prison because of this Charter that I signed it to show my support for him; by then I was among the third batch of signatures.

It's fair to say that as a political document, Charter 08 is not radical to the point of no return. It is in line with hopes that China might take a political line of reform and peaceful evolution, and seems moderate and rational. It can be considered an almost mundane political document with no special characteristics. In terms of concepts it mechanically applies some popular and empty truths or Western consensus on universal values, purposely avoiding a critical stance toward China's current situation, and it is in no way revolutionary in terms of culture or politics. But however one sees it, Charter 08 remains the only standpoint and voice of popular justice. It expresses the criticisms and demands of a generation or several generations toward political reality.

On Christmas Day 2009, the day Liu Xiaobo was sentenced to his final imprisonment, I went to the door of the courthouse along with several colleagues from my studio. Of course, I didn't go to the courthouse for Liu Xiaobo—I wasn't naïve enough to think the authorities would reconsider their actions because of people voicing support, nor was it for any so-called political movement; China basically has no political movements in any real sense. I went purely for myself, as some kind of basic expression in the face of injustice. Like all of my useless artistic expressions, it was merely frivolous posturing. The wind was harsh and cold that day, and the handful of emotional and indignant people who had gathered in front of the courthouse for the spectacle were greatly outnumbered by clusters of foreign journalists. I tossed them a few words and slipped away.

Thinking back, we simply expressed our helplessness and regret one word at a time. Liu Xiaobo was sentenced again, and it was a very harsh sentence. On Twitter I calculated the time he would spend in prison in minutes and seconds. At that time, it was still possible to post commentaries on the internet in China. We traded stories about Liu Xiaobo in hopes that more people would talk about him. Whether they took a position of criticism or praise, discussion was very important; discussion was a refusal to forget and a protest against aphasia and disappearance. All of this happened before my name completely vanished from the internet in China.

I wrote a lot about Liu Xiaobo, and I also criticized him a lot. That was in a stuttering era in which nothing could be said clearly. Liu Xiaobo's imprisonment was always closely bound with the helplessness and despair of Liu Xia, the person he loved the most; helplessness, despair, and terror are the most distinctive products of this era, purely Made in China.

When Liu Xiaobo was awarded the Nobel Peace Prize in 2010, I was in London preparing for an exhibition at the Tate Modern. In frequent interviews, I expressed my happiness for Liu Xiaobo, condemned his persecution by the totalitarian government and hoped he would soon be released from prison, even though I knew that the sole raison d'être of this regime was to kill off those emotional people of whom Liu Xiaobo was the prime example.

The more I heard of what happened afterwards, the more unreal it became. In 2017 Liu Xiaobo fell critically ill in prison, and in less than a month's time he mysteriously died. His death was clearly not that simple; accidental deaths under totalitarianism always challenge and question the longevity of totalitarianism while also sternly interrogating the democracy, freedom, and human rights of the post-globalized West. In spite of everyone's efforts, and no matter how many people shouted or wept for Liu Xiaobo or in his name, Liu Xiaobo still died. With him died people's subtle, covert, unspoken conjectures toward the West and Chinese politics. Some people felt cheated; some felt it was inevitable. Liu Xiaobo's halo for one last time cast light on the distorted features of those who survive in degradation.

Now that all of this is in the past, what has Liu Xiaobo left behind? The greatest political legacy that Liu Xiaobo has left for his era is that he has left nothing. Despite his efforts, China is still an authoritarian state, people's rights are even more restricted, and business continues on as usual between the West and China. After his death, there is only a boundless void.

*Translated by Stacy Mosher*

# Liu Xiaobo's Death and Chinese Regime's Fear

*Andrew J. Nathan*

What does the Chinese regime's treatment of Liu Xiaobo tell us about the regime itself? The way the Chinese government treated Liu at the end was gratuitously cruel. They denied treatment for liver cancer until it was too late for him to survive, then put on a propaganda show of providing palliative treatment and invaded his and his wife's privacy to circulate videos of their last moments together. After Liu died, the regime forced his widow, Liu Xia, to disappear, and as I write this she still is not free.

But these were just the final acts in a long series of cruelties. The regime gave Liu an extreme eleven-year sentence merely for exercising his rights, subjected Liu Xia to an illegal, ruthless, and maddening house arrest for the entire time of Xiaobo's imprisonment, punished Norway diplomatically and economically for being the host country for the committee that awarded Liu the Nobel Peace Prize, and blocked all mention of Liu and his doings from domestic media, so that few Chinese people today know anything about him. After his death the government cremated his body and forced his widow to scatter the ashes at sea so that there could be no place of pilgrimage for those who would wish to remember him.

Liu's case was uniquely prominent internationally but not unique as a case of repression in China. Many have suffered excessive punishment for peaceful and moderate acts. Xu Zhiyong served a four-year prison term for having led a New Citizens' Movement that used peaceful, lawful methods to promote rule of law. Since Xu's release he has disappeared from public view, which hints at what he must have suffered in prison. The rights protection movement of lawyers and activists tried to use the Chinese courts to protect victims of rights abuses. Some three hundred lawyers were rounded up in July 2015, and a number still remain in jail or in custody. Feminist activists demonstrated against sexual harassment and domestic violence; five were arrested in 2015. The poet Langzi (Wu Mingliang) was arrested in 2017 for writing poetry memorializing Liu Xiaobo, and a person who printed some of his work (Peng Heping) was arrested and both were charged with "illegal business activity."

While conditions in Chinese jails are bad in general, human rights and democracy activists are, like Liu, often singled out for harsh treatment and denial of medical care. In 2014 human rights activist Cao Shunli died in detention just before she was scheduled to go to Geneva to testify at the UN Human Rights Council.[1] Tibetan monk Tenzin Delek Rinpoche died in prison after mistreatment in 2015.[2] In 2016 the sister of imprisoned human rights lawyer Guo Feixiong reported that his medical condition was deteriorating and he was being denied medical treatment.[3] Examples could be multiplied.

Why is such a strong regime—which as I write this is heading triumphantly into its Nineteenth Party Congress with 6.7 percent growth rate, more than $3 trillion of foreign exchange, and a vast domestic market; is able to buy influence from Australia to Greece to Cambridge University Press; has total control of domestic media, academia, and public opinion; by all appearances has succeeded in purging all opposition within the party; and is preparing to crown its head as supreme leader of everything and apotheosize his thought in the party constitution—so scared of those few who dare to criticize it openly?

This is the central paradox of the Chinese regime. It really is strong, in my opinion. It is hard to know for sure, but the elite appears authentically unified around Xi Jinping, economic growth is sustainable, popular support is real, and the many problems that exist are being skillfully managed. Yet the regime remembers Tiananmen, the collapse of the Soviet Union, riots in Tibet and Xinjiang, the Umbrella Movement in Hong Kong, and the Sunflower Movement in Taiwan. And from this sequence of events it draws the lesson that its political support is fragile.

For a regime like this, I believe such a judgment is correct. By choice and design, this is a structurally isolated regime. The ruling, Leninist vanguard party, the Chinese Communist Party, claims as members about 6 percent of the population. The reason it is a vanguard party is that it doesn't trust those whom it calls "the masses." It doesn't trust them to vote. It doesn't trust them to write. It doesn't trust them to think. It doesn't trust professors to analyze politics, students to figure out for themselves what they think, journalists to report on official wrong doing, or judges to decide political cases.

Who then can supervise the party? The party's answer is that "the party can supervise itself." But the party doesn't really trust even itself because it suspects so many of its own members of misdoings—corruption, ambition, opportunism, abuse of power—and, despite their constant training in right thinking, of wrong thinking.

We must admit that in recent years the performance of the Chinese system has been impressive, and the performance of Western democratic systems has been poor. But the grotesque abuse of Liu Xiaobo, and of so many other people less well known than Liu, throws a sharp light on the core weakness of the Chinese type of system. Liu Xiaobo famously said that he had no enemies. But the vanguard authoritarian regime, by its nature, has many enemies.

## NOTES

This is a version of remarks that were delivered at a symposium on Liu Xiaobo and the Future of China at the National Endowment for Democracy, Washington DC, on September 7, 2017.

1. Jonathan Kaiman, "Chinese Activist Cao Shunli Dies after Being Denied Medical Help, Says Website," *Guardian*, March 14, 2014.—Ed.
2. Patrick Boehler, "Tenzin Delek Rinpoche, Tibetan Religious Leader, Dies in Chinese Custody," *New York Times*, July 13, 2015.—Ed.
3. Goh Fung, "Sister of Chinese Political Prisoner Guo Fixing Denied Prison Hospital Visit," *Radio Free Asia*, August 24, 2016.—Ed.

# Liu Xiaobo's Fight for Freedom

*Louisa Greve*

It was the Czech writer Milan Kundera who said, "The struggle of man against power is the struggle of memory against forgetting."[1] His fellow writer Liu Xiaobo, who died this summer under police guard while serving an eleven-year prison sentence, made a profoundly important and significant contribution to the struggle of memory against forgetting.

For four millennia, each new Chinese dynasty rewrote the history of the last. The ruler since 1949, the Chinese Communist Party, also believes it controls the truth. Liu Xiaobo's empty chair at his Nobel Prize ceremony in Oslo in 2010 told us all we needed to know of the authoritarian power that is exercised over history and remembrance by the China of our time. The poet, dissident, and Nobel laureate embodied what George Orwell called "the liberal habit of mind, which thinks of truth as something outside yourself, something to be discovered, and not as something you can make up as you go along."[2]

In August 1943, before it came to power, the Chinese Communist Party had already published an editorial in the *Liberation Daily* entitled, "Without the Communist Party There Would Be No China." Later that same year, the CCP created a propaganda song using this title. Mao Zedong later decided the song was to be called "Without the Communist Party, There Would Be No New China." But while, mercifully, Mao has been dead for more than four decades, the party has in our generation tried to combine material progress with Mao's revolutionary totalitarian control over history.

In 2006 a gigantic memorial to the song was unveiled in Beijing. The leadership now requires an oath of loyalty to the Communist Party from lawyers and judges, media workers and professors, schoolchildren and army generals alike.[3] Uyghur mosques are required to cover Islamic verses with large red banners that read, "Love the Party, Love the Country." But Liu Xiaobo steadfastly refused to participate in the CCP's version of history and reality. He was among the most confident advocates of a more humane world in all of Chinese literature and social commentary, for lives of dignity and authenticity. Upon his death of cancer at the age of sixty-one, government censors sprang into action to block the news of his passing and also to block publication of the tributes paid to him by his countrymen.

We can learn from the man whose chair sat empty at Oslo. Americans need to know more about him.

Liu Xiaobo said to a friend in 2000, "The beauty of written language is that, in the dark, it shines a light on truth; and beauty is the focal point of truth." He later said, regarding the explosion of the world wide web in China, "The Internet is like a magic engine. It has helped my writing to erupt like a geyser. Now I can even live on what I write."[4]

In his enthusiasm for the new medium of the internet—he even called it "God's gift to China"—Liu Xiaobo was truly prescient. For some nine years, between his release from his second prison term in 1999 and his detention in 2008, he was, by one calculation, able to publish more than a thousand articles promoting humanitarianism and democracy on Chinese-language websites based outside China. He was able to reach audiences in this way because he was no longer dependent on a job in the party-controlled universities or on party-controlled journals to circulate his trenchant social criticism.

He developed an audience of millions, not just outside his country but within it. Along with that avenue for freedom of expression, though, comes a certain discipline: there has to be a demand side. What that means is you can't just spout abstractions. You have to speak directly to people—you have to know the concerns and worries of your audience. Even more fundamentally, you have to build and nurture a readership, to bring citizens along to a new way of thinking when all the power of the modern authoritarian state is geared toward molding the minds of the young, engineering every psychological and material incentive to herd people into one of two paths: harmless individuality or loyal conformity. Whatever genuinely independent individuality manages not to disappear into the maw of this well-organized system is subject to brutal repression.

Liu Xiaobo's imprisonment in 2008, his third, coincides very nearly with the beginnings of the global authoritarian resurgence that reflects newfound confidence on the part of authoritarian governments to use the internet for surveillance and to disseminate propaganda. This new phase of the use of communications technology seeks not only to censor but also to monopolize the medium: any instrument can and will become an instrument of propaganda, oppression, or just "fake news." Of China in the pre-internet era, Liu said: "Unrelenting inculcation of Chinese Communist Party ideology has ... produced generations of people whose memories are blank."[5] In today's brave new world where every citizen has a twenty-four-seven tracking device in his pocket, and facial recognition software is slated for installation on every street corner in major Chinese cities, what chance does memory have?

Liu Xiaobo recognized that the direct communication from activists to followers is not worth much without what we call intermediating institutions. He was not only a poet, critic, and intellectual. He was not only a voice of conscience and a man of exceptional moral courage. He created a true legacy of flesh-and-blood human beings, people inspired by him and shaped by the aspirations he articulated, but also, just as importantly, by the experience of working together to build ideas, build institutions, and work on practical problems.

In particular I note the significance of two institutions with which Liu worked in the mid-2000s until his arrest in 2008, and which the National Endowment for Democracy, for which I worked at the time, was privileged to support through its grants program.

When Liu became a magazine editor, in 2006, it was not for a literary magazine but rather *Democratic China* magazine (*Minzhu Zhongguo*). This online publication featured the work of hundreds of authors, writing about all aspects of Chinese society and politics, encompassing cultural and political commentary. The mission of *Democratic China* has been to explore and foster freedom, democracy, human rights, the rule of law, and constitutionalism. These are not the topics of literary imagination first and foremost but practical problems of politics and governance.

Liu used this platform to cultivate the next generation of writers and readers. What he had already been doing as a teacher and leader of "salons" he now did as a mentor for all kinds of writers, who were encouraged to come forward and develop their insights and critical observations. The publication gave them space in a Chinese-language world that is otherwise harshly censored.

At the helm of *Democratic China*, Liu was able to resolve the inevitable difficulties of working not just with one but with two coeditors who lived on two continents and communicated closely despite a twelve-hour time difference. He reinforced a strong ethical foundation for the publication's internal guidelines. Editorial board members could not receive fees for the articles they wrote, for example. All this was against the culture: both of intellectuals, who can sometimes be self-absorbed and competitive, and of the CCP, which touted conformity and hierarchy. He did all this while coping with constant government harassment and also with the habits of self-censorship endemic to authoritarian regimes.

Liu was also a founder of the Independent Chinese PEN Center, the first and only membership organization of writers and journalists in China dedicated to championing freedom of expression. Elected president of Independent Chinese PEN in 2003, he served two terms, for a total of four years. He declined to be a candidate for a third term, making way for new leadership and ensuring there would be no conflict of interest with his role as an editor of *Democratic China*. Here too he fostered the next generation of Chinese intellectual talent, and here too he insisted that every board member faithfully observe the ethical standards of the institution.

In both endeavors, Liu fostered humanitarian assistance. ICPC has devoted much energy and precious financial resources to helping those in need, through Freedom to Write Fellowships and legal aid and human-itarian assistance to the families of writers languishing in labor camps as prisoners of conscience. In both, he was an institution builder, insisting on a division of responsibility and accountability for staff and volunteers roles, ground rules for proper board meetings, ground rules for elections and rotations in office, and consistent ethical guidelines to guard against self-dealing—in contrast to the ubiquitous culture of graft and corruption that dominates Chinese institutions, from schools to companies to the bureaucracies of the state.

As he carried out these duties, all the while writing so many articles of his own, Liu also received a constant stream of visitors who were victims of injustice. He spent countless hours, and often his own money, connecting them with lawyers, journalists, documentary filmmakers, and others who were willing to help.

So Liu Xiaobo was a thinker, and a writer, and an activist. He excelled at all; like no one else, he combined them in an exceptional life of service, shaping what we might call a program for democracy.

In all of this, he recognized that not everyone can be a hero or will want to be. Most people are not acute social critics, but they can take a look around themselves and perceive when something is wrong. Most people are not prolific writers, but they can insist on ethical rules in the institutions they serve. Most people may not become well known, but they can still cultivate the next generation (in their own little garden). Most people live under myriad forms of pressure and stress, and don't have extraordinary amounts of courage, but they can take time to pay respects to the dead and be personally generous to others in need.

Liu Xiaobo's example teaches all of us—Chinese democrats but also those struggling against tyranny everywhere in the world—to think, speak, and write, even under censorship and deprivation, even when you can't publish or when you have a tiny audience, even when you despair that nobody is listening. He teaches us that the act of remembering the dead, especially those who have lost their lives in service of the true, the good, and the just, is an act of resistance and an act of conscience.

In the example of his work as a writer, editor, and investigator and documentarian, Liu teaches us that any matter of social importance should not be regarded as beneath our notice or beyond our ability to recognize and act upon. His example teaches us to guard against idealism unconnected to the concerns of ordinary people and the most downtrodden—for example, his deep personal involvement in the case of the child slave-laborers in the brick kilns in 2007.[6] He was a professor of literature and a literary intellectual, but he didn't get caught up in mastering abstruse theory or endless debate over "isms." He focused his concern, especially after his first imprisonment, on daily struggles. He strongly believed that a true civic movement could be formed by Chinese people despite generations of authoritarian conditioning that actively fostered hatred, cynicism, and cruelty toward others for one's own survival.

Liu Xiaobo never succumbed to discouragement but emphasized always that the struggle for democracy is a generational struggle. When his wife, Liu Xia, was allowed to visit him in prison, and he learned that he would be given the Nobel Peace Prize, he told her he wished to dedicate the prize to those who lost their lives on June 4, 1989. He also asked that children participate in the ceremony. We learn from Liu Xiaobo to pay respects to those who have gone before us and to nurture those who will come after us, in the struggle for freedom and democracy.

It may be that for a while, the Chinese party-state will be able to "disappear" the memory of Liu Xiaobo into the black hole of amnesia that he did so much to fight. But the tributes that Chinese writers have managed to disseminate and the memorials that have been held in New York and in Taipei, London, Malmö, Oslo, and elsewhere, are at the very least a guarantee that the amnesia will not be complete. Orwell held out hope that "the liberal habit of mind" would have the strength to outlast the rule of the tyrants. Liu Xiaobo now belongs to history. His fight for the survival of conscience is ours to carry on.

## NOTES

This essay first appeared at Liberty Fund's *Law and Liberty* journal and is reprinted here with permission.

1. Milan Kundera, *The Book of Laughter and Forgetting,* translated from the French by Aaron Asher (New York: Harper Perennial, 1999), 167.—Ed.

2. George Orwell, "As I Please, 4 February 1944," in George Orwell, *As I Please, 1943– 1945: The Collected Essays, Journalism and Letters,* Vol. 3, ed. Sonia Orwell and Ian Angus (Nonpareil Books, 1968). George Orwell (1903–50) was an English novelist and journalist.—Ed.

3. Since 2012 Chinese lawyers have been obliged to swear this oath: "I promise to faithfully fulfil the sacred mission of socialism with Chinese characteristics . . . loyalty to the motherland, its people, and uphold the leadership of the Communist Party of China." Last year, President Xi Jinping visited the state-run media outlets and ordered their editors and reporters to show their fealty to the Chinese Communist Party. "All the work by the party's media must reflect the party's will, safeguard the party's authority, and safeguard the party's unity," he said; "they

must love the party, protect the party, and closely align themselves with the party leadership in thought, politics and action."

4. Quoted in Liao Yiwu, "In Letter, Writer Liao Yiwu Seeks Help from Angela Merkel," trans. Human Rights in China, 2010, https://www.hrichina.org/en/content/376.—Ed.
5. Liu Xiaobo, "The Spiritual Landscape of the Urban Young," trans. Michael S. Duke, in *Liu Xiaobo: No Enemies, No Hatred*, ed. Perry Link, Tienchi Martin-Liao, and Liu Xia (Cambridge MA: The Belknap Press of Harvard University Press, 2012), 51.—Ed.
6. "China Brickwork Slave Children May Number 1,000," *Reuters*, June 15, 2007, https://www.reuters.com/article/us-china-slaves/china-brickwork-slave-children -may-number-1000-idUSPEK22844720070615.—Ed.

# "They Killed Him"

DENIAL OF MEDICAL CARE IN CHINA AND
THE LITERARY CONSCIENCE

*James Tager*

When you meet a famous writer for the first time, what they say has a tendency to stick in your head. But I only remember one phrase from when I first met Paul Auster: "They killed him."

Auster was staring at a poster of Liu Xiaobo, the Nobel Peace Prize winner and Chinese writer. Liu had died that morning of liver cancer, only twenty-one days after being released from prison on medical parole, and Auster had come to a vigil and poetry reading to commemorate his life. "They killed him," Auster repeated to me. I knew exactly what he meant.

As a matter of medicine, it was of course cancer that took Liu's life. But the responsibility for his death must rest on the shoulders of the Chinese state. Liu Xiaobo was serving an eleven-year sentence for "subversion" when he died, and authorities waited until he was terminally ill before they released him from prison. His last few days became a micromanaged farce, with authorities releasing crass promotional videos while challenging the decisions of foreign doctors who said it was not too late for him to seek treatment abroad.

But while his last days were subjected to the indignity of medicine-as-propaganda, the real question is how and why Chinese authorities took action only when Liu's condition had become terminal. Liu suffered from hepatitis B, a condition that dramatically increases one's risk of liver cancer. And yet it seems that his jailers could be bothered to notice the state of his health only mere weeks before his death.

Weeks after Liu Xiaobo's death, we at PEN America learned that Yang Tongyan, another well-known Chinese writer who had similarly been convicted for dissident activities in connection to both his activism and his writing, had been diagnosed with a particularly fast-moving and malignant form of brain cancer. Yang was granted medical parole on August 16 and moved to a specialist hospital but was denied permission to leave the country for medical treatment due to his status as a "criminal," despite his family's wishes to pursue treatment abroad. He died on November 7.

Yang Tongyan was serving a twelve-year sentence. His family had sought medical parole for him twice and had been denied twice. Yang suffered from tuberculosis, diabetes, high blood pressure, and nephritis. He had previously been in critical condition—in 2009, Yang's sister visited him and said he had become so thin as to be "unrecognizable."

Both Yang and Liu were recipients of PEN America's Freedom to Write Award, given yearly in recognition of writers who have paid a high price for their refusal to self-censor. China has the dubious distinction of having the most Freedom to Write Award winners: seven. A third Freedom to Write Award winner from China, the Uyghur academic Ilham Tohti, is currently serving a life sentence on charges of "separatism." Tohti is also supposedly in ill health; he has lost significant weight in prison, in part because the prison provides insufficient amounts of halal food.

The Network of Chinese Human Rights Defenders noted in August 2017 that "dozens of political detainees and prisoners have reported being deprived of adequate medical treatment." It concluded that "deliberately depriving political prisoners of medical care . . . appears to be commonly used against political prisoners on China." Frances Eve, a researcher for the group, noted that there is "a real fear amongst prisoners of conscience and their families that authorities aren't afraid to let them die from lack of adequate medical care."

Nicholas Bequelin, East Asia director of Amnesty International, has offered a similar assessment: "In many cases seriously ill imprisoned activists are being granted medical parole late, and their families' wishes for treatment outside of detention or abroad are ignored. There seems to be no accountability for the pattern of death on medical parole for people labeled by the authorities as 'enemies of state.'"[1]

Whether through deliberation or through depraved indifference, Chinese authorities are wielding the denial of adequate medical care as a weapon against their dissidents, including writers and those who have been jailed simply for their peaceful exercise of free expression.

Yang Tongyan once wrote, in a 2005 jeremiad published in *The Epoch Times*, "fear flows everywhere in China. . . . Government officials are afraid of losing their power." Liu and Yang died of cancer. But they also died as a result of their government's fear of them: their words, their activism, and their strength as symbols of freedom and conscientious protest.

Health care as propaganda. The denial of health care as a weapon. The image of the party over the life of a sick individual.

I agree with you, Paul. They killed him. They killed him.

## NOTES

Originally published by James Tager, "'They Killed Him': Denial of Medical Care in China and the Literary Conscience," *Huffington Post*, November 15, 2017, https://www.huffingtonpost.com/entry/they-killed-him-denial-of-medical-care-in-china_us_5a0c5804e4b060fb7e59d50c.

1. "China: Veteran Democracy Activist Yang Tongyan Dies While on Medical Parole," *Amnesty International*, November 8, 2017, https://www.amnesty.org/en/press-releases/2017/11/china-democracy-activist-yang-tongyan-dies/.

# Remembering Liu Xiaobo
*Hu Jia*


Ever since July 13, 2017, from midsummer to late autumn while under continuous house arrest, on many days, again and again, a heavy feeling of remorse and disappointment arises at 5:35 p.m.—this was the moment when Liu Xiaobo regrettably passed away. It seemed that I heard Liu Xia choking with tears. It seemed that I saw with my own eyes Xiaobo on his deathbed, reluctant to part with his wife's love and the transition to a peaceful society. A warrior who sought and struggled for freedom and stood firm and fought bravely for sixty-one years, as the poet Du Fu wrote, "but before he could conquer, he was dead; / and heroes have wept on their coats ever since."[1] In 2017 a death that the whole world paid close attention to occurred in Shenyang, China. The conductor, however, was in Zhongnanhai in Beijing. The criminal ringleader directing the tragedy was the tyrant Xi Jinping.

The whole world and Liu Xiaobo's family had followed him with the small bit of hope that arose from rushing toward freedom, but in the end was shattered. That a Chinese citizen of global morality was sacrificed with his death in prison has proven to the world and to history the cold-bloodedness of the Chinese Communist Party and the ruthless hostility of the authoritarian regime to freedom and humanity. This is the true interpretation of the Nineteenth Party Congress's "beautiful new world," which is disguised in flowery language. A thick evidence file has been added to support the indictments of tyranny and tyrants in the moral and legal trials of the future.

Like Xiaobo I contracted hepatitis B with a history of eleven years of cirrhosis due to my having been disappeared and imprisoned. Moreover, I was also suspected of having liver cancer in prison after I had a fever that lasted a month and a liver cyst was detected. This gave me an even more conclusive basis for determining that Liu Xiaobo's death was a political assassination designed and carried out by the political and legal organs of the CCP. The routine physical exams and tumor screenings as shown by the video clips at Jinzhou Prison could definitely detect liver cancer. But his liver cancer developed to the terminal stage, when nothing could be done. This was a slow and invisible execution. In order to hide the responsibility for the cause of Xiaobo's death from the world, a rescue drama was staged at the end, sparing no expense. The process for releasing official information under calls for accountability and condemnation and the treatment of his suffering from illness while he was dying with each passing day was like a live-broadcast execution.

After Liu Xiaobo won the Nobel Peace Prize, the CCP listed him and Gao Zhisheng as its most important political opponents with "political ambition" and influence in Chinese society and the international community. In the authorities' political risk and prevention analysis, Liu Xiaobo and Gao Zhisheng were predicted to be among the most important formidable opponents of the CCP if the movement in Hong Kong for genuine universal suffrage ignited Chinese Mainland citizens to demand an end to the ban on political parties and free elections. They could become figures like Kim Dae-jung and Roh Moo-hyun in South Korea. Regarding political interests, the CCP's fundamental interests were served by causing such opponents to die early from manmade illness or accidents in keeping with the CCP's means of waging secret battles against its enemies.

It's been one hundred days since Liu Xiaobo was buried at sea, but his widow Liu Xia is still sealed off from the world under house arrest, as she has been for more than seven years. Liu Xia's body and spirit has been on the brink of collapse for a long time. Whether she will leave and follow Xiaobo is a very real problem. The Freedom for Xiaobo campaign has fully extended to Freedom for Liu Xia. However, diplomatic negotiations launched by the United States and Germany from April to June failed to make substantive progress. I was imprisoned at home and could not reach Liu Xia. Citizens commemorating Xiaobo in Dalian and Guangdong were detained one after another and sent back to their hometowns. The CCP's police empire fully demonstrated its power and arrogance. Liu Xia, whether at Tiger Beach in Dalian or Erhai Lake in Dali, can only be: "For the perils on Perilous Beach I have sighs; / On Lonely Ocean now I feel dreary and lonely."[2] As long as the territory is controlled by the CCP, whether Beijing or Hong Kong, such places are an abyss of misery for Liu Xia and Liu Hui (Liu Xia's brother) because they are guarded and isolated by the political police. Only in Germany or the United States can their trauma truly be healed.

The CCP's Nineteenth Party Congress was a feast of Xi Jinping's consolidation of imperial power and the ill-gotten gains of power; the Red Tsar is an enemy of democracy, freedom, and constitutionalism. He started as Xi-Hitler and may eventually end as Xi-Ceaucescu. In 2018 how will Xiaobo be comforted? Only if Liu Xia and Liu Hui obtain freedom and only if Charter 08, which he sacrificed his life for, becomes an extension of his ideal and pursuit to regain vitality.

Xiaobo, it's been more than one hundred years since so many Chinese people have trekked in the darkness of night, looking for a way out of the millennia of the great Gobi Desert of autocracy. Although generation after generation has collapsed in the frigid cold and parched desert, everyone believes and knows that the boundless sea of democracy is ahead. The only way to pursue freedom is usually to first throw oneself into prison as a sacrifice. Our mission is to be the brightest star in the dark sky before dawn.

*Translated by Andréa Worden*

NOTES

1. Du Fu (Tu Fu, 712–70), "The Temple of the Premier of Shu," trans. Witter Bynner (1881–1968), in *The Penguin Book of Chinese Verse*, ed. A. R. Davis (Baltimore: Penguin, 1962).—Trans.
2. Wen Tianxiang (1236–83), "Crossing Lonely Sea," trans. Xu Yuanzhong (b. 1921), *New World Encyclopedia*, December 15, 2007—Trans.

# Elegy for Liu Xiaobo

*Liao Yiwu*

As he is dead, what can it change?
The sun shines bright, and lingering Alpine snows are far away
Like flashing fish scales, his ashes thrown into the flashing sea
Like fish scales, is our remembrance of him
Drifting as scales going away?
What can it change? He is dead

A book was torn
And the wife an injured bookmark
Slipping off the bed. She watches him
Wanting to pounce on him and shout:
"Don't die! My dear, I don't want you to die, God!"
But she can only watch silently
Like the slipped bookmark watching the book being torn,
Page after page

The whole world watched him being murdered
The cage was surrounded by white-clad ghosts
This scholar who once would rather die than leave China
This prisoner of thought who had been imprisoned four times
Now said he preferred to die in the West. Did you hear it, world?
If you're deaf, at least you have a mouth
If you're dumb, at least you're still watching
If you're blind—will the blind be angry?
Will more than a billion blind Chinese be angry?
What can it change? He is dead.

I still awaited news that he would have taken off
A mass of birds cried in the wind, that late night
Petals were falling, grass growing, my wife and daughter sleeping
I was a ghost in the darkness. He drew closer
A silhouette like a comet crossed the sky
Is there a flight 8964 to heaven?
He released his wife's hands and told her to keep on living well.
That was many years ago
He was at Tiananmen, with roaring tanks, bursts of gunfire
Children fell in clusters, their souls climbing upward
To bid him farewell. They urged him to live on
To keep on living well for the lost souls of the massacre.

What can it change, as he is dead
Crucified by the Communist Party, eternal as Jesus
Resurrected in the slaughter
I still awaited news that he would have taken off
Waiting for him to finish the last love letter
He would send his wife thousands of miles away and then be buried
    in a foreign land
We would often go to see him. When night would fall
The past would cross the treetops like a river.

But all is shattered; he has no freedom
No freedom of life or death, of ashes, or of love
The world helplessly watched a noble man
Being slowly torn like the finest book
No one could stop this senseless atrocity
Though everyone hoped to stop it!
What can it change, dear God?
He is dead

*Translated by Yu Zhang and Stacy Mosher*

# Rebirth

TSERING WOESER

*To Liu Xiaobo*


A river

A river without beginning or end in the darkness . . .

As if on a river with a turbulent undercurrent but a still surface

Your long-unseen image gradually becomes clear

It seems that nothing but bones remain

And that those bones can also speak

Unless the deaf or deceptive—hollow men, hypocrites, executioners

—Turn a deaf ear

Compared with lips that yet open and close, your bones that would
    rather break than bend

Speak louder

And more eternally

Standing with my palms in anjali mudra

As if looking at that distant, I see on this all-too-silent river

You drifting to the other shore

To be reborn in death

*Translated by Yu Zhang and Stacy Mosher*

## NOTE

Chinese original published by *Radio of Free Asia*, July 14, 2017.

# My Brother, Why Have You Gone to Die?
*Du Daobin*

*In Imitation of Liu Xiaobo's "My Dear, My*
*Puppy Is Dead—To My Little Finger"*

Why are you dead, my good brother?
You had not even said hello
Before you died amid tyranny's terrors
Died in a calculating prison

Your voice calling "Daobin" still rings in my ears
You were the forerunner whose back I saw when facing the
    crossroads
The applause and laughter you gave me
Are deeply etched in my mind

That afternoon when abruptly reading news of your dying
I wanted at one to buy a plane ticket
To Shenyang to visit you in sickbed
And embrace you to warm your sick and weak body
The notion lasted a tenth of a second
Before being crushed by an iron fist
My dearest, gracious, intimate, good brother is dead
And I could not even pray before your body

Your liver was corroded by conspiracy soaked in snake venom
Your free thought sent into a fiery oven
My once stuttering and brawny brother
Has been scattered in the icy Pacific

My dearest, gracious, intimate, good brother is dead
Taking his leave without saying hello
And facing this insidious and cruel world
I still don't believe it's true

Why have you died with our wish to meet unfulfilled?
Where couldn't you go? Why returned here?
This has been a land rampant with tigers and wolves
Where any evil may occur; why didn't you believe it?

*Translated by Yu Zhang and Stacy Mosher*

# Poems

*Li Yongsheng*

## China's Road Map

Towering like a snowy night
over the border between brightness and darkness
using a snowy night's stature
and a snowy night's language
to put thousands of years of darkness
behind you
The brightness
is stretching, stretching before your eyes
while the yellow earth
adheres to your feet

Perhaps your appearance is truly cold
facing every transient
with the same
ruthless face as if your coldness
has been fed by
too much, too much hatred
But in fact, it is
the radiance shining forth
when you entered the inner realm of no enemies
Thus, holding it fast
is of priceless value
You therefore
coldly stand in position like a flag
Your bones like a forest
to guide China

in the direction of constitutional democracy
You therefore
coldly stand in position
like Everest
like the sun
coldly expressing
your boundless affection for this warm soil

## We Plant a Tree Called Liu Xiaobo

The spring month of March
is a good time to plant trees
For thousands of years, Chinese
have been sowing good seeds
into the parched land
and dreaming of the reincarnation
of the righteous Judge Bao
unaware that all that grows
throughout this land are corrupt officials

Tomorrow is March once again
We are going to plant trees
but no long plant superstition
and no longer plant illusion
Instead, we will plant the ideals of democracy and liberty
with human dignity
together
Then, blessing it with tolerance
we will grow it into a sheltering forest
and then push corrupt and arbitrary power
behind it
May democracy, rule of law and human rights
become second nature
in every heart
and then become sunshine
become air

become food

become necessities that no one can live without

*Translated by Stacy Mosher and Yu Zhang*

NOTE

Originally published in *Beijing Spring*, March 2009, and republished in July 2017, http://beijingspring.com/bj2/2010/400/72201754743.htm

# Conclusion

*Heart to Heart*

# Poems
*Liu Xia*


## A Road in Darkness

I know that sooner or later one day
You will leave me
And walk alone the road in darkness

I pray for the moment to reappear
For me to view the scene in memory
And hope in that scene, I
At the time of shocking panic
Will shine a light

But I could not do it
And just clutched my fists tightly
Not letting the slightest strength flow from my fingertips

*2010*


## The 2nd of June 1989
*—To Xiaobo*


This is not a good weather
I said to myself
under the brilliant sun

Standing behind you
I patted your head
While your hair pricked my palm
Feeling a bit strange.

Before I had time to say a word to you
You became a media figure
Looking up at you among the crowd
Made me rather tired
Instead I hid outside the crowd
Smoked a cigarette
And looked at the sky

Perhaps a legend was emerging then
But the sun was too bright
For me to see it
   *June 1989*


## Untitled

You speak you speak you speak the truth
You are talking day and night as long as you are awake
You talk and talk
You are in a closed room while your voice breaks out to spread
The death from twenty years ago has come back again
Come and gone as the time
You are short of many things but with you are the souls of the dead
You have lost daily life to join the outcry of the dead
There is no response and none

You speak you speak you speak the truth
You are talking day and night as long as you are awake
You talk and talk
You are in a closed room while your voice breaks out to spread
The wound from twenty years ago has been bleeding
Fresh and red as the life
You are fond of many things but more passionate accompanying the
   souls of the dead
You have made a promise to seek the truth with them
On the way there is no light and none

You speak you speak you speak the truth
You are talking day and night as long as you are awake
You talk and talk
You are in a closed room while your voice breaks out to spread
The gunfire of twenty years ago has decided your life
Always living in death
You are in love with your wife but more proud of the dark time with
    her you spent
You let her be but are more insistent that she continues to write you
    poems after her death
In the verses there is no sound and none
*September 4, 2009*

## Wind

You are destined in fate to be like the wind
Waving and flying
And playing games in the cloud

I ever imagined to be with you
But what home should there be
To accommodate you
As the walls will make you choke

You can only be a wind, but the wind
Has never told me
When to come and when to go

As the wind comes I cannot open my eyes
After the wind is gone there are dusts everywhere
*December 1992*

*Translated by Yu Zhang and edited by Bonny Cassi*

# Preface to Liu Xia's Photo Album

*Liu Xiaobo*

My praise may be an unforgivable toxin:

By the dim light of the table lamp, you gave me my first, dilapidated computer, probably a Pentium 586.

In that simple home that always cramped our loving gazes, you are sure to have read my short poem describing Shrimpie (my wife) as overbearing; she went to boil congee for me, demanding that I write the world's most drop-dead beautiful poem in 360 seconds.[1]

The dim light of the table lamp, our small, simple home, the flaking tea table and Shrimpie's peremptory order blended like a first, surprising encounter between stones and stars, a flawless intersection.

From then on, I was predestined to praise, perhaps as instinctively as the polar bear's enjoyment of hibernation in the vast, white snow.

One Bird after Another pierces my vision.[2] Seizing a person's aesthetic judgment means spending my life going through his life; Shrimpie's poems emerge from the intersection of ice and darkness, just as her photography shoots poems in black and white. Frenzy and tranquil facing of hardship, horrifying dolls scatter toward a smokescreen through a gaping chest cavity, wooden figures in black armbands may be widows coming from witnessing the resurrection of Jesus, or the witches in *Macbeth*.

No, no, none of those. It is Shrimpie's incomparable description of a solitary branch in the wilderness; it is a dust-laden lily on a murky horizon—offered to the dead souls.

From the time Shrimpie completed her first drawing, they became mourning for a fate that will never be fulfilled. Most regrettable is that up to now, I have not been able to hold a joint exhibition of Shrimpie's "Poems · Drawings · Photos—Black and White Entangled."

Love as intense as ice, love as remote as blackness; perhaps it is my cheap and vulgar praise that profanes this poetic sentiment, artistic style, and image; may G forgive me.

G: After several days' delay, I have the strength to complete your task.

*Translated by Stacy Mosher*

## NOTES

Chinese original published by *Initium Media*, July 14, 2017.

1. The first part of the word *xiami*, "dried shrimp," sounds the same as Liu Xia's name.—Trans.

2. "One Bird after Another" is a poem Liu Xia wrote to Liu Xiaobo when he was in prison during 1996–99. Its translation by Yu Zhang is available at Morton Grove Public Library, http://www.mgpl.org/poem-of-the-day-one-bird-after-another/.—Trans.

# Appendix

## Xiaobo, a Meteoroid in Darkness
*Independent Chinese PEN Center*

All the efforts cannot keep you in this world, Xiaobo. You finally left. These last days, the state of your illness touches the hearts of the good people all over the world. Everybody prays and wishes for your blessing. Maybe God does not want you to suffer anymore through the sickness. You shall not continuously be surrounded by various agents of the evil party so that God allows you to leave this world, which owes you so much, in arm with your beloved wife, Liu Xia.

When you were a young man, you started a fearless struggle against the hypocrisy in the Chinese tradition and the oppressive forces. Your clear, sharp thinking and beautiful and elegant writing has attracted countless youth and even elders, who have become your admirers and followers. In times of great change, you never fell back. You did not consider your personal safety. Determined, you participated in all kinds of social activities. For decades, you have been constantly criticizing by words and actions the deformed society of China, showing sympathy and helping the suffering people. You have never missed the chance to provoke the evil forces.

In the Independent Chinese PEN Center, you have been a beloved president for four years. With personal charm, big heart, and tolerance, you united a large group of dissident writers both at home and abroad, helping to make ICPC one of the most dynamic literary organizations that advocates for China's freedom of expression with particular support for writers in prison and their works. Charter 08 is a road map for democratization in China. It is a guiding light for our future but has pushed you into the abyss of darkness. Even the high honor such as the Nobel Peace Prize cannot free you.

Dear Xiaobo, your short life is like a meteor. You illuminated the darkness and burned yourself. You longed for freedom for the millions of your countrymen's liberty. You sacrificed your personal freedom at the end. The spiritual heritage you leave us is the example of a true intellectual, the free soul of a nation and the hope and courage that mankind will never give up in fighting for liberty.

Xiaobo, your soul is immortal. Your spirit will last forever!

## Liu Xiaobo—An Exceptional Life, Always Remembered
*PEN International*

The PEN community is deeply saddened to hear of Liu Xiaobo's death today. Liu Xiaobo, a Nobel Peace Prize winner, writer, literary critic, and human rights activist, spent the last eight years of his life in Jinzhou Prison in northeast China, with little or no access to friends, family or colleagues. A former president of the Independent Chinese PEN Center and an active PEN member, Liu was arrested in December 2009 and charged with "inciting subversion of state power," with a sentence of eleven years in prison.

His wife—the poet and photographer Liu Xia—was only allowed to visit him once a month under the supervision of prison guards. They would be forced to change the subject if they spoke about anything deemed offensive to the state. Liu Xia herself spent almost the entire duration of her husband's detention under house arrest, held without charge.

Despite this harsh and unjust treatment, Liu Xiaobo's continuing message to the outside world was one of peace, hope, and love. His poetry—written from within prison—spoke of his love for his wife and his hope for a China free from discrimination and human rights abuses. He used imagery rooted in nature and transformation, and his verse was rhythmic and lyrical.

At the December 2010 Nobel Peace Prize award ceremony in Oslo, Liu Xiaobo's medal and diploma were presented to an empty chair. It is a huge sadness to all of us who knew or were influenced by Liu Xiaobo—his resilient activism, his commitment to justice, his optimism and peaceful heart—that he will never have the opportunity to be recognized in person for all that he has done in the service of others. His empty chair was and remains a deep injustice, but just as he was remembered while locked behind bars, he will be remembered by us forever.

As well as sending our thoughts and love to Liu Xiaobo's family, we are calling on the authorities to grant complete freedom of movement to his wife, Liu Xia, at this difficult time and going forward.

If you would like to pay tribute to Liu Xiaobo, you can write a message in memory here.

Below, please find statements from PEN President Jennifer Clement, Executive Director Carles Torner, and Salil Tripathi, chair of PEN's Writers in Prison Committee, as well as a recent message of solidarity from UK poet laureate Carol Ann Duffy.

On this sad day I remember the 2010 image of the chairman of the Norwegian Nobel Committee, Thorbjørn Jagland, sitting beside Liu Xiaobo's medal and diploma on an empty chair—PEN's symbol for imprisoned writers. On that day the world honored and celebrated Liu Xiaobo's courage as it does again today. Liu once said, "I hope I will be the last victim in China's long record of treating words as crimes." We must continue to uphold his dream.

—*Jennifer Clement, PEN President*

Jan Patočka wrote that "the real test of a man is not how well he plays the role he has invented for himself, but how well he plays the role that destiny assigned to him." Patočka drafted and signed with Havel Charter 77 and died after a marathon interrogation by Czech police; he remains the symbol of freedom for Czechs. Dear Liu Xiaobo, dear PEN colleague, you have died today because of the treatment imposed on you by Chinese authorities after you signed Charter 08. Your PEN friends around the world will praise your destiny and your commitment; we will praise you every single day until China is free.

—*Carles Torner, PEN Executive Director*

In one of your poems, you write of the "cold and indifferent moon." The same sky with this moon in it reaches over all of us, over you and me, over my freedom and your oppression. What we have in common is as various as our differences, but one of thing we share is our belief in the power of writing to challenge those things that limit, oppress, destroy, and deny. I am sorry that you have experienced this denial, this oppression so directly, but I want you to know that—while your punishment has attempted to reduce you—in my eyes you are magnified inside your work, your power, your courage, and your love. Thank you for everything you have done in your fight for a better world.

—*Carol Ann Duffy, UK Poet Laureate*

China's callous treatment of political prisoners and dissidents reached lower depths today with the tragic passing of Nobel laureate Liu Xiaobo. Liu, a writer, poet, and democracy campaigner, had committed no crime—he wanted the Chinese government to respect the dignity of Chinese people and uphold their human rights. But his words threatened the authoritarian regime which attempted to silence him by jailing him. His words will resonate and will continue to inspire millions of people in China and beyond, and he will be remembered long after the unelected men temporarily in power are forgotten, and, as Liu dreamed and fought for, China will become a democracy.

—*Salil Tripathi, PEN International Writers in Prison Committee Chair*

NOTE

Originally published at PEN International, July 13, 2017, http://www.pen -international.org/newsitems/liu-xiaobo-an-exceptional-life-always-remembered/.

# Chinese Publisher's Afterword
*Wang Tiancheng*

The publication of this memorial collection is the result of unforeseen grief. In the beginning of 2017, Cai Chu, editor in chief of the *Democratic China* online magazine, urged me to write a plan on his behalf and apply for funding from a foundation to hold an international conference in October 2017, titled, Global Symposium on Solidarity with Liu Xiaobo.

In planning and submitting applications to funders, based on our understanding of the current Chinese authoritarian government, we did not expect Xiaobo to be released early from prison. However, we never expected that Xiaobo would be unable to wait until the conference in October that would focus on rallying support for him.

After the news of Xiaobo's critical illness broke, we had wanted to revise the plan and move the meeting up to early August. Even though it was hurried, we nevertheless needed to serve as a voice for him. However, Xiaobo did not wait until August.

The death of Xiaobo rendered the solidarity conference moot. After Cai Chu, Hu Ping, and I discussed the matter, we tentatively proposed to the foundation that the funds that had originally been agreed upon to support the conference could instead be used to publish the *Liu Xiaobo Memorial Collection*. This was actually an application different from what was originally planned. As expected, however, the foundation did not agree to our proposal.

However, Xiaobo's death was a major event in the contemporary Chinese opposition movement. In addition to all sorts of mourning activities, there should also be a long-lasting written record. Based on this kind of consideration, we decided to continue to promote the plan to edit and publish the memorial collection, and Democratic China and the Institute for China's Democratic Transition would figure out a way to share the cost.

I'm grateful to all of the authors who contributed to this collection. The dozens of articles compiled here recall or comment on Xiaobo's life, deeds, thought and spirit from different perspectives.

I have not written anything specifically for Xiaobo. This is truly a great regret for me. Here I would like to use a very limited space to mention the two times I had contact with Xiaobo.

The first time I saw Xiaobo was in 1987. At that time, Xiaobo was well known as a literary dark horse. I was a student in the law department of Peking University. Xiaobo was invited to Peking University to give a speech in a large hall, near the triangle, where movies were often shown. The entire hall, including the hallways and doorways were overflowing with people. I was among the numerous students in the audience who were deeply influenced by Xiaobo's passionate speech. I still remember a sentence from his speech: "For freedom, even if you would die once you stepped out of this gate, it's worth it!"

The last contact I had with Xiaobo was in December 2008. At that time, I was a visiting scholar at Columbia University in New York City. Xiaobo contacted me frequently and hoped that I could participate in certain aspects of the work of the Independent Chinese PEN Center. However, based on various considerations, I was very hesitant. On December 7 Xiaobo contacted me again on Skype. The next day, because of Charter 08, he was detained.

After the news broke, for a long time it was difficult to calm my mood. Had I known—perhaps ICPC's work was an arrangement or something he sought to entrust me with—I would definitely have put aside my misgivings and accepted.

Condensed into Xiaobo's life were the sorrow and pride, misery and hope of this era. He did not see the collapse of despotism in China, but his spirit has already overcome it. He has become part of history and will be admired forever by future generations.

*Institute for China's Democratic Transition*
*Translated by Andréa Worden*

# To Those Gathered for the Book Launch of Essays Commemorating Liu Xiaobo and Dialogue on His Legacy
*Marco Rubio and Chris Smith*

We send warm greetings on behalf of the Congressional-Executive Commission on China. We commend you for your participation in today's event honoring the life and work of the late Liu Xiaobo. In particular, we want to recognize the organizers of this important event—*Democratic China* and its president and editor in chief, Cai Chu, and the Institute for China's Democratic Transition and its president, Wang Tiancheng—for their work to gather, edit, and publish essays commemorating Liu Xiaobo and to bring all of you together this afternoon.

Further, we deeply appreciate the timing of today's event—it is not lost on us that Chinese authorities detained Liu Xiaobo on December 8, 2008, or that Charter 08 was issued on December 10, 2008, to mark the sixtieth anniversary of the Universal Declaration of Human Rights.

Nor will we ever forget that on December 10, 2010, Liu Xiaobo was the first Chinese national and resident in China to receive the prestigious Nobel Peace Prize (in absentia) for his "long and nonviolent struggle for fundamental human rights in China."

We at the commission were dismayed by the news in June of this year that Liu Xiaobo, unjustly imprisoned for his advocacy of political reform in China, had been diagnosed with late-stage liver cancer. We joined observers in questioning whether Liu received adequate medical care and appropriate health screenings in prison. We called for the Chinese government and Communist Party to accept the wishes of Liu Xiaobo and his wife, Liu Xia, to travel abroad for medical treatment. And we were profoundly saddened when Liu died on July 13 under state guard at a hospital in Shenyang, Liaoning Province. We have continued to demand Chinese authorities release Liu Xia from the illegal confinement that began when the Norwegian Nobel Committee named Liu Xiaobo recipient of the Nobel Peace Prize in October 2010.

At a time when Chinese President and Communist Party General Secretary Xi Jinping has claimed global leadership and legitimacy for China, Liu's treatment stands out as especially callous and cynical. The Chinese government and Communist Party's refusal to honor the Lius' wishes to receive medical care abroad, their manipulation and censorship in China of the news of Liu Xiaobo's final illness and death, and their decision to cremate his body and hold a sea burial laid bare the mechanisms of this repressive one-party state. The human rights situation in China continues to deteriorate with the escalating persecution of ethnic minorities and religious groups, rights lawyers and defenders, and citizen journalists; discrimination against migrant workers and their right to freedom of residence and livelihood; the criminalization of speech critical of the government; and countless other violations of human rights norms and aspirations.

Today's event, commemorating Liu Xiaobo's writing, his activism, and his interactions with many of you as fellow writers and advocates of political reform, is an important forum to consider Liu's reflections on pursuing responsibility, freedom, and tolerance in the face of a repressive regime. Liu advocated human rights, freedom of expression, peaceful political reform, and love to counter the toxic impact of hatred and an enemy mentality among citizens living in a repressive, authoritarian one-party state. We must never forget his words to the Chinese government and Communist Party: "I have no enemies and no hatred."

We hope and believe that China will one day be a democratic country where the rights of Chinese citizens are respected and protected. In our respective leadership roles on the U.S. Senate Foreign Relations Committee and the U.S. House Foreign Affairs Committee and as chairs of the bipartisan Congressional-Executive Commission on China, we support your efforts to honor Liu Xiaobo and assure you that we, too, will continue to promote his legacy in the future.

## Letter of Thanks to PEN International Congress
*Liu Xia*

As PEN International holds its congress in Pune, India, in October 2018, I would like to send you my deep gratitude and blessing.

Since the beginning of this century, when the Independent Chinese PEN Center became a member of PEN International, the leadership of PEN International and many sister PEN centers have provided strong support to ICPC, for which Liu Xiaobo was once president. Later, when Xiaobo was imprisoned for the fourth time, you fought tirelessly for his and my freedom. Before Xiaobo received the Nobel Peace Prize, PEN America, German PEN Center, and later PEN Canada granted him their own PEN awards.

All these are still fresh in my mind. Now Xiaobo has left us. After I suffered very much physically and psychologically, I am finally free. Because of my poor health, I cannot be with you and bring my gratitude to you personally, dearest friends.

I love you and miss you.

Thank you for your company.

# Additional Statements

We have not been able to include all the essays and tributes for Liu Xiaobo because of space constraints but list here many others who expressed support and admiration:

Thorbjørn Jagland, speech at Nobel Awards Ceremony

Berit Reiss-Andersen, chair of Norwegian Nobel Committee, statement

Zeid Ra'ad Al Hussein, UN high commissioner for human rights, statement

Jean-Claude Junker, president of European Commission, and Donald Tusk, president of European Council, joint statement

Suzanne Nossel, PEN American Center executive director, statement

Salil Shetty, secretary-general of Amnesty International, "Liu Xiaobo: A Giant of Human Rights Who Leaves a Lasting Legacy for China and the World"

Tsai Ing-wen, president of Republic of China, statement

Rex Tillerson, U.S. Secretary of State, Statement on the Passing of Liu Xiaobo

Nancy Pelosi, U.S. representative, Statement on the Death of Liu Xiaobo

Marco Rubio, U.S. senator, An Open Letter to Liu Xia, Widow of Liu Xiaobo

Chris Smith, U.S. representative, Statement on the Passing of Liu Xiaobo

Chen Pokong, "Liu Xiaobo's Death, Witnessing the Birth of Neo-Fascism"

Chien-Yuan Tseng, "China Couldn't Tolerate Liu Xiaobo, but He Coexists with the World"

Ding Jiaxi, "Journey to Shenyang: A Brief Account"

Han Sanzhou, "I Met Him Three Times"

He Qinglian, "Liu Xiaobo and His Course of Civil Disobedience"

Jiang Danwen, "Thinking of Xiaobo and the Day We Said Goodbye"

Leung Man-tao, "The Storyline after the Ending"

Li Hai, "Shedding Tears for My Friend Liu Xiaobo"

Li Jinfang, "Facing Grave Darkness"

Li Nanyang, "Li Xiaobo's Gone"

Peng Xiaoming, "From the Gas Chambers and Radiation to Liu Xiaobo's Terminal Liver Cancer"

Sangjey Kep, "May Liu Xiaobo's Life Awaken the Conscience of the Chinese People"

Wang Yumin, "Liu Xiaobo and the Sea Together Hold Up Tomorrow's Sun"

Wei Sheng, "Theological Thinking on Liu Xiaobo's Death"

Wen Kejian, "Recalling A Funeral Liu Xiaobo Managed"

Xie Yanyi, "What Did Liu Xiaobo Leave to the World?"

Zan Aizong, "West Lake's Gentle Waves Should Remember You"

Nicholas Kristof, "Liu Xiaobo Has Suffered so Others May Be Free"

Freedom for Liu Xiaobo Action Group, obituary for Liu Xiaobo

Mr. Liu Xiaobo Memorial Alliance, Announcing the Establishment of Mr. Liu Xiaobo Memorial Alliance

# Books by Liu Xiaobo

*Aesthetics and Human Freedom.* Beijing: Beijing Normal University Press, 1988.

*A Belle Gave Me a Knockout Drug.* Under pen name Lao Xia, coauthored with Wang Shuo. Wuhan: Changjiang Literature and Art Press, 2000.

*CCP's Unification Is Slavery: Liu Xiaobo on Taiwan, Hong Kong and Tibet.* Liu Xiaobo's Collected Works, Vol. 2. New Taipei City: Lordway Publishing, 2016.

*Civil Awakening—The Dawn of a Free China.* Laogai Research Foundation, 2005.

*Contemporary Politics and Intellectuals of China.* Taipei: Tangshan, 1990.

*Criticism of the Choice: Dialogues with Leading Thinker Li Zehou.* Shanghai: Shanghai People's Publishing House, 1989.

*Criticism of the Choice: Dialogues with Li Zehou.* Shanghai: Shanghai People's Publishing House, 1987.

*Criticism on Contemporary Chinese Intellectuals.* Japanese translation. Tokyo: Tokuma Bookstore, 1992.

*Falling of a Great Power: Memorandum to China.* Taipei: Yunchen Culture, October 2009.

*The Fog of Metaphysics.* Shanghai: Shanghai People's Publishing House, 1989.

*Freedom behind Iron Bars.* Liu Xiaobo's Collected Works, Vol. 3. New Taipei City: Lordway Publishing, 2017.

*From 64 to 08: Liu Xiaobo's Human Rights Path.* Liu Xiaobo's Collected Works, Vol. 1. New Taipei City: Lordway Publishing, 2016.

*From TianAnMen Incident to "Charter 08": Memorandum to China.* In Japanese. Tokyo: Fujiwara Bookstore, December 2009.

*Going Naked toward God.* Changchun: Time Literature and Art Publishing House, 1989.

*June Fourth Elegies.* Poems translated from the Chinese by Jeffrey Yang, with a foreword by His Holiness the Dalai Lama. Bilingual ed. Minneapolis: Graywolf Press, 2012.

*Liu Xiaobo: No Enemies, No Hatred.* Edited by Perry Link, Tienchi Martin-Liao, and Liu Xia. Cambridge MA: The Belknap Press of Harvard University Press, 2012.

*Mao Zedong: The Demon King of Chaos.* Liu Xiaobo's Collected Works, Vol. 4. New Taipei City: Lordway Publishing, 2017.

*The Monologues of a Doomsday's Survivor.* Taipei: China Times Publishing, 1993.
*Mysteries of Thought and Dreams of Mankind*, 2 vols. Taipei: Strom and Stress, 1989–90.
*A Nation That Lies to Conscience.* Taipei: Jie-jou, 2002.
*Selected Poems of Liu Xiaobo and Liu Xia.* Hong Kong: Xiafei'er International Press, 2000.
*A Single Blade and Toxic Sword: Critique on Contemporary Chinese Nationalism.* Sunnyvale: Broad Press, 2006.

# Liu Xiaobo's Awards and Honors

Human Rights Watch, Hellman-Hammett Grant, 1990, 1996

China Foundation on Democracy Education, Award for Outstanding Democratic Activist, 2003

Reporters without Borders, Foundation de France Prize, 2004

Hong Kong Human Rights, Press Award, 2004, 2005, 2006

Hong Kong Human Rights, Excellent Award, 2004, for "Corrupted News Is Not News," *Open Magazine*, January 2004 issue

Hong Kong Human Rights, Grand Prize, 2005, for "Paradise of the Powerful, Hell of the Vulnerable," *Open Magazine*, September 2004 issue

Hong Kong Human Rights, Excellent Award, 2006, for "The Causes and Ending of Shanwei Bloodshed," *Open Magazine*, January 2006 issue

Asia-Pacific Human Rights Foundation, Courage of Conscience Award, 2007

People in Need, Homo Homini Award, 2009

PEN/Barbara Goldsmith Freedom to Write Award, 2009

Independent Federation of Chinese Students and Scholars, Free Spirit Award, 2009

Human Rights Watch, Alison Des Forges Award for Extraordinary Activism, 2010

German PEN, Hermann Kesten Medal, 2010

Nobel Peace Prize, 2010

Geneva Institute for Democracy and Development, Giuseppe Motta Medal for Protection of Human Rights, 2010

PEN Canada, One Humanity Award, 2012

National Endowment for Democracy, Democracy Award, 2014

German, American, England, Scotland, Island, Portuguese, Czech, and Sydney PEN Centers, Honorary Member

Independent Chinese PEN Center, Honorary President

# Chronology

**December 28, 1955**  Liu Xiaobo is born in Changchun City, Jilin Province, China, the third of five sons to Liu Ling (1931–2011), a teacher at Northeast Normal University, and Zhang Suqin (d. 1999), a worker at the university's nursery.

**May 2, 1956**  At a Supreme State Conference, Mao Zedong (1893–1976) formally declares his guiding principle for artistic and scholarly issues: "Let one hundred flowers bloom and one hundred schools of thought contend."

**May 1957**  The CCP Central Committee launches its Rectification Campaign against bureaucratism, factionalism, and subjectivism within the CCP and invites the public to assist with a "free airing of views."

**June 8, 1957**  Publication of the *People's Daily* editorial entitled "Why Is This?" (later revealed to have been penned by Mao himself) shifts the emphasis from the CCP to its critics, who become targets of the Anti-Rightist Campaign affecting more than three million intellectuals, students, cadres, and members of prodemocratic parties.

**1958**  The CCP Central Committee launches the Great Leap Forward campaign with the slogan "To Surpass Britain and Catch Up with America" in major industrial output within fifteen years. The People's Commune Movement results in a massive nationwide famine that kills tens of millions in the following three years.

**September 1962**  Liu Xiaobo is admitted to the primary school affiliated with Northeast Normal University.

**November 10, 1965**  *Wenhui Bao* publishes "A Critique of the New Historical Play *Hai Rui Dismissed from Office*," which serves as the prelude to the Great Proletarian Cultural Revolution.

May 7, 1966   Mao Zedong writes his May 7 Directive to Lin Biao, promoting his idea for the People's Liberation Army to serve as a great school in multiple capacities.

May 16, 1966   The CCP Politburo holds an enlarged meeting to issue its May 16 Notice, effectively launching the Great Proletarian Cultural Revolution.

1967   Liu Xiaobo is admitted to the middle school affiliated with Northeast Normal University.

October 5, 1968   *People's Daily* publishes a full-page report on the implementation of Mao's May 7 Directive, demoting cadres to labor in the fields through the establishment of May 7 Cadre Schools.

December 22, 1968   *People's Daily* publishes a report in which Mao calls on "educated youth" to "go down to the countryside and receive re-education from the poor and lower-middle peasants."

1969   China's universities are closed down for the Cultural Revolution. Liu Xiaobo's family is transferred to the Dashizhai People's Commune in the Horqin Right Front Banner of the Inner Mongolia Autonomous Region.

1973   Liu Xiaobo follows his parents back to Changchun and returns to his middle school as his father, Liu Ling, resumes his work at Northeast Normal University.

1974   Liu Xiaobo graduates from middle school in July and is sent to the countryside as an educated youth to be reeducated at Shan'gang People's Commune in Nong'an County, Jilin Province.

January 8, 1976   Premier Zhou Enlai (1898–1976) dies. Mao Zedong selects Politburo member, Vice Premier, and Public Security Minister Hua Guofeng (1921–2008) as acting premier and begins publicly criticizing Deng Xiaoping (1904–1997) for his reformist economic policies and rectification measures.

April 5, 1976   Crowds throng Tiananmen Square to commemorate Zhou Enlai during the Qing Ming Festival. Police are sent in the following day to clear the square, resulting in mass protests, arrests, and beatings in what later comes to be known as the April 5 Movement.

April 7, 1976   The CCP Central Committee formally appoints Hua Guofeng as first vice chairman of the CCP and premier of the State Council and passes a resolution removing Deng Xiaoping from all of his official postings.

September 9, 1976   Mao Zedong dies.

October 6, 1976   Hua Guofeng leads a coup d'état resulting in the arrest of the Gang of Four, including Mao's widow Jiang Qing (1914–1991). On the following day, a Politburo meeting elects Hua Guofeng chairman of the Central Committee and of the Central Military Commission, ending the Cultural Revolution.

November 1976   Liu Xiaobo is recruited as a plastering apprentice at the Changchun City Construction Company.

July 1977   The Third Plenum of the Tenth Central Committee of the CCP restores Deng Xiaoping to the posts of vice chairman of the Central Committee and of the Central Military Commission, vice premier of the State Council, and chief of the general staff of the People's Liberation Army, paving the way for Deng to become China's supreme leader.

October 21, 1977   *People's Daily* publishes an editorial announcing a decision by the National Higher Education Recruitment Conference to reform the higher education admissions system, including a plan to resume the National Higher Education Entrance Examination, which was suspended during the ten-year Cultural Revolution.

March 13, 1978   Liu Xiaobo registers as a new student at the Chinese Department of Jilin University after passing the national examination in December 1977.

April 5, 1978   The CCP Central Committee authorizes the United Front Department and Ministry of Public Security's "Report Requesting Instructions on the Removal of All Rightist Labels," after which the rehabilitation of "wrongfully labeled Rightists" commences.

November 14, 1978   The Beijing Municipal Party Committee, with the authorization of the Politburo Standing Committee, declares the rehabilitation of the April 5 Tiananmen Incident. Days later, big-character posters on a bus station wall at Xidan call for "science, democracy, and rule of law," launching the Xidan Democracy Wall Movement.

December 5, 1978   Wei Jingsheng (b. 1950), founder and editor of the independent magazine *Exploration* (*Tansuo*), puts up on the Xidan Democracy Wall his own poster "The Fifth Modernization," calling for democracy and for the Four Modernizations set forth by Chinese government to strengthen the fields of agriculture, industry, national defense, and science and technology as its goals toward the end of twentieth century.

March 25, 1979    Wei Jingsheng posts on the Xidan Democracy Wall his essay "Do We Want Democracy or a New Dictatorship?" warning that Deng Xiaoping might degenerate into a dictator. Wei is arrested four days later.

March 30, 1979    Deng Xiaoping gives a speech proclaiming the Four Cardinal Principles: upholding the socialist path, the people's democratic dictatorship, the leadership of the CCP, and Marxism-Leninism and Mao Zedong Thought, providing official approval of the ongoing crackdown of the Democracy Wall Movement.

April 17, 1980    The China PEN Center is formed in Beijing and elects Ba Jin (1904–2005), president of China Writers Association, as its chairman.

1982    Liu Xiaobo graduates with a BA in Chinese literature from Jilin University in January and later becomes a graduate student in Chinese literature at Beijing Normal University.

December 4, 1982    The Fifth Session of the Fifth NPC adopts a revision of the PRC Constitution that includes Deng's Four Cardinal Principles in its preamble.

October 12, 1983    Deng Xiaoping gives a speech launching a campaign against "spiritual pollution" that targets dissident writers.

1984    Liu Xiaobo graduates with an MA in Chinese classical literature and joins the faculty of Beijing Normal University. He is married to Tao Li, his girlfriend since they were schoolmates at middle school.

1985    Liu Xiaobo's son, Liu Tao, is born.

September 7–12, 1986    The Institute of Literature at the Chinese Academy of Social Sciences holds a symposium on Ten Years of New Period Literature with hundreds of participants, including many celebrities, such as the head of the institute Liu Zaifu (b. 1941), philosopher Li Zehou (b. 1930), and newly appointed minister of culture Wang Meng (b. 1934). Liu Xiaobo creates waves by giving a speech entitled "The New Period Literature Is Facing a Crisis," which is published by *Shenzhen Youth Daily* on October 3 and reprinted by many presses, earning him the title of "literary dark horse."

December 5, 1986    Students at the China University of Science and

Technology in Hefei, Anhui Province, protest school authorities' interference in student participation in district People's Congress elections. Students in other cities begin voicing discontent on a variety of matters, giving rise to the 1986 student movement.

December 30, 1986   Deng Xiaoping calls for "representative figures of bourgeois liberalization" Fang Lizhi (1936–2012), Liu Binyan (1925–2005), and Wang Ruowang (1918–2001) to be expelled from the party.

January 1987   CCP General Secretary Hu Yaobang (1915–1989) is removed from office as a nationwide campaign against "bourgeois liberalization" is launched.

January 1988   Liu Xiaobo's first book, *The Critique of Choice: Dialogue with Li Zehou*, is published and soon becomes a bestseller.

June 1988   Liu Xiaobo publishes his doctoral dissertation, *Aesthetics and Human Freedom*, defends it before hundreds of students, and obtains the unanimous approval of a panel of nine prominent literary critics and aestheticians to receive his PhD in literature and become a lecturer in the same faculty.

August 1988   Liu Xiaobo leaves China to serve as a visiting scholar at the University of Oslo and is also invited to study at the University of Hawaii and Columbia University.

April 15, 1989   Former CCP general secretary Hu Yaobang dies, and university students in Beijing, Shanghai, and other major cities stage mass protests "against corruption and for freedom" in his memory.

April 26, 1989   *People's Daily* publishes a front-page editorial, based on a decision by the CCP's Politburo Standing Committee that effectively defines the student movement as a destabilizing anti-party revolt that should be resolutely opposed at all levels of society. This provokes the student protesters to stage a much larger demonstration the following day and widens the chasm between the students and the CCP leadership. Eventually the CCP's general secretary, Zhao Ziyang (1919–2005), is dismissed after urging for the editorial to be "toned down" or rescinded.

April 27, 1989   Liu Xiaobo cancels his plan to study in the United States until 1990 and arrives in Beijing to support the student movement.

May 20, 1989   The authorities declare martial law in Beijing, eventually mobilizing as many as 250,000 troops to the capital to disassemble the protesters and clear Tiananmen Square "by all means necessary."

June 2, 1989   Liu Xiaobo, Zhou Duo, Gao Xin, and Taiwanese singer Hou Derchien declare a hunger strike that earns the trust of the protesting students, who call them the Four Gentlemen of Tiananmen Square.

June 3–4, 1989   The government sends in People's Liberation Army martial law troops to forcefully remove protesters from Tiananmen Square, causing the deaths of hundreds or thousands people (the death toll remains undisclosed to this day), known as the June Fourth Incident or Tiananmen massacre. In the early hours of June 4, Liu Xiaobo and his colleagues successfully negotiate with students and troop commanders to allow the peaceful withdrawal of thousands of protesters from the square.

June 6, 1989   Liu Xiao is arrested and detained in Beijing's Qincheng Prison. He is soon announced in official media as a "black hand" manipulating the student movement to overthrow the government and socialist system and is particularly criticized in late June with a government-published anthology, *Liu Xiaobo: The Man and His Deeds*.

September 1989   Liu Xiaobo is expelled from the Beijing Normal University.

August 1990   Liu Xiaobo and Tao Li divorce.

January 26, 1991   The Beijing Intermediate People's Court pronounces Liu Xiaobo guilty of "counter-revolutionary propaganda and incitement" but exempts him from further punishment due to his "major meritorious act" of persuading the students to leave the Tiananmen Square.

January–May 1993   Liu Xiaobo is invited to Australia and the United States for showings of a documentary film, *The Gate of Heavenly Peace* but declines to seek political asylum and returns to China.

May 1995–January 1996   Liu Xiaobo is detained under residential surveillance in the suburbs of Beijing for his participation in a series of petitioning campaigns.

October 8, 1996   Liu Xiaobo is detained for issuing the Double Ten Declaration, drafted jointly with another well-known dissident, Wang Xizhe (b. 1948), and is sentenced to three years of reeducation through labor for "disturbing social order."

November 1996   Liu Xiaobo and Liu Xia are formally married at the Dalian

RTL center where Liu Xiao is serving his sentence, and Liu Xiao is allowed to visit him afterward.

March 14, 1997   The Fifth Session of the Eighth NPC approves the revision of the Criminal Law of PRC, effective from October 1, 1997, abolishing counterrevolutionary offenses and replacing them with offenses of endangering state security.

October 27, 1997   The PRC signs the International Covenant on Economic, Social and Cultural Rights.

October 5, 1998   The PRC signs the International Covenant on Civil and Political Rights. It has not ratified the covenant as of 2019.

October 7, 1999   Liu Xiaobo is released and allowed to join Liu Xia in Beijing and resumes his freelance writing.

March 27, 2001   The PRC ratifies the International Covenant on Economic, Social and Cultural Rights.

July 2001   The Independent Chinese PEN Center is founded by a group of Chinese writers worldwide, including Liu Xiaobo and his wife, Liu Xia, as the only two residing in Mainland China. ICPC is approved as a chapter of International PEN at its Sixty-Seventh Congress in November and later elects Liu Binyan as its chairman and Zheng Yi as vice chairman.

October 2003   The ICPC holds its first internet congress of its membership assembly, approving its charter and electing a board of directors that includes President Liu Xiaobo, vice presidents Cai Chu and Chen Maiping, and directors Yu Jie, Liao Yiwu, and others.

March 14, 2004   The Second Session of the Tenth NPC approves an amendment to the PRC Constitution that states, "The State respects and preserves human rights."

September–October 2005   The ICPC holds its second internet congress of its membership assembly, approving the revision of its charter and electing its board of directors, including President Liu Xiaobo, vice presidents Yu Jie and Chen Kuide, and directors Wang Yi, Cai Chu, Zhao Shiying, Tienchi Martin-Liao, and others.

October 2006   Liu Xiaobo is invited to become chief editor of the U.S.-based website Democratic China.

September–October 2007   The ICPC holds its third internet congress of its membership assembly, electing its board of directors, including

President Zheng Yi, vice presidents Emily Wu and Jiang Qisheng, and directors Liu Xiaobo, Wang Yi, Yu Jie, Cai Chu, Tienchi Martin-Liao, and Zhao Shiying.

December 8, 2008    Liu Xiaobo is detained by the Beijing Municipal Public Security Bureau for his role in drafting Charter 08, a manifesto calling for human rights and political reform initially signed by Liu Xiaobo and 302 other intellectuals and activists and released in celebration of the sixtieth anniversary of the Universal Declaration of Human Rights.

December 23, 2009    Liu Xiaobo is tried at the Beijing Municipal First Intermediate People's Court for "inciting subversion of state power" and is sentenced to eleven years' imprisonment two days later.

October 8, 2010    Liu Xiaobo wins the Nobel Peace Prize and receives the award in absentia in Oslo on December 10.

July 13, 2017    Liu Xiaobo dies of terminal liver cancer and multiple organ failure in the First Affiliated Hospital of China Medical University in Shenyang at the age of sixty-one.

July 15, 2017    Liu Xiaobo is cremated in the morning and his ashes are buried at sea at noon.

# Charter 08

## I. Foreword

A hundred years have passed since the writing of China's first constitution. 2008 also marks the sixtieth anniversary of the promulgation of the Universal Declaration of Human Rights, the thirtieth anniversary of the appearance of Democracy Wall in Beijing, and the tenth of China's signing of the International Covenant on Civil and Political Rights. We are approaching the twentieth anniversary of the 1989 Tiananmen massacre of prodemocracy student protesters. The Chinese people, who have endured human rights disasters and uncountable struggles across these same years, now include many who see clearly that freedom, equality, and human rights are universal values of humankind and that democracy and constitutional government are the fundamental framework for protecting these values.

By departing from these values, the Chinese government's approach to "modernization" has proven disastrous. It has stripped people of their rights, destroyed their dignity, and corrupted normal human intercourse. So we ask: Where is China headed in the twenty-first century? Will it continue with "modernization" under authoritarian rule, or will it embrace universal human values, join the mainstream of civilized nations, and build a democratic system? There can be no avoiding these questions.

The shock of the Western impact upon China in the nineteenth century laid bare a decadent authoritarian system and marked the beginning of what is often called "the greatest changes in thousands of years" for China. A "self-strengthening movement" followed, but this aimed simply at appropriating the technology to build gunboats and other Western material objects. China's humiliating naval defeat at the hands of Japan in 1895 only confirmed the obsolescence of China's system of government. The first attempts at modern political change came with the ill-fated summer of reforms in 1898, but these were cruelly crushed by ultraconservatives at China's imperial court. With the revolution of 1911, which inaugurated Asia's first republic, the authoritarian imperial system that had lasted for centuries was finally supposed to have been laid to rest. But social conflict inside our country and external pressures were to prevent it; China fell into a patchwork of warlord fiefdoms and the new republic became a fleeting dream.

The failure of both "self-strengthening" and political renovation caused many of our forebears to reflect deeply on whether a "cultural illness" was afflicting our country. This mood gave rise, during the May Fourth Movement of the late 1910s, to the championing of "science and democracy." Yet that effort, too, foundered as warlord chaos persisted and the Japanese invasion [beginning in Manchuria in 1931] brought national crisis.

Victory over Japan in 1945 offered one more chance for China to move toward modern government, but the Communist defeat of the Nationalists in the civil war thrust the nation into the abyss of totalitarianism. The "new China" that emerged in 1949 proclaimed that "the people are sovereign" but in fact set up a system in which "the Party is all-powerful." The Communist Party of China seized control of all organs of the state and all political, economic, and social resources, and, using these, has produced a long trail of human rights disasters, including, among many others, the Anti-Rightist Campaign (1957), the Great Leap Forward (1958–1960), the Cultural Revolution (1966–1969), the June Fourth [Tiananmen Square] Massacre (1989), and the current repression of all unauthorized religions and the suppression of the weiquan rights movement [a movement that aims to defend citizens' rights promulgated in the Chinese constitution and to fight for human rights recognized by international conventions that the Chinese government has signed]. During all this, the Chinese people have paid a gargantuan price. Tens of millions have lost their lives, and several generations have seen their freedom, their happiness, and their human dignity cruelly trampled.

During the last two decades of the twentieth century the government policy of "Reform and Opening" gave the Chinese people relief from the pervasive poverty and totalitarianism of the Mao Zedong era, and brought substantial increases in the wealth and living standards of many Chinese as well as a partial restoration of economic freedom and economic rights. Civil society began to grow, and popular calls for more rights and more political freedom have grown apace. As the ruling elite itself moved toward private ownership and the market economy, it began to shift from an outright rejection of "rights" to a partial acknowledgment of them.

In 1998 the Chinese government signed two important international human rights conventions; in 2004 it amended its constitution to include the phrase "respect and protect human rights"; and this year, 2008, it has promised to promote a "national human rights action plan." Unfortunately most of this political progress has extended no further than the paper on which it is written. The political reality, which is plain for anyone to see, is that China has many laws but no rule of law; it has a constitution but no constitutional government. The ruling elite continues to cling to its authoritarian power and fights off any move toward political change.

The stultifying results are endemic official corruption, an undermining of the rule of law, weak human rights, decay in public ethics, crony capitalism, growing inequality between the wealthy and the poor, pillage of the natural environment as well as of the human and historical environments, and the exacerbation of a long list of social conflicts, especially, in recent times, a sharpening animosity between officials and ordinary people.

As these conflicts and crises grow ever more intense, and as the ruling elite continues with impunity to crush and to strip away the rights of citizens to freedom, to property, and to the pursuit of happiness, we see the powerless in our society—the vulnerable groups, the people who have been suppressed and monitored, who have suffered cruelty and even torture, and who have had no adequate avenues for their protests, no courts to hear their pleas—becoming more militant and raising the possibility of a violent conflict of disastrous proportions. The decline of the current system has reached the point where change is no longer optional.

## II. Our Fundamental Principles

This is a historic moment for China, and our future hangs in the balance. In reviewing the political modernization process of the past hundred years or more, we reiterate and endorse basic universal values as follows:

Freedom. Freedom is at the core of universal human values. Freedom

of speech, freedom of the press, freedom of assembly, freedom of association, freedom in where to live, and the freedoms to strike, to demonstrate,
and to protest, among others, are the forms that freedom takes. Without
freedom, China will always remain far from civilized ideals.

Human rights. Human rights are not bestowed by a state. Every person is born with inherent rights to dignity and freedom. The government
exists for the protection of the human rights of its citizens. The exercise of
state power must be authorized by the people. The succession of political
disasters in China's recent history is a direct consequence of the ruling
regime's disregard for human rights.

Equality. The integrity, dignity, and freedom of every person—regardless
of social station, occupation, sex, economic condition, ethnicity, skin color,
religion, or political belief—are the same as those of any other. Principles
of equality before the law and equality of social, economic, cultural, civil,
and political rights must be upheld.

Republicanism. Republicanism, which holds that power should be bal-
anced among different branches of government and competing interests
should be served, resembles the traditional Chinese political ideal of "fairness in all under heaven." It allows different interest groups and social
assemblies, and people with a variety of cultures and beliefs, to exercise
democratic self-government and to deliberate in order to reach peaceful
resolution of public questions on a basis of equal access to government
and free and fair competition.

Democracy. The most fundamental principles of democracy are that the
people are sovereign and the people select their government. Democracy
has these characteristics: (1) Political power begins with the people and
the legitimacy of a regime derives from the people. (2) Political power is
exercised through choices that the people make. (3) The holders of major
official posts in government at all levels are determined through periodic
competitive elections. (4) While honoring the will of the majority, the fundamental dignity, freedom, and human rights of minorities are protected.
In short, democracy is a modern means for achieving government truly
"of the people, by the people, and for the people."

Constitutional rule. Constitutional rule is rule through a legal system
and legal regulations to implement principles that are spelled out in a

constitution. It means protecting the freedom and the rights of citizens, limiting and defining the scope of legitimate government power, and providing the administrative apparatus necessary to serve these ends.

## III. What We Advocate

Authoritarianism is in general decline throughout the world; in China, too, the era of emperors and overlords is on the way out. The time is arriving everywhere for citizens to be masters of states. For China the path that leads out of our current predicament is to divest ourselves of the authoritarian notion of reliance on an "enlightened overlord" or an "honest official" and to turn instead toward a system of liberties, democracy, and the rule of law, and toward fostering the consciousness of modern citizens who see rights as fundamental and participation as a duty. Accordingly, and in a spirit of this duty as responsible and constructive citizens, we offer the following recommendations on national governance, citizens' rights, and social development:

1. A New Constitution. We should recast our present constitution, rescinding its provisions that contradict the principle that sovereignty resides with the people and turning it into a document that genuinely guarantees human rights, authorizes the exercise of public power, and serves as the legal underpinning of China's democratization. The constitution must be the highest law in the land, beyond violation by any individual, group, or political party.

2. Separation of Powers. We should construct a modern government in which the separation of legislative, judicial, and executive power is guaranteed. We need an Administrative Law that defines the scope of government responsibility and prevents abuse of administrative power. Government should be responsible to taxpayers. Division of power between provincial governments and the central government should adhere to the principle that central powers are only those specifically granted by the constitution and all other powers belong to the local governments.

3. Legislative Democracy. Members of legislative bodies at all levels should be chosen by direct election, and legislative democracy should observe just and impartial principles.

4. An Independent Judiciary. The rule of law must be above the interests of any particular political party and judges must be independent. We need to establish a constitutional supreme court and institute procedures for constitutional review. As soon as possible, we should abolish all of the Committees on Political and Legal Affairs that now allow Communist Party officials at every level to decide politically sensitive cases in advance and out of court. We should strictly forbid the use of public offices for private purposes.

5. Public Control of Public Servants. The military should be made answerable to the national government, not to a political party, and should be made more professional. Military personnel should swear allegiance to the constitution and remain nonpartisan. Political party organizations must be prohibited in the military. All public officials including police should serve as nonpartisans, and the current practice of favoring one political party in the hiring of public servants must end.

6. Guarantee of Human Rights. There must be strict guarantees of human rights and respect for human dignity. There should be a Human Rights Committee, responsible to the highest legislative body, that will prevent the government from abusing public power in violation of human rights. A democratic and constitutional China especially must guarantee the personal freedom of citizens. No one should suffer illegal arrest, detention, arraignment, interrogation, or punishment. The system of "Reeducation through Labor" must be abolished.

7. Election of Public Officials. There should be a comprehensive system of democratic elections based on "one person, one vote." The direct election of administrative heads at the levels of county, city, province, and nation should be systematically implemented. The rights to hold periodic free elections and to participate in them as a citizen are inalienable.

8. Rural—Urban Equality. The two-tier household registry system must be abolished. This system favors urban residents and harms rural residents. We should establish instead a system that gives every citizen the same constitutional rights and the same freedom to choose where to live.

9. Freedom to Form Groups. The right of citizens to form groups must be guaranteed. The current system for registering nongovernment groups, which requires a group to be "approved," should be replaced by a system in which a group simply registers itself. The formation of political parties should be governed by the constitution and the laws, which means that we must abolish the special privilege of one party to monopolize power and must guarantee principles of free and fair competition among political parties.

10. Freedom to Assemble. The constitution provides that peaceful assembly, demonstration, protest, and freedom of expression are fundamental rights of a citizen. The ruling party and the government must not be permitted to subject these to illegal interference or unconstitutional obstruction.

11. Freedom of Expression. We should make freedom of speech, freedom of the press, and academic freedom universal, thereby guaranteeing that citizens can be informed and can exercise their right of political supervision. These freedoms should be upheld by a Press Law that abolishes political restrictions on the press. The provision in the current Criminal Law that refers to "the crime of incitement to subvert state power" must be abolished. We should end the practice of viewing words as crimes.

12. Freedom of Religion. We must guarantee freedom of religion and belief, and institute a separation of religion and state. There must be no governmental interference in peaceful religious activities. We should abolish any laws, regulations, or local rules that limit or suppress the religious freedom of citizens. We should abolish the current system that requires religious groups (and their places of worship) to get official approval in advance and substitute for it a system in which registry is optional and, for those who choose to register, automatic.

13. Civic Education. In our schools we should abolish political curriculums and examinations that are designed to indoctrinate students in state ideology and to instill support for the rule of one party. We should replace them with civic education that advances universal values and citizens' rights, fosters civic consciousness, and promotes civic virtues that serve society.

14. Protection of Private Property. We should establish and protect the right to private property and promote an economic system of free and fair markets. We should do away with government monopolies in commerce and industry and guarantee the freedom to start new enterprises. We should establish a Committee on State-Owned Property, reporting to the national legislature, that will monitor the transfer of state-owned enterprises to private ownership in a fair, competitive, and orderly manner. We should institute a land reform that promotes private ownership of land, guarantees the right to buy and sell land, and allows the true value of private property to be adequately reflected in the market.

15. Financial and Tax Reform. We should establish a democratically regulated and accountable system of public finance that ensures the protection of taxpayer rights and that operates through legal procedures. We need a system by which public revenues that belong to a certain level of government—central, provincial, county or local—are controlled at that level. We need major tax reform that will abolish any unfair taxes, simplify the tax system, and spread the tax burden fairly. Government officials should not be able to raise taxes, or institute new ones, without public deliberation and the approval of a democratic assembly. We should reform the ownership system in order to encourage competition among a wider variety of market participants.

16. Social Security. We should establish a fair and adequate social security system that covers all citizens and ensures basic access to education, health care, retirement security, and employment.

17. Protection of the Environment. We need to protect the natural environment and to promote development in a way that is sustainable and responsible to our descendants and to the rest of humanity. This means insisting that the state and its officials at all levels not only do what they must do to achieve these goals, but also accept the supervision and participation of nongovernmental organizations.

18. A Federated Republic. A democratic China should seek to act as a responsible major power contributing toward peace and development in the Asian Pacific region by approaching others in a spirit of equality and fairness. In Hong Kong and Macao, we should support

the freedoms that already exist. With respect to Taiwan, we should declare our commitment to the principles of freedom and democracy and then, negotiating as equals and ready to compromise, seek a formula for peaceful unification. We should approach disputes in the national-minority areas of China with an open mind, seeking ways to find a workable framework within which all ethnic and religious groups can flourish. We should aim ultimately at a federation of democratic communities of China.

19. Truth in Reconciliation. We should restore the reputations of all people, including their family members, who suffered political stigma in the political campaigns of the past or who have been labeled as criminals because of their thought, speech, or faith. The state should pay reparations to these people. All political prisoners and prisoners of conscience must be released. There should be a Truth Investigation Commission charged with finding the facts about past injustices and atrocities, determining responsibility for them, upholding justice, and, on these bases, seeking social reconciliation.

China, as a major nation of the world, as one of five permanent members of the United Nations Security Council, and as a member of the UN Council on Human Rights, should be contributing to peace for humankind and progress toward human rights. Unfortunately, we stand today as the only country among the major nations that remains mired in authoritarian politics. Our political system continues to produce human rights disasters and social crises, thereby not only constricting China's own development but also limiting the progress of all of human civilization. This must change, truly it must. The democratization of Chinese politics can be put off no longer.

Accordingly, we dare to put civic spirit into practice by announcing Charter 08. We hope that our fellow citizens who feel a similar sense of crisis, responsibility, and mission, whether they are inside the government or not, and regardless of their social status, will set aside small differences to embrace the broad goals of this citizens' movement. Together we can work for major changes in Chinese society and for the rapid establishment of a free, democratic, and constitutional country. We can bring to reality the goals and ideals that our people have incessantly been seeking for more than a hundred years, and can bring a brilliant new chapter to Chinese civilization.

*Translated by Perry Link*

NOTE

*New York Review of Books*, January 15, 2009, http://www.nybooks.com/articles/2009/01/15/chinas-charter-08/. Perry Link was authorized as the official translator of the Charter 08 by Liu Xiaobo on behalf of all initiators several days before his detention. The translation here is the original of the official version. It was planned to publish both the Chinese and English version on December 10, 2008, but the Chinese version was published by someone unknown one day earlier on December 9, 2008, when the English version was not ready. After Liu Xiaobo was taken away by the police on December 8, Human Rights in China was very fast to translate and publish the Charter in English first some hours later. However, Link's version is frequently used and referred to as it is the authorized translation.

# I Have No Enemies

MY FINAL STATEMENT

*Liu Xiaobo*


Nobel Lecture in Absentia, December 10, 2010

*Statement of December 23, 2009, Read by Liv Ullmann*

In the course of my life, for more than half a century, June 1989 was the major turning point. Up to that point, I was a member of the first class to enter university when college entrance examinations were reinstated following the Cultural Revolution (Class of '77). From BA to MA and on to PhD, my academic career was all smooth sailing. Upon receiving my degrees, I stayed on to teach at Beijing Normal University. As a teacher, I was well received by the students. At the same time, I was a public intellectual, writing articles and books that created quite a stir during the 1980s, frequently receiving invitations to give talks around the country, and going abroad as a visiting scholar upon invitation from Europe and America. What I demanded of myself was this: whether as a person or as a writer, I would lead a life of honesty, responsibility, and dignity. After that, because I had returned from the U.S. to take part in the 1989 movement, I was thrown into prison for "the crime of counter-revolutionary propaganda and incitement." I also lost my beloved lectern and could no longer publish essays or give talks in China. Merely for publishing different political views and taking part in a peaceful democracy movement, a teacher lost his lectern, a writer lost his right to publish, and a public intellectual lost the opportunity to give talks publicly. This is a tragedy, both for me personally and for a China that has already seen thirty years of Reform and Opening Up.

When I think about it, my most dramatic experiences after June 4 have been, surprisingly, associated with courts: my two opportunities to address the public have both been provided by trial sessions at the Beijing Municipal Intermediate People's Court, once in January 1991 and again today. Although the crimes I have been charged with on the two occasions are different in name, their real substance is basically the same-both are speech crimes.

Twenty years have passed, but the ghosts of June 4 have not yet been laid to rest. Upon release from Qincheng Prison in 1991, I, who had been led onto the path of political dissent by the psychological chains of June 4, lost the right to speak publicly in my own country and could only speak through the foreign media. Because of this, I was subjected to year-round monitoring, kept under residential surveillance (May 1995 to January 1996) and sent to reeducation through labor (October 1996 to October 1999). And now I have been once again shoved into the dock by the enemy mentality of the regime. But I still want to say to this regime, which is depriving me of my freedom, that I stand by the convictions I expressed in my "June 2nd Hunger Strike Declaration" twenty years ago—I have no enemies and no hatred. None of the police who monitored, arrested, and interrogated me, none of the prosecutors who indicted me, and none of the judges who judged me are my enemies. Although there is no way I can accept your monitoring, arrests, indictments, and verdicts, I respect your professions and your integrity, including those of the two prosecutors, Zhang Rongge and Pan Xueqing, who are now bringing charges against me on behalf of the prosecution. During interrogation on December 3, I could sense your respect and your good faith.

Hatred can rot away at a person's intelligence and conscience. Enemy mentality will poison the spirit of a nation, incite cruel mortal struggles, destroy a society's tolerance and humanity, and hinder a nation's progress toward freedom and democracy. That is why I hope to be able to transcend my personal experiences as I look upon our nation's development and social change, to counter the regime's hostility with utmost goodwill, and to dispel hatred with love.

Everyone knows that it was Reform and Opening Up that brought about our country's development and social change. In my view, Reform and Opening Up began with the abandonment of the "using class struggle as guiding principle" government policy of the Mao era and, in its place, a commitment to economic development and social harmony. The process of abandoning the "philosophy of struggle" was also a process of gradual weakening of the enemy mentality and elimination of the psychology of hatred, and a process of squeezing out the "wolf's milk" that had seeped into human nature. It was this process that provided a relaxed climate, at home and abroad, for Reform and Opening Up, gentle and humane grounds for restoring mutual affection among people and peaceful coexistence among those with different interests and values, thereby providing encouragement in keeping with humanity for the bursting forth of creativity and the restoration of compassion among our countrymen. One could say that relinquishing the "anti-imperialist and anti-revisionist" stance in foreign relations and "class struggle" at home has been the basic premise that has enabled Reform and Opening Up to continue to this very day. The market trend in the economy, the diversification of culture, and the gradual shift in social order toward the rule of law have all benefited from the weakening of the "enemy mentality." Even in the political arena, where progress is slowest, the weakening of the enemy mentality has led to an ever-growing tolerance for social pluralism on the part of the regime and substantial decrease in the force of persecution of political dissidents, and the official designation of the 1989 movement has also been changed from "turmoil and riot" to "political disturbance." The weakening of the enemy mentality has paved the way for the regime to gradually accept the universality of human rights. In [1997 and] 1998 the Chinese government made a commitment to sign two major United Nations international human rights covenants, signaling China's acceptance of universal human rights standards. In 2004 the National People's Congress amended the constitution, writing into the constitution for the. first time that "the state respects and guarantees human rights," signaling that human rights have already become one of the fundamental principles of China's rule of law. At the same time, the current regime puts forth the ideas of "putting people first" and "creating a harmonious society," signaling progress in the CPC's concept of rule.

I have also been able to feel this progress on the macro level through my own personal experience since my arrest.

Although I continue to maintain that I am innocent and that the charges against me are unconstitutional, during the one -plus year since I have lost my freedom, I have been locked up at two different locations and gone through four pretrial police interrogators, three prosecutors, and two judges, but in handling my case, they have not been disrespectful, overstepped time limitations, or tried to force a confession. Their manner has been moderate and reasonable; moreover, they have often shown goodwill. On June 23 I was moved from a location where I was kept under residential surveillance to the Beijing Municipal Public Security Bureau's No. 1 Detention Center, known as Beikan. During my six months at Beikan, I saw improvements in prison management.

In 1996 I spent time at the old Beikan (located at Banbuqiao). Compared to the old Beikan of more than a decade ago, the present Beikan is a huge improvement, both in terms of the "hardware"—the facilities—and the "software"—the management. In particular, the humane management pioneered by the new Beikan, based on respect for the rights and integrity of detainees, has brought flexible management to bear on every aspect of the behavior of the correctional staff, and has found expression in the "comforting broadcasts," *Repentance* magazine, and music before meals, on waking and at bedtime. This style of management allows detainees to experience a sense of dignity and warmth and stirs their consciousness in maintaining prison order and opposing the bullies among inmates. Not only has it provided a humane living environment for detainees; it has also greatly improved the environment for their litigation to take place and their state of mind. I've had close contact with correctional officer Liu Zheng, who has been in charge of me in my cell, and his respect and care for detainees could be seen in every detail of his work, permeating his every word and deed, and giving one a warm feeling. It was perhaps my good fortune to have gotten to know this sincere, honest, conscientious, and kind correctional officer during my time at Beikan.

It is precisely because of such convictions and personal experience that I firmly believe that China's political progress will not stop, and I, filled with optimism, look forward to the advent of a future free China. For there is no force that can put an end to the human quest for freedom, and China will in the end become a nation ruled by law, where human rights reign supreme. I also hope that this sort of progress can be reflected in this trial as I await the impartial ruling of the collegial bench—a ruling that will withstand the test of history.

If I may be permitted to say so, the most fortunate experience of these past twenty years has been the selfless love I have received from my wife, Liu Xia. She could not be present as an observer in court today, but I still want to say to you, my dear, that I firmly believe your love for me will remain the same as it has always been. Throughout all these years that I have lived without freedom, our love was full of bitterness imposed by outside circumstances, but as I savor its aftertaste, it remains boundless. I am serving my sentence in a tangible prison, while you wait in the intangible prison of the heart. Your love is the sunlight that leaps over high walls and penetrates the iron bars of my prison window, stroking every inch of my skin, warming every cell of my body, allowing me to always keep peace, openness, and brightness in my heart, and filling every minute of my time in prison with meaning. My love for you, on the other hand, is so full of remorse and regret that it at times makes me stagger under its weight. I am an insensate stone in the wilderness, whipped by fierce wind and torrential rain, so cold that no one dares touch me. But my love is solid and sharp, capable of piercing through any obstacle. Even if I were crushed into powder, I would still use my ashes to embrace you.

My dear, with your love I can calmly face my impending trial, having no regrets about the choices I've made and optimistically awaiting tomorrow. I look forward to [the day] when my country is a land with freedom of expression, where the speech of every citizen will be treated equally well; where different values, ideas, beliefs, and political views . . . can both compete with each other and peacefully coexist; where both majority and minority views will be equally guaranteed, and where the political views that differ from those currently in power, in particular, will be fully respected and protected; where all political views will spread out under the sun for people to choose from, where every citizen can state political views without fear, and where no one can under any circumstances suffer political persecution for voicing divergent political views. I hope that I will be the last victim of China's endless literary inquisitions and that from now on no one will be incriminated because of speech.

Freedom of expression is the foundation of human rights, the source of humanity, and the mother of truth. To strangle freedom of speech is to trample on human rights, stifle humanity, and suppress truth.

In order to exercise the right to freedom of speech conferred by the constitution, one should fulfill the social responsibility of a Chinese citizen. There is nothing criminal in anything I have done. [But] if charges are brought against me because of this, I have no complaints.

Thank you, everyone.

*Translated by Human Rights in China, based on*
*a translation by J. Latourelle.*

NOTE

Available at "Liu Xiaobo: Nobel Lecture," Nobel Prize, https://www.nobelprize.org/nobel _prizes/peace/laureates/2010/xiaobo-lecture.html.

# Contributors

Ai Weiwei is a Chinese artist and activist. He now lives and works in Berlin, Germany.

Ai Xiaoming holds a PhD in literature and is a retired professor of Sun Yat-sen University, Guangzhou. She is a scholar of women's issues and public affairs, and an independent documentary filmmaker. She has received numerous awards, including the Simone de Beauvoir Award and ICPC's Lin Zhao Memorial Award.

Bao Tong is a Beijing writer, former central committee member of the Chinese Communist Party, and political secretary of General Secretary Zhao Ziyang. In 1989, because he supported Zhao Ziyang and opposed the use of force by the authorities to suppress the prodemocracy movement, he was sentenced to seven years in prison for the crime of "revealing state secrets" and "counterrevolutionary propaganda and incitement."

Jean-Philippe Béja is a French sinologist, honorary research fellow at the French National Center for Scientific Research, and a consultant of *Democratic China*.

Teng Biao is a U.S.-based Chinese scholar and human rights lawyer with a PhD in law, a legal advisor to ICPC's Writers in Prison Committee and former lecturer at the China University of Political Science and Law.

Cai Chu is a Chinese American poet and editor, publisher and editor in chief of *Democratic China* online magazine and honorary director and former vice president of ICPC (under President Liu Xiaobo).

Chen Kuide is a Chinese scholar, writer, and editor based in the United States with a PhD in philosophy and is executive chair of the Princeton China Initiative, publisher and editor in chief of *China Perspectives* online magazine, and former vice president of ICPC (under President Liu Xiaobo).

Cui Weiping is a Chinese visiting scholar in the United States, a retired professor of the Beijing Film Academy, and a recipient of ICPC's Lin Zhao Memorial Award.

Du Daobin is Hubei writer and a director of ICPC and recipient of its Writers in Prison Award in 2008. He served a sentenced of three years' imprisonment for "inciting subversion of state power."

Carl Gershman is the president of the National Endowment for Democracy.

Louisa Greve has worked on human rights in Asia for three decades and written most recently on Tibetan and Uyghur human rights in the *Journal of Democracy*.

He Depu is a freelance writer and human rights activist in Beijing. In 1979 he participated in Xidan Democracy Wall and was the convener of the *Beijing Youth* magazine. He participated in the 1989 Democracy Movement, and in 1998 he was involved in the founding of the China Democracy Party. For publishing articles expressing dissent, he was sentenced to eight years in prison, a term he served from 2003 to 2011. The year he was released from prison, He Depu joined the Independent Chinese PEN Center and currently serves as director of ICPC's Writers in Prison and Freedom to Write Committee.

Albert Ho Chun-yan is a solicitor and politician in Hong Kong. He is the chairman of the Hong Kong Alliance in Support of Patriotic Democratic Movements in China, former chairman of the Democratic Party in 2006–2012, and a former member of the Legislative Council of Hong Kong in 1998–2016.

Hori Takeaki is a Japanese writer and anthropologist, as well as a vice president and former international secretary of PEN International.

Hu Jia, a Beijing dissident and social activist, spent three and a half years in prison, from 2008 to 2011, for "inciting subversion." The European Parliament awarded him the Sakharov Prize for Freedom of Thought.

Hu Ping is a U.S.-based Chinese writer. He is editor in chief emeritus of *Beijing Spring* and an honorary director of the ICPC.

Cary S. Hung is a U.S.-based Taiwanese American writer, editor, political activist, and editor in chief of the Democracy Forum website. Hung has a PhD in civil engineering.

Jiang Qisheng is a Beijing writer, scholar, and former vice president of ICPC. He participated in the 1989 student movement and served on the standing committees of the Beijing University Student Dialogue Delegation and China People's University Autonomous Student Union. After the June Fourth Massacre, he was detained for five months; from 1999 to 2003, he was imprisoned for "inciting subversion of state power."

Jin Zhong is the founder and chief editor of *Open* Magazine in Hong Kong.

Joanne Leedom-Ackerman, novelist, short story writer, and journalist, is vice president emeritus of PEN International, where she served as international secretary and chair of the Writers in Prison Committee. She is also an emeritus board member of Human Rights Watch and former chair of its Asia Advisory Committee.

Li Yongsheng was Sichuan poet, editor, screenwriter, and a member of ICPC; he passed away on October 4, 2017.

Liao Yiwu is a Chinese author and poet exiled in Germany, a former and honorary director of ICPC, and a recipient of the Peace Prize of the German Book Trade and other international awards.

Perry Link is an American sinologist, professor emeritus of Princeton University, and consultant of *Democratic China*.

Liu Di is a Beijing-based freelance writer and translator and a columnist for Radio of Free Asia. After enrolling in the Psychology College at Beijing Normal University in 1999, she became active on the internet writing under the pen name Stainless Steel Rat after the antihero character in Harry Harrison's science fiction series. She was detained for more than a year in 2002–3 on the allegation of subverting state power, then released without indictment for "minor offenses." She has been a member of ICPC's board since October 2013 and is now a director of its Youth Committee.

Liu Xia, the widow of Liu Xiaobo, is an artist, poet, founding member of ICPC, and honorary member of many PEN centers. On July 10, 2018, three days before the anniversary of Liu Xiaobo's death, she left China for medical treatment in Germany. She resides in Berlin.

Lu Yang, born Zhang Guiqi, is a Shandong poet and writer and a member of ICPC.

Makino Seishu is a Japanese politician, president of the Human Rights Foundation, former member of the House of Representatives of the Japan Diet, and former president of the Japan Parliamentary Alliance in Support of Liu Xiaobo.

Tienchi Martin-Liao is a Chinese author, editor, and translator in Germany and president of ICPC (2009–2013 and 2016–present).

Mo Zhixu, born Zhao Hui, is a Beijing writer and former director of ICPC.

Andrew J. Nathan is a U.S. sinologist, professor of political science, and chair of the steering committee for the Center for the Study of Human Rights at Columbia University.

Kaiser Abdurusul ÖzHun is a Sweden-based Uyghur writer and artist with a PhD in cultural anthropology; he is project director, international secretary, and former president of Uyghur PEN Center.

Pan Yongzhong is a German Chinese author, journalist, publisher, deputy secretary-general of ICPC, and secretary-general of the Federation for a Democratic China.

Pei Yiran is a U.S.-based Chinese scholar and writer, professor emeritus of the Shanghai University of Finance and Economics, and a member of ICPC.

Qi Jiazhen is a Chinese Australian author, former vice president and director of ICPC, and chair of its Women Writers Committee.

Qian Yuejun is a Chinese German engineer, scholar, writer, and editor with a PhD in aero-acoustics and is publisher and chief editor of *Layin Tongxin* and *Ouhua Daobao* (*Chinese European Post*) and a member of ICPC.

Qin Geng is a writer based in Hainan, China, and member of ICPC.

Shao Jiang is a UK-based Chinese scholar, political scientist, human rights activist, and founder of Chinese Uighur and Tibetan Solidarity UK. At the time of the 1989 student movement, he was a student in mathematics at Peking University and served on the standing committee of the Beijing College and Universities

Student Autonomous Federation. He was detained for a year and a half after the June Fourth Massacre.

Sha Yexin was a Shanghai playwright, former vice president of ICPC, former president of Shanghai People's Art Theater, and honorary vice chair of the Chinese Theatre Literature Association. Sha passed away on July 26, 2018.

Shi Tao is a Chinese journalist, poet, member of ICPC, and a recipient of the World Association of Newspapers Golden Pen of Freedom Award and other international awards. Due to his use of Yahoo email to send his short notes of CCP documents to overseas websites for publication, he was sentenced to ten years' imprisonment for illegally providing state secrets overseas. He served eight years and nine months in several prisons before his release on August 23, 2013.

Su Xiaokang is a Chinese writer based in the United States and the former chief editor of *Democratic China.*

Sun Wenguang is a retired professor of Shandong University and honorary director of ICPC.

James Tager is the senior manager of Free Expression Programs at PEN America.

Tsering Woeser, known in Chinese as Cheng Wensa, is a Beijing-based Tibetan poet and writer and a recipient of ICPC's Lin Zhao Memorial Award, International Women's Media Foundation's Courage in Journalism Award, and U.S. Secretary of State's International Women of Courage Award, among others.

Tsoi Wing-Mui is a Hong Kong writer, former editor at *Open* Magazine, and coordinator of ICPC's Women Writers Committee.

Wang Dan is a Chinese exiled scholar in the United States, author, chairman of the board of *Beijing Spring*, president of the New School for Democracy, member of Independent Chinese PEN Center, and a leader of the 1989 student movement with a PhD in history. After the June Fourth Massacre, Wang was twice convicted— first of the crime of "counter-revolutionary propaganda and incitement" and then "conspiracy to overthrow the government"—sentenced to a total of fifteen years in prison, and served nearly seven years before his release on medical parole and exile to the United States.

Wang Debang is a Beijing-based writer and member of ICPC. During the 1989 student movement, he was a student of philosophy at Beijing Normal University and represented the university on the Universities Dialog Delegation as well as being a leader of the theory and propaganda group of the BNU Autonomous Student Union.

Wang Jinbo is a Beijing writer and director and secretary-general of ICPC, and he previously served four years in prison for "inciting subversion of state power."

Wang Jinzhong is a Chinese journalist based in Japan, human rights activist, and former director of the Independent Chinese PEN Center.

Wang Wei is a Chinese American poet and writer with an MA in linguistics and a former Chinese language lecturer.

Emily Wu is a Chinese American writer and former vice president of the Independent Chinese PEN Center.

Wu Zuolai is a U.S.-based Chinese scholar and writer. He was formerly deputy director of the research department of the Chinese Academy of Arts and publisher of the journal *Theory and Criticism of Literature and Art.*

Xiao Qiao, born Li Jianhong, is a Shanghai writer, former coordinator of ICPC's Writers in Prison Committee, and a winner of the Lin Zhao Memorial Award in 2007. She was a writer-in-residence of Stockholm City, Sweden, for a year and a half in 2008–9.

Xu Lin is an architect, internet writer, and lyricist in Guangdong Province, China, and a member of ICPC. Due to his collaboration with others in creating rights defense songs, he has been detained since September 26, 2017 on "suspicion of creating trouble."

Xu Youyu is a Chinese philosopher, resident scholar of the New School in New York, retired researcher of the Chinese Academy of Social Sciences, one of the initiators of the New Citizen Movement, and recipient of the Olof Palme Prize in Sweden.

Yan Jiawei is a Sichuan-based writer and a retired "employee" of a labor reform team. He was sentenced to fifteen years in prison for "counterrevolutionary crimes" during the 1957 Anti-Rightist Movement.

Yang Guang is a Hubei-based scholar and writer and deputy secretary-general of ICPC.

Ye Du, born Wu Yangwei, is a Guangdong writer, editor, and former deputy secretary-general of ICPC and coordinator of its Internet Work Committee.

Yi Ping, born Li Jianhua, is a U.S.-based Chinese poet, writer, editor, and former director of ICPC's Freedom to Write and Literary Exchange Committee.

Yu Jianrong, doctor of law, is a researcher at the Rural Development Institute, Chinese Academy of Social Sciences, and director of the Social Issues Research Center.

Yu Jie is a U.S.-based Chinese writer and former vice president of ICPC (under President Liu Xiaobo).

Yu Ying-Shih is a Chinese American intellectual historian, sinologist, retired professor, and fellow of Academia Sinica and the American Philosophical Society.

Yu Zhang is a Chinese citizen based in Sweden, a retired research fellow with a PhD in technology. As a scholar, editor, and translator, he is now the coordinator of ICPC's Writers in Prison and Freedom to Write Committee.

Zhang Zuhua is a Beijing-based scholar, writer, and editor, director and editor of *Democratic China*, and the main drafter of Charter 08. He served on the standing committee of the central committee of the Communist Youth League and as secretary of the Central State Organs Youth League Committee before being dismissed following the June Fourth Incident.

Zhao Changqing is a Shaanxi dissident, social activist, member of the Independent Chinese PEN Center, and member of the New Citizen Movement. Since 1989 he has been detained or sentenced five times for "inciting subversion of state power" and "gathering crowds to disrupt public order," totaling about eleven years in prison.

Zhao Dagong, born Zhao Shiying, is a Shenzhen-based writer and vice president and former secretary-general of the ICPC. In January 2010 he was detained under residential surveillance for two weeks on suspicion of "inciting subversion of state power."

Zheng Yi is a Chinese writer living in exile in the United States and former president and honorary director of ICPC.

Zhou Duo, one of the Four Gentlemen of Tiananmen Square in 1989, is Beijing-based writer and a member of ICPC.

Zi Kang, born Liu Kangxiu, is a poet in Guangdong Province, China, and a member of ICPC.

CPSIA information can be obtained
at www.ICGtesting.com
Printed in the USA
LVHW080109010220
645508LV00002BA/5